Lecture Notes in Computer Scie

T0237810

Commenced Publication in 1973
Founding and Former Series Editors:
Gerhard Goos, Juris Hartmanis, and Jan van Leeuwen

Germán Puebla (Ed.)

Logic-Based Program Synthesis and Transformation

16th International Symposium, LOPSTR 2006
Venice, Italy, July 12-14, 2006
Revised Selected Papers

 Springer

Volume Editor

Germán Puebla
Technical University of Madrid (UPM), School of Computer Science
Campus de Montegancedo, 28660 Boadilla del Monte (Madrid), Spain
E-mail: german@fi.upm.es

Library of Congress Control Number: 2007922566

CR Subject Classification (1998): F.3.1, D.1.1, D.1.6, D.2.4, I.2.2, F.4.1

LNCS Sublibrary: SL 1 – Theoretical Computer Science and General Issues

ISSN   0302-9743
ISBN-10   3-540-71409-X Springer Berlin Heidelberg New York
ISBN-13   978-3-540-71409-5 Springer Berlin Heidelberg New York

Springer is a part of Springer Science+Business Media

springer.com

© Springer-Verlag Berlin Heidelberg 2007
Printed in Germany

Typesetting: Camera-ready by author, data conversion by Scientific Publishing Services, Chennai, India
Printed on acid-free paper   SPIN: 12035236   06/3142   5 4 3 2 1 0

Preface

This volume contains a selection of papers presented at LOPSTR 2006, the 16th International Symposium on Logic-Based Program Synthesis and Transformation, held in Venice, Italy, July, 12-14 2006.

The aim of the LOPSTR series is to stimulate and promote international research and collaboration on logic-based program development. Previous LOPSTR events were held in London (2005, 2000), Verona (2004), Uppsala (2003), Madrid (2002), Paphos (2001), Venice (1999), Manchester (1998, 1992, 1991), Leuven (1997), Stockholm (1996), Arnhem (1995), Pisa (1994), and Louvain-la-Neuve (1993).

We would like to thank all those who submitted contributions to LOPSTR. Overall, we received 41 submissions (29 full papers and 12 extended abstracts). Each submission received at least three reviews. The committee decided to accept nine of these full papers for presentation and for inclusion in the final conference proceedings. In addition, eight extended abstracts, including two tool demonstrations, were accepted for presentation only. After the conference, authors of extended abstracts describing research judged to be mature enough for possible publication in the present volume were invited to submit full papers. In this second reviewing process, five additional papers were accepted for publication in the current LNCS volume, together with revised versions of the nine full papers previously accepted.

We would also like to thank Shaz Qadeer and Massimo Marchiori for agreeing to give invited talks and for their contribution to these proceedings.

I am very grateful to the authors of the papers, the reviewers, and in particular to the members of the Program Committee for their invaluable help. Thanks also to Andrei Voronkov for his support with the use of EasyChair, which greatly simplified the submission, reviewing and discussion process, as well as the preparation of the proceedings.

LOPSTR 2006 was co-located with PPDP 2006 (ACM Symposium on Principles and Practice of Declarative Programming) and ICALP 2006 (International Colloquium on Automata, Languages and Programming).

My warmest thanks go to Sabina Rossi (Local Arrangements Chair), who was always willing to help in any aspect of the organization of the event. Special thanks also to Annalisa Bossi and Michele Bugliesi who, together with Sabina, took care of the overall planning and local organization of LOPSTR 2006.

December 2006   Germán Puebla

Conference Organization

Program Chair

Germán Puebla

Program Committee

Slim Abdennadher
Roberto Bagnara
Gilles Barthe
John Gallagher
Robert Glück
Michael Hanus
Patricia M. Hill
Kazuhiko Kakehi
Andy King
Michael Leuschel
Fred Mesnard
Sabina Rossi
Grigore Rosu
Wim Vanhoof
Germán Vidal

Local Organization

Sabina Rossi (Local Arrangements Chair)
Annalisa Bossi
Michele Bugliesi

External Reviewers

James Avery, Bernd Braßel, Diego Calvanese, Stephen Bond, Alvaro Cortes, Guillaume Dufay, Santiago Escobar, Marc Fontaine, Samir Genaim, Mark Hills, Frank Huch, Dongxi Liu, Wafik Boulos Lotfallah, Thomas Lukasiewicz, Damiano Macedonio, Claude Marché, Viviana Mascardi, Thierry Massart, Kazutaka Matsuda, Nancy Mazur, Antoine Miné, Torben Mogensen, Akimasa Morihata, Klaus Ostermann, Etienne Payet, Andrea Pescetti, Alberto Pettorossi, Carla Piazza, David Pichardie, Andrei Popescu, Maurizio Proietti, Traian Florin Serbanuta, Fausto Spoto, Xavier Urbain, Brent Venable, Tetsuo Yokoyama, Enea Zaffanella.

Table of Contents

Debugging and Testing

Termination and Analysis

How to Talk to a Human: The Semantic Web and the Clash of the Titans

Massimo Marchiori[1,2]

[1] University of Padua (UNIPD)
`massimo@math.unipd.it`
[2] Utility Labs (UTILABS)
`massimo@utilabs.org`

Abstract. The Semantic Web has managed to produce an enormous buzzword. However, despite it cannot be considered a new technology anymore, it didn't fly off yet, and has remained unexpressed in its potentials. In this article we try to analyze the possible reasons, and also the tension that the Semantic Web has with XML. We emphasize the need for consideration of the more comprehensive social environment, together with a more formal modeling of the mechanics of the Web and its information flows.

1 The Semantic Web and XML: The Eternal Quest

The Semantic Web (mostly, in its RDF [1] incarnation) and XML have been often seen as two distinct worlds, and as such, each of them has a community of people who think the other side of the fence is doing things "the wrong way".

Given XML's success, and the current dual lack of success of the Semantic Web/RDF, it is normal that the latter has been often criticized, using the following "fundamental question":

Q: What can you do with RDF that you can't do with XML?

The fundamental question is both tricky and crucial. This question has been source of embarrassment, and of misunderstandings, for both worlds, and has somehow contributed to the lack of proper understanding of the potential of the Semantic Web in the context of the bigger XML world.

We were saying the question is tricky. The classic general answer which is given is:

Q: What can you do with RDF that you can't do with XML?

A: Semantics!

This usually leaves the XML-World unsatisfied, because this is in fact a very fuzzy answer. Saying that with RDF you can do semantics, equals more or less to say that with the Semantic Web you can do... semantics, which doesn't sound too good to critical eyes. So then, the "socratic dialogue" goes on, and the XML-World usually replies with

G. Puebla (Ed.): LOPSTR 2006, LNCS 4407, pp. 1–14, 2007.

XML-World: What do you mean?

More or less, the debate between RDF-World and XML-World then goes on like this:

RDF-World: With RDF I can do X.

XML-World, Well, I can do X with XML too, so what?

RDF-World: But, with RDF I can do Y.

XML-World, Well, I can do Y with XML as well, so what?

(and so on, and so on...)

The point is that the answer is in fact quite easy, and it is one that few people in RDF-World would dare to mention explicitly:

Q: What can you do with RDF that you can't do with XML?

A: Nothing!

This comes trivially from the fact that RDF is XML, and therefore, there's no magic in RDF: RDF is just a dialect of XML, and as such, there's nothing RDF can do "more" than XML: the question, posed this way, is just bogus.

But so, does this mean the XML world is right, and that the Semantic Web is superfluous?

2   The Semantic Web to the Rescue: Closed vs. Open Worlds

The answer to the previous question is not that easy: it really depends on what level of precision we want to analyze. It is certainly true that with XML you can do anything you want, but that doesn't prevent RDF (and the related tower of technologies) to be a successful dialect/specialization of XML, like there are many around. But specialization for what, precisely?

XML has been labeled as the best invention after peanut butter: versatile, flexible, powerful. However, there is one thing for which XML, at least apparently, doesn't work so well: aggregating information.

XML's strength is its specialization capabilities: given an information locale, everybody can easily write a local dialect to express that information. In other words, XML works extremely well in the *closed world* context: an environment where there is a centralized vocabulary control. However, there is another scenario, which didn't fit the original design of XML: the *open-world model*, where there is no centralized vocabulary control. In such scenarios, everybody can develop its own local dialect, and then the big problem is how to exchange information between the different vocabularies, integrating various information sources that have no control over each other. Like for the Tower of Babel, where the multitude of languages has been the disgrace of Humanity, in the open-world model the different languages can provoke heavy interoperability problems (what linguistics call very appropriately the Lost in translations effect).

RDF, more or less consciously, was designed with this fundamental goal in mind (besides the related "give more semantics" mantra): reducing almost to zero the complexity of aggregating information (which, essentially, becomes a merge of graphs). The connections among information pieces are established via the URIs: so, when merging graphs, nodes are considered equal if they have the same URI. Therefore, URIs become the fundamental key to distinguish web object. This choice is compatible, and actually stems from, one of the very first Web Axioms stated by Tim Berners-Lee (the so-called Universality 2 axiom, cf. [2] and compare with the later [3]): meaningful resources on the Web should be identified by URIs.

Thus, RDF is (also) XML, but RDF has been designed to work in the open-world model: while XML works better in the closed-world model, RDF does in the open-world model.

3   Just Aggregation?

So, a first important point that distinguishes "generic" XML from RDF is the complexity of information aggregation. While being an important point, that alone doesn't give the whole picture.

In fact, the Web is, as a whole, semantically speaking, a huge open-world model: so, how come that the Semantic Web didn't rapidly gain success? Something must have gone wrong, and to trace that, we need to start back from the original definition that Tim Berners-Lee gave of the Semantic Web: an extension of the current web in which information is given well-defined meaning, better enabling computers and people to work in cooperation". Computers. . . and people! What about the people?

4   The Benefits

What is missing in the equation is the *utilization model*, i.e., the complete benefits (goals) that the new technology is supposed to provide.

Saying that RDF "works better" in the open-world model is a simplistic assertion, as we haven't quite defined what "better" means. If better means aggregating information, the assertion is correct. But aggregation alone isn't what the Semantic Web promise to do (if it were so, the benefits alone wouldn't be quite clear): the goals of the Semantic Web are more ambitious, and for that reason, the original idea of the Semantic Web includes the well-known "Semantic Web tower" (see for example [4]), i.e., a full tower of technologies that better describe the operational model, and therefore help clarifying the benefits.

So for instance, aggregation of information isn't much helpful if we don't have a clear working model that allows us to benefit from that feature. In order to exploit information aggregation we can then for example also include a logic into the picture: a logic allows to make deductions, and so in principle augments by far the benefits of having aggregated information on the Web. Initial step into this direction have been done with the RDF Semantics, RDF-Schema, OWL, and this line has been continuing more recently with the work of W3C's RIF effort, devoted to specify a Rules Interchange Format that will allow even more flexibility in "programming" the rules shaping web information. This is all consistent with the big view of the Semantic Web Tower.

5   The Costs

But then, there is also the other side of the coin, the dual part that has to be considered every time that we want to analyze the behavior of a successful technology: the *cost factor*.

The overall cost is in general a complex thing to compute, but roughly, it can be seen as the sum of two components: the *technological cost* (the cost for the machine), and the *social cost* (the cost for the people). We can summarize the concept this way:

$$\text{Cost} = \text{Technology} + \text{Society}$$

Both aspects, technology and society, are equally very important. What have happened so far is that the societal cost of the Semantic Web hasn't been object of much attention, and the whole design has been centered on the technological cost, making best efforts to ensure that the technologies in the Semantic Web Tower would have a relatively low technological cost. But in the overall Semantic Web operational model, the scenario is much bigger than just the computational complexity of a logic: it includes the much wider scenario of the Web, its information flows, machines, and the people. Therefore, we need to rethink the situation and not just wear the eyeglasses of the technologist, caring mostly about the computers (classic semantic web stack). Sure, there is the need to monitor and balance the technical cost, but also to consider at least another dimension for the social cost (what has been called the *P axis*, P as Perception/People, in [5]).

Only when we have a complete measure for the cost we can proceed to measure the cost/benefit ratio (shortly, C/B), which is a major indicator of success, especially in environment like the Web.

5.1   The C/B Ratio

The C/B ratio provides a uni-dimensional space that can give a rough estimate of the chances of success of a technology (ranging from 0, the optimum, to infinity, the worst). Minimizing the cost/benefit can happen in a variety of ways, depending on the balance between C and B. In the Web, the important thing to take into account is the dynamics of C and B within the web environment and the users. For instance, in a web-wide application cost usually grows at least linearly with the size of the web (or of the sub-web/community taken into consideration), which can be extremely dangerous. On the other hand, B also in such applications usually depends on the size of the user base, which is very low in the starting adoption phase. Therefore, if we are not careful the corresponding dynamic system will not lead to a success situation, because the too high C/B in the initial phases will prevent an evolution that makes the C/B decrease and reach a wide enough user base. So, in order to produce a network effect, either the initial cost has to be extremely low, or the initial benefit has to be very high.

5.2   The Cost of URIs

The previous C/B discussion then naturally leads to consider: what are the costs of the Semantic Web? An interesting exercise is to measure the technological cost for the semantic web architecture (e.g. in the Semantic Web tower). The analysis will then reveal, in fact, a nice result: the technological (computational) cost is usually low/moderate according to where one sits in the Tower (although interestingly, even in this respect, computational cost has started to grow a lot, see for instance the logic behind the higher layer of OWL). However, when one views at the historical progression of the Semantic Web (still ongoing...), the situation is that there is an overgrowing set of specifications: RDF Model & Syntax / RDF Schema / RDF/XML Syntax revised / RDF Vocabulary Description Language / RDF Concepts and Abstract Syntax / RDF Semantics / OWL (OWL-DL / OWL-Full)/ SPARQL / RDF-A / Rules... and the list is still growing.

So, what has been happening here? Will the user be able to sustain the social complexity that these layers are going to produce? The answer, for the moment, is in front of everybody: not yet. The overall cost seems too high for the moment. And this comes from a variety of factor, given that as said, the scenario to consider is much bigger than what has been formally analyzed so far (computational complexity of logics): the Web, the people, information flows.

For instance, let's just revisit the basic association mechanism of the semantic web: aggregation via URIs. An old gag that used to be around in the semantic web circles was the following:

Q: How many Semantic Web scientists does it take to change a light bulb?
A: Ten. One to screw the bulb, and nine to agree on what a light bulb is.

This gag is significant for the suggestion it is giving: it's hard to all agree on a concept. If URIs are meant to be identification names, they are the centralized part of an otherwise decentralized and distribute environment, the web. But how to achieve consensus without control? In other words, there is a significant *social problem* with URIs when they are used as universal aggregators of information. This gives raise to the *URI Variant problem*: in general, there can be many variants (URI) for the same concept. The URI Variant problem is particularly bad in view of the *URI Variant Law*: utility of a URI can decrease exponentially with the number of its variants (in other words, the worst-case is exponential).

This is not enough, because the social problem is not just on what common URI to agree, among many. There is also the other side of the coin, which is much more difficult: how to agree on the semantics of a specific URI. This is sometimes called the *URI meaning problem*: in other words, for two different people in the web the same URI might well mean different things (after all, there is no centralized interpretation for URIs). This problem is rather severe, because it does not simply affect computational complexity (like the URI variant), but deeply touch the relationship between the web and the people who interact with/in it.

So, all in all, what seemed a strength of the Semantic Web, i.e., almost zero cost for aggregating information, is now revealing deeper faces: while the direct technological cost is indeed very low, there is an underlying social cost that is in fact quite high.

Therefore, this extra variable of the social cost, makes the original simplistic observation, that information aggregation in the Semantic Web is very easy and effective, not quite true any more, and emphasizes the lack of a precise operational model and consequent cost/benefit analysis that have occurred so far.

5.3   Another Perspective: Lost in Navigation

Social costs are not limited to URIs, of course, but they can pervade the same data model. Data structures can have a rigid architecture, or lean towards a more liberal framework, therefore going from the areas of structured data, passing thru the intermediate realm of semi-structured data, and ending in the opposite extreme, the area of unstructured data. Within this wide spectrum, we find for instance in small-size data management on one extreme (structured) spreadsheets and the table model, and on the other extreme (unstructured) things like Zig-Zag, the innovative (for the time) concept by Ted Nelson (cf. [6]. In large(r)-size data management, going on with the parallelism, we find relational databases and the relational model (structured), then we can proceed with XML (semi-structured), then ending with RDF (unstructured).

It is therefore interesting to follow the parallelism, and note that the previous unstructured models (like Zig-Zag) didn't have much success, while the more structured ones did. What are the main reasons? This can be explained by using the so-called *Heisenberg Principle for data handling*: If you stretch the flexibility aspect (benefit), you lose in efficiency (cost).

Note that here efficiency doesn't just mean computational efficiency, but efficiency in-the-large, also for the user. In fact, preliminary studies by the author shows that one can quantify the degree of lost in navigation (that is to say, informally, the capability by the user to grasp the data structure, and to navigate without errors in it): the lost in navigation effect increases (not surprisingly) from structured to semi-structured to unstructured. What is more surprising is that there is quite a gap when passing to unstructured models like RDF and graph-like ones. In other words, the amount of flexibility that these kinds of models give, has a very high price that the user needs to pay. This can explain more formally why unstructured data didn't gain so far the wide success they were expected to. What this also means is that, in order to lower the cost/benefit ratio, there is the need for extra efforts to raise the benefit.

On a related side, the gap occurring inbetween structured and semi-structured data is comparatively rather small, which might also explain why technologies like XML managed to gain success, despite the initial dominant position of structured data approaches.

5.4 Technologies Examples: The Good and the Bad

Let's sweep out of the XML / Semantic Web scenario, and for the sake of illustration, try to see some other examples of more specific technologies and their related cost/benefit.

A first pair of examples is interesting, and comes from privacy technologies developed by the author: P3P and APPEL.

P3P (standing for Platform for Privacy Preferences) is the world standard for Privacy on the Web ([7]). Analyzing the P3P specification will easily show that the P3P technical cost is very low (in fact, not surprisingly, as this was a crucial requirement). As far as the Social Cost is concerned, it is moderate for site maintainers: the moderate complexity essentially stems from building the privacy policy for the site, although this can be ameliorated by specific tools, and in any case approximate policies can be written that are much easier; complementary, publishing the privacy policy is very easy and has a very low cost.

Now let's turn our attention to the benefits side. The benefit is moderate for users (this can be evaluated by using the many privacy surveys available), whereas, interestingly enough, it is very high for site maintainers. The reason? When Internet Explorer passed from version 5 to version 6, it actually incorporated the P3P technology, and in a very stringent way: sites not P3P compliant had severe problems and their cookies were essentially blocked by the browsers. This crucial step provoked a huge rise in the benefit of implementing P3P (even if just at the site maintainers side), and therefore boosted the C/B ratio of P3P, despite cost wasn't low (this C/B boost can be also verified by using the statistical P3P dashboards published by Ernst&Young on the subject).

Now, we want also to consider the other side of the coin, as we said initially that we were going to consider a pair of technologies: P3P and APPEL. APPEL [8] is the companion technology to P3P: the acronym stands for A Privacy Preference Language, and it is a language that enables users (via their browser, for instance), to program on a fine level whether or not to enter a web site, according to the privacy level the site itself provides.

The technological cost for APPEL is moderate, as it can be easily seen. On the other hand, the social cost is high: users need to get knowledge of the privacy possibilities, and to adequately shape a set of preferences. This was too much, given both the relative user interest in privacy (versus content, for instance), and the complexity of programming/shaping a fine level behavior. On the other hand, the benefit here was also relatively small, as the additional privacy control wasn't enough more than for instance some easy pre-defined levels (that Internet Explorer in fact implemented). As a result, the C/B ratio never got sufficiently low, and APPEL didn't fly (in fact, it was never promoted to W3C Recommendation, and remains a proposed technology).

On a wider historical perspective, it would have been much better for W3C, if still wanting to target fine privacy user control, to use a more general-purpose reasoning tool (so to at least try to increase the benefit), either in the Semantic Web area (viewing privacy policies as RDF data), or in the more classic XML data handling area (using technologies like XQuery for instance).

5.5   Talk to a Human: Blogs and the Grillo Case

Leaving aside privacy, another good example to consider is a mainstream one: *blogs*. Blogs have been so successful that it's interesting to see what the reasons are, especially given that, historically, they had been greeted with much scepticism. Why? Because, from the technological viewpoint, blogs are a relatively trivial technology. This is the reason why in the technological world, blogs had initially received so little attention: trivial technology, no real innovation, and why should people bother about writing a diary online?

Things went differently than those critics planned. Sure, the technological level of blogs might well be low, but what really matters is the C/B ratio. Let's see things deeper. The benefit, at least initially, was moderate (now the blog networking/echo effect has raised this initial value to high). The technical cost for blogs is very low. And, even more important, the social cost is extremely low (what is easiest than writing?). As a result, in the initial step a moderate benefit was more than adequately counterbalanced by very low costs, which made the C/B ratio low enough to make blogs spread. A paradigmatic social example that well illustrates the blog C/B power is one of the Times magazine *European Heros* for the year 2005: Beppe Grillo. Grillo is a famous Italian comic actor, which at a point of his career became totally against computers, arriving, in his shows, to smash a computer with a hammer. Then, he discovered blog technology. The entry level was so easy, that he could approach the technology without the complexity that had lead him to previously hammer down computers. And, in his own words, he gave that thing a try, even if the benefits weren't clear at all to him. Nowadays, Grillo's opinion on the Internet, thanks to the blog, have radically changed, and he is an Internet evangelist (!), with his blog (cf. [9]) ranked as the number 1 blog in Europe and among the top ones in the world (first non-USA blog, number 28 world-wide).

Talk to a human, talk to humans.

6   The Web and the Information Flows

Trying to grasp the operational model in which the Semantic Web operates is a significant task: as seen, entering people in the loop makes the C/B analysis far from trivial, and can lead to important insight. But as we have said, the overall operational scenario is bigger, involving the Web, its information flows, machines, and the people. A natural goal would be to have a more formal way to discuss the operational model, so to be able to do more precise and scientific kinds of analysis. This also implies that we need to fill in what are the information flows present in the Web: before even starting to formally discussing properties of an operational model living in the Web, we ought to have a formal model that we can reason upon, describing the information flows mechanics that underline every higher-level handling of information.

7   Towards a Web Algebra

Going alone the line of a more formal approach, the reason why it's not easy to answer the question "what is the Semantic Web" is that the semantic web is essentially a way to build a *shared information system.* "Shared" here means essentially that the distributed nature of the Web enables information to be spread out on the Web, and then *composed* together. Therefore, the problem here is that to define how the semantic web works, we need to take into account in the big picture not just the specific language (XML dialect), like RDF, that is used to encode knowledge. We also need to take into account the way information is composed, that is to say, we need to consider in the picture the Web and the related process model. In other words, the fundamental equation to take into account, when wholly describing the semantic web (from the technical viewpoint), can be roughly stated as

$$Semantic\ Web = Semantics + Web$$

So far, just the "Semantics" part has been considered, and the "Web" part has mostly been left out, or considered as an appendix.

7.1   Infoshares and Infostructures

We then proceed with somehow more formal definition. First, we need to set the stage for a general logical setting, where reasoning takes place:

Definition 1. *An* information system *is a poset* $(S, \vdash_S)$.

So, given an information system $(S, \vdash_S)$, and two elements a and b of S ($a \in S \ni b$), we say that "b follows from a", or also that "from a we can infer b, when $a \vdash_S b$.

Then, we go on with the definition of the more general environment where the various shared reasonings can take place:

Definition 2 *(Infoshare)*
Given an ordinal k, a k-infoshare is composed by:

- *A gateways set Λ, which is a semi-lattice.*
- *A shared spaces set **SSS***
- *For each i, $0 < i \le k$:*
  - *An information system $\mathcal{A}_i$*
  - *A map $TAKE_{\mathcal{A}_i} : \Lambda \times \textbf{SSS} \to \mathcal{A}_i$*
  - *A map $PUB_{\mathcal{A}_i} : \Lambda \times \textbf{SSS} \times \mathcal{A}_i \to \textbf{SSS}$*

We will usually omit the index k in a k-infoshare, and just talk of an *infoshare*. Also, given an infoshare, we will refer to members of its gateways set as "gateways", and to members of its shared spaces set as "shared spaces". In the gateway set, we indicate with $\perp$ the non-interference relationship (i.e., we write $\lambda \perp \lambda'$ to state that two gateways do not intersect).

En passant, note that in the above definition the $TAKE_{A_i}$ and PUB_{A_i} are total (always defined): a relaxation of these assumptions is provided for illustration in the Appendix at the end of the paper.

An infoshare alone is little more than an algebraic container of the information flows: in order to have an information algebra, we need to enrich the structure with more axioms, that give some basic rules on the behavior of the information handling:

Definition 3 *(Infostructure)*
An infostructure is an infoshare such that the following axioms hold:

- ***Incrementality:***
  $\lambda \geq \lambda' \Rightarrow TAKE_A(\lambda, S) \geq TAKE_A(\lambda', S)$
- ***Locality:***
  $\lambda \perp \lambda' \Rightarrow TAKE_A(\lambda', PUB_B(\lambda, S, x)) = TAKE_A(\lambda', S)$
- ***Echo:***
  $TAKE_A(\lambda, PUB_A(\lambda, S, x)) = x$
- ***Update:***
  $\lambda \geq \lambda' \Rightarrow PUB_A(\lambda, PUB_B(\lambda', S, y), x) = PUB_A(\lambda, S, x)$
- ***Separation:***
  $\lambda \perp \lambda' \Rightarrow PUB_A(\lambda, PUB_B(\lambda', S, y), x) = PUB_B(\lambda', PUB_A(\lambda, S, x), y)$
- ***Freedom:***
  $\forall \lambda \in \Lambda. \exists \lambda' \in \Lambda. \lambda \perp \lambda'$

The axioms that constitute the infostructure can be described as follows:

- Incrementality: this states that the more gateways we use, the more information we get. This is what makes *partial evaluation* possible (sound), and so makes reasoning scalable in-the-large.
- Locality:this expresses the fact that if two gateways sets are in non-interference (w.r.t. the semi-lattice structure of the gateways set, i.e., they don't have a common component) then even if some publication occurs in a set, the information that can be taken out of the other set stays unchanged. So, separate areas/teams can safely work independently, and legacy information is preserved if appropriate separate gateways are used.
- Echo: if something is published, and then retrieved, there is no loss of information. This expresses safety of the publication process: every bit of information that is put in the SIS, can be retrieved, with no losses.
- Update: if something is published, this overrides previous publishing in the gateways. So, this axiom corresponds to the possibility to update old/ incomplete/ incorrect information.

- Separation publishing at two gateways sets that are in non-interference is independent on the order. This allows asynchronous processing between different teams and different applications: they don't have to "wait on each other" to publish information. With no cycles lost, this enables for a true parallel information system.
- Freedom: given a gateway set, there is always another gateway set that doesn't interfere. In simpler words, there's always room to expand and put new information.

Of course, the proposed modeling is an approximation of the simple information system, and more refined axiomatic systems can be introduced, depending on the level of details we want to analyze and model. Nevertheless, even such a simplified model can give quite some hints. For example, a consequence of the fact that the $TAKE_{A_i}$ functions are total (i.e., always defined) is the *information compression property*, which says, roughly speaking, that the amount of information is independent on the gateways (even more informally, one can "compress" information coming from many gateways into fewer gateways). In the case of the Web (with URL sets as gateways), this means that one can also aggregate information within a single page (so, the semantic layer and URLs are somehow orthogonal). It is interesting to note that RDF has the compression property (and so, it is indeed an aggregator language), while XML (cf. [10])does not, due to the in-famous unique root constraint. This shows that aggregation of information wasn't at all one of the design priorities of XML. In fact, given that compression is an essential feature for data handling, the compression property has later been re-introduced "under the hood" in the XML world, either using dummy root elements to do aggregation, or using the concept of XML collection (like for instance in the XQuery language, cf. [11]).

7.2   Info-extensions

As an example of use of infostructures, we can for example start to model a simplified open-world scenario, where there are several systems that publish and retrieve information: what are some conditions that ensure a certain degree of consistency of the information, i.e., that allows safe aggregation between different information worlds? To answer this question, we can introduce a relationship that information system can satisfy:

Definition 4. *Given two information systems* $\mathcal{A}, \mathcal{B} \in \textbf{\textit{IS}}$, *we say that* $\mathcal{B}$ *is a info-extension (briefly, i-extension) of* $\mathcal{A}$, *and write* $\mathcal{A} \triangleleft \mathcal{B}$, *iff*
$\forall \lambda, \lambda' \in \Lambda, S \in \textbf{\textit{SSS}}, x \in \mathcal{A}.$
$$TAKE_{\mathcal{A}}(\lambda, S) \vdash_{\mathcal{A}} x \Rightarrow TAKE_{\mathcal{B}}(\lambda, S) \vdash_{\mathcal{B}} TAKE_{\mathcal{B}}(\lambda', PUB_{\mathcal{A}}(\lambda', S, x))$$

The following two lemmata show that $\triangleleft$ provides an ordering structure:

Lemma 1 *($\triangleleft$-transitivity)*
The relationship $\triangleleft$ *is transitive.*

Lemma 2 *($\triangleleft$-reflexivity)*
The relationship $\triangleleft$ *is reflexive.*

Before going on, we now need a few definitions.

Definition 5. *Given an infoshare, we can construct the corresponding term algebra, which we call the infoalgebra. Thenn, given a term τ in the infoalgebra, we denote with:*

- *Active(τ) the set of all the λ ∈ Λ that appear as an argument of any PUB in τ.*
- *Passive(τ) the set of all the λ ∈ Λ that appear as an argument of any TAKE in τ.*
- *Before(τ) the initial element S ∈ **SSS** used to build τ*
- *After(τ) the element S' ∈ **SSS** obtained by "evaluating" τ, i.e. by applying all the functions TAKE and PUB present in τ.*

We then have the fundamental:

Theorem 1 *(Passive-Active)*
Suppose to have a term τ in the infoalgebra (say, τ), and the involved information systems form an info-extensionn chain, with $\mathcal{A}$ as top. Then we have:

$$TAKE_{\mathcal{A}} \left(\bigvee Passive(\tau), Before(\tau) \right) \vdash_{\mathcal{A}} TAKE_{\mathcal{A}} \left(\bigvee Active(\tau), After(\tau) \right)$$

Note the importance of the Passive-Active theorem, that essentially shows that info-extensions provide a well-formed layering structure: in an infoshare there is a top $\mathcal{A}$, then $\mathcal{A}$ "stays the same" (remain consistent), unregarding of what has been happening on the infoshares below. This regulation of the information flows allows for a successful integration of information.

It is interesting to compare the information flow behavior of info-extensions with the current information modeling of the Semantic Web Tower, where no general information extension concept had been defined, for lack of a basic operational model to start with. As a result, extensions have been first interpreted as strict logical extensions, and then somehow "patched" so to ensure consistency of information in a web-free embedding modeling. Info-extensions, on the other hand, provide for a more flexible general mechanism that allows more flexibility, allowing to deal more nicely with scenarios where one can't enforce a one-solution-fits-all, but where there will be many competing solutions (at the same time, and also over time), possibly sharing common knowledge grounds.

8   The Future: From Towers to Trees?

We hope to have given some hints on what are the crucial issues that should lead the discussion in judging how the Semantic Web can be an effective way of better handling information on the Web. What is needed is a much wider perspective, including the definition of operational models that take into account the technological structure (the Web, the machines) as well as its interactions with the societal structure (the information flows, the people). Here we have just started to scratch the surface, but it is obvious that a better science of successful information handling for the Web should come from a refined analysis that underlines models, axioms, principles and human factors. Such analysis would help a lot in shaping successful standards and solution for web information, and also help to understand what are the real principles to focus on. For instance, coming back to the original "XML versus RDF" clash described at the beginning, it is interesting to note how once identified an operational model, alternative possible solutions naturally arise: nobody prevents for instance to lower the cost for people that publish (PUB) information, by directly using XML instead of RDF. If this solution is chosen, then suitable interpretations of XML documents can be provided, so to define an infostructure (on this point, remember the basic discussion on the compression property in subsection 7.1). Then, infostructures can be assembled by using infoextensions, in a scenario where information flows grow like a tree, with several possible branches and leaves. Given the relative drop in the cost factor, that avoids information duplication/reshaping in RDF, this might prove to be quite a viable approach for the future. In fact, this approach can be brought even further, by considering not just XML but also XHTML and HTML, so making the initial cost factor for publication of information radically drop: sure, the initial benefits would be lower too, but to start the network effect, after all, we maybe need to talk to humans first. And nobody prevents from then having more specialized semantic web solutions, in the spirit of RDF and the Semantic Web Tower, grow as a branch of the bigger *Web Tree*.

Acknowledgments

I would like to thank German Puebla for his extreme kindness and support.

References

1. W3C: Resource description framework (RDF). http://www.w3.org/RDF/ (1997)
2. Berners-Lee, T.: Universal resource identifiers – axioms of web architecture. http://www.w3.org/DesignIssues/Axioms.html (1996)
3. Berners-Lee, T., et al.: Architecture of the World Wide Web, volume one. http://www.w3.org/TR/webarch/ (2004)
4. Berners-Lee, T., Hendler, J., Lassila, O.: The semantic web. Scientific American **284** (2001) 34–43
5. Marchiori, M.: The semantic web made easy. http://www.w3.org/RDF/Metalog/docs/sw-easy (2003)
6. Nelson, T.: Zig-Zag® Software. http://xanadu.com/zigzag/ (1999)
7. Cranor, L., Langheinrich, M., Marchiori, M., Presler-Marshall, M., Reagle, J.: The platform for privacy preferences 1.0 (p3p1.0) specification. http://www.w3.org/TR/P3P/ (2002)
8. Cranor, L., Langheinrich, M., Marchiori, M.: A P3P preference exchange language 1.0 (APPEL1.0). http://www.w3.org/TR/P3P-preferences (2002)
9. Grillo, B.: Beppe Grillo's Blog. http://www.beppegrillo.it/ (2005)
10. Bray, T., et al.: Extensible markup language (XML) 1.0 (fourth edition). http://www.w3.org/TR/REC-xml/ (2006)
11. Boag, S., et al.: XQuery 1.0: An XML query language. http://www.w3.org/TR/xquery/ (2006)

Appendix: Deeper Modeling

The fact each PUB function in an infostructure is supposed to be a *total* function is quite an assumption. This, because from the Echo axiom, if a $PUB_{\mathcal{A}}$ is always defined (as, $TAKE_{\mathcal{A}}$ is always defined too) then information in $\mathcal{A}$ can't know about the gateway it came from. In other words, $\mathcal{A}$ is in a sense "separated" from the gateway structure, which is good as it makes for a simpler modeling, but also limitative in some scenarios.

The assumption of totality for the publication functions can be be relaxed, and a more sophisticated modeling taken into consideration. For instance, the infostructures axioms can be rewritten using a $Def()$ functor that checks whether or not the specific instance of a publication function is defined:

- **Incrementality**:
  $$\lambda \geq \lambda' \Rightarrow TAKE_{\mathcal{A}}(\lambda', S) \geq TAKE_{\mathcal{A}}(\lambda, S)$$
- **Locality**:
  $$\lambda \perp \lambda' \wedge Def(PUB_{\mathcal{B}}(\lambda, S, x)) \Rightarrow TAKE_{\mathcal{A}}(\lambda', PUB_{\mathcal{B}}(\lambda, S, x)) = TAKE_{\mathcal{A}}(\lambda', S)$$
- **Echo**:
  $$Def(PUB_{\mathcal{A}}(\lambda, S, x)) \Rightarrow TAKE_{\mathcal{A}}(\lambda, PUB_{\mathcal{A}}(\lambda, S, x)) = x$$
- **Update**:
  $$\lambda \leq \lambda' \wedge Def(PUB_{\mathcal{A}}(\lambda, S, x)) \Rightarrow PUB_{\mathcal{A}}(\lambda, PUB_{\mathcal{B}}(\lambda', S, y), x) = PUB_{\mathcal{A}}(\lambda, S, x)$$
- **Separation**:
  $$\lambda \perp \lambda' \wedge Def(PUB_{\mathcal{A}}(\lambda, PUB_{\mathcal{B}}(\lambda', S, y), x)) \Rightarrow PUB_{\mathcal{A}}(\lambda, PUB_{\mathcal{B}}(\lambda', S, y), x) =$$
  $$PUB_{\mathcal{B}}(\lambda', PUB_{\mathcal{A}}(\lambda, S, x), y)$$
- **Freedom**:
  $$\forall \lambda \in \Lambda. \forall S \in \mathbf{SSS}. \exists x \in \mathcal{A}. \exists \lambda' \in \Lambda. \lambda \perp \lambda' \wedge Def(PUB_{\mathcal{A}}(\lambda', S, x))$$

More sophisticated modeling would also include the time variable (which now is implicit in the axioms), making the axiomatization more similar, in spirit, to a modal logic (although, somehow complicating the analysis). Note that this only concerns the modeling of the web environment: a comprehensive formal modeling would also properly take into account the social aspects of the population dynamics, and formalize the concept of Cost and Benefit discussed in Sections 5 and 4.

CHESS: Systematic Stress Testing of Concurrent Software

Madan Musuvathi and Shaz Qadeer

Concurrency is a fundamental attribute of systems software. Asynchronous computation is the norm in important software components such as operating systems, databases, and web servers. As multi-core architectures find their way into mainstream desktop computers, we are likely to see an increasing use of multi-threading in application software as well. Unfortunately, the design of concurrent programs is a very challenging task. The main intellectual difficulty of this task lies in reasoning about the interaction between concurrently executing threads. Nondeterministic thread scheduling makes it extremely difficult to reproduce behavior from one run of the program to another. As a result, the process of debugging concurrent software becomes tedious resulting in a drastic decrease in the productivity of programmers. Since concurrency is both important and difficult to get right, it is imperative that we develop techniques and tools to automatically detect and pinpoint errors in concurrent programs.

The current state-of-the-art in testing concurrent software is unsatisfactory for two reasons. The first problem is that testing is not systematic. A concurrent test scenario is executed repeatedly in the hope that a bad thread schedule will eventually happen. Testers attempt to induce bad schedules by creating thousands of threads, running the test millions of times, and forcing context switches at special program locations. Clearly, these approaches are not systematic because there is no guarantee that one execution will be different from another. The second problem is that a bad schedule, if found, is not repeatable. Consequently, the programmer gets little debugging help once a bug has been detected.

The CHESS project at Microsoft Research attempts to address these limitations by providing systematic, repeatable, and efficient enumeration of thread schedules. CHESS instruments the program execution in order to get control of the scheduling. The instrumentation allocates a semaphore for each thread that is created, and preserves the invariant that at any time every thread but one is blocked on its semaphore. Thus, the underlying operating system scheduler is forced to schedule the one thread that is not blocked. When this thread reaches the next point in its execution that is instrumented, a different thread can be scheduled by performing appropriate operations on their respective semaphores. This mechanism allows CHESS to implement a simple depth-first search of thread schedules, thereby providing the guarantee that each thread schedule generated is different. Moreover, if a schedule results in an error, it can be replayed ad infinitum.

Clearly, the number of possible schedules for realistic concurrent programs is huge. For example, the number of executions for a program with n threads, each

G. Puebla (Ed.): LOPSTR 2006, LNCS 4407, pp. 15–16, 2007.
© Springer-Verlag Berlin Heidelberg 2007

of which executes k steps can be as large as $\Omega(n^k)$. CHESS uses two techniques to manage the complexity of exploring such a large search space.

Iterative context-bounding. In previous work on analysis of concurrent software, we have observed that many subtle concurrency errors are manifested in executions with a small number of context switches [6,5]. At the same time, the total number of executions with at most c context switches is $O(n^{2c}k^c)$. While the total number of executions is exponential in k, the number of executions for any fixed context-switch bound is polynomial in k. CHESS enumerates thread schedules in order of increasing number of context switches. We believe that this strategy for prioritizing search increases the likelihood of finding erroneous executions.

Partial-order reduction. This technique exploits the fact that events in a multithreaded execution are partially rather than totally ordered. All linearizations of a partially-ordered execution are equivalent and it suffices to explore any one of them. In order to avoid enumerating equivalent executions, the partial order corresponding to a linearization must be computed. This partial order, also known as the happens-before relation [3], has traditionaly been computed using clock vectors [4]. We have recently proposed a new algorithm [1] for computing the happens-before relation that is significantly more efficient in practice compared to the clock vector algorithm. CHESS combines this algorithm with a dynamic partial-order reduction strategy due to Flanagan and Godefroid [2] to systematically and efficiently enumerate non-equivalent executions.

References

1. Tayfun Elmas, Shaz Qadeer, and Serdar Tasiran. Goldilocks: Efficiently computing the happens-before relation using locksets, 2006. Full version available at http://www.research.microsoft.com/~qadeer/fatesrv06-fullversion.ps.
2. C. Flanagan and P. Godefroid. Dynamic partial-order reduction for model checking software. In *POPL 05: Principles of Programming Languages*, pages 110–121. ACM Press, 2005.
3. Leslie Lamport. Time, clocks, and the ordering of events in a distributed system. *Communications of the ACM*, 21(7):558–565, 1978.
4. Friedemann Mattern. Virtual time and global states of distributed systems. In *International Workshop on Parallel and Distributed Algorithms*, pages 215–226. North-Holland, 1989.
5. S. Qadeer and J. Rehof. Context-bounded model checking of concurrent software. In *TACAS 05: Tools and Algorithms for the Construction and Analysis of Systems*, volume 3440 of *Lecture Notes in Computer Science*, pages 93–107. Springer, 2005.
6. S. Qadeer and D. Wu. KISS: Keep it simple and seqeuential. In *PLDI 04: Programming Language Design and Implementation*, pages 14–24. ACM, 2004.

ARM: Automatic Rule Miner

Slim Abdennadher, Abdellatif Olama, Noha Salem, and Amira Thabet

Department of Computer Science, German University in Cairo
{slim.abdennadher, abdellatif.olama, noha.salem, amira.thabet}@guc.edu.eg
http://www.cs.guc.edu.eg

Abstract. Rule-based formalisms are ubiquitous in computer science. However, a difficulty that arises frequently when specifying or programming the rules is to determine which effects should be propagated by these rules. In this paper, we present a tool called ARM (Automatic Rule Miner) that generates rules for relations over finite domains.

ARM offers a rich functionality to provide the user with the possibility of specifying the admissible syntactic forms of the rules.

Furthermore, we show that our approach performs well on various examples, e.g. generation of firewall rules or generation of rule-based constraint solvers. Thus, it is suitable for users from different fields.

1 Introduction

Historically, developing rules has been the province of the human experts. Typically, learning the rules in any application domain requires a long apprenticeship. However, when a new knowledge domain immerses then it becomes actually an unaffordable luxury to spend time developing rules in the conventional manner.

Therefore, the trend towards generating the rules in an automated manner is rapidly expanding. To introduce the different available techniques it is important to present the general steps of automatic rule generation.

The first step is the *knowledge acquisition*, which is the action of collecting the data and representing it in the appropriate form as input to the second step. This process is indispensable to build either self-learning or expert systems. The knowledge collection is done with the aid of a field expert and involves a lot of computer science irrelevant details, however the representation of the knowledge has to be thought through in order to better serve the data-mining/rule-inference process. The second and most important step, which is the center of this paper is the *knowledge elicitation*, which involves inferring more information than extensionally provided in the knowledge base, i.e. the generation of general rules that are induced from the given data. This procedure is carried out by experts, who employ usually one of three options:

1. Human manual classification, where experts spend a lot of time studying the technical as well as the practical aspects of the knowledge base and work out the clusters manually.
2. Semi-automatic structuring, where the computer scientists are required to build up an entire expert system manually and then use this expert system afterwards in the induction process.

G. Puebla (Ed.): LOPSTR 2006, LNCS 4407, pp. 17–25, 2007.

3. Automatic selection and generation, where there exists some kind of a system that carries out the process with no - or minor - human intervention.

The motivation for automatic rule generation lies in the advantages offered thereby. The automated generation process is indispensable if no knowledge engineers exist to mine the data manually in order to acquire the deep knowledge. Automatic generation of rules is needed in the fields where it is important to assess and *validate* experts knowledge in a faster and more reliable manner, especially in applications where the lack of reliability is dangerous.

Last but not least, the knowledge provided in most of the application fields is incomplete and sometimes it is useful to be able to induce the rules automatically each time the knowledge base has to be updated. Such updates, if done manually, highly affect the cost.

As mentioned before, automatic rule generation - sometimes referred to as data mining - is a way of extracting rules directly from data and presenting them in an easily understood format. Some of the intelligent techniques that are used include *Neural Networks*, *Genetic Algorithms*, *Fuzzy Logic* and also *Neurofuzzy Logic* [10].

In this paper, we present a tool that is based on an algorithm previously proposed to generate rule-based constraint solvers [1,2]. However, the algorithm turned out to be of great use in different fields that provide crucial services to the various sectors in research as well as in industry and medicine. The power of the tool is accentuated by its high *expressivity* and beneficial *flexibility*. It is more expressive than usual automatic rule generation tools implemented in applications based on Artificial Intelligence since the rules inferred from the knowledge base do not propagate only equality constraints. Using ARM it is possible to propagate *all* sorts of constraints provided that the required constraint solvers exist. Thus, it is possible to customize the generated rules according to any type of application (further elaboration in Section 2).

The paper is organized as follows: In Section 2 the representation of the knowledge base as well as the algorithm is briefly described. Three different applications that benefit from the algorithm implemented in ARM are elaborated in Section 3. In Section 4, an explicit and detailed explanation of the tool ARM is presented, where eventually in Section 5, future perspectives and conclusions are discussed.

2 Algorithm

Knowledge is classified into *facts*, statements that are always true, and *rules*, more complicated and more general statements. Facts are considered to be extensional definitions of some sort of relations. Rules, which denote the intensional definition of the relation, are conditionable; in the sense that they are customized to condition-action situations, like expert and prediction systems.

There are two main different types of rules that could be generated given a specific knowledge base: *propagation rules* and *simplification rules*. Simplification rules, as the name suggests, simplify the knowledge base by removing one or more facts and replacing them by other simpler ones, whereas propagation rules induce a process of deriving new facts from given ones and adding them to the existing knowledge.

Our algorithm generates first only propagation rules. Often, some propagation rules can be transformed into simplification rules. Thus, in a second step a post-processing approach based on a confluence test is performed [2]. The algorithm for generating propagation rules has been developed based on previous work done in the field of *knowledge discovery*.

The algorithm of the tool at hand allows the user to define the form of the rules to be generated. As mentioned before, this tool accepts any type of constraints on both sides of the rule. Technically a rule consists of two parts, called the left-hand side (LHS) and the right-hand side (RHS). The antecedent is written first and called the *head* of the rule, the consequent is called the *body*.

Simplification rules are rules of the form $LHS \Leftrightarrow RHS$ and propagation rules are rules of the form $LHS \Rightarrow RHS$, where LHS and RHS are sets of constraints.

Using ARM the user has the possibility to specify the admissible syntactic forms of the rules. The user determines the relation for which rules have to be generated, i.e. the LHS, and chooses the candidate constraints to form conjunctions together with the left hand side. Usually, these candidate constraints are simply equality constraints. For the right hand side of the rules the user specifies also the form of candidate constraints she/he wants to see there. Finally, the user determines the semantics of the constraint on the LHS by means of its extensional definition which must be finite, and provides the semantics of the candidate constraints and the candidate RHS by two constraint theories. Furthermore, it is assumed that the constraints defined are handled by an appropriate constraint solver.

To compute the rules the algorithm enumerates each possible LHS constraint (noted C_{lhs}) and for each determines the corresponding RHS constraint (noted C_{rhs}).

For each LHS C_{lhs} the corresponding RHS C_{rhs} is computed in the following way:

1. if C_{lhs} has no solution then $C_{rhs} = \{false\}$ and we have the failure rule $C_{lhs} \Rightarrow \{false\}$.
2. if C_{lhs} has at least one solution then C_{rhs} is the set of all atomic constraints which are candidates for the RHS part and that are true for all solution of C_{lhs}. If C_{rhs} is not empty we have the rule $C_{lhs} \Rightarrow C_{rhs}$.

The algorithm uses pruning strategies to reduce the number of rules generated. This way it becomes much more efficient if during the enumeration of all possible rule LHS, a given LHS is considered before any of its supersets. So a specific ordering for this enumeration is imposed in the algorithm. Moreover, this ordering allows to discover early covering rules avoiding then the generation of many uninteresting covered rules.

3   Application

Many applications require data-mining and rule generation. In this section, three applications from three different domains are presented to endorse the generality of the proposed tool for automated generation of rules.

3.1   Firewall Design

The function of a firewall is to examine each packet that attempts to enter a private network and decide whether to accept the packet and allow it to proceed or to discard it. A typical firewall design consists of a sequence of rules. To make a decision concerning some packets, the firewall rules are compared, one by one, with the packet until one rule is found to be satisfied by the packet: this rule determines the fate of the packet. The first method ever for designing the sequence of rules in a firewall to be consistent, complete, and compact using Firewall Decision Diagram was proposed by [7]. Using ARM it is possible to use the extensional definitions of a packet to generate the firewall rules. There are usually five primary fields that describe the packet in any firewall and are used for deciding the course of a packet: discard or accept. The following is an excerpt of the knowledge base of a firewall with simplified representation of a network packet pack(F0,F1,A) with only two parameter fields, F0 and F1 together with the action A to be taken upon the arrival of this packet, where a stands for accept and d stands for discard:

```
pack(4, 2, a).    pack(4, 3, a).    pack(4, 5, a).    pack(4, 6, a).
pack(4, 7, a).    pack(4, 0, d).    pack(4, 1, d).    pack(4, 4, d).
pack(4, 8, d).    pack(4 ,9, d).    pack(5, 2, a).    pack(5, 3, a).
pack(5, 5, a).    pack(5, 6, a).    pack(5, 7, a).    pack(5, 0, d).
pack(5, 1, d).    pack(5, 4, d).    pack(5, 8, d).    pack(5, 9, d).
pack(6, 2, a).    pack(6, 3, a).    pack(6, 5, a).    pack(6, 6, a).
pack(6, 7, a).    pack(6, 0, d).    pack(6, 1, d).    pack(6, 4, d).
pack(6, 8, d).    pack(6, 9, d).    pack(7, 2, a).    pack(7, 3, a).
pack(7, 5, a).    pack(7, 6, a).    pack(7, 7, a).    pack(7, 0, d).
pack(7, 1, d).    pack(7, 4, d).    pack(7, 8, d).    pack(7, 9, d).
pack(0, 0, d).    pack(0, 1, d).    pack(0, 2, d).    pack(0, 3, d).
pack(0, 4, d).    pack(0, 5, d).    pack(0, 6, d).    pack(0, 7, d).
pack(0, 8, d).    pack(0, 9, d).    pack(1, 0, d).    pack(1, 1, d).
pack(1, 2, d).    pack(1, 3, d).    pack(1, 4, d).    pack(1, 5, d).
pack(1, 6, d).    pack(1, 7, d).    pack(1, 8, d).    pack(1, 9, d).
pack(2, 0, d).    pack(2, 1, d).    pack(2, 2, d).    pack(2, 3, d).
pack(2, 4, d).    pack(2, 5, d).    pack(2, 6, d).    pack(2, 7, d).
pack(2, 8, d).    pack(2, 9, d).    pack(3, 0, d).    pack(3, 1, d).
pack(3, 2, d).    pack(3, 3, d).    pack(3, 4, d).    pack(3, 5, d).
pack(3, 6, d).    pack(3, 7, d).    pack(3, 8, d).    pack(3, 9, d).
pack(8, 0, d).    pack(8, 1, d).    pack(8, 2, d).    pack(8, 3, d).
pack(8, 4, d).    pack(8, 5, d).    pack(8, 6, d).    pack(8, 7, d).
pack(8, 8, d).    pack(8, 9, d).    pack(9, 0, d).    pack(9, 1, d).
pack(9, 2, d).    pack(9, 3, d).    pack(9, 4, d).    pack(9, 5, d).
pack(9, 6, d).    pack(9, 7, d).    pack(9, 8, d).    pack(9, 9, d).
```

For this knowledge base of the firewall, ARM will automatically generate among others the following propagation rule provided the user specifies that the right hand side of the rules may consist of a conjunction of equality constraints.

```
pack(F0,9,A) ⇒ A=d.
pack(F0,8,A) ⇒  A=d
...
pack(7,7,A)⇒ A=a.
pack(7,6,A)⇒ A=a.
...
```

The first rule means that for any values for F0, if the second field has the value 9, then the packet should be discarded.

The ARM tool can generate a more compact representation of the rules, if the user specifies to have membership constraints in the left hand side of the rules:

```
pack(F0,F1,A), F1 in[0,1,4,8,9]⇒ A=d.
pack(F0,F1,A), F0 in[0,1,2,3,8,9] ⇒ A=d.
pack(F0,F1,A), F0 in [4,5,6,7], F1 in [2,3,5,6,7] ⇒ A=a.
```

3.2 Generation of Constraint Solvers

Originally the algorithm presented in Section 2 was introduced to generate rule-based constraint solvers for finite constraints given their extensional representation [1]. The generated rules can be executed using the Constraint Handling Rules framework [5,6].

For example, for the logical operator *and* that can be defined extensionally by the triples $\{(0,0,0),(0,1,0),(1,0,0),(1,1,1)\}$ and for the logical operator *neg* that can be defined by the pairs $\{(0,1),(1,0)\}$, where 1 stands for truth and 0 for falsity, the algorithm can generate, among other, the following rules:

$$and(0,Y,Z) \Leftrightarrow Z=0.$$
$$and(1,Y,Z) \Leftrightarrow Y=Z.$$
$$and(X,X,Z) \Leftrightarrow X=Z.$$
$$neg(X,0) \Leftrightarrow X=1.$$
$$neg(X,X) \Rightarrow false.$$
$$and(X,Y,Z), neg(X,Y) \Leftrightarrow Z=0, neg(X,Y).$$

The algorithm performs well on various examples, including Boolean constraints, multi-valued logic, Allen's qualitative approach to temporal logic and qualitative spatial reasoning with the Region Connection Calculus [1].

4 Arm Features

4.1 How to Run ARM

ARM can be run as an application. The application version of ARM requires the installation of SICStus Prolog version 3.8.6 or later as well as the Java to Prolog interface package Jasper (se.sics.jasper). If ARM was started successfully, the start screen shown in Figure 1 appears. On the start screen one has to choose either of the two available options which will determine how ARM will specify the domain for each of the parameters of a relation. Choosing the N-to-1 option will result in setting a single domain which is applied to each of the parameters of the relation based on the values that were used in the specified tuples. The N-to-N option sets a separate domain for each parameter of the relation. This feature will suppress the generation of a huge number of failure rules. For example, for the firewall design example, if the user will choose the N-to-1 option, then rules like

```
pack(F0,F1,4)  ⇒   false.
```

will be generated, although it is clear from the begining that the third argument of the predicate pack cannot take the value 4. Thus for the firewall design example, the user should specify the values of each parameter using the N-to-N option. For the constraint solving example, all arguments have the domain $\{0,1\}$, thus the user should choose the N-to-1 option.

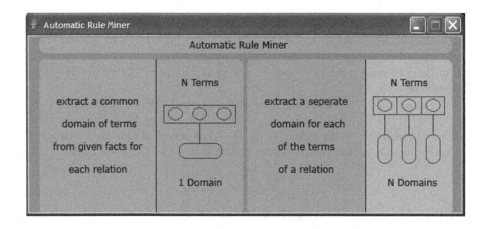

Fig. 1. Start-up Window

After choosing either option by clicking the appropriate button, the main view of ARM will appear as shown in Figure 2.

From the relations menu one can add rules to the relations list. By clicking on the add button a pop-up window will appear where the name of the relation can be entered. By clicking the name of a relation from the relations list the tuples associated with the selected relation will be displayed in the tuples list, part of the tuples menu. Tuples associated with a relation can be added or removed using the add and remove buttons. By clicking the add button of the `tuples menu` a pop-up window containing a text field will appear where a space-separated list of values should be entered to represent a tuple to be associated with the highlighted relation of the `relations menu`.

Each of the two drop-down lists at the bottom of the main view window contains available constraints that could be added to the list of constraints to be added to the right-hand-side and left-hand-side of the generated rules. Choosing a constraint from the drop-down list and clicking the `add` button will add the constraint to the specified side of the rules.

After finalizing the selection of relations, associated tuples and constraints, the `generate rules` button should be clicked to display the result of generating the rules according to the specified input.

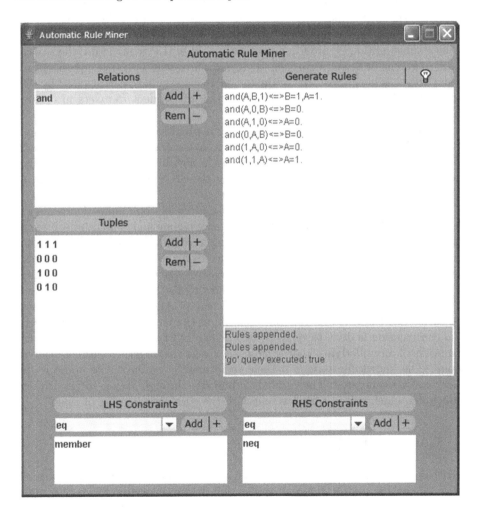

Fig. 2. ARM's Main View

4.2   Implementation of ARM

ARM's graphical user interface is implemented in Java using the Java Software Development Kit (J2SDK) version 1. The underlying generation of rules is implemented partly in Java, however the main part is implemented in SICStus Prolog.

As described in Section 2, ARM needs to enumerate LHS constraints. Our implementation follows the idea of direct extraction of association rules by exploring a tree corresponding to the LHS search space. This tree is expanded and explored using a depth first strategy, in a way that constructs only necessary LHS candidates and allows to remove uninteresting candidates by cutting whole branches of the tree. The branches of the tree are developed using a partial ordering on the LHS candidates such that the more general LHS are examined before more specialized ones. The partial ordering used in our implementation is the θ-subsumption [9] ordering commonly used in ILP to structure the search space (e.g., the WARMR algorithm [4] to mine frequent DATALOG queries). To prune branches in the tree, one of the two main criteria has been inspired by the CLOSE algorithm [8] devoted to the extraction of frequent *itemsets* in dense[1] data sets.

The interaction between Java and Prolog is provided using the bidirectional interface Jasper. Jasper is used as a Java package (se.sics.jasper) for the purposes of ARM since the interaction is needed only in one direction, more specifically, the Java graphical user interface will query the SICStus Prolog and obtain a result which will be displayed by Java again.

SICStus Prolog performs the role of a base layer for communication between the knowledge base on one side and the inference engine and constraint solver on the other side. As a rule-based programming language, Prolog helps in simplifying this task. SICStus provides several choices for developing user interfaces, however Java stands out among other alternatives like C and Tcl/Tk especially because of the portability issue which is overcome by default when using Java.

Through the Java-Prolog interaction, the user of ARM will be able to generate rules. The rules will be generated based on the facts provided by the user. The construction is done through the graphical interface which will trigger the formation of an underlying knowledge base of relations together with associated tuples. The knowledge base will then be formatted by Java, the appropriate query will be generated. The result is submitted through Jasper to the Prolog interpreter which will in turn respond with the corresponding list of rules.

5   Conclusion

ARM is a tool for generating rules from relational data. We have shown that this tool can be used in different application fields: generation of firewall rules and rule-based constraint solvers.

The tool can be run as an application under `http://cs.guc.edu.eg/arm`

---

[1] e.g., data sets containing many strong correlations.

Future work includes the extension of the tool to generate rules for relations defined intensionally eventually over non finite domains. A first preliminary step in this direction has recently been proposed in [3].

References

1. S. Abdennadher and C. Rigotti. Automatic generation of propagation rules for finite domains. In *6th International Conference on Principles and Practice of Constraint Programming, CP'00*, LNCS 1894. Springer-Verlag, 2000.
2. S. Abdennadher and C. Rigotti. Automatic generation of rule-based constraint solvers over finite domains. *ACM Transactions on Computational Logic*, 5(2), 2004.
3. S. Abdennadher and C. Rigotti. Automatic generation of CHR constraint solvers. *Journal of Theory and Practice of Logic Programming (TPLP)*, 5(2), 2005.
4. Luc Dehaspe and Hannu Toivonen. Discovery of frequent DATALOG patterns. *Data Mining and Knowledge Discovery*, 3(1):7–36, 1999.
5. T. Frühwirth. Theory and practice of constraint handling rules, special issue on constraint logic programming. *Journal of Logic Programming*, 37(1-3), October 1998.
6. T. Frühwirth and S. Abdennadher. *Essentials of Constraint Programming*. Springer-Verlag, 2003.
7. X. A. Liu M. G. Gouda. Firewall design: Consistency, completeness, and compactness. In *24th IEEE International Conference on Distributed Computing Systems*, 2004.
8. Nicolas Pasquier, Yves Bastide, Rafik Taouil, and Lotfi Lakhal. Efficient mining of association rules using closed itemset lattices. *Information Systems*, 24(1):25–46, 1999.
9. Gordon Plotkin. A note on inductive generalization. In *Machine Intelligence*, volume 5, pages 153–163. Edinburgh University Press, 1970.
10. P. Smyth U. Fayyad, G. Piatestsky. From data mining to knowledge discovery in databases. *American Association for Artificial Intelligence*, 1996.

Constructing Consensus Logic Programs

Chiaki Sakama[1] and Katsumi Inoue[2]

[1] Department of Computer and Communication Sciences
Wakayama University, Sakaedani, Wakayama 640-8510, Japan
sakama@sys.wakayama-u.ac.jp
[2] National Institute of Informatics
2-1-2 Hitotsubashi, Chiyoda-ku, Tokyo 101-8430, Japan
ki@nii.ac.jp

Abstract. In this paper, we suppose an agent which has a knowledge base represented by a logic program under the answer set semantics. We then consider the following two problems: given two programs P_1 and P_2, which have the sets of answer sets $\mathcal{AS}(P_1)$ and $\mathcal{AS}(P_2)$, respectively; (i) find a program Q which has the answer sets as the minimal elements of $\{\, S \cap T \mid S \in \mathcal{AS}(P_1) \text{ and } T \in \mathcal{AS}(P_2) \,\}$; (ii) find a program R which has the answer sets as the maximal elements of the above set. A program Q satisfying (i) is called *minimal consensus* between P_1 and P_2; and R satisfying (ii) is called *maximal consensus* between P_1 and P_2. Minimal/maximal consensus extracts common beliefs that are included in an answer set of every program. Consensus provides a method of program development under a specification of constructing a program that reflects the meaning of two or more programs. In application, it contributes to a theory of building consensus in multi-agent systems.

1 Introduction

Logic programming provides a formal language for representing knowledge and belief of an agent. The declarative semantics of a program is given by a set of canonical models which represent belief sets of an agent. Our primary interest in this paper is: what are the suitable conclusions drawn from a *collection* of programs, and how to synthesize a program having such a collective semantics. Those problems become especially important when there exist more than one agent in multi-agent environments. In a multi-agent community, multiple agents generally have different beliefs and intentions. To make decision and act as a whole community, they must seek *consensus* which is acceptable to every individual agent. Suppose a multi-agent system in which each agent has a knowledge base represented by a logic program under the answer set semantics [8]. Answer sets represent sets of literals corresponding to beliefs which can be built by a rational reasoner on the basis of a program [2]. An agent may have (conflicting) alternative sets of beliefs, which are represented by multiple answer sets of a program. Different agents have different collections of answer sets in general. We then capture building consensus among multiple agents as the problem of finding a new program which has consequences common to all programs.

Before formally stating the problem, suppose the following scenario: John and Mary are a couple. John wants to buy a new personal computer. To achieve the goal, he considers two options to save money. The first option is to stop bar-hopping. The second

G. Puebla (Ed.): LOPSTR 2006, LNCS 4407, pp. 26–42, 2007.

one is to give up a family trip this year. These two options are indefinite at the moment. John's belief is represented by the program:

$$P_1 : \quad \leftarrow not\ pc,$$
$$pc \leftarrow money,$$
$$money \leftarrow \neg bhop,$$
$$money \leftarrow \neg trip,$$
$$bhop;\ \neg bhop \leftarrow,$$
$$trip;\ \neg trip \leftarrow,$$

where ";" represents disjunction and *not* represents negation as failure. On the other hand, Mary plans to save money to buy her new dress. She also has two options: giving up a family trip or going to no restaurant. She usually does not go to a restaurant. If the family gives up a trip, however, she wants to have a special dinner at a restaurant, instead. She also has indefinite belief on giving up a trip. Mary's belief is represented by the program:

$$P_2 : \quad \leftarrow not\ dress,$$
$$dress \leftarrow money,$$
$$money \leftarrow \neg trip,$$
$$money \leftarrow \neg restaurant,$$
$$\neg restaurant \leftarrow not\ restaurant,$$
$$restaurant \leftarrow \neg trip,$$
$$trip;\ \neg trip \leftarrow .$$

In this situation, P_1 has three answer sets: $S_1 = \{ pc, money, \neg bhop, trip \}$, $S_2 = \{ pc, money, bhop, \neg trip \}$, and $S_3 = \{ pc, money, \neg bhop, \neg trip \}$. And P_2 has two answer sets: $T_1 = \{ dress, money, \neg restaurant, trip \}$ and $T_2 = \{ dress, money, \neg trip, restaurant \}$. Then, which conclusions should be drawn as consensus of the couple? Since *money* is included in every answer set of two programs, it seems no doubt to have $\{ money \}$ as a result of consensus. In fact, John and Mary agree to save money, although their purposes are different. On the other hand, $\{ money, trip \}$ is a subset of both S_1 and T_1, and $\{ money, \neg trip \}$ is a subset of S_2, S_3 and T_2. So these two sets are also considered as admissible results of consensus. In the set $\{ money, trip \}$, the couple agrees with both saving money and having a trip. In this case, each person considers another way to save money. In the set $\{ money, \neg trip \}$, the couple agrees with giving up a trip to save money.

This example illustrates that there are two different types of consensus. The first one collects minimal sets of beliefs that are included in an answer set of every program. By contrast, the second one collects maximal sets of beliefs that are included in an answer set of every program. These two types of consensus provide different results in general. The purpose of this paper is to develop a theory of such consensus among multiple logic programs.

Formally, the problems considered in this paper are described as follows:

Given : two programs P_1 and P_2;

Find : (1) a program Q satisfying
$$AS(Q) = min(\{ S \cap T \mid S \in AS(P_1) \text{ and } T \in AS(P_2) \});$$
   (2) a program R satisfying
$$AS(R) = max(\{ S \cap T \mid S \in AS(P_1) \text{ and } T \in AS(P_2) \}),$$

where $min(X) = \{ Y \in X \mid \neg\exists Z \in X \text{ s.t. } Z \subset Y \}$ and $max(X) = \{ Y \in X \mid \neg\exists Z \in X \text{ s.t. } Y \subset Z \}$.

The program Q satisfying (1) is called *minimal consensus* between P_1 and P_2; and the program R satisfying (2) is called *maximal consensus* between P_1 and P_2. We investigate the declarative nature of these two types of consensus, and develop methods for constructing consensus programs from multiple programs.

The rest of this paper is organized as follows. Section 2 presents basic notions used in this paper. Section 3 introduces a framework of consensus among logic programs. Section 4 provides a method for constructing consensus programs. Section 5 addresses applications to multi-agent systems. Section 6 discusses related issues, and Section 7 summarizes the paper.

2   Preliminaries

A *program* considered in this paper is an *extended disjunctive program* (EDP) which is a set of *rules* of the form:

$$L_1 ; \cdots ; L_l \leftarrow L_{l+1}, \ldots, L_m, \, not \, L_{m+1}, \ldots, \, not \, L_n \quad (n \geq m \geq l \geq 0)$$

where each L_i is a positive/negative literal, i.e., A or $\neg A$ for an atom A, and *not* is *negation as failure* (NAF). $not\,L$ is called an *NAF-literal*. The symbol ";" represents disjunction. The left-hand side of the rule is the *head*, and the right-hand side is the *body*. For each rule r of the above form, $head(r)$, $body^+(r)$ and $body^-(r)$ denote the sets of literals $\{L_1, \ldots, L_l\}$, $\{L_{l+1}, \ldots, L_m\}$, and $\{L_{m+1}, \ldots, L_n\}$, respectively. Also, $not\_body^-(r)$ denotes the set of NAF-literals $\{not\,L_{m+1}, \ldots, not\,L_n\}$. A disjunction of literals and a conjunction of (NAF-)literals in a rule are identified with its corresponding sets of literals. A rule r is often written as $head(r) \leftarrow body(r)$ where $body(r) = body^+(r) \cup not\_body^-(r)$. A rule r is *disjunctive* if $head(r)$ contains more than one literal. A rule r is an *integrity constraint* if $head(r) = \emptyset$; and r is a *fact* if $body(r) = \emptyset$. A rule r is a *conditional fact* if $body^+(r) = \emptyset$. A program is *NAF-free* if no rule contains NAF-literals. A program is a *kernel form* if it consists of conditional facts only. A program with variables is considered a shorthand for its ground instantiation, and this paper handles ground programs unless stated otherwise.

The semantics of EDPs is given by the *answer set semantics* [8]. Let Lit be the set of all ground literals in the language of a program. A set $S(\subseteq Lit)$ *satisfies* a ground rule r if $body^+(r) \subseteq S$ and $body^-(r) \cap S = \emptyset$ imply $head(r) \cap S \neq \emptyset$. In particular, S satisfies a ground integrity constraint r with $head(r) = \emptyset$ if either $body^+(r) \not\subseteq S$ or $body^-(r) \cap S \neq \emptyset$. S satisfies a ground program P if S satisfies every ground rule in P. Let P be a ground NAF-free EDP. Then, a set $S(\subseteq Lit)$ is an *answer set* of P if S is a minimal set such that (i) S satisfies P; and (ii) if S contains a pair of complementary literals L and $\neg L$, $S = Lit$. Next, let P be any ground EDP and $S \subseteq Lit$. For every ground rule r in P, the rule $head(r) \leftarrow body^+(r)$ is included in the *reduct* P^S if $body^-(r) \cap S = \emptyset$. Then, S is an *answer set* of P if S is an answer set of P^S. A program has none, one, or multiple answer sets in general. The set of all answer sets of P is written as $\mathcal{AS}(P)$. Note that the collection $\mathcal{AS}(P)$ is an *anti-chain* set, i.e., no element $S \in \mathcal{AS}(P)$ is a proper subset of another element $T \in \mathcal{AS}(P)$. A program having a single answer set is called *categorical* [2]. Categorical programs include important classes of programs such as *definite programs*, *stratified programs*, and *call-consistent programs*. An answer set is *consistent* if it is not Lit. A program P is *consistent* if it has a consistent answer set; otherwise, P is *inconsistent*. An inconsistent program has either no answer set (*incoherent*) or the single answer set Lit (*contradictory*). A literal L is a consequence of *skeptical reasoning* (resp. *credulous reasoning*) in P if L is included in every (resp. some) answer set of P. The set of all literal consequences under skeptical (resp. credulous) reasoning in P is written as $skp(P)$ (resp. $crd(P)$). By the definition, $skp(P) = Lit$ and $crd(P) = \emptyset$ if P is incoherent; and $skp(P) = crd(P) = Lit$ if P is contradictory. Clearly, $skp(P) \subseteq crd(P)$ for any consistent program P.

Example 2.1. Let P be the program:

$$p \,; q \leftarrow,$$
$$r \leftarrow p,$$
$$r \leftarrow q,$$

where $\mathcal{AS}(P) = \{\{p, r\}, \{q, r\}\}$. Then, $crd(P) = \{p, q, r\}$ and $skp(P) = \{r\}$.

3   Consensus Logic Programs

In this section, we introduce a framework of consensus among multiple programs. Throughout the paper, different programs are assumed to have the same underlying language. This implies that every program has the same set Lit of all ground literals in the language.

Definition 3.1. Let P_1 and P_2 be two programs. Then, define

$$cons(P_1, P_2) = \{ S \cap T \mid S \in \mathcal{AS}(P_1) \text{ and } T \in \mathcal{AS}(P_2) \}.$$

In particular, $cons(P_1, P_2) = \emptyset$ if $\mathcal{AS}(P_1) = \emptyset$ or $\mathcal{AS}(P_2) = \emptyset$.

Definition 3.2. Let P_1 and P_2 be two programs. A program Q is called *minimal consensus* (between P_1 and P_2) if it satisfies the condition

$$\mathcal{AS}(Q) = min(cons(P_1, P_2))$$

where $min(X) = \{ Y \in X \mid \neg \exists Z \in X \text{ s.t. } Z \subset Y \}$. On the other hand, a program R is called *maximal consensus* (between P_1 and P_2) if it satisfies the condition

$$\mathcal{AS}(R) = max(cons(P_1, P_2))$$

where $max(X) = \{ Y \in X \mid \neg \exists Z \in X \text{ s.t. } Y \subset Z \}$. Each element in $\mathcal{AS}(Q)$ (resp. $\mathcal{AS}(R)$) is called a *result* of minimal (resp. maximal) consensus (between P_1 and P_2).

We will often omit "between P_1 and P_2" when it is clear from the context. The above program Q or R is also called a (minimal or maximal) *consensus program*.

Intuitively, a result of minimal consensus represents a minimal agreement. That is, an answer set of Q is a minimal set of beliefs which are included in both an answer set of P_1 and an answer set of P_2. By contrast, a result of maximal consensus represents a maximal agreement. A minimal/maximal consensus is a program which has the meaning as a collection of such minimal/maximal agreement.

Example 3.1. For $\mathcal{AS}(P_1) = \{\{p,s\},\{q\}\}$ and $\mathcal{AS}(P_2) = \{\{p,t\},\{r\}\}$, $cons(P_1, P_2) = \{\emptyset, \{p\}\}$. Then, the result of minimal consensus is $\emptyset$, while the result of maximal consensus is $\{p\}$.

The following properties directly hold by Definition 3.2.

Proposition 3.1. *Let P_1 and P_2 be two programs, Q a minimal consensus, and R a maximal consensus. Consensus programs have the following properties.*

1. *Q and R are consistent iff both P_1 and P_2 are consistent, or one is consistent and the other is contradictory. In particular, if P_1 is contradictory, $\mathcal{AS}(Q) = \mathcal{AS}(R) = \mathcal{AS}(P_2)$.*
2. *Q and R are contradictory iff both P_1 and P_2 are contradictory.*
3. *Q and R are incoherent iff either P_1 or P_2 is incoherent.*

Proposition 3.2. *When two programs P_1 and P_2 are both categorical, minimal and maximal consensus coincide.*

By Proposition 3.1, when one of two programs is inconsistent, the results of consensus are rather trivial. We thus consider consensus of consistent programs hereafter.

Proposition 3.3. *Let P_1 and P_2 be two consistent programs, Q a minimal consensus, and R a maximal consensus. Then,*

1. *$\forall U \in \mathcal{AS}(Q), \exists S \in \mathcal{AS}(P_1)$ and $\exists T \in \mathcal{AS}(P_2)$ such that $U \subseteq S$ and $U \subseteq T$.*
2. *$\forall V \in \mathcal{AS}(R), \exists S \in \mathcal{AS}(P_1)$ and $\exists T \in \mathcal{AS}(P_2)$ such that $V \subseteq S$ and $V \subseteq T$.*
3. *$\forall S \in \mathcal{AS}(P_1)$ and $\forall T \in \mathcal{AS}(P_2), \exists U \in \mathcal{AS}(Q)$ such that $U \subseteq S$ and $U \subseteq T$.*

Proof. Since $U = S \cap T$ for some $S \in \mathcal{AS}(P_1)$ and $T \in \mathcal{AS}(P_2)$, $U \subseteq S$ and $U \subseteq T$ hold. Thus, 1 and 2 hold. As U is a minimal element of $cons(P_1, P_2)$, the result 3 follows.   □

Proposition 3.3 asserts that a result of minimal/maximal consensus reflects a part of beliefs included in an answer set of every program. Conversely, beliefs included in an answer set of every program are partly reflected as a result of minimal consensus. By contrast, beliefs included in an answer set of a program may not be reflected as a result of maximal consensus.

Example 3.2. In Example 3.1, the result of maximal consensus $\{p\}$ reflects a part of beliefs in the answer set $\{p,s\}$ of P_1 and a part of beliefs in the answer set $\{p,t\}$ of P_2. But beliefs in the answer set $\{q\}$ of P_1 and $\{r\}$ of P_2 is not reflected as a result of maximal consensus.

Comparing results of minimal consensus and maximal consensus, a result of maximal consensus generally contains more information than a result of minimal consensus. A result of minimal consensus easily becomes an empty set as in Example 3.1.

It may happen that the results of consensus coincide with answer sets of one of the original programs.

Definition 3.3. For two programs P_1 and P_2, let Q be a minimal consensus and R a maximal consensus. When $\mathcal{AS}(Q) = \mathcal{AS}(P_1)$ (resp. $\mathcal{AS}(R) = \mathcal{AS}(P_1)$), P_1 *dominates* P_2 under minimal (resp. maximal) consensus.

Every consistent program dominates contradictory programs under minimal/maximal consensus (Proposition 3.1(1)). When P_1 dominates P_2 under minimal/maximal consensus, we can easily have a consensus program as P_1. The next proposition presents a situation in which such domination happens.

Proposition 3.4. *Let P_1 and P_2 be two consistent programs. Then,*

1. *If $S \subseteq T$ for any $S \in \mathcal{AS}(P_1)$ and for any $T \in \mathcal{AS}(P_2)$,*
   P_1 dominates P_2 under minimal/maximal consensus.
2. *If $S \subseteq T$ for any $S \in \mathcal{AS}(P_1)$ and for some $T \in \mathcal{AS}(P_2)$,*
   P_1 dominates P_2 under maximal consensus.

Proof. (1) If $S \subseteq T$ for any $S \in \mathcal{AS}(P_1)$ and for any $T \in \mathcal{AS}(P_2)$, it holds that $cons(P_1, P_2) = \mathcal{AS}(P_1)$. Then, $\mathcal{AS}(Q) = \mathcal{AS}(R) = \mathcal{AS}(P_1)$ and P_1 dominates P_2 under minimal/maximal consensus. (2) If $S \subseteq T$ for any $S \in \mathcal{AS}(P_1)$ and for some $T \in \mathcal{AS}(P_2)$, $S \cap T = S$ holds for such T. For any $T' \in \mathcal{AS}(P_2)$ such that $S \not\subseteq T'$, $S \cap T' \subset S$ holds. As $S \cap T' \subset S \cap T$, $\mathcal{AS}(R) = \mathcal{AS}(P_1)$. Hence, P_1 dominates P_2 under maximal consensus. □

Skeptical/credulous inference in consensus programs has the following properties.

Proposition 3.5. *Let P_1 and P_2 be two consistent programs, Q a minimal consensus, and R a maximal consensus. Then,*

1. $skp(Q) = skp(P_1) \cap skp(P_2)$.
2. $skp(Q) \subseteq skp(R)$.
3. $crd(R) = crd(P_1) \cap crd(P_2)$.
4. $crd(Q) \subseteq crd(R)$.

Proof. 1. For any $L \in Lit$, $L \in skp(Q)$
iff $\forall U \in min(cons(P_1, P_2))$, $L \in U$
iff $\forall V \in cons(P_1, P_2)$, $L \in V$
iff ($\forall S \in \mathcal{AS}(P_1)$, $L \in S$) and ($\forall T \in \mathcal{AS}(P_2)$, $L \in T$)
iff $L \in skp(P_1) \cap skp(P_2)$.
   2. For any $L \in Lit$, $L \in skp(Q)$
iff $\forall U \in min(cons(P_1, P_2))$, $L \in U$
only if $\forall V \in max(cons(P_1, P_2))$, $L \in V$
iff $L \in skp(R)$.

3. For any $L \in Lit$, $L \in crd(R)$
iff $\exists U \in max(cons(P_1, P_2))$, $L \in U$
iff $\exists V \in cons(P_1, P_2)$, $L \in V$
iff ($\exists S \in AS(P_1)$, $L \in S$) and ($\exists T \in AS(P_2)$, $L \in T$)
iff $L \in crd(P_1) \cap crd(P_2)$.
  4. For any $L \in Lit$, $L \in crd(Q)$
iff $\exists U \in min(cons(P_1, P_2))$, $L \in U$
only if $\exists V \in max(cons(P_1, P_2))$, $L \in V$
iff $L \in crd(R)$. $\square$

Thus, minimal consensus extracts skeptical consequences that are common between two programs. By contrast, maximal consensus extracts credulous consequences that are common between two programs. The converse inclusion relations in the second and fourth items of Proposition 3.5 do not hold in general.

Example 3.3. Let $AS(P_1) = \{\{p, q\}, \{q, r\}\}$ and $AS(P_2) = \{\{p, q\}\}$ where $skp(P_1) = \{q\}$, $crd(P_1) = \{p, q, r\}$, and $skp(P_2) = crd(P_2) = \{p, q\}$. The result of minimal consensus is $AS(Q) = \{\{q\}\}$ and the result of maximal consensus is $AS(R) = \{\{p, q\}\}$. Then, $crd(Q) \subseteq crd(R)$ and $skp(Q) \subseteq skp(R)$.

Proposition 3.5 shows that minimal consensus (resp. maximal consensus) is appropriate for making consensus among skeptical (resp. credulous) reasoners. In building consensus, the problem of interest is the case where one program does not dominate the other and the result of consensus is consistent. In the next section, we present methods for computing consensus programs.

4 Computing Consensus Programs

This section assumes function-free logic programs which are instantiated to finite ground programs. The following transformations are applied to a finite ground EDP P.

- (Elimination of tautologies)
  Delete a rule r from P if $head(r) \cap body^+(r) \neq \emptyset$.
- (Elimination of non-minimal rules)
  Delete a rule r from P if there is another rule r' in P such that $head(r') \subseteq head(r)$, $body^+(r') \subseteq body^+(r)$ and $body^-(r') \subseteq body^-(r)$.
- (Partial evaluation) [3,11] If P contains a rule $head(r) \leftarrow body(r)$ such that $L \in body^+(r)$, and contains r_i ($i = 1, \ldots, n$) with $L \in head(r_i)$, replace r with the following n rules: $head(r) \cup (head(r_i) \setminus \{L\}) \leftarrow (body(r) \setminus \{L\}) \cup body(r_i)$.
- (Elimination of unfired rules)[1]
  Delete a rule r from P if $head(r') \cap body^+(r) = \emptyset$ for any rule r' in P.

Let $T(P)$ be a program which is obtained from P by applying one of the transformations presented above. Also, let $T^{k+1}(P) = T(T^k(P))$ ($k \geq 0$) where $T^0(P) = P$. Iterative application of transformations reaches a fixpoint $T^n(P) = T^{n-1}(P)$ ($n \geq 1$) and satisfies the following property.

---

[1] This transformation is considered a special case of partial evaluation in clausal logic [7]. We separate this one here as extended disjunctive programs are outside of clausal logic.

Proposition 4.1. *([3]) Let P be a program, and T transformations presented above. Then, there is a fixpoint $T^n(P) = T^{n-1}(P)$. Moreover, for any such n, $T^n(P)$ is a kernel form and $\mathcal{AS}(P) = \mathcal{AS}(T^n(P))$.*

In what follows, a fixpoint $T^n(P)$, which is in a kernel form, is represented by $ker(P)$.

Definition 4.1. Let P_1 and P_2 be two programs, and $\Sigma \subseteq 2^{Lit}$ an anti-chain over Lit.

1. Compute kernel forms $ker(P_1)$ and $ker(P_2)$.
2. Let $S \in \Sigma$. For any rule $r \in ker(P_1) \cup ker(P_2)$ satisfying $head(r) \cap S \neq \emptyset$, construct a rule r^* such that
   - $head(r^*) = head(r) \cap S$,
   - $body(r^*) = body(r) \cup \{\, not\, L \mid L \in head(r) \setminus S \,\}$
     $\qquad\qquad \cup \{\, not\, M \mid M \in T \setminus S \text{ for any } T \in \Sigma \,\}.$

   Put $R(S) = \{r^*\}$ as the set of all such rules.
3. For any $S \in \Sigma$, collect $R(S)$ as $\bigcup_{S \in \Sigma} R(S)$.

We define $P_1 \diamond_\Sigma P_2 = \bigcup_{S \in \Sigma} R(S)$.

The intuitive meaning of the transformation is as follows. First, kernel forms of P_1 and P_2 are computed by the fixpoint construction of T. In the second step, from $ker(P_1)$ and $ker(P_2)$, any rule r which derives each literal in S is first selected. The rule r is transformed to r^* by (1) restricting disjuncts in the $head(r)$ to those literals appearing in S, (2) literals in $head(r) \setminus S$ are shifted to the body as the set of NAF-literals, and (3) any literal appearing in $T \in \Sigma$ but not in S is appended as the set of NAF-literals. The newly appended NAF-literals do not contribute to the derivation of literals in S. Finally, in the third step, those generated rules r^* are collected as a single program. Note that $P_1 \diamond_\Sigma P_2$ contains no integrity constraint. Integrity constraints do not contribute to producing any element included in a set $S \in \Sigma$. The program $P_1 \diamond_\Sigma P_2$ may contain non-minimal rules which are redundant. In this case, those rules are eliminated according to the second transformation in T.

Example 4.1. Consider two programs:

$$P_1 : \; p \leftarrow q,$$
$$q \leftarrow not\, r,$$
$$r \leftarrow not\, q,$$
$$P_2 : \; p \leftarrow r,$$
$$q\,;\,r \leftarrow,$$

and $\Sigma = \{\{p\}, \{q\}, \{r\}\}$. First, $ker(P_1)$ and $ker(P_2)$ become

$$ker(P_1): \quad p \leftarrow not\, r,$$
$$q \leftarrow not\, r,$$
$$r \leftarrow not\, q,$$
$$ker(P_2): \quad p\,;\,q \leftarrow,$$
$$q\,;\,r \leftarrow .$$

For $\{p\} \in \Sigma$, the first rule in $ker(P_1)$ and the first rule in $ker(P_2)$ are transformed to the same rule:

$$R(\{p\}): \quad p \leftarrow not\, q,\, not\, r\,.$$

Likewise, for $\{q\} \in \Sigma$ and $\{r\} \in \Sigma$, transformed rules become

$$R(\{q\}): \quad q \leftarrow not\, p,\, not\, r\,,$$
$$R(\{r\}): \quad r \leftarrow not\, p,\, not\, q\,.$$

As a result, $P_1 \diamond_\Sigma P_2$ becomes

$$p \leftarrow not\, q,\, not\, r,$$
$$q \leftarrow not\, p,\, not\, r,$$
$$r \leftarrow not\, p,\, not\, q.$$

The operator $\diamond_\Sigma$ has the following properties.

Proposition 4.2. *The operation $\diamond_\Sigma$ is commutative and associative.*

Proof. The commutative law $P_1 \diamond_\Sigma P_2 = P_2 \diamond_\Sigma P_1$ is straightforward. To see the associative law, both $(P_1 \diamond_\Sigma P_2) \diamond_\Sigma P_3$ and $P_1 \diamond_\Sigma (P_2 \diamond_\Sigma P_3)$ consist of rules r^* build from any $r \in ker(P_1) \cup ker(P_2) \cup ker(P_3)$. As Σ is common, two programs contain the same transformed rules. Hence, $(P_1 \diamond_\Sigma P_2) \diamond_\Sigma P_3 = P_1 \diamond_\Sigma (P_2 \diamond_\Sigma P_3)$. □

The proposition implies that the operation $\diamond_\Sigma$ is confluent; given an anti-chain set Σ and a set of programs, the operation produces the same program independent of the order of computation.

Lemma 4.3. *Let P be a program, and S a consistent answer set of P. Then, for any $L \in Lit$, $L \in S$ iff there is a rule $r \in ker(P)$ such that $L \in head(r)$, $S \cap (head(r) \setminus \{L\}) = \emptyset$, and $S \cap body^-(r) = \emptyset$.*

Proof. Suppose that for some literal $L \in S$, there is no rule $r \in ker(P)$ satisfying the condition. Then, for every rule $r \in ker(P)$, $L \notin head(r)$ or $S \cap (head(r) \setminus \{L\}) \neq \emptyset$ or $S \cap body^-(r) \neq \emptyset$. Thus, for every rule $r \in ker(P)$, $S \cap body^-(r) = \emptyset$ implies either $L \notin head(r)$ or $S \cap (head(r) \setminus \{L\}) \neq \emptyset$ (†). Next, consider the reduct $ker(P)^S$. Since S is an answer set of $ker(P)$ (Proposition 4.1), S is a minimal set satisfying $ker(P)^S$. For any rule $r' \in ker(P)^S$, (†) implies either $L \notin head(r')$ or $S \cap (head(r') \setminus \{L\}) \neq \emptyset$. In this case, $S' = S \setminus \{L\}$ satisfies r'. This contradicts the fact that S is a minimal set satisfying $ker(P)^S$.

Conversely, suppose $L \notin S$ in the presence of a rule $r \in ker(P)$ satisfying the condition. Then, $L \in head(r)$, $S \cap (head(r) \setminus \{L\}) = \emptyset$, and $S \cap body^-(r) = \emptyset$ imply that S does not satisfy r. This contradicts the fact that S satisfies $ker(P)$. □

Lemma 4.4. *Let P_1 and P_2 be two consistent programs, and $\Sigma \subseteq cons(P_1, P_2)$ an anti-chain over 2^{Lit}. Then, $\mathcal{AS}(P_1 \diamond_\Sigma P_2) = \Sigma$.*

Proof. Let $U \in \Sigma$. For any $r^* \in P_1 \diamond_\Sigma P_2$, if $r^* \in R(U')$ for $U' \in \Sigma$ with $U' \neq U$, $body(r^*)$ includes $not\, L$ for $L \in U \setminus U'$. Every such rule is eliminated in $(P_1 \diamond_\Sigma P_2)^U$.

Then, $(P_1 \diamond_\Sigma P_2)^U$ consists of facts: $head(r) \cap U \leftarrow$ where $body^-(r) \cap U = \emptyset$. Thus, U satisfies $(P_1 \diamond_\Sigma P_2)^U$. Suppose that there is a set $V \subseteq U$ which satisfies $(P_1 \diamond_\Sigma P_2)^U$. Then, there is a literal $L \in U \backslash V$. For any fact $head(r^*) \leftarrow$ in $(P_1 \diamond_\Sigma P_2)^U$, $V \cap (head(r^*) \backslash \{L\}) \neq \emptyset$. By $V \subseteq U$, this implies $U \cap (head(r^*) \backslash \{L\}) \neq \emptyset$ (†). On the other hand, by $U = S \cap T$ for some $S \in \mathcal{AS}(P_1)$ and $T \in \mathcal{AS}(P_2)$, $L \in S \cap T$ implies that there is a rule $r_1 \in ker(P_1)$ such that $L \in head(r_1)$, $S \cap (head(r_1) \backslash \{L\}) = \emptyset$, and $S \cap body^-(r_1) = \emptyset$; and there is a rule $r_2 \in ker(P_2)$ such that $L \in head(r_2)$, $T \cap (head(r_2) \backslash \{L\}) = \emptyset$, and $T \cap body^-(r_2) = \emptyset$ (Lemma 4.3). As $U \subseteq S$ and $U \subseteq T$, $U \cap (head(r_1) \backslash \{L\}) = \emptyset$ and $U \cap body^-(r_1) = \emptyset$; and $U \cap (head(r_2) \backslash \{L\}) = \emptyset$ and $U \cap body^-(r_2) = \emptyset$. Such r_1 and r_2 are transformed to r_1^* and r_2^* in $R(U) \subseteq P_1 \diamond_\Sigma P_2$, where $head(r_1^*) = head(r_2^*) = L$; and $body^-(r_1^*) = body^-(r_1) \cup (head(r_1) \backslash \{L\}) \cup \{ M \mid M \in U' \backslash U \text{ for any } U' \in \Sigma \}$ and $body^-(r_2^*) = body^-(r_2) \cup (head(r_2) \backslash \{L\}) \cup \{ M \mid M \in U' \backslash U \text{ for any } U' \in \Sigma \}$. By $U \cap body^-(r_1^*) = U \cap body^-(r_2^*) = \emptyset$, $(P_1 \diamond_\Sigma P_2)^U$ includes the fact $L \leftarrow$. Thus, $U \cap (head(r_1^*) \backslash \{L\}) = U \cap (head(r_2^*) \backslash \{L\}) = \emptyset$ for the fact $L \leftarrow$ in $(P_1 \diamond_\Sigma P_2)^U$. This contradicts the assertion (†). Hence, there is no such L, thereby $U = V$. Therefore, U is a minimal set satisfying $(P_1 \diamond_\Sigma P_2)^U$, and an answer set of $P_1 \diamond_\Sigma P_2$.

Conversely, let $U \in \mathcal{AS}(P_1 \diamond_\Sigma P_2)$. Then, for any $L \in U$ there is a rule r^* in $P_1 \diamond_\Sigma P_2$ such that $L \in head(r^*)$, $U \cap (head(r^*) \backslash \{L\}) = \emptyset$, and $U \cap body^-(r^*) = \emptyset$ (Lemma 4.3). As $L \in head(r^*)$ implies $L \in V$ for some $V \in \Sigma$, $L \in U$ implies $L \in V$ for some $V \in \Sigma$ (‡). Suppose that there is no $V \in \Sigma$ such that $U \subseteq V$. Then, for any $V \in \Sigma$, there is a literal $L' \in U \backslash V$. Since L' is included in some $V' \in \Sigma$ (by (‡)), every $r^* \in R(V)$ contains $not\, L'$ in $body(r^*)$. Then, $R(V)^U$ becomes $\emptyset$, so $(P_1 \diamond_\Sigma P_2)^U = \bigcup_{V \in \Sigma} R(V)^U = \emptyset$. Thus, $U \notin \mathcal{AS}(P_1 \diamond_\Sigma P_2)$. Contradiction. Hence, there is $V \in \Sigma$ such that $U \subseteq V$. By the above proof, $V \in \Sigma$ is an answer set of $P_1 \diamond_\Sigma P_2$. Hence, $U \subseteq V$ implies $V \subseteq U$. Therefore, $U = V$ and $U \in \Sigma$.   □

Given two programs P_1 and P_2, let Q be a minimal consensus and R a maximal consensus. By Definition 3.2, both $\mathcal{AS}(Q)$ and $\mathcal{AS}(R)$ are anti-chains over 2^{Lit}, and $\mathcal{AS}(Q) \subseteq cons(P_1, P_2)$ and $\mathcal{AS}(R) \subseteq cons(P_1, P_2)$ hold. So we can apply the procedure of Definition 4.1 for $\Sigma = \mathcal{AS}(Q)$ and $\Sigma = \mathcal{AS}(R)$. For notational simplicity, we write $\diamond_{\mathcal{AS}(Q)}$ as $\diamond_Q$, and $\diamond_{\mathcal{AS}(R)}$ as $\diamond_R$.

Theorem 4.5. *Let P_1 and P_2 be two consistent programs. Then, a minimal consensus Q is given as the program $P_1 \diamond_Q P_2$, and a maximal consensus R is given as the program $P_1 \diamond_R P_2$.*

Proof. The results follow from Lemma 4.4.   □

The result of Theorem 4.5 presents that the program $P_1 \diamond_Q P_2$ realizes minimal consensus, and $P_1 \diamond_R P_2$ realizes maximal consensus.

Example 4.2. In Example 4.1, Σ is the result of maximal consensus $\mathcal{AS}(R)$ between P_1 and P_2. Hence, $\mathcal{AS}(R) = \mathcal{AS}(P_1 \diamond_R P_2)$ holds.

A consensus program $P_1 \diamond_Q P_2$ or $P_1 \diamond_R P_2$ is constructed inductively by the result of consensus $\mathcal{AS}(Q)$ or $\mathcal{AS}(R)$. The need of a consensus program, in addition to the results of consensus, is explained as follows. A result of consensus represents common beliefs included in an answer set of every program. However, it brings no information on which the consensus is ground. A consensus program includes sufficient conditions in the original programs to derive beliefs included in the results of consensus. In the next section, we illustrate the use of consensus programs using an example.

By Definition 4.1, the procedure for computing $P_1 \diamond_\Sigma P_2$ includes computation of kernel forms of P_1 and P_2 at the first step, which requires exponential computation in the worst case. Once kernel forms are computed, the second and third steps are executed in time polynomial to $|ker(P_1) \cup ker(P_2)| \times |\Sigma|$, where $|ker(P)|$ represents the number of rules in $ker(P)$ and $|\Sigma|$ represents the number of sets in Σ. In practice, the computation of kernel programs could be done as a compilation process. On the other hand, in runtime environments the computation could be done only for the part of rules that are required to build consensus. The latter case is formally stated below.

Definition 4.2. Let P_1 and P_2 be two programs, and C a minimal/maximal consensus program. Given a set D of literals, a program $C' \subseteq C$ is called a *consensus program with respect to D* if $C' = \{ r \mid r \in C$ and $head(r) \cap D \neq \emptyset \}$.

A consensus program with respect to a particular set D is obtained as

$$\sigma_D(P_1 \diamond_\Sigma P_2) = \{ r \mid r \in P_1 \diamond_\Sigma P_2 \text{ and } head(r) \cap D \neq \emptyset \}$$

where Σ is either $\mathcal{AS}(Q)$ or $\mathcal{AS}(R)$, and $D \cap S \neq \emptyset$ for some $S \in \Sigma$. Generally, $\sigma_D(P_1 \diamond_\Sigma P_2)$ has a computational advantage over $P_1 \diamond_\Sigma P_2$. This is because we are interested in a particular set D of literals, there is no need for computing the whole kernel programs $ker(P_1)$ and $ker(P_2)$ in the first step of Definition 4.1. Instead, for every rule $r \in P_1$ satisfying $head(r) \cap D \neq \emptyset$, iteratively applying the program transformations $\mathcal{T}$ produces the set of conditional facts such that

$$\Gamma_1 = \{ r \mid head(r) \cap D \neq \emptyset \text{ and } body^+(r) = \emptyset \}$$

where $\Gamma_1 \subseteq ker(P_1)$ holds. Likewise, a set $\Gamma_2(\subseteq ker(P_2))$ of conditional facts is produced by P_2. Then, for such Γ_1 and Γ_2, the procedure of Definition 4.1 is modified as follows.

Definition 4.3. Let P_1 and P_2 be two programs, and $\Sigma \subseteq 2^{Lit}$ an anti-chain over Lit. Given a set D of literals such that $D \cap S \neq \emptyset$ for some $S \in \Sigma$;

1. Compute sets of conditional facts Γ_1 and Γ_2 as presented above.
2. Let $S \in \Sigma$. For any rule $r \in \Gamma_1 \cup \Gamma_2$ satisfying $head(r) \cap S \neq \emptyset$, construct a rule r^* as in Definition 4.1, and put $R'(S) = \{r^*\}$ as the set of all such rules.
3. For any $S \in \Sigma$, collect $R'(S)$ as $\bigcup_{S \in \Sigma} R'(S)$.
   Put $\sigma_D(\bigcup_{S \in \Sigma} R'(S)) = \{ r \mid r \in \bigcup_{S \in \Sigma} R'(S)$ and $head(r) \cap D \neq \emptyset \}$.

Proposition 4.6. $\sigma_D(P_1 \diamond_\Sigma P_2) = \sigma_D(\bigcup_{S \in \Sigma} R'(S))$.

Proof. Any $r^* \in \sigma_D(P_1 \diamond_\Sigma P_2)$ satisfies $head(r^*) \cap D = head(r) \cap S \cap D \neq \emptyset$ for $r \in ker(P_1) \cup ker(P_2)$ and $S \in \Sigma$. On the other hand, any $r^* \in \sigma_D(\bigcup_{S \in \Sigma} R'(S))$ satisfies $head(r^*) \cap D = head(r) \cap S \cap D \neq \emptyset$ for $r \in \Gamma_1 \cup \Gamma_2$ and $S \in \Sigma$. Since $\Gamma_i = \{ r \mid r \in ker(P_i)$ and $head(r) \cap D \neq \emptyset \}$ $(i = 1, 2)$, the result holds. $\square$

Example 4.3. In Example 4.1, let $D = \{p\}$. Then,

$$\Gamma_1 : \; p \leftarrow not\, r\,,$$
$$\Gamma_2 : \; p\,;\, q \leftarrow$$

are obtained as conditional facts with respect to D from P_1 and P_2, respectively. Each rule in $\Gamma_1 \cup \Gamma_2$ is transformed to

$$p \leftarrow not\, q,\, not\, r,$$
$$q \leftarrow not\, p,\, not\, r$$

in $P_1 \diamond_\Sigma P_2$. As a result, $\sigma_D(P_1 \diamond_\Sigma P_2)$ contains the single rule

$$p \leftarrow not\, q,\, not\, r\,.$$

5   Application to Multi-agent Consensus

In multi-agent systems, consensus could be achieved in different ways. In one way, agents have their own knowledge bases and build consensus through communication. In this case, every agent can share the result of consensus. In another way, there is a master agent who coordinates slave agents. In this case, the master agent builds consensus but slave agents are not necessarily share the result of consensus. In both cases, a consensus program serves as a social knowledge base which best reflects belief of individual agents. As shown in Proposition 4.2, the operation $\diamond_\Sigma$ is applied to more than two programs. Thus, minimal/maximal consensus are considered in multi-agent systems in which agents have knowledge bases represented by logic programs. In this section, we give an example to illustrate a process of building consensus among such agents.

Example 5.1. There are three agents, John, Mary, and Susie, who cook dinner together. Each agent has different preference as follows:

1. John wants to have either meat or fish. If he eats meat, he wants to have salad. Else if he eats fish, he wants to have soup. Concerning drinks, he prefers red wine in case of meat, and white wine in case of fish.
2. Mary is vegetarian, so she eats neither meat nor fish. Instead, she wants to have both salad and soup. She likes wine, but no preference between red and white.
3. Susie likes meat and wants to take either salad or soup. She usually drinks beer, but she will give up beer if other two agents agree with drinking red wine. She do not want white wine.

The three agents can communicate on-line. They do not share all their knowledge, but they are informed of results of consensus.

Beliefs of those agents are encoded by the following three logic programs.

$$P_j : \; meat \leftarrow not\, fish,$$
$$fish \leftarrow not\, meat,$$

$$salad \leftarrow meat,$$
$$soup \leftarrow fish,$$
$$red \leftarrow meat,$$
$$white \leftarrow fish,$$

P_m : $salad \leftarrow,$

$$soup \leftarrow,$$
$$red\,;white \leftarrow,$$
$$\leftarrow meat,$$
$$\leftarrow fish,$$

P_s : $meat \leftarrow,$

$$salad\,;soup \leftarrow,$$
$$beer \leftarrow not \neg beer,$$
$$\neg beer \leftarrow red,$$
$$\leftarrow white.$$

Here, P_j, P_m, and P_s correspond to John, Mary, and Susie, respectively. Each program has the answer sets:

$$\mathcal{AS}(P_j):\ \{\,meat,\,salad,\,red\,\},\ \ \{\,fish,\,soup,\,white\,\};$$
$$\mathcal{AS}(P_m):\ \{\,salad,\,soup,\,red\,\},\ \ \{\,salad,\,soup,\,white\,\};$$
$$\mathcal{AS}(P_s):\ \{\,meat,\,salad,\,beer\,\},\ \ \{\,meat,\,soup,\,beer\,\}.$$

In this situation, the result of minimal consensus is the empty set, while the result of maximal consensus is $\{\,salad\,\}$ or $\{\,soup\,\}$. If three agents are credulous reasoners, every agent agrees with cooking either salad or soup. The maximal consensus program $P_j \diamond_R P_m \diamond_R P_s$ then becomes

$$salad \leftarrow not\ soup,$$
$$soup \leftarrow not\ salad,$$

after eliminating non-minimal rules. The program represents common knowledge agreed by the agents.

The story goes on. Three agents notice that there is no consensus about drink. However, Susie can change her preference if the other two agents agree with drinking red wine. Then, she asks John and Mary to let her know their consensus about drinking. In response to this, John and Mary construct a consensus program with respect to drinking. The maximal consensus results in $\{\{\,salad,\,red\,\},\{\,soup,\,white\,\}\}$. Then, for $D = \{\,red,\,white\,\}$, the maximal consensus program with respect to D becomes $\sigma_D(P_j \diamond_R P_m)$:

$$red \leftarrow not\ soup,\ not\ white,$$
$$white \leftarrow not\ red,\ not\ salad,$$

after eliminating non-minimal rules. As a result, John and Mary inform Susie of their consensus program with respect to D. Susie then updates her program as $P_s^+ = P_s \cup \sigma_D(P_j \diamond_R P_m)$:

$$
\begin{aligned}
P_s^+ : \quad & meat \leftarrow, \\
& salad; \, soup \leftarrow, \\
& beer \leftarrow not \,\neg\, beer, \\
& \neg\, beer \leftarrow red, \\
& \leftarrow white, \\
& red \leftarrow not \, soup, \, not \, white, \\
& white \leftarrow not \, red, \, not \, salad.
\end{aligned}
$$

The updated program has the single answer set: $\{\, meat, \, salad, \, \neg beer, \, red \,\}$. The result of maximal consensus among P_j, P_m and P_s^+ then becomes $\{\, salad, \, red \,\}$. That is, three agents now agree with preparing salad and red wine.

Note that in making the final consensus, the consensus program plays an important role. This is because John and Mary agree on drinking red wine on the condition that they do not take both soup and white wine. The consensus program $\sigma_D(P_j \diamond_R P_m)$ contains this information. So, if Susie took soup, the agreement (drinking red wine) could not be reached. On the other hand, a simple result of consensus, red or $white$, does not bring information on which the consensus is ground. This explains the need of constructing a consensus program, even after obtaining the results of consensus.

6 Related Work

Several studies argue the semantic issue of multiple logic programs. Baral et al. [1] introduce algorithms for combining multiple logic programs. Given two stratified logic programs P_1 and P_2, they produce a program which has an answer set as a subset of an answer set of the program union $P_1 \cup P_2$. Program union or *merging* is the simplest operation for combining different theories. When programs are nonmonotonic, however, merging does not always produce consensus among agents, even though they do not contradict one another. Consider the following example from [8]. A brave driver crosses railway tracks in the absence of information on an approaching train:

$$cross \leftarrow not \, train \, .$$

On the other hand, a careful driver crosses railway tracks in the presence of information on no approaching train:

$$cross \leftarrow \neg\, train \, .$$

Simply merging these two programs produces the single solution $\{cross\}$, which would be unacceptable for the careful driver. In our framework, both minimal and maximal consensus produce the empty set.

Brogi et al. [4] introduce meta-level operations for composing normal logic programs. Among them, the intersection operation combines two programs by merging pair of rules with unifiable heads. For instance, given two programs:

$$P_1 : \quad likes(x, y) \leftarrow not\ bitter(y),$$
$$hates(x, y) \leftarrow sour(y),$$
$$P_2 : \quad likes(Bob, y) \leftarrow sour(y),$$

the program $P_1 \cap P_2$ consists of the single rule:

$$likes(Bob, y) \leftarrow not\ bitter(y),\ sour(y).$$

The produced rule specifies information which is common to the original two programs. However, the operation is performed on individual rules, so that resulting rules do not always produce common conclusions. For instance, suppose two programs $P_1 = \{ p \leftarrow q,\ not\ r, \quad q \leftarrow \}$ and $P_2 = \{ p \leftarrow not\ q,\ r, \quad r \leftarrow \}$. Applying intersection operation, the result becomes $P_1 \cap P_2 = \{ p \leftarrow q,\ r,\ not\ q,\ not\ r \}$, which never produces the common conclusion p. By contrast, the consensus program becomes $P_1 \diamond_Q P_2 = P_1 \diamond_R P_2 = \{ p \leftarrow not\ q, \quad p \leftarrow not\ r \}$, which has the single answer set $\{p\}$.

Buccafurri and Gottlob [5] introduce a framework of *compromise logic programs* which aims at reaching common conclusions. Given a collection of programs $T = \{P_1, \ldots, P_n\}$, the *joint fixpoint semantics* of T is defined as the set of minimal elements of $JFP(T) = FP(P_1) \cap \cdots \cap FP(P_n)$ where $FP(P_i)$ is the set of all fixpoints of P_i. For instance, when two programs $P_1 = \{ p \leftarrow \}$ and $P_2 = \{ p \leftarrow p \}$ are given, by $FP(P_1) = \{\{p\}\}$ and $FP(P_2) = \{\emptyset, \{p\}\}$ the joint fixpoint semantics becomes $\{p\}$. Thus, in their framework a tautology $p \leftarrow p$ has a special meaning that "if p is required by another agent, let it be". With this reading, however, $P_1 = \{ p \leftarrow \}$ and $P_3 = \{ p \leftarrow p, \quad q \leftarrow \}$ have the joint fixpoint semantics $\emptyset$, that is, P_3 does not tolerate p when another irrelevant fact q exists in the program. By contrast, the result of minimal/maximal consensus is not affected by the existence of tautologies and the result is $P_1 \diamond_Q P_2 = P_1 \diamond_R P_2 = P_1 \diamond_Q P_3 = P_1 \diamond_R P_3 = \emptyset$.

Consensus is a result of agreement among multiple agents, and the process of reaching agreement is called *negotiation*. Meyer et al. [10] introduce a logical framework for negotiating agents. They introduce two different modes of negotiation: *concession* and *adaptation*. They characterize such negotiation by rational postulates and provide methods for constructing outcomes. In their framework each agent is represented by classical propositional theories, so that those postulates are not generally applied to nonmonotonic theories. Moreover, their negotiation outcome coincides with the result of merging when two propositional theories are consistent with each other. This is different from our results of consensus as discussed above. Foo et al. [6] introduce a theory of multi-agent negotiation in answer set programming. Starting from the initial agreement set $S \cap T$ for an answer set S of an agent and an answer set T of another agent, each agent extends this set to reflect its own demand while keeping consistency with demand of the other agent. When two answer sets S and T do not contradict each other, their algorithm just returns the union $S \cup T$ as the trivial deal. In the "cross-train" example, the algorithm returns $\{ cross \}$ as the solution, which would be unsatisfactory as stated above. Wooldridge and Parsons [14] provide conditions for multiple agents to reach an agreement. Given formulas ψ_i $(1 \leq i \leq n)$ as *proposals* made by n agents on the final round of negotiation, an agreement is reached if $\psi_1 \wedge \cdots \wedge \psi_n$ is satisfiable. Another stronger condition requires convergence to equivalent proposals $\psi_1 \Leftrightarrow \cdots \Leftrightarrow \psi_n$. For instance, given two proposals $\psi_1 = p \vee q$ and $\psi_2 = p \vee \neg q$, the first type of agreement succeeds as $\psi_1 \wedge \psi_2 \equiv p$, while the second type of agreement fails as $\psi_1 \not\equiv \psi_2$. In the context of logic programming, two programs $\{\, p \,;\, q \leftarrow \,\}$ and $\{\, p \,;\, \neg q \leftarrow \,\}$ has the result of maximal consensus $\{p\}$ and the result of minimal consensus $\emptyset$. Thus, two types of agreement correspond to different results of consensus. Such correspondence does not hold in general, however. When $\psi_1 = p$ and $\psi_2 = q$, the first type of agreement produces $\psi_1 \wedge \psi_2 \equiv p \wedge q$. The result corresponds to merging two theories and is different from the result of minimal/maximal consensus.

Sakama and Inoue [12] introduce a framework of coordination between logic programs. Given two programs P_1 and P_2, they construct (i) a program Q which has the set of answer sets such that $\mathcal{AS}(Q) = \mathcal{AS}(P_1) \cup \mathcal{AS}(P_2)$; and (ii) a program R which has the set of answer sets such that $\mathcal{AS}(R) = \mathcal{AS}(P_1) \cap \mathcal{AS}(P_2)$. The program Q is called *generous coordination* and R is called *rigorous coordination* of two programs. Compared with the framework of consensus in this paper, generous/rigorous coordination does not change answer sets of the original programs. That is, generous one collects every answer set of each program, while rigorous one picks up answer sets that are common to each program. By contrast, the result of consensus in this paper extracts partial information that are commonly included in an answer set of every program. Thus, coordination and consensus result in different effects, and are used for different purposes. Sakama and Inoue [13] propose a method of combining answer sets of different programs. Given two programs P_1 and P_2, they construct a program Q satisfying $\mathcal{AS}(Q) = min(\mathcal{AS}(P_1) \uplus \mathcal{AS}(P_2))$ where $\mathcal{AS}(P_1) \uplus \mathcal{AS}(P_2) = \{\, S \uplus T \mid$ for $S \in \mathcal{AS}(P_1)$ and $T \in \mathcal{AS}(P_2)$, $S \uplus T = S \cup T$ if $S \cup T$ is consistent; otherwise, $S \uplus T = Lit \,\}$. The program Q is called a *composition* of P_1 and P_2. The result of composition combines answer sets of two programs, and extends some answer sets of one program by additional information of another program. This is in contrast to our present work which takes intersection of answer sets of two programs. Coordination, composition, and consensus are thus all intended to formalize different types of social behaviors of multiple agents in logic programming. A recent study [9] reveals that those theories have close relations to a theory of generalization in answer set programming.

7   Conclusion

This paper introduced the notion of consensus that extracts common beliefs from answer sets of multiple logic programs. Two different types of consensus, minimal consensus and maximal consensus, were considered, and a method of constructing consensus programs was developed. We applied the framework to building consensus in multi-agent systems. From the viewpoint of program synthesis, construction of consensus programs is considered as a program development under a specification that requests a program reflecting the meanings of two or more programs. In application, it serves as a step on understanding social behaviors of multiple agents by means of logic programming.

The procedure for constructing consensus programs requires computation of all answer sets of programs. This may often be infeasible when a program possesses an exponential number of answer sets. The same problem, however, arises in computing answer sets by existing answer set solvers. In future work, we will refine the present framework and investigate formulation of other types of social behaviors among logic programming agents.

References

1. C. Baral, S. Kraus, and J. Minker. Combining multiple knowledge bases. *IEEE Transactions of Knowledge and Data Engineering*, 3(2):208–220, 1991.
2. C. Baral and M. Gelfond. Logic programming and knowledge representation. *Journal of Logic Programming*, 19/20:73–148, 1994.
3. S. Brass and J. Dix. Semantics of (disjunctive) logic programs based on partial evaluation. *Journal of Logic Programming*, 40(1):1–46, 1999.
4. A. Brogi, S. Contiero, and F. Turini. Programming by combining general logic programs. *Journal of Logic and Computation*, 9(1):7–24, 1999.
5. F. Buccafurri and G. Gottlob. Multiagent compromises, joint fixpoints, and stable models. *Computational Logic: Logic Programming and Beyond*, Lecture Notes in Artificial Intelligence 2407, pp. 561–585, Springer, 2002.
6. N. Foo, T. Meyer, Y. Zhang, and D. Zhang. Negotiating logic programs. *Proceedings of the 6th Workshop on Nonmonotonic Reasoning, Action and Change*, 2005.
7. P. A. Gardner and J. C. Shepherdson. Unfold/fold transformations of logic programs. in: J-L. Lassez and G. Plotkin (eds.), *Computational Logic, Essays in Honor of Alan Robinson*, pp. 565-583, MIT Press, 1991.
8. M. Gelfond and V. Lifschitz. Classical negation in logic programs and disjunctive databases. *New Generation Computing*, 9(3/4):365–385, 1991.
9. K. Inoue and C. Sakama. Generality relations in answer set programming. *Proceedings of the 22nd International Conference on Logic Programming*, Lecture Notes in Computer Science 4079, pp. 211–225, Springer, 2006.
10. T. Meyer, N. Foo, R. Kwok, and D. Zhang. Logical foundation of negotiation: outcome, concession and adaptation. *Proc. AAAI-04*, pp. 293–298, MIT Press, 2004.
11. C. Sakama and H. Seki. Partial deduction in disjunctive logic programming. *Journal of Logic Programming*, 32(3):229–245, 1997.
12. C. Sakama and K. Inoue. Coordination between logical agents. *Proceedings of the 5th International Workshop on Computational Logic in Multi-Agent Systems*, Lecture Notes in Artificial Intelligence 3487, pp. 161–177, Springer, 2005.
13. C. Sakama and K. Inoue. Combining answer sets of nonmonotonic logic programs. *Proceedings of the 6th International Workshop on Computational Logic in Multi-Agent Systems*, Lecture Notes in Artificial Intelligence 3900, pp. 320–339, Springer, 2006.
14. M. Wooldridge and S. Parsons. Languages for negotiation. *Proceedings of the 14th European Conference on Artificial Intelligence*, pp. 393–397, IOS Press, 2000.

Supervising Offline Partial Evaluation of Logic Programs Using Online Techniques*

Michael Leuschel, Stephen-John Craig, and Dan Elphick

Institut für Informatik, Universität Düsseldorf
D-40225, Düsseldorf, Germany
leuschel@cs.uni-duesseldorf.de

Abstract. A major impediment for more widespread use of offline partial evaluation is the difficulty of obtaining and maintaining annotations for larger, realistic programs. Existing automatic binding-time analyses still only have limited applicability and annotations often have to be created or improved and maintained by hand, leading to errors. We present a technique to help overcome this problem by using online control techniques which supervise the specialisation process in order to detect such errors. We discuss an implementation in the LOGEN system and show on a series of examples that this approach is effective: very few false alarms were raised while infinite loops were detected quickly. We also present the integration of this technique into a web interface, which highlights problematic annotations directly in the source code. A method to automatically fix incorrect annotations is presented, allowing the approach to be also used as a pragmatic binding time analysis. Finally we show how our method can be used for efficiently locating errors with built-ins inside Prolog source code.

1 Introduction

Partial evaluation [11] is a source-to-source program transformation technique which specialises programs by fixing part of the input of some source program P and then pre-computing those parts of P that only depend on the fixed part of the input. The so-obtained transformed programs are less general than the original but often more efficient. The part of the input that is fixed is referred to as the *static* input, while the remainder of the input is called the *dynamic* input. The research into controlling partial evaluation can be broadly partitioned into two schools of thought: the *offline* and the *online* approach. In the online approach all control decisions (i.e., deciding which parts of the input are static and which parts of the program should be pre-computed) are made online, during the specialisation process. The idea of the offline approach is to separate the specialisation process into two phases (cf. Fig. 1):

- First a *binding-time analysis* (BTA for short) is performed which, given a program and an approximation of the input available for specialisation,

---

* This research has been carried out as part of the EU funded project IST-2001-38059 ASAP (Advanced Specialization and Analysis for Pervasive Systems).

G. Puebla (Ed.): LOPSTR 2006, LNCS 4407, pp. 43–59, 2007.

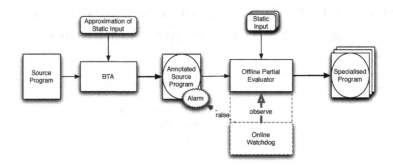

Fig. 1. Offline Partial Evaluation and the new watchdog mode

approximates all values within the program and generates annotations that
steer (or control) the specialisation process.
– A (simplified) *specialisation phase*, which is guided by the result of the *BTA*.
A short summary of the advantages and disadvantages of offline specialisation
wrt to online specialisation is as follows:

– The offline approach is in principle less precise (see, however, [6]) as it has
to make decisions before the actual static values are known.
– The offline approach leads to simpler specialisers, thus making self-application
easier and leading to more efficient specialisation. Especially the specialisation phase proper (i.e., after the BTA has been performed) is usually considerably faster than specialisation using an online specialiser. This is relevant
in situations where the same source program is re-specialised multiple times
w.r.t. the same approximation of the static data.
– The offline approach is more predictable, as it is relatively clear from the
annotation which parts of the code will be pre-computed. This also means
that it is easier to tune the offline approach by editing the annotations.

An offline system for logic programming is the LOGEN system [19]. LOGEN has
successfully been applied to non-trivial interpreters, and can be used to achieve
Jones-optimality [23]. for a variety of interpreters [17], i.e., completely removing
the interpretation overhead.[1] As such, LOGEN is of potential interest for many
logic programming areas and applications; for example, LOGEN has been applied
to optimise access control checks in deductive databases [2], to compile denotational semantics language specifications into abstract machine code [31], or to
pre-compile Object Petri nets for later model checking. However, the learning
curve for LOGEN is still considerable and the LOGEN system has up until now
still proven to be too difficult to be used by non-experts in partial evaluation.
The main difficulty lies in coming up with the correct annotations (and then
maintaining them as the source program evolves). Indeed, while some errors
(i.e., annotating an argument as static even though it is dynamic) can be easily

---

[1] Achieving this predictably for a variety of interpreters using online approaches is not
yet fully understood; see, however, [30].

identified by various abstract interpretation schemes (see, e.g., [5,8]), ensuring termination of the specialisation process is a major obstacle. Recent work has led to a fully automatic BTA [8], but unfortunately the BTA still only provides partial termination guarantee[2]; is sometimes overly conservative, especially for the more involved (and more interesting) applications; and can be too costly to apply for larger, real-life Prolog programs. Finally, the BTA of [8] does not yet deal with many of Prolog's built-ins and non-logical control constructs.

In this paper we present a way to tackle and solve this problem from a new angle. The main idea is to use online techniques to *supervise* an offline specialiser. The central idea is that the user can turn on a *watchdog* mode which activates powerful online control methods to supervise the offline specialiser (see Fig. 1). If the online control detects a potential infinite loop (or some other problem such as incorrectly calling a built-in) an *alarm* is raised, helping the user to identify and fix errors in the annotation. This watchdog mode will obviously slow down the specialisation process, invalidating one of the advantages of the offline approach. However, it is the intention that this watchdog would only be activated in the initial development or maintenance phase of the annotation or when an error (e.g., apparent non-termination) arises: it is not our intention to have the watchdog mode permanently enabled (in that case an online partial evaluator would be more appropriate). In this paper we formally develop this idea, present an implementation inside the LOGEN system [19] and evaluate its performance on a series of examples. We show that on most correct annotations no false alarms are raised, while on incorrect annotations the problems are spotted quickly and useful feedback is given. We also present a web interface that can further help the user to quickly spot and automatically fix the problems identified by the watchdog. We thus hope that this new technique will make it possible for users to quickly find errors in their annotations. This hope is underpinned by several initial case studies within the ASAP project.

2   Offline Partial Evaluation

We now describe the process of offline partial evaluation of logic programs. Throughout this paper we suppose familiarity with basic notions in logic programming. We follow the notational conventions of [22]. Formally, evaluating a logic program P for an atom A consists in building a so-called *SLD-tree* and then extracting the *computed answer substitutions* from every non-failing branch of that tree. Take for example the following program to match a regular expression against a (difference) list of characters:

```
re(empty,T,T).                          re(ch(X),[X|T],T).
re(or(X,Y),H,T) :- re(X,H,T).           re(or(X,Y),H,T) :- re(Y,H,T).
re(star(X),T,T).
re(star(X),H,T) :- re(X,H,T1),re(star(X),T1,T).
re(cat(X,Y),H,T) :- re(X,H,T1),re(Y,T1,T).
```

---

[2] [9] does provide full termination guarantees for functional programs but is not available in a running system and does seem not cope very well with interpreters.

As an example, the SLD-tree for `re(star(ch(a)),[C],[])` is presented on the left in Fig. 2. The underlined atoms are called selected atoms. Here there is only one branch, and its computed answer is `C = a`.

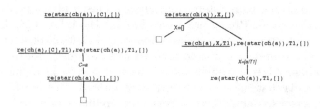

Fig. 2. Complete and Incomplete SLD-trees for the regular expression program

Partial evaluation (also sometimes called partial deduction) for logic programs proceeds by building possibly *incomplete* SLD-trees, i.e., trees in which it is possible *not* to select certain atoms. The right side of Fig. 2 contains such an incomplete SLD-tree, where the call `re(star(ch(a)),T1,[])` is not selected. Formally, partial evaluation builds a series of incomplete SLD-trees for a set of atoms $\mathcal{A}$ that is chosen in such a way that all unselected leaf atoms (such as `re(star(ch(a)),T1,[])` in Fig. 2) as well as all user queries of interest are an instance of some atom in $\mathcal{A}$. The specialised program is then extracted from those trees by producing one new specialised predicate for every atom in $\mathcal{A}$, with one clause constructed per non-failing branch. The arguments of the specialised predicate are the variables of the corresponding atom in $\mathcal{A}$. E.g., for $\mathcal{A} = \{$ `re(star(ch(a)),X,[])`$\}$ and for the SLD-tree in Fig. 2, we would get:

    re__0([]).   re__0([a|A]) :- re__0(A).

Partial evaluation techniques for logic programs often start off with an initial atom A_0 of interest: $\mathcal{A} = \{A_0\}$. For every atom in $\mathcal{A}$ an SLD-tree is built, and then all unselected leaf atoms which are not an instance of an atom in $\mathcal{A}$ are added to $\mathcal{A}$. This is repeated until all unselected leaf atoms are an instance of some atom in $\mathcal{A}$. To ensure termination, generalisation techniques have to be applied; i.e., atoms in $\mathcal{A}$ may be replaced by a more general atom. The control of partial evaluation for logic programs is thus naturally separated into two components [24] (see also [16]): The *local control* controls the construction of the SLD-trees for the atoms in $\mathcal{A}$ and thus determines *what* the residual clauses for the atoms in $\mathcal{A}$ are. The process of constructing these trees is also called *unfolding*. The *global control* controls the content of $\mathcal{A}$, it decides *which* specialised predicates are present in the residual program and ensures that all unselected leaf atoms are an instance of some atom in $\mathcal{A}$.

In offline partial deduction the local and global control are guided by annotations. The LOGEN system [19] uses two kinds of annotations for this:

– *Filter declarations*, which declare which arguments (or subarguments) to which predicates are static and which ones dynamic. This influences the global control only. More precisely, for unselected leaf atoms the dynamic (sub-)arguments are replaced by fresh variables; it is then checked whether a variant of this generalised atom already exists in $\mathcal{A}$; if not the generalised atom is added to $\mathcal{A}$.

- *Clause annotations*, which indicate for every call in the body how that call should be treated during unfolding; i.e., it influences the local control only. For now, we assume that a call is either annotated by **memo** — indicating that it should not be selected – or by **unfold** — indicating that it should be selected. Built-ins (or predicates whose source is not available) can be annotated as either **call** — indicating that the call should be executed at specialization time — or as **rescall** — indicating that the call should not be executed at specialization time.

First, let us consider, e.g., an annotated version of the regular expression program above in which the filter declarations annotate the first and third arguments as static while the second one is dynamic: `:- filter re(static,dynamic,static)`. Then let the clause annotations annotate the call `re(star(X),T1,T)` in the last clause as **memo** and all the other calls as **unfold**. Given a specialisation query `re(star(ch(a)),X,[])`, offline partial deduction would proceed as follows:

1. The atom `re(star(ch(a)),X,[])` is generalised by replacing the dynamic arguments by variables. In this case, the second argument is already a variable.
2. The generalised atom is added to $\mathcal{A}$ and then unfolded. This generates exactly the right SLD-tree depicted in Fig. 2.
3. The leaf atoms of the tree are again generalised and are added to $\mathcal{A}$ if no variant is already in $\mathcal{A}$. In this case there is only one leaf atom—namely `re(star(ch(a)),T1,[])`—whose second argument is again already a variable and a variant of which is already in $\mathcal{A}$. Thus no further unfolding is required.
4. The specialised code is produced by mapping each atom in $\mathcal{A}$ to a fresh predicate whose arguments are the variables of the atoms. In this case `re(star(ch(a)),X,[])` would be mapped to, e.g., `re__0(X)` resulting in the same specialised code as above:

```
re__0([]).              re__0([a|A]) :-  re__0(A).
```

3   Watchdog Mode

Below we show how offline partial evaluation can be supervised by online techniques, in order to identify non-terminating annotations. We first need the concept of a well-quasi order, which is used for many online techniques:

Definition 1. *A* quasi order $\leq_S$ *on a set* S *is a reflexive and transitive binary relation on* $S \times S$. *A sequence of elements* $s_1, s_2, \ldots$ *in* S *is called* **admissible** **with respect to** $\leq_S$ *iff there are no* $i < j$ *such that* $s_i \leq_S s_j$. *The relation* $\leq_S$ *is a* **well-quasi order** *(wqo) on* S *iff there are no infinite admissible sequences with respect to* $\leq_S$.

A widely used wqo is the homeomorphic embedding relation $\trianglelefteq$. The following is an adaptation of the definition from [28] (see, e.g., [14, 15] for a summary of its use in online control). In what follows, we define an *expression* to be either a term, an atom, a conjunction, or a goal.

Definition 2. *The* (pure) homeomorphic embedding *relation $\trianglelefteq$ on expressions is inductively defined as follows (i.e. $\trianglelefteq$ is the least relation satisfying the rules):*

   1. $X \trianglelefteq Y$ for all variables X, Y
   2. $s \trianglelefteq f(t_1, \ldots, t_n)$ if $s \trianglelefteq t_i$ for some i
   3. $f(s_1, \ldots, s_n) \trianglelefteq f(t_1, \ldots, t_n)$ if $n \geq 0$ and $\forall i \in \{1, \ldots, n\} : s_i \trianglelefteq t_i$.

Notice that n is allowed to be 0 and we thus have $c \trianglelefteq c$ for all constant and proposition symbols. When $s \trianglelefteq t$ we also say that s is *embedded in* t or t is *embedding* s. By $s \triangleleft t$ we denote that $s \trianglelefteq t$ and $t \ntrianglelefteq s$. The intuition behind the above definition is that $A \trianglelefteq B$ iff A can be obtained from B by "striking out" certain parts. E.g., we have $p(0) \triangleleft p(s(0))$ and $f(a, b) \triangleleft h(f(g(a)), b)$.

For a finite set of function symbols, $\trianglelefteq$ is a well-quasi order, i.e., for every infinite sequence of expressions $s_1, s_2, \ldots$ there exists $i < j$ such that $s_i \trianglelefteq s_j$. This property has been used in various online control algorithms (first in [28] for supercompilation and then in [20] for partial evaluation of logic programs and then in various other techniques, e.g., [1]). Its main use is to ensure termination by stopping unfolding/specialisation when a new expression to specialise s_j embeds some earlier expression s_i of the specialisation history.

In the case of specialisation we know that the function symbols occurring within a given program (text) are finite. Thus for pure logic programs without built-ins, $\trianglelefteq$ is a well-quasi order for calls that can occur at runtime or at specialisation time. However, certain built-ins (such as `is/2` or `functor/3`) permit a program to generate an unbounded number of new function symbols. For this we employ the solution from [20, 15]: all function symbols not occurring within the original program text are classified as *dynamic* and we add the rule: $f(s_1, \ldots, s_n) \trianglelefteq g(t_1, \ldots, t_m)$ if f/n and g/m are dynamic function symbols.[3]

We now show how we have used $\trianglelefteq$ to act as a "watchdog" in offline specialisation which is used to supervise both the unfolding process and the memoisation. Let us first discuss the supervision of the local control. Suppose that we are constructing the SLD-tree for a given atom A. A simple solution would be, whenever an atom is unfolded, to check whether the sequence of selected literals starting from A up to (and including) the currently selected atom is admissible wrt $\trianglelefteq$.

However, it is well known ([4], see also [16]) in online partial evaluation of logic programs that examining the sequence of selected atoms does give rise to suboptimal techniques. Indeed, this sequence does not contain the information which selected atom actually descends from which other selected atom. This shortcoming can be remedied by working on the sequence of *covering ancestors* of the selected atom, i.e., only those atoms from which the selected atom descends

---

[3] It would be possible to refine this slightly by adding the requirement that there exists a subsequence of $t_1, \ldots, t_m$ which embeds the arguments to $s_1, \ldots, s_n$.

(via resolution). More formally, covering ancestors [4] can be captured in the following definitions.

Definition 3. *If a program clause $H \leftarrow B_1, \dots, B_n$ is used in a derivation step with selected atom A then, for each i, A is the **parent** of the instance of B_i in the resolvent and in each subsequent goal where an instance originating from B_i appears (up to and including the goal where B_i is selected). The **ancestor** relation is the transitive closure of the parent relation. Let G_0, G_1, $\dots$, G_n be an SLD-derivation with selected atoms A_1, A_2, $\dots$, A_n. The **covering ancestor sequence** of A_i, a selected atom, is the maximal subsequence A_{j_1}, A_{j_2}, $\dots A_{j_m} = A_i$ of A_1, A_2, $\dots$, A_i such that all atoms in the sequence have the same predicate symbol and, $\forall 1 \leq k < m$ it holds that A_{j_k} is an ancestor of $A_{j_{k+1}}$.*

For every atom that is unfolded the supervisor will check whether the covering ancestor sequence of the selected atom is admissible wrt $\trianglelefteq$. If it is then specialization will proceed normally. Otherwise, an alarm will be raised: e.g., a warning message will be printed and the specialization process will suspend, allowing the user to choose between aborting or continuing the specialisation process. For example, in the SLD-tree on the left in Fig. 2, when selecting the call re(star(ch(a)),[],[])) the watchdog will check whether the sequence ⟨re(star(ch(a)),[C],[]) re(star(ch(a)),[],[])⟩ is admissible wrt $\trianglelefteq$. As it is admissible, no alarm is raised.

Let us now examine the global control, which builds up the set $\mathcal{A}$ of atoms to be specialised. To achieve more refined control, the set $\mathcal{A}$ is often structured as a tree [24, 20], called a *specialisation tree*. Basically, if after unfolding some atom A_j we have to add one of the unselected leaf atoms A_k in the SLD-tree to the set $\mathcal{A}$, then we register A_k as a child of A_j in the specialisation tree. We can thus do the following for atoms annotated as **memo**: we first build up the global specialisation tree, i.e., when a call A_k gets memoed during unfolding of A_i, and A_k is not an instance of another atom that has already been specialised, then we add A_k as a child of A_i in the specialisation tree. Furthermore, we check whether the sequence of ancestors of A_k in the tree is admissible wrt $\trianglelefteq$. If it is not, we raise an alarm and allow the user to choose between aborting or continuing the specialisation process.

The Implementation. We have integrated the above idea and technique into the LOGEN system. The LOGEN system uses the so-called "cogen" approach to specialisation, i.e., given an annotated source program it directly generates a specialised specialiser for this source program and the annotation (called a *generating extension*). In particular, for every clause of the source program LOGEN derives an "unfolder" clause in the generating extension, having an extra argument to compute the residual code. Similarly, memoisation predicates are constructed for the memoised predicates. To implement our watchdog mode the unfolder predicates do not carry enough information to determine whether unfolding the body literals is actually safe or not: we need access to the covering ancestor sequence. For memoised calls, we additionally need the global specialisation tree. We have adapted the compilation strategy of LOGEN so that in watchdog mode an extra argument is maintained by the unfolder and memoisation predicates, where both the covering ancestor sequence and the specialisation tree are built up. In Section 4, we examine empirically whether our approach is efficient enough to be practical and precise enough to be useful.

Let us now use the watchdog on our regular expression example. First, we annotate all calls as unfold and run LOGEN from the command line with the watchdog mode enabled:

```
% logen re.pl "re(star(ch(a)),X,[])" -w
<| HOMEOMORPHIC WARNING |> : UNFOLDING re(star(ch(a)),A,[]),
History: [re(star(ch(a)),B,[])]
A predicate is possibly being unfolded infinitely often.
You may want to annotate the call as memo.
Type 'c' to continue unfold, 'F' to fail branch,
'C' to continue without further intervention, anything else to abort:
```

As can be seen, the watchdog has correctly spotted (after a few ms) that we were about to infinitely unfold the atom re(star(ch(a)),X,[]). If we now correct our annotation, as suggested, by memoing the last call to re/2 in the last clause we get the following:

```
% logen re.pl "re(star(ch(a)),X,[])" -w
/* re(star(ch(a)),A,[]) :-re__0(A). */
re__0([]).
re__0([a|A]) :- re__0(A).
```

I.e., this time the watchdog has not raised an alarm, and indeed our specialisation now terminates.

4 Experiments

In the first series of experiments we ran our watchdog technique on a series of *correctly annotated*, terminating examples. We have gathered some simple programs as well as a variety of successful applications of the LOGEN system documented in the literature. The purpose was twofold: first, test whether, despite the overhead, the approach is practical, and second, whether the number of false alarms is low enough for the approach to be useful.

The results of the experiments are summarised in Table 1. All experiments were run using Ciao Prolog 1.13 on a Macintosh PowerPC Dual G5, 2.7 GHz with 4.5 GB of RAM running Mac OS X 10.4. The cogen time in the second column is the time needed to run the cogen of the LOGEN system to generate the generating extension. Column three contains the same figure for the watchdog mode. The fourth column then contains the time needed to run the generating extension on a single specialisation query. Column five contains the same figure for the watchdog mode. The sixth column contains the number of alarms, and thus the number

Table 1. The watchdog approach for correct annotations

Benchmark	Cogen	Cogen watch	Spec.	Spec. watch	False Alarms	Overhead One Shot	Overhead Just Spec.
match	43 ms	65 ms	1.4 ms	1.7 ms	0	1.50	1.21
transpose	44 ms	66 ms	0.5 ms	0.8 ms	0	1.50	1.60
ex_depth	45 ms	68 ms	1.7 ms	2.3 ms	0	1.51	1.35
inter_medium	48 ms	71 ms	0.4 ms	12.5 ms	0	1.73	31.25
vanilla_list	44 ms	67 ms	1.0 ms	1.3 ms	0	1.52	1.30
liftsolve	49 ms	74 ms	1.7 ms	72.3 ms	0	2.89	42.53
lambdaint	60 ms	92 ms	1.6 ms	11.7 ms	0	1.68	7.31
db_access	115 ms	145 ms	1.2 ms	10.8 ms	1	1.34	9.00
matlab	94 ms	146 ms	3.4 ms	40.0 ms	0	1.91	11.76
pascal	70 ms	107 ms	3.0 ms	27.3 ms	0	1.84	9.10
picsim	258 ms	390 ms	145.8 ms	1999.4 ms	0	5.92	13.71
Average					0.09	2.12	11.83

of false alarms (as all annotations ensure termination). The overhead of the watchdog mode in "one-shot" situations (i.e., a single specialisation) is presented in column seven, while the overhead of the specialisation process without the cogen time is presented in the last column. The benchmark programs are as follows. First, match is the semi-naive pattern matcher from [13], specialised for the pattern [a,a,b]. transpose and ex_depth are also taken from [13], while inter_medium is taken from [8]. vanilla_list is a variation of the vanilla interpreter (see [17]) specialised for an object program which is in turn the same interpreter but with the append as object program. liftsolve is the interpreter for the ground representation from [13] specialised for the append program. lambdaint is the interpreter for a small functional language presented in [17], specialised for the Fibonacci function. db_access is the interpreter for access control from [2] specialised for a particular policy and query pattern (query Q4 in [2]). matlab is the interpreter for a subset of the Matlab language also used in [21], specialised for the factorial function. pascal is the denotational semantics interpreter for a small Pascal like language used in [31], specialised for a small Pascal program so as to obtain assembly like code. picsim is an emulator for the machine language of PIC processors written by Kim Henriksen and John Gallagher [10], specialised for a particular machine program (so as to extract analysis information by further abstract interpretation).

In summary the results are very satisfactory. The overhead on the specialisation is usually an order of magnitude (this is to be expected, as every unfolding step and memoisation step is supervised and checked against the history of unfoldings and earlier memoisations respectively), even though the overhead on the total time in "one-shot" situations (i.e. time for both the cogen and the specialisation) is often much less, e.g., 84 % for the pascal experiment or 50 % for the match benchmark. What is most encouraging, however, is the low number of false alarms: on only one of the experiments false alarms were raised, and even there only a single alarm was raised.

We now examine how our approach fares when the annotations are *erroneous* and do not ensure termination of the specialiser. This is probably a more typical use case, as the watchdog would usually be turned on in exactly those circumstances. It is, however, more difficult to present empirical data in that setting: the notion of overhead makes no sense as the offline approach does not terminate; it is also difficult to quantify the earliest possible moment when non-termination can be "detected." Still, we will try to show on a series of examples that our watchdog technique does find the problem and does so quickly.

In Section 3 we have already looked at a simple example. Let us now examine the behaviour of the watchdog method on some more realistic examples. Take the ex_depth interpreter used in the previous section, counting the depth of SLD-trees, but marking this time the depth argument as static rather than dynamic.[4] Termination is no longer guaranteed, and this is a common annotation mistake in offline partial evaluation. This is spotted quickly by our technique (after less than 5 ms):

```
% logen ex_depth_nonterm.pl "solve([inboth(X,Y,Z)],0,Depth)." -w
<| HOMEOMORPHIC WARNING|> : MEMO Atom solve([member(A,B)],s(s(s(0))),C),
History: [solve([member(D,E)],s(s(0)),F),solve([member(G,H),member(I,J)],
 s(0),K), solve([inboth(L,M,N)],0,0)]
```

Let us now take the same annotation, but this time unfold all calls to solve. As above, this is correct from the point of view of binding times (i.e., all arguments marked as static are really static). However, termination is not guaranteed, something which our technique spots quickly (again after less than 6 ms):

```
% logen ex_depth_nonterm_local.pl "solve([inboth(X,Y,Z)],0,Depth)." -w
<| HOMEOMORPHIC WARNING |> : UNFOLDING solve([member(A,B)],s(s(s(C))),D),
History: [solve([member(E,F)],s(s(G)),H),solve([member(I,J),member(I,K)],
 s(L),M), solve([inboth(N,O,P)],Q,R)]
```

The problems above were spotted at a very early stage, where it is easy for the user to identify the causes. In both cases the specialiser without watchdog mode will not terminate. Finally, we have tried two bigger examples: the lambdaint and pascal interpreters from the previous subsection. In the former we annotated the apply construct and in the latter the while construct as unfoldable. After less than 25 ms and 60 ms and 9 and 11 unfolding steps respectively the problem was detected by the watchdog.

5   The Web Interface and Semi-automatic Correction

Further Error Conditions. In addition to non-termination there are various other errors that often arise in hand-crafted annotations. First, a common mistake is to annotate built-ins as **call** even though they are not guaranteed to be sufficiently instantiated at specialisation time. Another common mistake is to

---

[4] This required adapting one clause for the binding times to be correct.

make the filter declarations too narrow, so that not all memoised calls are covered by the filter declaration. We have extended our watchdog technique so that these conditions are detected. This means that all calls to built-ins are explicitly checked by the watchdog, and the filter errors are also caught and presented to the user.[5] Another common mistake relates to *backpropagation* of bindings [26] in the context of non-logical built-ins and connectives. Here the watchdog uses co-routining to detect those backpropagations.

Graphical Web Interface. In [18] we have presented a graphical web interface for the LOGEN system, which allows the user to edit annotations for a given Prolog program in a user friendly way: the Prolog program to be annotated is presented with comments and formatting intact and colour coding (as well as "mouse over" information) is used to display the annotation. The annotations can be edited using an intuitive point and click interface.

In order to make it easier for users to understand and act upon the feedback provided by the watchdog, it would make sense to provide the watchdog information by highlighting the problematic annotations directly in the source code frame of the web interface. For this we had to extend the scheme presented in Section 3, in that the generating extensions also need to keep track of program points (in addition to the covering ancestor sequence and the specialisation tree). This information (along with a description of the error) is then fed back in XML format to the web interface to locate the source of the error and highlight it. Once this framework was in place, it was possible to extend the XML format to convey further information, such as how to fix an incorrect annotation. Below we show how these suggestions can be computed, again using online control techniques. To use this information the web interface uses XSLT to translate LOGEN's XML suggestions into Javascript statements for fixing the annotations, which are executed if the user presses the "fix" button.

Correcting Annotations. Let us first summarise the four classes of problems that our watchdog can catch, along with a summary of the fixes that can be applied. Note that there could be alternate ways to fix the problems below; e.g., by unfolding more user predicates to make more things static. Our underlying assumption here is that the user will progress from more aggressive annotations to less aggressive ones (with less calls marked as unfold and call).

- Problem 1: dangerous unfolding is detected by $\trianglelefteq$. Fix: mark this call as **memo**.
- Problem 2: a built-in is marked as **call** but is not sufficiently instantiated (or throws an exception). Fix: mark the built-in as **rescall**.
- Problem 3: a call marked as **memo** is not covered by its filter declaration. Fix: generalise the filter declaration to cover the call. Details are presented below.
- Problem 4: $\trianglelefteq$ has detected a potential infinite memoisation. Fix: generalise the filter declaration to throw part of the static information away.

---

[5] The filter errors are now actually also caught in normal mode as this extra checking does not incur a significant overhead.

For the first two entries the fix is straightforward; for the latter two the computation of the updated filter declarations is more subtle. There are various ways this could be achieved. Below we present solutions inspired by online control techniques.

We first need to recall some background on LOGEN's filter declarations: a filter declaration assigns every argument of every predicate a binding-type. A *binding type* is a generalisation of the classical binding-times (static, dynamic; see, e.g., [11]), making it possible to precisely specify which subarguments are static or dynamic (rather than having to declare the entire argument as either static or dynamic).   LOGEN's binding types are expressed using the standard formalism employed by polymorphically typed languages (e.g. [27]). Formally, a *type* is either a *type variable* or a *type constructor* of arity $n \geq 0$ applied to n types. We presuppose the existence of three 0-ary type constructors: static, dynamic, and nonvar. These constructors are given a pre-defined meaning.

Definition 4. *A* type definition *for a type constructor c of arity n is of the form*

$$c(V_1, \ldots, V_n) \longrightarrow f_1(T_1^1, \ldots, T_1^{n_1}) \; ; \; \ldots \; ; \; f_k(T_k^1, \ldots, T_k^{n_k})$$

with $k \geq 1, n, n_1, \ldots, n_k \geq 0$ and where $f_1, \ldots, f_k$ are distinct function symbols, $V_1, \ldots, V_n$ are distinct type variables, and T_i^j are types which only contain type variables in $\{V_1, \ldots, V_n\}$.
A type system Γ is a set of type definitions, exactly one for every type constructor c different from static, dynamic, and nonvar.

From now on we will suppose that the underlying type system Γ is fixed. LOGEN also allows function symbols to be used as type constructors and we thus also suppose that every function symbol of arity n is also a type constructor of arity n, defined by $f(V_1, \ldots, V_n) \longrightarrow f(V_1, \ldots, V_n)$ in Γ. As an example, the parametric type list(T) can be declared as follows in LOGEN (following the notations of Mercury): :- type list(T) ---> [ ] ; [T | list(T)].

We define *type substitutions* to be finite sets of the form $\{V_1/\tau_1, \ldots, V_k/\tau_k\}$, where every V_i is a type variable and τ_i a type. Type substitutions can be applied to types (and type definitions) to produce *instances* in exactly the same way as substitutions can be applied to terms. For example, $list(V)\{V/\text{static}\} = list(\text{static})$. A type or type definition is called *ground* if it contains no type variables.

Definition 5. *We now define* type judgements *relating terms to types in Γ.*
  - *$t : $ dynamic holds for any term t*
  - *$t : $ static holds for any ground term t*
  - *$t : $ nonvar holds for any non-variable term t*
  - *$f(t_1, \ldots, t_n) : c(\tau_1', \ldots, \tau_k')$ if there exists a ground instance of a type definition in Γ which has the form $c(\tau_1', \ldots, \tau_k') \longrightarrow \ldots f(\tau_1, \ldots, \tau_n) \ldots$ and where $t_i : \tau_i$ for $1 \leq i \leq n$.*

Here are a few examples, using the type system Γ_1 above. First, we have $s(0) : $ static, $s(0) : $ nonvar, and $s(0) : $ dynamic. Also, $s(X) : $ nonvar, $s(X) : $ dynamic but not $s(X)$: static. A few examples with lists are: $[s(0)]$: $list(\text{static})$, $[X, Y]$: $list(\text{dynamic})$.

The following fixes problem 3 identified earlier, i.e., it computes a new binding type for an argument t which has incorrectly been assigned a binding type τ:

Definition 6. *Let t be a term and τ a binding type.* $tgen(t, \tau) =$
  - τ *if $t : \tau$;*
  - dynamic   *if $\neg(t : \tau)$ and t is a variable;*
  - $f(tgen(t_1, \tau_1), \ldots, tgen(t_k, \tau_k))$ *if $t = f(t_1, \ldots, t_n)$ and $\tau = f(\tau'_1, \ldots, \tau'_k)$ and $\neg(t : \tau)$;*
  - nonvar *otherwise.*

For example, $tgen(s(0), \text{static}) = \text{static}$, $tgen(p(X), \text{static}) = \text{nonvar}$, and $tgen(X, \text{static}) = \text{dynamic}$. Also $tgen(p(s(X), 0), p(\text{static}, \text{static})) = p(\text{nonvar}, \text{static})$, and $tgen([a, X], list(\text{nonvar})) = \text{nonvar}$. The above algorithm does not try to invent new types and the last example shows that there are ways to make the algorithm more precise (by inferring $list(\text{dynamic})$ rather than nonvar). However, the algorithm does guarantee termination and correctness in the following sense:

Proposition 1. *For every infinite sequence of terms $t_1, t_2, \ldots$ and for every binding type τ_0 the sequence $\tau_1, \tau_2, \ldots$ with $\tau_i = tgen(t_i, \tau_{i-1})$ stabilises and there exists a $k > 0$ such that for all $j > k$ we have $t_j : \tau_j$.*

The proposition follows from the fact that by construction $t : tgen(t, \tau)$ and for any given type τ only finitely many more general types can be obtained by applying $tgen$.

Dangerous Memoisation. The watchdog flags a memoisation of a call as dangerous if it can find an ancestor in the specialization tree which is embedded in the call. To fix this (potential) problem detected by the watchdog we make use of the following definition:

Definition 7. *Let $a = p(a_1, \ldots, a_n)$ and $b = p(t_1, \ldots, t_n)$ be two atoms such that $a \trianglelefteq b$. Then the growing argument positions of b wrt a are all indices i such that t_i is not a variant of a_i.*

It can be seen that for every growing argument position i we have $a_i \lhd b_i$. A simple solution is now to compute all growing argument positions and adapt the filter declaration so that the corresponding arguments are given the binding-type dynamic (i.e., these arguments will be replaced by fresh variables during memoisation). This is the solution that we have currently implemented within LOGEN. A more subtle solution could be developed by employing most specific generalisation (msg) [12] a common technique used for controlling generalisation in online specialisation [16]: the msg of a set of terms S is the most specific term such that all expressions in S are instances of it. We can now compute the msg on the growing arguments and then only replace the variables by dynamic. For example, given the memoised call $p(b, p(s(s(0)), 1)), [W])$ with filter declaration :- filter p(static,static,list(dynamic)) and with covering ancestor $p(a, p(s(0), 1), [V])$ we have $msg(\{p(s(s(0)), 1), p(s(0), 1)\}) = p(s(Z), 1)$ and thus obtain the new declaration: :- filter p(static,p(s(dynamic),static),list(dynamic)).

Pragmatic BTA, Debugging and ASAP Case Studies. The above new methods and the accompanying web interface make it now much easier for users to fix their incorrect annotations. Furthermore, it also enables a *pragmatic BTA* to be performed. Basically, the idea is to start off with an initial annotation where all user predicates are marked as **unfold** and all built-ins as **call**. The specialiser is then run in watchdog mode on a series of representative specialisation queries. Every time a problem is detected the fix computed by LOGEN is applied. This is repeated until all sample queries can be specialised without error. One should also combine this process with the filter propagation algorithm of [8] to ensure that the annotations are correct wrt static information. It is easy to see that this process must terminate. However, the approach does obviously not guarantee that specialisation will terminate for all queries. Still, this approach has proven to be successful on some larger case studies within the European project ASAP. In the first study, LOGEN was used to specialise an interpreter for a process language with the aim of automatic task scheduling on pervasive devices. In another case study a complete emulator for PIC assembly [10] was successfully specialised by LOGEN for arbitrary PIC programs (for further analysis such as dead code detection). In both cases the automatic BTA was not applicable (due to the size of the interpreters and due to the various built-ins used), but the watchdog mode enabled us to annotate the programs with much less effort (e.g. a few hours for the process language interpreter) than was previously possible. Note that once the annotation was developed, the watchdog mode was turned off allowing the offline specialiser to run at full speed for the various applications.

Another application of our method and web interface is debugging. For instance, we had a version of the task scheduling interpreter containing a built-in error (calling T2 =.. [Op,V0|V1] instead of T2 =.. [Op,V0,V1]). When one executes the main method of this program one simply gets the following message: ERROR: illegal arithmetic expression, without any indication about the call or the location of the error. Using a debugger to locate such errors is often not practical: the error was reached after 175 steps (and more tricky problems will easily require thousands or millions of steps given that current Prolog systems can exceed 20 Million logical inferences per second) and when using the debugger's leap command one gets the same message as above, without any indication about the problematic built-in nor its location. Our watchdog approach can be used as an automatic debugger to locate those problems (as well as locating loops). The idea is to use a simple BTA which annotates all calls to user predicates as unfold and all calls to built-ins as call (this BTA is available via the web interface). Specializing then corresponds to supervised execution, where checks and program point information has been weaved into the source program. We thus get information about the actual call that causes the problem (as well as precise program point information which is used by the web interface to highlight the location of the error):

```
% logen task_csp_scheduler_err.pl "main([2,3,4])" -wb
<| BUILT-IN ERROR |> : CALL Atom _7966=..[+,2|10]
```

The -wb option tells LOGEN to check only built-ins and not user predicates for potential loops (in order to reduce the overhead). Some experimental data for the overhead of this approach can be seen in the table below. As can be seen, the overhead is very reasonable.

Benchmark	original (consulted)	original (compiled)	LOGEN (normal)	LOGEN -wb (watch)
lambdaint	2.18 ms	1.22 ms	1.29 ms	4.48 ms
task_scheduler	1.15 ms	0.61 ms	0.59 ms	2.83 ms

6   Related Work and Conclusion

We believe that our idea to use online techniques to supervise an offline specialiser to be new. However, in the past several researchers have investigated hybrid strategies[6] (e.g., [3, 7, 11]) where offline partial evaluators were augmented with online constructs. The aim there was different (to augment specialisation power) and only very few actual techniques or implementations exist ([29] is one). Another related work is [25] where program transformations are used to construct justifications for computed answers.

We have presented the idea of using online techniques in general and the homeomorphic embedding relation in particular to supervise an offline specialiser, in an effort to help the development of correct annotations by identifying error conditions. We have implemented this technique within the LOGEN system and have shown that this technique turned out to be very effective: very few false alarms were raised and the overhead was low enough for the technique to be practically usable. We have presented an improved web interface that feeds back this information to the user in an intuitive way, and we have presented techniques to automatically computed fixes for the spotted problems. We have applied our ideas to various case studies, and the techniques have enabled us to annotate and specialise much larger programs than was previously possible. These new features of LOGEN can also be tried out at using a web interface at http://stups.cs.uni-duesseldorf.de/~pe/weblogen.

Our technique can also be used as a pragmatic BTA: one simply starts with a maximally aggressive annotation and then lets the watchdog find and fix the errors. While this does not produce termination guarantees, it has proven very effective in practice and can easily deal with larger source programs and with many built-ins. Another application of our watchdog mode is to locate built-in errors or non-termination problems in user programs, and highlight those errors directly within the user's source program.

The LOGEN system has found many uses; from specialising PIC assembly code emulators, to point cut languages for aspect orientation over to CTL model

---

[6] Sometimes called mixline annotations.

checkers. But so far using LOGEN required considerable expertise in partial evaluation, hampering a more widespread usage. With this work we hope to make LOGEN and the underlying technology accessible to a broader community.

Acknowledgements. We would like to thank Marc Fontaine for useful feedback.

References

1. M. Alpuente, M. Falaschi, and G. Vidal. Partial Evaluation of Functional Logic Programs. *ACM Transactions on Programming Languages and Systems*, 20(4):768–844, 1998.
2. S. Barker, M. Leuschel, and M. Varea. Efficient and flexible access control via logic program specialisation. In *Proceedings PEPM'04*, pages 190–199. ACM Press, 2004.
3. A. Bondorf. Towards a self-applicable partial evaluator for term rewriting systems. In D. Bjørner, A. P. Ershov, and N. D. Jones, editors, *Partial Evaluation and Mixed Computation*, pages 27–50. North-Holland, 1988.
4. M. Bruynooghe, D. De Schreye, and B. Martens. A general criterion for avoiding infinite unfolding during partial deduction. *New Generation Computing*, 11(1):47–79, 1992.
5. M. Bruynooghe, M. Leuschel, and K. Sagonas. A polyvariant binding-time analysis for off-line partial deduction. In C. Hankin, editor, *Proceedings ESOP'98*, LNCS 1381, pages 27–41. Springer-Verlag, April 1998.
6. N. H. Christensen and R. Glück. Offline partial evaluation can be as accurate as online partial evaluation. *ACM Transactions on Programming Languages and Systems*, 26(1):191–220, 2004.
7. C. Consel. Binding time analysis for high order untyped functional languages. In *LFP '90: Proceedings of the 1990 ACM conference on LISP and functional programming*, pages 264–272, New York, NY, USA, 1990. ACM Press.
8. S.-J. Craig, J. Gallagher, M. Leuschel, and K. S. Henriksen. Fully automatic binding-time analysis for Prolog. In S. Etalle, editor, *Proceedings LOPSTR 2004*, LNCS 3573, pages 53–68. Springer-Verlag, August 2004.
9. A. J. Glenstrup and N. D. Jones. BTA algorithms to ensure termination of off-line partial evaluation. In *Perspectives of System Informatics: Proceedings of the Andrei Ershov Second International Memorial Conference*, LNCS 1181, pages 273–284. Springer-Verlag, 1996.
10. K. S. Henriksen and J. P. Gallagher. Analysis and specialisation of a PIC processor. In *Proceedings of the IEEE International Conference on Systems, Man & Cybernetics (2)*, pages 1131–1135, The Hague, The Netherlands, 2004.
11. N. D. Jones, C. K. Gomard, and P. Sestoft. *Partial Evaluation and Automatic Program Generation*. Prentice Hall, 1993.
12. J.-L. Lassez, M. Maher, and K. Marriott. Unification revisited. In J. Minker, editor, *Foundations of Deductive Databases and Logic Programming*, pages 587–625. Morgan-Kaufmann, 1988.
13. M. Leuschel. The ECCE partial deduction system and the DPPD library of benchmarks. Obtainable via http://www.ecs.soton.ac.uk/~mal, 1996-2002.
14. M. Leuschel. On the power of homeomorphic embedding for online termination. In G. Levi, editor, Static Analysis. *Proceedings of SAS'98*, LNCS 1503, pages 230–245, Pisa, Italy, September 1998. Springer-Verlag.

15. M. Leuschel. Homeomorphic embedding for online termination of symbolic methods. In T. Æ. Mogensen, D. Schmidt, and I. H. Sudborough, editors, *The Essence of Computation - Essays dedicated to Neil Jones*, LNCS 2566, pages 379–403. Springer-Verlag, 2002.

16. M. Leuschel and M. Bruynooghe. Logic program specialisation through partial deduction: Control issues. *Theory and Practice of Logic Programming*, 2(4 & 5):461–515, July & September 2002.

17. M. Leuschel, S. Craig, M. Bruynooghe, and W. Vanhoof. Specializing interpreters using offline partial deduction. In M. Bruynooghe and K.-K. Lau, editors, *Program Development in Computational Logic*, LNCS 3049, pages 341–376. Springer-Verlag, 2004.

18. M. Leuschel, D. Elphick, M. Varea, S. Craig, and M. Fontaine. The Ecce and Logen partial evaluators and their web interfaces. In F. T. John Hatcliff, editor, *Proceedings of PEPM'06*, pages 88–94. IBM Press, Januar 2006.

19. M. Leuschel, J. Jørgensen, W. Vanhoof, and M. Bruynooghe. Offline specialisation in Prolog using a hand-written compiler generator. *Theory and Practice of Logic Programming*, 4(1):139–191, 2004.

20. M. Leuschel, B. Martens, and D. De Schreye. Controlling generalisation and polyvariance in partial deduction of normal logic programs. *ACM Transactions on Programming Languages and Systems*, 20(1):208–258, January 1998.

21. M. Leuschel and G. Vidal. Forward slicing by conjunctive partial deduction and argument filtering. In M. Sagiv, editor, *Proceedings ESOP 2005*, LNCS 3444, pages 61–76. Springer-Verlag, April 2005.

22. J. W. Lloyd. *Foundations of Logic Programming*. Springer-Verlag, 1987.

23. H. Makholm. On Jones-optimal specialization for strongly typed languages. In W. Taha, editor, *Semantics, Applications, and Implementation of Program Generation*, LNCS 1924, pages 129–148. Springer-Verlag, 2000.

24. B. Martens and J. Gallagher. Ensuring global termination of partial deduction while allowing flexible polyvariance. In L. Sterling, editor, *Proceedings ICLP'95*, pages 597–613, Kanagawa, Japan, June 1995. MIT Press.

25. G. Pemmasani, H.-F. Guo, Y. Dong, C. R. Ramakrishnan, and I. V. Ramakrishnan. Online justification for tabled logic programs. In *Proceedings FLOPS 2004*, LNCS 2998, pages 24 – 38. Springer-Verlag, January 2004.

26. D. Sahlin. Mixtus: An automatic partial evaluator for full Prolog. *New Generation Computing*, 12(1):7–51, 1993.

27. Z. Somogyi, F. Henderson, and T. Conway. The execution algorithm of Mercury: An efficient purely declarative logic programming language. *The Journal of Logic Programming*, 29(1–3):17–64, 1996.

28. M. H. Sørensen and R. Glück. An algorithm of generalization in positive supercompilation. In J. W. Lloyd, editor, *Proceedings of ILPS'95, the International Logic Programming Symposium*, pages 465–479, Portland, USA, 1995. MIT Press.

29. M. Sperber. Self-applicable online partial evaluation. In O. Danvy, R. Glück, and P. Thiemann, editors, *Partial Evaluation, International Seminar*, LNCS 1110, pages 465–480, Schloß Dagstuhl, 1996. Springer-Verlag.

30. W. Vanhoof and B. Martens. To parse or not to parse. In N. Fuchs, editor, *Logic Program Synthesis and Transformation. Proceedings of LOPSTR'97*, LNCS 1463, pages 322–342, Leuven, Belgium, July 1997.

31. Q. Wang, G. Gupta, and M. Leuschel. Towards provably correct code generation via Horn logical continuation semantics. In M. V. Hermenegildo and D. Cabeza, editors, *Proceedings PADL'05*, of *LNCS 3350*, pages 98–112. Springer, 2005.

Improving Offline Narrowing-Driven Partial Evaluation Using Size-Change Graphs*

Gustavo Arroyo, J.Guadalupe Ramos, Josep Silva, and Germán Vidal

Technical University of Valencia,
Camino de Vera s/n, 46022 Valencia, Spain
{garroyo,guadalupe,jsilva,gvidal}@dsic.upv.es

Abstract. An offline approach to narrowing-driven partial evaluation (a partial evaluation scheme for first-order functional and functional logic programs) has recently been introduced. In this approach, program annotations (i.e., the expressions that should be generalised at partial evaluation time to ensure termination) are based on a simple syntactic characterisation of quasi-terminating programs. This work extends the previous offline scheme by introducing a new annotation strategy which is based on a combination of size-change graphs and binding-time analysis. Preliminary experiments point out that the number of program annotations is significantly reduced compared to the previous approach, which means that faster residual programs are often produced.

1 Introduction

Narrowing [30] extends the reduction principle of functional languages by replacing matching with unification (as in logic programming). Narrowing-driven partial evaluation (NPE) [1] is a powerful specialisation technique for the first-order component of many functional and functional logic languages like Haskell [28] or Curry [18]. In NPE, some refinement of narrowing is used to perform symbolic computations. Currently, *needed narrowing* [4], a narrowing strategy that only selects a function call if its reduction is necessary to compute a value, is the strategy that presents better properties. In general, the narrowing space (i.e., the counterpart of the SLD search space in logic programming) of a term may be infinite. However, even in this case, NPE may still terminate when the original program is *quasi-terminating* w.r.t. the considered narrowing strategy, i.e., when only finitely many different terms—modulo variable renaming—are computed. The reason is that the (partial) evaluation of multiple occurrences of the same term (modulo variable renaming) in a computation can be avoided by inserting a call to some previously encountered variant (a technique known as *specialisation-point insertion* in the partial evaluation literature).

* This work has been partially supported by the EU (FEDER) and the Spanish MEC under grant TIN2005-09207-C03-02, by the Mexican SEIT-ANUIES and DGEST *beca-comisión* and by the ICT for EU-India Cross-Cultural Dissemination Project ALA/95/23/2003/077-054.

G. Puebla (Ed.): LOPSTR 2006, LNCS 4407, pp. 60–76, 2007.

Recently, [29] identified a class of quasi-terminating rewrite systems (w.r.t. needed narrowing) that are called *non-increasing*. This characterisation is purely syntactic and very easy to check, though too restrictive to be useful in practice. Therefore, [29] introduces an offline scheme for NPE by

- annotating the program expressions *that violate the non-increasingness property* and
- considering a slight extension of needed narrowing to perform partial computations so that annotated subterms are *generalised* at specialisation time (which ensures the termination of the process).

In this work, we improve on the simpler characterisation of non-increasing rewrite systems by using *size-change graphs* [24] to approximate the changes in parameter sizes from one function call to another. In particular, we use the information in the size-change graphs to identify a particular form of quasi-termination, called PE-termination, which implies that only finitely many different *function calls* (modulo variable renaming) can be produced in a computation. For this purpose, the output of a standard binding-time analysis is also used in order to have information on which function arguments are *static* (and thus ground) and which are *dynamic*. When the information gathered from the combined use of size-change graphs and binding-time analysis does not allow us to infer that the rewrite system quasi-terminates, we proceed as in [29] and annotate the problematic subterms to be generalised at partial evaluation time.

Related Work

Regarding quasi-termination, we find relatively few works devoted to quasi-termination analysis of functional or logic programs (and no previous work on quasi-termination of functional logic programs). The notion of quasi-termination was originally introduced in term rewriting by Dershowitz [12], where a rewrite derivation is called quasi-terminating when it only contains finitely many different terms. Within logic programming, one of the first approaches is [11], where the authors introduce the notion of *quasi-acceptability*, a sufficient and necessary condition for quasi-termination. This work has been extended in [32].

As for size-change analysis, this approach was originally introduced in [24] in the context of functional programming. The scheme was later adapted to term rewriting in [31].

Finally, regarding the use of quasi-termination analysis for ensuring the termination of offline partial evaluation, there are a few related approaches. Quasi-termination was soon recognised as an essential property to guarantee the termination of partial evaluation (see, e.g., the pioneering work of Holst [20]). In particular, we share many similarities with the approach introduced by Glenstrup and Jones [16], where a quasi-termination analysis based on size-change graphs is used to ensure the termination of an offline partial evaluator for first-order functional programs. However, transferring Glenstrup and Jones' scheme to function logic programming is not straightforward because narrowing computations propagate bindings forward in the computations (as logic programming does). As a consequence, several additional conditions should be introduced in order to preserve the termination of partial evaluation. Furthermore, we consider simpler size-change graphs (i.e., the "may-increase" relation of [16] is not used in this work). This may somewhat weaken the power of our size-change analysis, but it could be straightforwardly extended along the lines of [16].

Plan of the Paper

This paper is structured as follows. After providing some preliminary definitions in Sect. 2, we recall the original approach to offline narrowing-driven partial evaluation in Sect. 3. Then, Sect. 4 introduces a quasi-termination analysis based on size-change graphs and states the main result of the paper. Section 5 presents the new annotation procedure and illustrates it with an example. Section 6 describes an experimental evaluation of our approach by using a prototype implementation of the offline partial evaluator. Finally, Sect. 7 concludes and points out some directions for future work. More details and missing proofs can be found in [5].

2   Preliminaries

Term rewriting [6] offers an appropriate framework to model the first-order component of many functional and functional logic programming languages. Therefore, we follow the standard framework of term rewriting for developing our results.

A set of rewrite rules (or oriented equations) $l \to r$ such that l is a nonvariable term and r is a term whose variables appear in l is called a *term rewriting system* (TRS for short); terms l and r are called the left-hand side and the right-hand side of the rule, respectively. Given a TRS $\mathcal{R}$ over a signature $\mathcal{F}$, the *defined* symbols $\mathcal{D}$ are the root symbols of the left-hand sides of the rules and the *constructors* are $\mathcal{C} = \mathcal{F} \setminus \mathcal{D}$. We restrict ourselves to finite signatures and TRSs. We denote the domain of terms and *constructor terms* by $\mathcal{T}(\mathcal{F}, \mathcal{V})$ and $\mathcal{T}(\mathcal{C}, \mathcal{V})$, respectively, where $\mathcal{V}$ is a set of variables with $\mathcal{F} \cap \mathcal{V} = \emptyset$.

A TRS $\mathcal{R}$ is *constructor-based* if the left-hand sides of its rules have the form $f(s_1, \ldots, s_n)$ where s_i are constructor terms, i.e., $s_i \in \mathcal{T}(\mathcal{C}, \mathcal{V})$, for all $i = 1, \ldots, n$. The set of variables appearing in a term t is denoted by $Var(t)$. A term t is *linear* if every variable of $\mathcal{V}$ occurs at most once in t. $\mathcal{R}$ is left-linear (resp. right-linear) if l (resp. r) is linear for all rules $l \to r \in \mathcal{R}$. The *definition* of f in $\mathcal{R}$ is the set of rules in $\mathcal{R}$ whose root symbol in the left-hand side is f. A function $f \in \mathcal{D}$ is left-linear (resp. right-linear) if the rules in its definition are left-linear (resp. right-linear).

The root symbol of a term t is denoted by $root(t)$. A term t is *operation-rooted* (resp. *constructor-rooted*) if $root(t) \in \mathcal{D}$ (resp. $root(t) \in \mathcal{C}$). As it is common practice, a *position* p in a term t is represented by a sequence of natural numbers, where ϵ denotes the root position. Positions are used to address the nodes of a term viewed as a tree: $t|_p$ denotes the *subterm* of t at position p and

$t[s]_p$ denotes the result of *replacing the subterm* $t|_p$ by the term s. A term t is *ground* if $Var(t) = \emptyset$. A term t is a *variant* of term t' if they are equal modulo variable renaming. A *substitution* σ is a mapping from variables to terms such that its domain $Dom(\sigma) = \{x \in \mathcal{V} \mid x \neq \sigma(x)\}$ is finite. The identity substitution is denoted by *id*. A substitution σ is *constructor*, if $\sigma(x)$ is a constructor term for all $x \in Dom(\sigma)$. Term t' is an *instance* of term t if there is a substitution σ with $t' = \sigma(t)$. A syntactic object s_1 is *more general* than a syntactic object s_2, denoted $s_1 \leqslant s_2$, if there exists a substitution θ such that $s_2 = s_1\theta$. A *unifier* of two terms s and t is a substitution σ with $\sigma(s) = \sigma(t)$; furthermore, σ is the *most general unifier* of s and t, denoted by $mgu(s, t)$ if, for every other unifier θ of s and t, we have that $\sigma \leqslant \theta$. In the following, we write $\overline{o_n}$ for the *sequence of objects* $o_1, \ldots, o_n$.

Inductively sequential TRSs [3] are a subclass of left-linear constructor-based TRSs. Essentially, a TRS is *inductively sequential* when all its operations are defined by rewrite rules that, recursively, make on their arguments a case distinction analogous to a data type (or structural) induction. Inductive sequentiality is not a limiting condition for programming. In fact, the first-order component of many functional (logic) programs written in, e.g., Haskell, ML or Curry, are inductively sequential.

Example 1. Consider the following rules which define the less-or-equal function on natural numbers (built from *zero* and *succ*):

$$
\begin{array}{rcl}
zero \leqslant y & \rightarrow & true \\
succ(x) \leqslant zero & \rightarrow & false \\
succ(x) \leqslant succ(y) & \rightarrow & x \leqslant y
\end{array}
$$

This function is inductively sequential since its left-hand sides can be hierarchically organised as follows:

$$
\boxed{n} \leqslant m \Longrightarrow
\begin{cases}
zero \leqslant m \\
succ(x) \leqslant \boxed{m} \Longrightarrow
\begin{cases}
succ(x) \leqslant zero \\
succ(x) \leqslant succ(y)
\end{cases}
\end{cases}
$$

where arguments in a box denote a case distinction (this is similar to the notion of definitional tree in [3]).

The evaluation of terms w.r.t. a TRS is formalised with the notion of *rewriting*. A *rewrite step* is an application of a rewrite rule to a term, i.e., $t \rightarrow_{p,R} s$ if there exists a position p in t, a rewrite rule $R = (l \rightarrow r)$ and a substitution σ with $t|_p = \sigma(l)$ and $s = t[\sigma(r)]_p$ (p and R will often be omitted in the notation of a reduction step). The instantiated left-hand side $\sigma(l)$ is called a *redex*. A term t is called *irreducible* or in *normal form* if there is no term s with $t \rightarrow s$. We denote by $\rightarrow^+$ the transitive closure of $\rightarrow$ and by $\rightarrow^*$ its reflexive and transitive closure. Given a TRS $\mathcal{R}$ and a term t, we say that t *evaluates* to s iff $t \rightarrow^* s$ and s is in normal form.

Functional *logic* programs mainly differ from purely functional programs in that function calls may contain *free* variables. In order to evaluate such terms containing variables, narrowing nondeterministically instantiates the variables such that a rewrite step is possible [17]. Formally, $t \leadsto_{p,R,\sigma} t'$ is a *narrowing step* iff p is a nonvariable position of t and $\sigma(t) \to_{p,R} t'$ (we sometimes omit p, R and/or σ when they are clear from the context). The substitution σ is very often the *most general unifier*[1] of $t|_p$ and the left-hand side of (a variant of) R, restricting its domain to $\mathcal{V}ar(t)$. As in proof procedures for logic programming, we assume that the rules of the TRS always contain fresh variables if they are used in a narrowing step. We denote by $t_0 \leadsto_\sigma^* t_n$ a sequence of narrowing steps $t_0 \leadsto_{\sigma_1} \ldots \leadsto_{\sigma_n} t_n$ with $\sigma = \sigma_n \circ \cdots \circ \sigma_1$ (if $n = 0$ then $\sigma = id$).

In order to avoid unnecessary computations and to deal with infinite data structures, a demand-driven generation of the search space has been advocated by a number of *lazy* narrowing strategies [15,26,27]. Because of its optimality properties w.r.t. the length of derivations and the number of computed solutions, we consider *needed narrowing* [4] in the following.

We say that $s \leadsto_{p,R,\sigma} t$ is a *needed narrowing step* iff $\sigma(s) \to_{p,R} t$ is a *needed rewrite* step in the sense of Huet and Lévy [21], i.e., in every computation from $\sigma(s)$ to a normal form, either $\sigma(s)|_p$ or one of its *descendants* must be reduced. Here, we are interested in a particular needed narrowing strategy, denoted by λ in [4, Def. 13], which is based on the notion of a *definitional tree* [3] (a hierarchical structure containing the rules of a function definition, which is used to guide the needed narrowing steps). This strategy is basically equivalent to *lazy narrowing* [27] where narrowing steps are applied to the outermost function, if possible, and inner functions are only narrowed if their evaluation is *demanded* by a constructor symbol in the left-hand side of some rule (i.e., a typical call-by-name evaluation strategy). The main difference is that needed narrowing does not compute the *most general unifier* between the selected redex and the left-hand side of the rule but only a unifier. The additional bindings are required to ensure that only "needed" computations are performed (see, e.g., [4]) and, thus, needed narrowing generally computes a smaller search space.

Example 2. Consider again the rules defining function "$\leqslant$" of Example 1. In a term like $t_1 \leqslant t_2$, needed narrowing proceeds as follows: First, t_1 should be evaluated to some *head normal form* (i.e., a free variable or a constructor-rooted term) since all three rules defining "$\leqslant$" have a non-variable first argument. Then,

1. If t_1 evaluates to *zero* then the first rule is applied.
2. If t_1 evaluates to $succ(t_1')$ then t_2 is evaluated to head normal form:
   (a) If t_2 evaluates to *zero* then the second rule is applied.
   (b) If t_2 evaluates to $succ(t_2')$ then the third rule is applied.
   (c) If t_2 evaluates to a free variable, then it is instantiated to a constructor-rooted term, here *zero* or $succ(x)$ and, depending on this instantiation, we proceed as in cases (a) or (b) above.
3. Finally, if t_1 evaluates to a free variable, needed narrowing instantiates it to a constructor-rooted term (*zero* or $succ(x)$). Depending on this instantiation, we proceed as in cases (1) or (2) above.

---

[1] Some narrowing strategies (e.g., needed narrowing) compute unifiers that are not the most general, see below.

A precise definition of inductively sequential TRSs and needed narrowing is not necessary in this work (the interested reader can find detailed definitions in [3,4]). In the following, we use *needed narrowing* to refer to the particular strategy λ in [4, Def. 13].

3 A Simple Offline NPE Scheme

In this section, we briefly present the offline approach to NPE from [29]. Given an inductively sequential TRS $\mathcal{R}$, the *first stage* of the process consists in computing the annotated TRS. In [29], annotations were added to those subterms that violate the non-increasingness condition, a simple syntactic characterisation of programs that guarantees the quasi-termination of computations. Nevertheless, annotations can be based on other, more refined, analyses—the goal of this paper—as long as the annotated program still ensures the termination of the specialisation process.

For the annotation stage, the signature $\mathcal{F}$ of a program is extended with a fresh symbol: "•". A term t is then annotated by replacing t by $\bullet(t)$.

Then, the *second stage*, i.e., the proper partial evaluation, proceeds as follows:

- it takes the annotated TRS, together with an initial term t,
- and constructs its associated (finite) *generalising* needed narrowing tree (see below) where, additionally, a test is included to check whether a variant of the current term has already been computed and, if so, stop the derivation.

Finally, a residual—partially evaluated—program is extracted from the generalising needed narrowing tree. Essentially, a *generalising needed narrowing derivation* $s \rightsquigarrow_{\sigma}^{*} t$ is composed of

a) *proper needed narrowing steps*, for operation-rooted terms with no annotations,
b) *generalisations*, for annotated terms, e.g., $f(\bullet(g(y)), x)$ is reduced to both $f(w, x)$ and $g(y)$, where w is a fresh variable, and
c) *constructor decompositions*, for constructor-rooted terms with no annotations, e.g., $c(f(x), g(y))$ is reduced to $f(x)$ and $g(y)$ when $c \in \mathcal{C}$ and $f, g \in \mathcal{D}$.

The substitution in $s \rightsquigarrow_{\sigma}^{*} t$ is the composition of the substitutions labelling the proper needed narrowing steps of $s \rightsquigarrow_{\sigma}^{*} t$. Consider, for instance, the following definitions of the addition and product on natural numbers built from *zero* and *succ*:

$$
\begin{array}{ll}
add(zero, y) \rightarrow y & prod(zero, y) \rightarrow zero \\
add(succ(x), y) \rightarrow succ(add(x, y)) & prod(succ(x), y) \rightarrow add(prod(x, y), y)
\end{array}
$$

According to [29], this program is not non-increasing because of the nested functions in the right-hand side of the second rule of function *prod*. Therefore, it is annotated as follows:

$$
\begin{array}{ll}
add(zero, y) \rightarrow y & prod(zero, y) \rightarrow zero \\
add(succ(x), y) \rightarrow succ(add(x, y)) & prod(succ(x), y) \rightarrow add(\bullet(prod(x, y)), y)
\end{array}
$$

E.g., the following needed narrowing computation is not quasi-terminating w.r.t. the original program (the selected function call is underlined):

$$\underline{prod(x,y)} \leadsto_{\{x \mapsto succ(x')\}} add(\underline{prod(x',y)},y)$$
$$\leadsto_{\{x' \mapsto succ(x'')\}} add(add(\underline{prod(x'',y)},y),y) \leadsto \ldots$$

In contrast, the corresponding computation by *generalising* needed narrowing is quasi-terminating (generalisation steps are denoted by "$\leadsto^{\bullet}$"):

$$\underline{add(w,y)} \leadsto \ldots$$

$$\underline{prod(x,y)} \leadsto_{\{x \mapsto succ(x')\}} add(\bullet(prod(x',y)),y)$$

$$\underline{prod(x',y)} \leadsto \ldots$$

Our generalisation step is somehow equivalent to the splitting operation of *conjunctive partial deduction* (CPD) of logic programs [10]. While CPD considers conjunctions of atoms, we deal with terms possibly containing nested function symbols. Therefore, flattening a nested function call is basically equivalent to splitting a conjunction (in both cases some information is lost). A similar relation between term generalisation and CPD is also pointed out in [2,23].

We skip the details of the extraction of residual programs from generalising needed narrowing trees since it is orthogonal to the topic of this paper (a more detailed description can be found in [29]).

4   Ensuring Quasi-termination with Size-Change Graphs

In this section, we first recall some basic notions on size-change graphs from [31], where the original scheme of [24] is adapted to term rewriting, and, then, we introduce our new approach for ensuring quasi-termination.

A transitive and antisymmetric binary relation $\succ$ is an *order* and a transitive and reflexive binary relation $\succsim$ is a *quasi-order*. A binary relation $\succ$ is *well founded* iff there exist no infinite decreasing sequence $t_0 \succ t_1 \succ t_2 \succ \ldots$ In the following, we say that a given order "$\succ$" is *closed under substitutions* (or *stable*) if $s \succ t$ implies $\sigma(s) \succ \sigma(t)$ for all $s, t \in \mathcal{T}(\mathcal{F}, \mathcal{V})$ and substitution σ.

Size-change graphs are parameterized by a so called reduction pair:

Definition 1 (reduction pair). *We say that $(\succsim, \succ)$ is a reduction pair if $\succsim$ is a quasi-order and $\succ$ is a well-founded order on terms where both $\succsim$ and $\succ$ are closed under substitutions and compatible (i.e., $\succsim \circ \succ \subseteq \succ$ and $\succ \circ \succsim \subseteq \succ$ but $\succsim \subseteq \succ$ is not necessary, where "$\circ$" is defined on binary relations R and R' as follows: $R \circ R' = \{(a,c) \mid (a,b) \in R \text{ and } (b,c) \in R'\}$). We also require that $s \, R \, t$ implies $\mathcal{V}ar(t) \subseteq \mathcal{V}ar(s)$ for all $R \in \{\succsim, \succ\}$ and terms s and t.*

Informally speaking, the restriction $\mathcal{V}ar(t) \subseteq \mathcal{V}ar(s)$ above is necessary in order to correctly propagate groundness information through narrowing steps.

Definition 2 (size-change graph). *Let* $(\succsim, \succ)$ *be a reduction pair. For every rule* $f(\overline{s_n}) \to r$ *of a TRS* $\mathcal{R}$ *and every subterm* $g(\overline{t_m})$ *of* r *where* $g \in \mathcal{D}$*, we have a size-change graph as follows:*

- *The graph has* n *output nodes marked with* $\{1_f, \ldots, n_f\}$ *and* m *input nodes marked with* $\{1_g, \ldots, m_g\}$.
- *If* $s_i \succ t_j$*, then there is a directed edge marked with* $\succ$ *from* i_f *to* j_g*. Otherwise, if* $s_i \succsim t_j$*, then there is an edge marked with* $\succsim$ *from* i_f *to* j_g.

A size-change graph is thus a bipartite labelled graph $G = (V, W, E)$ *where* $V = \{1_f, \ldots, n_f\}$ *and* $W = \{1_g, \ldots, m_g\}$ *are the labels of the output and input nodes, respectively, and we have edges* $E \subseteq V \times W \times \{\succsim, \succ\}$.

Size-change graphs are used to represent the way each function parameter changes from one call to another, according to a given reduction pair. In order to analyse the termination (or quasi-termination) of a program, it suffices to focus on its loops. For this purpose, we now compute the transitive closure of the size-change relations as follows:

Definition 3 (multigraph, concatenation). *Every size-change graph of* $\mathcal{R}$ *is a multigraph of* $\mathcal{R}$ *and if*

$$G = (\{1_f, \ldots, n_f\}, \{1_g, \ldots, m_g\}, E_1)$$

and

$$H = (\{1_g, \ldots, m_g\}, \{1_h, \ldots, p_h\}, E_2)$$

are multigraphs of $\mathcal{R}$ *w.r.t. the same reduction pair* $(\succsim, \succ)$*, then the concatenation*

$$G \cdot H = (\{1_f, \ldots, n_f\}, \{1_h, \ldots, p_h\}, E)$$

is also a multigraph of $\mathcal{R}$*. For* $1 \leq i \leq n$ *and* $1 \leq k \leq p$*,* E *contains an edge from* i_f *to* k_h *iff* E_1 *contains an edge from* i_f *to some* j_g *and* E_2 *contains an edge from* j_g *to* k_h*. Furthermore, if some of the edges are labelled with "*$\succ$*", then the edge in* E *is labelled with "*$\succ$*" as well. Otherwise, it is labelled with "*$\succsim$*".*

A multigraph G is idempotent if $G = G \cdot G$ (which implies that its input and output nodes are both labelled with $\{1_f, \ldots, n_f\}$ for some f). In the following, we will only focus on the idempotent multigraphs of a program, since they represent its (potential) loops.

Example 3. Consider the following example which computes the reverse of a given list:

$$
\begin{array}{ll}
rev([\,]) \quad \to [\,] & app([\,], y) \quad \to y \\
rev(x : xs) \to app(rev(xs), x : [\,]) & app(x : xs, y) \to x : app(xs, y)
\end{array}
$$

where "$[\,]$" and "$:$" are the list constructors. In this example, we consider a particular reduction pair $(\succsim, \succ)$ defined as follows:

- $s \gtrsim t$ iff $Var(t) \subseteq Var(s)$ and for all $x \in Var(t)$, $dv(t, x) \leqslant dv(s, x)$;
- $s \succ t$ iff $Var(t) \subseteq Var(s)$ and for all $x \in Var(t)$, $dv(t, x) < dv(s, x)$.

where the depth of a variable x in a constructor term t [8], $dv(t, x)$, is defined as follows:

$$
\begin{aligned}
dv(c(\overline{t_n}), x) &= 1 + max(\overline{dv(t_n, x)}) & \text{if } x \in Var(c(\overline{t_n})) \\
dv(c(\overline{t_n}), x) &= -1 & \text{if } x \notin Var(c(\overline{t_n})) \\
dv(y, x) &= 0 & \text{if } x = y \\
dv(y, x) &= -1 & \text{if } x \neq y \\
dv(t, x) &= -1 & \text{if } t \text{ is not a constructor term}
\end{aligned}
$$

with $c \in \mathcal{C}$ a constructor symbol of arity $n \geqslant 0$. The corresponding size-change graphs of this program are the following:

$$
G_1 : 1_{rev} \xrightarrow{\;\succ\;} 1_{rev} \qquad G_2 : 1_{rev} \xrightarrow{\quad} \begin{array}{c} 1_{app} \\ \searrow^{\gtrsim} \\ 2_{app} \end{array} \qquad G_3 : \begin{array}{c} 1_{app} \xrightarrow{\;\succ\;} 1_{app} \\ \\ 2_{app} \xrightarrow{\;\gtrsim\;} 2_{app} \end{array}
$$

where G_1 and G_3 are also the idempotent multigraphs of the program.

Definition 4 (PE-termination, PE-terminating TRS). *A needed narrowing computation is PE-terminating if only a finite number of nonvariant function calls (i.e., redexes) have been unfolded. A TRS is PE-terminating if every possible needed narrowing computation is PE-terminating.*

Observe that a PE-terminating TRS does not ensure the quasi-termination of its computations. For instance, given the TRS of Example 3 and the initial call *rev(xs)*, we have the following needed narrowing derivation:

$$
\begin{aligned}
\underline{rev(xs)} &\rightsquigarrow_{\{xs \mapsto y:ys\}} app(\underline{rev(ys)}, y : [\,]) \\
&\rightsquigarrow_{\{ys \mapsto z:zs\}} app(app(\underline{rev(zs)}, z : [\,]), y : [\,]) \\
&\rightsquigarrow_{\{zs \mapsto w:ws\}} \cdots
\end{aligned}
$$

Although this derivation contains an infinite number of different terms, there is only a finite number of nonvariant function calls. Fortunately, this is sufficient to ensure termination in many partial evaluation schemes because they often include some form of memoisation.

Online methods for partial evaluation usually consider a distinction between the so called *local* and *global* control levels. The *local* control should ensure that function (or procedure) calls are not unfolded infinitely, while the *global* control should take care of not unfolding infinitely many function (or procedure) calls. In fact, this distinction can be applied to both online or offline partial evaluators. In some cases, the distinction is made explicit (e.g., in the online partial evaluationscheme for logic programs of [13]) and in some other cases it is left implicit.[2] The main difference between these partial evaluators is that, in the online case, both the local and the global control take decisions on-the-fly, while in the offline case all decisions are taken before the actual specialisation starts (i.e., offline partial evaluators mainly follow the program annotations).

In this work, we consider a simple offline partial evaluation procedure as follows:

- *Local control*: here, we stop generalising needed narrowing derivations (i.e., needed narrowing derivations where annotated subterms are replaced by fresh variables) when the selected function call is a variant of a previously reduced function call in the same derivation. Observe that our local control examines the previous function calls in order to determine if a given function call should be unfolded or not. This should not be considered an online strategy but a simple memoisation technique. Furthermore, one could also consider cheaper (though less precise) strategies like, e.g., a depth-k unfolding strategy where narrowing computations stop after k function unfoldings and no variant checking is necessary.
- *Global control*:once the unfolding of a function call stops, the non-constructor terms in the leaves of the generalising needed narrowing tree are fully flattened before adding them to the set of (to be) partially evaluated calls. For instance, given the term $f(g(x), h(y))$, the function calls $f(w_1, w_2)$, $g(x)$ and $h(y)$ are added to the current set of (to be) partially evaluated calls, where w_1, w_2 are fresh variables. This flattening step is required in order for PE-termination to imply the termination of the partial evaluation process.

Now, we consider that the output of a simple (monovariant) binding-time analysis (BTA) is available. Informally speaking, given a TRS and the information on which parameters of the initial function call are static and which are dynamic, a BTA maps each program function to a list of static/dynamic values. Here, we consider that a static parameter is definitely known at specialisation time (hence it is ground), while a dynamic parameter is possibly unknown at specialisation time. The output of the BTA must be *congruent* [22]: the value of every static parameter is determined by the values of other static parameters (and thus ultimately by the available input).

In the following, we will also require the component $\succsim$ of a reduction pair $(\succsim, \succ)$ to be *bounded*, i.e., the set $\{s \mid t \succsim s\}$ must contain a finite number of nonvariant terms for any term t. Some closely related notions are that of *rigidity* [7] and *instantiated enough* [25], both defined w.r.t. a so called *norm*. These notions are used in many termination analyses for logic programs (e.g., [9,14,25]).

---

[2] For instance, many partial evaluators for functional programs (see, e.g., [22]) include an algorithm that iteratively (1) takes a function call, (2) performs some symbolic evaluations, and (3) extracts from the partially evaluated expression the set of pending function calls—the so-called *successors* of the initial function call—to be processed in the next iteration of the algorithm. Steps (1) and (3) would correspond to the global control while step (2) would correspond to the local control.

The following theorem states sufficient conditions to ensure PE-termination. The proof of correctness is based on Ramsey's Theorem (see [5]).

Theorem 1. *Let $\mathcal{R}$ be a TRS and $(\succsim, \succ)$ a reduction pair. $\mathcal{R}$ is PE-terminating w.r.t. any linear term if every idempotent multigraph associated to a function f/n contains either*

(i) at least one edge $i_f \xrightarrow{\succ} i_f$ for some $i \in \{1, \ldots, n\}$ such that i_f is static, or

(ii) an edge $i_f \xrightarrow{R} i_f$, $R \in \{\succsim, \succ\}$, for all $i = 1, \ldots, n$, such that $\succsim$ is bounded.

Also, we require $\mathcal{R}$ to be right-linear w.r.t. the dynamic variables, i.e., no repeated occurrence of the same dynamic variable may occur in a right-hand side.

Boundedness of "$\succsim$" in the second case (ii) above is necessary to ensure that no infinite sequences of nonvariant function calls with arguments of the same "size" according to $\succsim$ are allowed. Consider, for instance, an order $\succsim$ which is based on the length of a list, i.e., $t_1 \succsim t_2$ if t_1 and t_2 are lists and the number of elements of t_2 is less than or equal to the number of elements of t_1. In this case, $\succsim$ is not bounded: consider, e.g, the term $[x]$ so that the set $\{s \mid [x] \succsim s\}$ contains infinitely many nonvariant terms. Therefore, one can have infinite sequences of calls with nonvariant arguments where each argument is less than or equal to the previous one in the sequence:

$$f([x]) \rightsquigarrow f([succ(x)]) \rightsquigarrow f([succ(succ(x))]) \rightsquigarrow \ldots$$

with $[x] \succsim [succ(x)] \succsim [succ(succ(x))] \succsim \ldots$.

Example 4. The last condition of Theorem 1 on right-linearity of dynamic variables is required in order to avoid situations like the following one: given the TRS

$$
\begin{aligned}
double(x) &\ \rightarrow add(x, x) \\
add(zero, y) &\ \rightarrow y \\
add(succ(x), y) &\ \rightarrow succ(add(x, y))
\end{aligned}
$$

although *double* and *add* seem clearly terminating (and thus quasi-terminating), the following infinite computation is possible:

$$
\begin{aligned}
\underline{double(x)} \rightsquigarrow_{\{\}} &\quad \underline{add(x, x)} \\
\rightsquigarrow_{\{x \mapsto succ(x')\}} &\quad succ(\underline{add(x', succ(x'))}) \\
\rightsquigarrow_{\{x' \mapsto succ(x'')\}} &\quad succ(succ(\underline{add(x'', succ(succ(x'')))})) \\
\rightsquigarrow_{\{x'' \mapsto succ(x''')\}} &\quad \cdots
\end{aligned}
$$

which is not quasi-terminating nor PE-terminating.

5 Annotation Procedure

In this section, we introduce our new annotation procedure for offline narrowing-driven partial evaluation. Analogously to [29], rather than requiring source programs to fulfil the conditions of Theorem 1, we use this result to determine which subterms (if any) violate the conditions of this theorem.

The annotation procedure proceeds as follows: it considers every function symbol f/n of the program such that f has an associated idempotent multigraph (i.e., there is a potential loop that involves function f), and performs one of the following actions:

1. if the conditions of Theorem 1 hold, no annotation is added to the program;
2. otherwise, each argument t_j of every function call $f(t_1, \ldots, t_j, \ldots, t_n)$ with no edge $j_f \xrightarrow{R} j_f$, $R \in \{\succsim, \succ\}$, is annotated as follows: $f(t_1, \ldots, \bullet(t_j), \ldots, t_n);$[3]
3. finally, if there is more than one occurrence of the same dynamic variable (not yet annotated) in the right-hand side of a program rule, then all occurrences but one (e.g., the leftmost one) are annotated.

Roughly speaking, the correctness of the annotation procedure follows from the following facts:

- Let us consider a function call f/n with an associated idempotent multigraph (note that, by Theorem 1, termination can be ensured by focusing only on those program functions that have an associated idempotent multigraph).
- If the conditions of Theorem 1 hold, we have that from every call $f(t_1, \ldots, t_n)$ to the next call $f(s_1, \ldots, s_n)$ in a computation the following conditions hold:

  • there exists some $i \in \{1, \ldots, n\}$ such that $t_i \succ s_i$ and the i-th argument of f is static (i.e., both t_i and s_i are ground), which means that only finitely many different calls to f can be produced;[4]
  • otherwise, we have that either $t_i \succsim s_i$ or s_i is annotated (and thus generalising needed narrowing replaces this argument by a fresh variable) for all $i = 1, \ldots, n$, which means that only finitely many nonvariant calls to function f can be produced since $\succsim$ is bounded.

- Finally, the only exception to the above reasoning comes from the possible non right-linearity of the program w.r.t. dynamic variables, which is avoided by also annotating all but one such variables, so that situations like the one illustrated by Example 4 are no longer possible.

Let us illustrate the complete process with an example.

Example 5. Consider the well known Ackermann function:

$$
\begin{aligned}
ack(zero, n) &\rightarrow succ(n) \\
ack(succ(m), zero) &\rightarrow ack(m, succ(zero)) \\
ack(succ(m), succ(n)) &\rightarrow ack(m, ack(succ(m), n))
\end{aligned}
$$

First, we compute the size-change graphs of this program (here, we consider the same reduction pair of Example 3):

$$G_1 : 1_{ack} \xrightarrow{\succ} 1_{ack} \qquad G_2 : 1_{ack} \xrightarrow{\succ} 1_{ack} \qquad G_3 : 1_{ack} \xrightarrow{\succsim} 1_{ack}$$

$$2_{ack} \qquad 2_{ack} \qquad 1_{ack} \qquad 2_{ack} \qquad 2_{ack} \xrightarrow{\succ} 2_{ack}$$

---

[3] Analogously to [29], we use a fresh symbol, denoted by •, to annotate problematic subterms that should be generalised at partial evaluation time.

[4] This case is similar to the bounded anchoring principle of [16].

where graph G_1 is associated to the second rule and graphs G_2 and G_3 are associated to the third rule. In this example, these graphs coincide with the idempotent multigraphs of the program.

Assume that we want to specialise this program w.r.t. the initial function call $ack(succ(succ(succ(zero))), y)$, i.e., the first argument is static (ground). Clearly, the binding-time analysis returns the division $\{ack \mapsto [S, D]\}$, which means that the first argument of every call to ack is static and the second argument is dynamic. In this case, we have that

- the first condition of Theorem 1 holds for G_1 and G_2 since the first argument of ack is static and there is an edge $1_{ack} \xrightarrow{\;\succ\;} 1_{ack}$, and
- the second condition of Theorem 1 holds for G_3 since there is an edge associated to each argument (and $\succsim$ is bounded).

Furthermore, the right-linearity condition also holds since the only repeated occurrences of the same variable are the repeated occurrences of variable m in the third rule. However, no annotation is required in this case since variable m is static according to the output of the binding-time analysis. Therefore, the annotated program coincides with the original one.

Consider now that we want to specialise function ackermann w.r.t. the initial call $ack(x, succ(succ(succ(zero))))$, i.e., the second argument is static (ground). Here, the binding-time analysis returns the division $\{ack \mapsto [D, D]\}$ (because of the nested calls in the third rule). In this case, we have that

- the second condition of Theorem 1 holds for G_3 since there is an edge associated to each argument,
- but, since no condition holds for both G_1 and G_2, we should annotate the second argument of every call to function ack.

The annotated program is thus as follows:

$$
\begin{aligned}
ack(zero, n) \quad&\rightarrow succ(n)\\
ack(succ(m), zero) \quad&\rightarrow ack(m, \bullet(succ(zero)))\\
ack(succ(m), succ(n)) \quad&\rightarrow ack(m, \bullet(ack(succ(m), \bullet(n))))
\end{aligned}
$$

Observe that there is no violation of the right-linearity condition since one of the repeated occurrences of variable m in the third rule is already inside a $\bullet$.

6   Experimental Evaluation

We have undertaken an implementation of the improved annotation procedure. In particular, we have included the new annotation procedure into an offline partial evaluator for Curry programs [29]. This partial evaluator has been implemented in Curry itself [18]. In its current form, only a subset of Curry is considered. The extension to the remaining features of Curry (e.g., constraints, higher-order functions, built-ins, etc) is planned. The sources of the partial

Table 1. Benchmark results

benchmark	codesize	original	simple peval	speedup1	improved peval	speedup2
ackermann	739	3363	1077	3.12	688	4.89
allones	662	1522	1444	1.05	1452	1.05
dec_list	825	589	587	1.00	525	1.12
gauss	2904	308	320	0.96	252	1.22
inc_list	817	937	834	1.12	730	1.28
insert_sort	1005	1953	1280	1.53	1322	1.48
kmpA*B	30580	428	298	1.44	227	1.89
kmpB*A	30582	86	80	1.08	72	1.21
power	794	591	602	0.98	571	1.03
Average	**7656**	**1086**	**725**	**1.36**	**649**	**1.68**

evaluator and a detailed explanation of the benchmarks considered below are publicly available from

http://www.dsic.upv.es/users/elp/german/offpeval/

Table 1 shows the results of some benchmarks. For each benchmark, we show the size (in bytes) of each program (`codesize`), the run time of the original program (`original`), the run time for executing the residual program specialised with the previous offline partial evaluator which uses the simpler annotation procedure (`simple peval`), the run time for executing the residual program produced with the partial evaluator which includes the new annotation procedure (`improved peval`), and the speedup achieved by each partial evaluator; speedups are given by *orig/spec*, where *orig* and *spec* are the absolute run times of the original and specialised programs, respectively. Times are expressed in milliseconds and are the average of 10 executions on a 2.4 GHz Linux-PC (Intel Pentium IV with 512 KB cache). Run time input goals were chosen to give a reasonably long overall time. All programs (including the partial evaluators) were executed with the Curry to Prolog compiler of PAKCS [19].

As it can be seen in Table 1, residual programs obtained with the improved partial evaluator run (in the average) 7% faster than the residual programs obtained with the previous partial evaluator. This is not an impressive improvement but demonstrates that the novel annotation procedure is able to produce faster specialised programs. Analysis and specialisation times are not shown because they are generally very small. We note that the current partial evaluator is rather simple (i.e., it follows the simple strategy mentioned in Sect. 4). We expect to produce faster residual programs by improving the control procedures involved in the specialisation phase.

7   Conclusions and Future Work

This work introduced a new annotation procedure for the offline partial evaluation of functional logic programs. This procedure combines the information gathered from a simple binding-time analysis and a size-change analysis [24]. In contrast to previous approaches like [16], several extensions were necessary to cope with the logic component of the considered functional logic language (e.g., the conditions of boundedness and right-linearity in Theorem 1 were not needed in [16]). Preliminary experiments point out the improved performance of a partial evaluator which included the new annotation procedure.

In order to further improve the precision of the partial evaluator, we are currently implementing a *polyvariant* version of the program annotation stage. In this case, every function call is treated separately according to the information gathered from the associated idempotent multigraph. The resulting algorithm would be more expensive but also more precise.

Acknowledgements

We gratefully acknowledge the anonymous referees as well as the participants of LOPSTR 2006 for many useful comments and suggestions.

References

1. E. Albert and G. Vidal. The Narrowing-Driven Approach to Functional Logic Program Specialization. *New Generation Computing*, 20(1):3–26, 2002.
2. M. Alpuente, M. Falaschi, and G. Vidal. Partial Evaluation of Functional Logic Programs. *ACM TOPLAS*, 20(4):768–844, 1998.
3. S. Antoy. Definitional trees. In *Proc. of the 3rd Int'l Conference on Algebraic and Logic Programming (ALP'92)*, pages 143–157. Springer LNCS 632, 1992.
4. S. Antoy, R. Echahed, and M. Hanus. A Needed Narrowing Strategy. *Journal of the ACM*, 47(4):776–822, 2000.
5. G. Arroyo, J.G. Ramos, J. Silva, and G. Vidal. Improving Offline Narrowing-Driven Partial Evaluation Using Size-Change Graphs. Technical report, Technical University of Valencia, 2006. Available from the following URL: http://www.dsic.upv.es/users/elp/german/papers.html.
6. F. Baader and T. Nipkow. *Term Rewriting and All That*. Cambridge University Press, 1998.
7. A. Bossi, N. Cocco, and M. Fabris. Proving Termination of Logic Programs by Exploiting Term Properties. In S. Abramsky and T.S.E. Maibaum, editors, *Proc. of TAPSOFT'91*, pages 153–180. Springer LNCS 494, 1991.
8. W.N. Chin and S.C. Khoo. Better Consumers for Program Specializations. *Journal of Functional and Logic Programming*, 1996(4), 1996.
9. Michael Codish and Cohavit Taboch. A semantic basis for the termination analysis of logic programs. *J. Log. Program.*, 41(1):103–123, 1999.
10. D. De Schreye, R. Glück, J. Jørgensen, M. Leuschel, B. Martens, and M.H. Sørensen. Conjunctive Partial Deduction: Foundations, Control, Algorihtms, and Experiments. *Journal of Logic Programming*, 41(2&3):231–277, 1999.
11. S. Decorte, D. De Schreye, M. Leuschel, B. Martens, and K.F. Sagonas. Termination Analysis for Tabled Logic Programming. In *Proc. of LOPSTR'97*, pages 111–127. Springer LNCS 1463, 1998.

12. N. Dershowitz. Termination of Rewriting. *Journal of Symbolic Computation*, 3(1&2):69–115, 1987.
13. J. Gallagher. Tutorial on Specialisation of Logic Programs. In *Proc. of the ACM Symp. on Partial Evaluation and Semantics-Based Program Manipulation (PEPM'93)*, pages 88–98. ACM, New York, 1993.
14. S. Genaim, M. Codish, J.P. Gallagher, and V. Lagoon. Combining Norms to Prove Termination. In *Proc. of 3rd Int'l Workshop on Verification, Model Checking, and Abstract Interpretation (VMCAI'02)*, pages 126–138. Springer LNCS 2294, 2002.
15. E. Giovannetti, G. Levi, C. Moiso, and C. Palamidessi. Kernel Leaf: A Logic plus Functional Language. *Journal of Computer and System Sciences*, 42:363–377, 1991.
16. A.J. Glenstrup and N.D. Jones. Termination analysis and specialization-point insertion in offline partial evaluation. *ACM Trans. Program. Lang. Syst.*, 27(6):1147–1215, 2005.
17. M. Hanus. The Integration of Functions into Logic Programming: From Theory to Practice. *Journal of Logic Programming*, 19&20:583–628, 1994.
18. M. Hanus. Curry: An Integrated Functional Logic Language. Available at: http://www.informatik.uni-kiel.de/~mh/curry/, 2003.
19. M. Hanus (ed.), S. Antoy, M. Engelke, K. Höppner, J. Koj, P. Niederau, R. Sadre, and F. Steiner. PAKCS 1.6.0: The Portland Aachen Kiel Curry System—User Manual. Technical report, University of Kiel, Germany, 2004.
20. C.K. Holst. Finiteness Analysis. In *Proc. of Functional Programming Languages and Computer Architecture*, pages 473–495. Springer LNCS 523, 1991.
21. G. Huet and J.J. Lévy. Computations in orthogonal rewriting systems, Part I + II. In J.L. Lassez and G.D. Plotkin, editors, *Computational Logic – Essays in Honor of Alan Robinson*, pages 395–443, 1992.
22. N.D. Jones, C.K. Gomard, and P. Sestoft. *Partial Evaluation and Automatic Program Generation*. Prentice-Hall, Englewood Cliffs, NJ, 1993.
23. L. Lafave and J.P. Gallagher. Constraint-based Partial Evaluation of Rewriting-based Functional Logic Programs. In *Proc. of the 7th Int'l Workshop on Logic Programming Synthesis and Transformation (LOPSTR'97)*, pages 168–188. Springer LNCS 1463, 1997.
24. C.S. Lee, N.D. Jones, and A.M. Ben-Amram. The Size-Change Principle for Program Termination. In *ACM Symposium on Principles of Programming Languages (POPL'01)*, volume 28, pages 81–92. ACM press, 2001.
25. Naomi Lindenstrauss and Yehoshua Sagiv. Automatic termination analysis of logic programs. In *ICLP*, pages 63–77, 1997.
26. R. Loogen, F. López-Fraguas, and M. Rodríguez-Artalejo. A Demand Driven Computation Strategy for Lazy Narrowing. In *Proc. of 5th Int'l Symposium on Programming Language Implementation and Logic Programming (PLILP'93)*, pages 184–200. Springer LNCS 714, 1993.
27. J.J. Moreno-Navarro and M. Rodríguez-Artalejo. Logic Programming with Functions and Predicates: The language Babel. *J. Logic Programming*, 12(3):191–224, 1992.
28. S. Peyton-Jones, editor. *Haskell 98 Language and Libraries—The Revised Report*. Cambridge University Press, 2003.
29. J.G. Ramos, J. Silva, and G. Vidal. Fast Narrowing-Driven Partial Evaluation for Inductively Sequential Systems. *ACM SIGPLAN Notices (Proc. of ICFP'05)*, 40(9):228–239, 2005.
30. J.R. Slagle. Automated Theorem-Proving for Theories with Simplifiers, Commutativity and Associativity. *Journal of the ACM*, 21(4):622–642, 1974.

31. R. Thiemann and J. Giesl. The size-change principle and dependency pairs for termination of term rewriting. *Appl. Algebra Eng. Commun. Comput.*, 16(4):229–270, 2005.
32. S. Verbaeten, K. Sagonas, and D. De Schreye. Termination Proofs for Logic Programs with Tabling. *ACM Transactions on Computational Logic*, 2(1):57–92, 2001.

Towards Description and Optimization of Abstract Machines in an Extension of Prolog*

José F. Morales[1], Manuel Carro[2], and Manuel Hermenegildo[2,3]

[1] U. Complutense de Madrid (UCM)
`jfmc@fdi.ucm.es`
[2] T. University of Madrid (UPM)
`{mcarro,herme}@fi.upm.es`
[3] U. of New Mexico (UNM)
`herme@unm.edu`

Abstract. Competitive abstract machines for Prolog are usually large, intricate, and incorporate sophisticated optimizations. This makes them difficult to code, optimize, and, especially, maintain and extend. This is partly due to the fact that efficiency considerations make it necessary to use low-level languages in their implementation. Writing the abstract machine (and ancillary code) in a higher-level language can help harness this inherent complexity. In this paper we show how the semantics of basic components of an efficient virtual machine for Prolog can be described using (a variant of) Prolog which retains much of its semantics. These descriptions are then compiled to C and assembled to build a complete bytecode emulator. Thanks to the high level of the language used and its closeness to Prolog the abstract machine descriptions can be manipulated using standard Prolog compilation and optimization techniques with relative ease. We also show how, by applying program transformations selectively, we obtain abstract machine implementations whose performance can match and even exceed that of highly-tuned, hand-crafted emulators.

Keywords: Prolog, Abstract Machines, Compilation, Optimization, Program Transformation.

1 Introduction

Designing and implementing competitive "abstract" (or "virtual") machines is not without difficulties. In particular, the extensive code optimizations required for performance make development and, especially, maintenance and further

---

* This work was funded in part by the Information Society Technologies program of the European Commission, Future and Emerging Technologies under the IST-15905 *MOBIUS* project, by the Spanish Ministry of Education under the TIN-2005-09207 *MERIT* project, and the Madrid Regional Government under the *PROMESAS* project. Manuel Hermenegildo is also supported by the Prince of Asturias Chair in Information Science and Technology at UNM.

G. Puebla (Ed.): LOPSTR 2006, LNCS 4407, pp. 77–93, 2007.

modification non-trivial. Implementing or testing new optimizations is often involved, as decisions previously taken need to be revisited and low level and tedious recoding is often necessary to test a new idea.

Systems based on virtual machines are typically composed of a compiler from the source language ($\mathcal{L}_P$) to bytecode language ($\mathcal{L}_B$, aimed at being fast to interpret, for which an intermediate-level symbolic representation $\mathcal{L}_A$ usually exists), plus an emulator for $\mathcal{L}_B$ written in a lower-level language $\mathcal{L}_C$. In our particular case, $\mathcal{L}_P$ is Prolog, $\mathcal{L}_A$ is symbolic WAM code, and $\mathcal{L}_C$ is C.

Complexity of virtual machines and low level of $\mathcal{L}_C$ has led to several proposals in order to raise the level at which the virtual machine is written, while trying to maintain the possibility of translating it to the in principle more efficient $\mathcal{L}_C$ language. A particularly interesting possibility when $\mathcal{L}_P$ is a general-purpose language (as in our case) is to use $\mathcal{L}_P$ itself to write its virtual machine. This has been done for example in JavaInJava [1] and PyPy [2]. However, making these implementations competitive with existing hand-tuned abstract machines is undoubtedly a challenge: JavaInJava reports initial slowdowns of approximately 700 times w.r.t. then-current implementations, and PyPy started at the 2000× slowdown level.

This slowdown is largely due to the "semantic gap" existing between $\mathcal{L}_P$ and $\mathcal{L}_C$, even in the case of imperative and O.O. languages such as Java or Python. $\mathcal{L}_P$ should be precise enough to describe the algorithms underlying the basic operations of the abstract machine with, at most, a constant slowdown (i.e., with no penalty regarding computational complexity). In order to achieve this, and in addition to using improved compilation technology, we made changes to the initial $\mathcal{L}_P$ in the form of extensions which make it easier to reflect (or control) $\mathcal{L}_C$ characteristics not originally available such as, e.g., data sizes, alignments, unboxing, etc. We will refer to this extended version of $\mathcal{L}_P$ as $\mathcal{L}_I$. A similar approach has made it possible to, for example, reduce the slowdown of PyPy to $3.5 \div - 11.0 \div$ in more recent versions [2].

The approach of coding completely the whole abstract machine in $\mathcal{L}_P$ or $\mathcal{L}_I$ at once has the disadvantage of making it almost inevitable (as illustrated by, e.g., PyPy) to start from a large slowdown and then work slowly towards regaining performance. This makes it difficult to use the generated virtual machines as "production" software (which would therefore be routinely tested) and, especially, it makes it difficult to study how a certain optimization will carry over to a complete, optimized abstract machine.

We propose herein another possibility which is to proceed the other way around by starting from a highly optimized abstract machine, keeping some key elements coded in $\mathcal{L}_C$ and gradually replacing different pieces of code with code written in $\mathcal{L}_I$, making sure that no performance is lost at each step. In our implementation, and following this approach, we have chosen to generate the bytecode fetching and decoding loop directly in $\mathcal{L}_C$ using the emulator generator of [3]. This automates the generation of efficient emulators, makes devising and generating bytecode easy, and, notwithstanding, it makes it possible to write the definitions of the abstract machine instructions in $\mathcal{L}_I$. This is not at odds with compilation to native code and just-in-time systems, where a sizable part of the emulator machinery is still there in the form of runtime libraries.

We started with an efficient, WAM-based abstract machine for Prolog initially coded in C and we rewrote parts of it in a variant of Prolog ($\mathcal{L}_I$) which we have termed ImProlog and which both extends and restricts Prolog. ImProlog can be translated into very efficient C and at the same time its semantics is close enough to Prolog so as to be able to reuse many compilation techniques (certain analyses, specialization, etc.). This allows obtaining highly optimized and specialized emulators while avoiding obscure, redundant implementations or overuse of C macros. In addition, the combination of this approach with an emulator generator makes it possible to carry out non-trivial optimizations, such as instruction merging, automatically.

2   A Prolog Variant to Describe Virtual Machines

In this section we will describe our $\mathcal{L}_I$ language, ImProlog, and the analysis and code generation techniques used to produce highly efficient code from it.

2.1   New Features in the Language

ImProlog adds two features to Prolog that can be modeled as new language constructs (expressible, however, within standard Prolog):

Native types and operations on them: They are opaque ("hidden" types in terms of the Ciao module system and assertion language [4]), and used to reflect in $\mathcal{L}_I$ the basic data representations of $\mathcal{L}_C$ and the data types required by the abstract machine (e.g., integers, floats, tagged words, etc.).

Mutable variables (mutvars): They associate an identifier (which can be any first-order *ground* term) with an arbitrary term.

Two operations are defined over mutable variables:

Access: @$MutVar$ acts as a *function* which returns the value previously stored in $MutVar$.

Assignment: $MutVar <= Value$ assigns $Value$ to the identifier $MutVar$. The assignment is imperative and non-backtrackable. If $MutVar$ is a free variable then a new, unique identifier is allocated for it. If it is a ground term, it is used as identifier. Its behavior remains unspecified otherwise.

Figure 1 shows an example of ImProlog code which defines how to dereference a variable to reach a term. Similarly to the standard algorithm, it follows a reference chain and stops when the value pointed to is the same as the pointing term. Note the use of mutable variables and the operations on native types `tagof/2` and `tagval/2`, which check the tag of a tagged word and retrieve the value of the tagged word, respectively.

The extensions included in ImProlog can easily be defined in full Prolog, as shown in Figure 2 (we assume that `new_id/1` returns a new, unique identifier in

```
deref(Reg) :-
   ( tagof(@Reg,ref) ->
       tagval(@Reg,V), T = @V,
       ( @Reg = T -> true
       ; Reg <= T, deref(Reg) )
   ; true ).
```

```
tagof(tagged(Tag,Val),Tag).
tagval(tagged(Tag,Val),Val).
:- dynamic (@)/2.
Id <= V :-
   ( var(Id) -> new_id(Id) ; true ),
   retract(@(Id,_)), assertz(@(Id,V)).
```

Fig. 1. Dereference operation

Fig. 2. Prolog semantics of extensions

each call and that a trivial syntactic transformation makes goals @(X, Y) and Y = @X equivalent). As @/2 can be expressed in Prolog, we would not need any additional machinery to write (and run) our virtual machine in a Prolog system and as a Prolog program, should we want to make that experiment. But that would clearly not be without an immense performance penalty (at least without complex optimizations), which is against our initial aims. By making these new constructs natively known by the compiler, and restricting their application to the cases which are useful to describe the virtual machine, we can compile them efficiently time- and memory-wise, and they become easy to map onto low-level primitive constructs of $\mathcal{L}_C$.

2.2   Conditions to Ensure Efficient Code Generation

As shown in [5,6,7] and other work (see [8] for more references), generation of highly efficient executables from logic programs heavily depends on reducing the computational overhead that supports the extended semantic capabilities of Prolog for the specific cases in which the full power of the language is not needed. This generally requires a wealth of compile-time information regarding types, modes, determinism, non-failure, and other properties of the program.

This information is generally inferred by means of static analysis.[1] When such information can be inferred, optimizations are performed, and less efficient code is generated otherwise. However, since our initial goal was to *ensure* efficiency, we will, instead of allowing the generation of suboptimal code, impose a number of constraints on the ImProlog code that can be written when describing the abstract machine: precisely those that will allow an almost direct (often one-to-one) translation to $\mathcal{L}_C$ code. The compiler will raise an (efficiency-related) error while processing the code that describes the virtual machine and abort its generation if the necessary conditions are not met. This is obviously too drastic a solution for general programs, but a good compromise in our application.

Program analysis combined with program assertions allows the compiler to identify when it is safe (or possible) to generate code based on these constraints. The conditions that must hold after analysis are that code must be deterministic (with optional support for failure continuations, as in if-then-else constructs,

---

[1] It can be also provided by program annotations written by the user, which will indeed be necessary in some cases in practice.

but not for full non-determinism), and that no garbage collection, trailing, or boxing should be required. The analyses used to ensure that those restrictions hold are listed in the next section.

2.3   Analysis

Following the order in which they are applied in the compiler, the analyses used can be divided into three main groups.

Traditional Prolog Analyses: These include analyses for types, modes, determinism, and non-failure. They are instrumental to decide the best data representation and to detect which pieces of code may require choice points or failure continuations. They are performed using the abstract interpretation-based analyzer in CiaoPP [9]. As CiaoPP was designed with extensibility in mind, knowledge about ImProlog native types and associated operations can be given to CiaoPP via (Ciao) assertions, without having to actually change the analyzer. Assertions are also used to state the types, modes, etc. of externally defined facilities and routines (so that they can be taken into account by the analyzers) and to declare properties to be met at the entry point of each abstract machine instruction, which is typically written as a predicate. This information includes implementation decisions such as the use of short or long native integers, etc.

In addition to assertions, the type of some mutable variables may be further restricted by knowledge about the location they refer to or by type-constraining program calls. For example, mutables for X(i) registers are always bound to elements of type 'tagged'. A typed specification of the assignment operation could be written as follows:

```
Id <= Val :- id_type(Id, Type), Type(Val),
             retract(@(Id, _)), assertz(@(Id, Val)).
```

where id_type/2 relates an identifier with the name of its type, and Type(Val) is a higher-order call which states the type of Val. As we will see later, this knowledge helps in unboxing and analysis of mutables. Type analysis can ensure that Type(Val) always holds and it can therefore be harmlessly removed. This additional information makes mapping to C much easier.

Imperative State Analysis: Analysis of the value of mutable variables requires tracking their (imperative) state, which is updated using rules that reflect the actual operational semantics (i.e., sequential execution of OR-alternatives, etc.). Since $\mathcal{L}_I$ programs are limited to the deterministic case, the complexity of this analysis is reduced with respect to a more general case. The domains used are precise enough to identify an abstraction of some properties of mutable variables (e.g., whether they represent an X register, a Y register, a heap location, etc.). Strict type restrictions for some identifiers are applied here, thereby increasing the performance of the analysis. The analysis is conservative: every time a mutable may be written to (directly or by code which is externally available, and therefore difficult of impossible to access and analyze) its state is set to the *top* value of the domain lattice. Different mutable variables may be aliased (i.e., they can point to the same location), and only a limited alias analysis is performed; it takes advantage of the knowledge of the compiler regarding the memory location of the variable: e.g., a mutable variable living in X(0) cannot share with a mutable variable living in Y(1). This simple approach was effective enough for the purpose of this work.

Analysis for Unboxing: This analysis tries to determine whether the type of some variable is known at all points where it is reachable. If so, then there is no need to reserve space for a tag to check its type at runtime. This requires a previous pass to determine the *scope* of the identifiers for mutable variables in order to establish in which program points they may be accessed. This is also needed in order to assign memory locations at compile time to the mutable variables created within the body of a predicate and which are not allocated on the heap. Since non-determinism is not allowed, and according to the compilation scheme we follow, if a variable name cannot be reached outside the scope of a predicate it can be safely mapped to a (local) C variable. A conservative approximation, which is easier to check and precise enough, is the following: the variable name can be read from, assigned to, and passed as argument to other predicates, but it cannot be assigned to anything else than other local variables.

2.4   Code Generation

The information provided by the analysis is used to optimize code generation, especially in order to partially evaluate away whole sections of code (e.g., simplifying conditionals, reducing calls to true/noop, etc.). The algorithm extends that of ciaocc [7] to support ImProlog and also simplifies it in view of the constraints on the code specified in Section 2.2.

Predicates that may or may not fail are mapped to C functions with boolean or void return types, respectively. Generation of code for several clauses or predicates in the same C function and jumping to C labels is also supported (e.g., to transform recursions into loops). Additionally, an interface to internal compiler modules is provided. This makes it possible to invoke instruction compilation from within the emulator generator.

Schematically, compilation distinguishes among control constructs, external C functions, and builtins. Compilation of control is as follows:

– A block G1, G2 is translated to the code for G1 having its success continuation pointing to G2, followed by the code for G2.
– The construct G1 -> G2 ; G3 is compiled into an if-then-else, where G1 is compiled in a context where the failure continuation points to G3. G2 and G3 are compiled in the same context where the whole construct appeared (i.e., success / failure continuations point to where G1 -> G2 ; G3 did).

For a goal G which calls a C function f(), arguments are compiled (see later) and then f() is called. If the predicate is semi-deterministic, the emitted code checks the return code and, if necessary, a jump to the failure continuation is made. When G corresponds to a built-in, its compilation proceeds as follows:

- `true` does nothing.
- `fail` is translated to a jump to the failure continuation.
- `A <= B` is translated into assignment instructions. If `A` was not initialized it is declared.
- `A = B` is handled as follows:

  - When `A` is unbound and `B` is ground (and also for the symmetrical case), the builtin is translated into the declaration of `A` plus an assignment statement that moves the value of executing the compiled code corresponding to `B` to the memory location associated with `A`.
  - When `A` and `B` are both ground, the builtin is translated into a comparison of the values resulting from executing the compiled code of both expressions.

Note that although full unification may be assumed during program transformations, it is ultimately reduced to the two cases above. This has to be possible in order to avoid bootstrapping problems: e.g., (full) unification, also defined in ImProlog, should not be based itself on a full unification built-in.

Prolog logical variables and mutable variables are mapped to C variables (which can be global, local, or be passed as function arguments). The type of those C variables is extracted from the declarations and using type inference. Due to the determinism of ImProlog, trailing is unnecessary.

During compilation a symbol table keeps track of the type and memory location (or C variable) associated to each variable. All variables have to have an associated type in order to perform unboxing (an error is flagged otherwise), and all types are either native types or mutables whose value is of a native type. For a variable whose associated C type is `Tc`, a declaration of variable named `V`, with C type `Vt`, is emitted, and the associated memory location is set to `Mem`, as follows:

- If the variable is not mutable, `Vt` is `Tc` and `Mem` is `V`.
- If the variable is mutable:
  - if its scope is local, then `Vt` is `Tc` and `Mem` is `V`, or
  - `Vt` is `(Tc *)` and `Mem` is `*V`, otherwise.

For simplicity we assume that goal arguments have been normalized and only variables or @ expressions appear. Compilation of arguments, assuming that the memory location for `A` is `Mem`, is as follows:

- `@A` is translated to `Mem` (and `A` must be a mutable variable in this case).
- `A` is translated to `&Mem` (if `A` is mutable), or
- `A` is translated to `Mem` otherwise.

3   Generating Emulators with ImProlog

We now sketch how WAM instructions can be described using ImProlog and how the full emulator is assembled using a generic abstract machine generator.

3.1   Defining WAM Instructions in ImProlog

The definition of every WAM instruction in ImProlog looks just like a regular predicate, and the types, modes, etc. of each of their arguments have to be declared using (Ciao) assertions. Figure 3 shows the definition of an instruction which tries to unify a term and a constant. The `pred/1` declaration states that the first argument is a mutable variable and that the second is a tagged word containing a constant. The predicates `deref/1` (from Figure 1) and `bind/2` (also a defined predicate) are used in the instruction definition.

```
:- pred u_cons(mutable, cons).
u_cons(A, Cons) :-
    T <= @A, deref(T),
    ( tagof(@T, ref) -> bind(@T,Cons) ; @T = Cons ).
```

Fig. 3. Unification with a constant

The general compilation process to C, described later, is able to unfold (if so desired) the definition of the predicates called by `u_cons/2` and to propagate information from the code inside the instruction in order to optimize the resulting piece of the emulator. After the set of transformations instruction definitions are subject to, the generated C code is of high quality.

Our approach has been to define a reduced number of instructions (50 is a ballpark figure) and let the merging and specialization process (see Section 4) generate all instructions needed to have a competitive emulator. Note that efficient emulators tend to have a large number of instructions (hundreds or even thousands) and many of them are variations (obtained through specialization, merging, etc.) on common blocks [10,11]. These common blocks are the simple instructions we aim at representing explicitly in ImProlog.

In the experiments we performed (Section 5) the emulator with a larger number of instructions had 199 different opcodes (not counting those which result from padding some other instruction with zeroes to ensure a correct alignment in memory). Starting with a simple instruction set makes it easier to maintain instruction sets and to make sure that they are consistent. Complex instructions are generated automatically in a (by construction) correct way.

3.2   Assembling the Emulator

To avoid the burden associated with the coding and $\mathcal{L}_C$-dependent details of the emulator, we chose to use here the framework previously described in [3], where instruction semantics and bytecode representation are independently handled and assembled together using an emulator compiler. Using the terminology of [3] we define the relation between $\mathcal{L}_A$ and $\mathcal{L}_B$ by means of several pieces:[2]

---

[2] A complete description, not included due to space constraints, would detail all expected elements for a WAM: X and Y registers, atoms, numbers, functors, etc.

$\mathcal{M}_{enc}$ which declares how bytecode encodes $\mathcal{L}_A$ instructions and data (e.g. X(0) is encoded as the number 0).

$\mathcal{M}_{dec}$ which declares how bytecode should be decoded to return the initial instruction format in $\mathcal{L}_A$ (e.g., for an instruction which uses as argument an X register, a 0 means X(0)).

$\mathcal{M}_{arg}$ which expresses how $\mathcal{L}_A$ expressions are translated to $\mathcal{L}_C$, e.g., how X(0) goes to x[0] (assuming X registers end up in an array).

Higher-level instruction definitions in $\mathcal{L}_I$ (which abstract away bytecode representation issues) and program assertions are processed to generate:

$\mathcal{M}_{def}$ which contains the definition of each instruction in the language $\mathcal{L}_A$ in terms of $\mathcal{L}_C$ code.

$\mathcal{M}_{ins'}$ which describes the instruction set with opcode numbers and the format of each instruction, i.e., the type in $\mathcal{L}_A$ for each instruction argument.

The instruction set $\mathcal{M}_{ins'}$ is generated by reading the information for each instruction contained in the assertions, interpreting types as $\mathcal{L}_A$ elements, and assigning opcodes to each instruction, either automatically or via user annotations. The definition of $\mathcal{M}_{def}$ is based on cgen, that generates $\mathcal{L}_C$ code from $\mathcal{L}_I$ as defined in Figure 4. In this figure, *mem_storage* stands for a look-up table which relates each $\mathcal{L}_A$-level variable arg_i with its type and location in $\mathcal{L}_C$, a_i. The pseudo-instruction *failure_ins* takes care of causing a failure. Some $\mathcal{L}_A$ instructions are not supposed to fail (e.g., pushing a choicepoint), while others, such as performing a unification, can fail. In the former case cgen is able to discard the *else* part and simplify the *then* part; in the latter case, jumps to *failure_ins* are inserted in the appropriate places.

The components $\mathcal{M}_{enc}$ and $\mathcal{M}_{ins'}$ are used to generate the $\mathcal{L}_A$ to $\mathcal{L}_B$ compiler back-end. The rest of the components and $\mathcal{M}_{ins'}$ are used by the emulator compiler. The emulator has to understand $\mathcal{L}_B$ and therefore it has to agree in its format with what the compiler back-end emits. Note that the overall emulator structure is largely independent of the code of the instructions.[3] A summarized definition of the emulator compiler and how it uses the different pieces in $\mathcal{M}$ can be found in Figure 4. The scheme of the generated emulator code is somewhat similar to what the Janus compilation scheme [12] produces, although in the Janus case the continuation to every call (in the source code) is known statically. The compiler can therefore generate a direct jump to a fixed label, while in our case the continuation can in principle be any program point which comes from the bytecode program itself and is not known until the emulator is being executed.

Example 1. Code for a specialized instruction. From the instruction in Figure 3, which unifies a term living in some variable with a constant, we can derive a specialized version in which the term is supposed to live in an X register. The declaration:

---

[3] Assuming that no global transformations are done, which we are not addressing here.

$emucomp(\mathcal{M}) =$
$[\, \textbf{emu}_B(p, prg) \equiv$
   $case\ get\_opcode(p, prg)\ of$
     $opcode_1 : inscomp(opcode_1, \mathcal{M})$
     $\ldots$
     $opcode_n : inscomp(opcode_n, \mathcal{M})]$
   $where\ opcode_i \in domain(\mathcal{M}_{ins'})$

$inscomp(opcode, \mathcal{M}) =$
$[\mathcal{M}_{def}(p', cont, name, \mathcal{M}_{args}(args));\ cont(p')]$
   $where$
   $\langle name, format \rangle = \mathcal{M}_{ins'}(opcode)$
   $\langle args, p' \rangle = decode_{ins}(format, [p], [prg], \mathcal{M})$
   $cont = \lambda a.[\textbf{emu}_B(a, prg);\ return]$

$\mathcal{M}_{def}(next, cont, name, [arg1, \ldots, arg_n]) =$
   $[\![\textsf{cgen}]\!](name(a_1, \ldots, a_n) \rightarrow true; failure\_ins)$
   $where\ mem\_storage[a_1 : arg_1, \ldots, a_n : arg_n]$

Fig. 4. Emulator compiler

```
loop:
    switch(Op(short,P,0)) {
    ...
    case 97: goto ux_cons;
    ...
    }
```
```
void deref(tagged_t *a0) {
deref:
    if (tagged_tag(*a0) == REF) {
        tagged_t t0;
        t0 = *(tagged_val(*a0));
        if ((*a0) != t0) {
            *a0 = t0;
            goto deref; }}}
```
```
    ...
    ux_cons:
        tagged t;
        t = X(Op(short,P,2));
        deref(&t);
        if (TagOf(t) == REF) {
            bind(t, Op(tagged,P,4));
        } else {
            if (t != Op(tagged,P,4))
                goto failure_ins;
        }
        P = Skip(P,8);
        goto loop;
        ...
```

Fig. 5. Schema for the code generated for a simple instruction

```
:- ins_alias(ux_cons, u_cons(xreg_mutable, any)).
```

states precisely that, assigns the (symbolic) name ux_cons to the new instruction, and specifies that the first argument lives in an X register. The declaration:

```
:- ins_entry(97, ux_cons).
```

indicates that the emulator has an entry with opcode 97 for that instruction.[4] Figure 5 shows the code generated for the instruction (right) and a fragment of the emulator generated by the emulator compiler in Figure 4.

We want to note that we deliberately stay within standard C: the use of C extensions (such as storing labels in variables, which are provided by gcc and used, for example, in [13,14]), is outside the scope of this paper.

---

[4] In fact, different assignments of instruction numbers to opcodes can have an impact on the final performance, as they dictate how the code is laid out in the emulator switch. This affects, for example, the behavior of the cache.

4 Automatic Generation of Abstract Machine Variations

Substantial work has been devoted to abstract machine generation strategies such as, e.g., [10,11], which explore different design variations with the objective of achieving highly optimized emulators. By making the semantics of the abstract machine instructions explicit in a language like ImProlog, which can be easily processed automatically, such variations can be formulated mostly as automatic transformations. Adding new transformation rules and testing them together with the existing ones becomes a relatively easy task.

We will briefly describe some of these transformations, which will be experimentally evaluated in Section 5. Each transformation is identified by a two-letter code. We make a distinction between transformations which change the instruction set (e.g., creating new instructions) and those which only affect the way code is generated.

4.1 Instruction Set Transformations

New instructions are currently synthesized from existing ones by explicitly unfolding shared pieces of code, by merging instructions (different or not), and by performing specialization for some operand values, types, or locations.

Instruction Merging [om]: Merging generates larger instructions from sequences of smaller ones, and aims at saving fetch cycles at the expense of an increased `switch` size. This technique has been used extensively in high-performance systems (e.g., Quintus Prolog, SICStus, Yap, etc.). The performance of different combinations has been studied empirically [10], but in that paper new instructions were generated by hand, although deciding which instructions had to be created was done by means of profiling. In our framework all that is needed in order to emit code for a merged instruction is a single declaration. Merging is done automatically through code unfolding based on the definitions of the component instructions. This makes it possible to define a set of optimal user rules for merging.

Instructions with a Variable Number of Operands [vo]: For some instruction families a number of instructions (e.g., `unify with void`) can be collapsed into a single instruction with a variable number of operands. Code generation emits a loop whose internal iteration code comes directly from the single instruction definition.

Instructions for Built-ins [ib]: Calling external library code or built-ins often requires ad-hoc instructions (to make the appropriate parameter conversion, etc.). A single family of instructions that call a foreign C function can be used to do that, and this is the default option. The same instruction can then be specialized for a predefined set of built-ins, thus generating a special instruction set that includes faster calls to, e.g., arithmetic operations.

4.2   Transformations of Instruction Code

Some transformations do not create new instructions, but perform instead different optimizations on already existing instructions by manipulating the code or choosing alternative translation schemes.

Unfolding Rules [ur]: Simple predicates are unfolded throughout the code before compilation. In the case of instruction merging, unfolding is used to merge the code of two or more instructions into a single piece of code. In some cases unfolding can be limited so that common pieces of instructions can be shared. This transformation enables or disables a set of predefined unfolding rules.

Different Tag Switching Schemes [ts]: Tags are used to detect dynamically the type of basic data (atom, structure, number, variable, etc.) contained in a machine word, so that different actions can be taken depending on this type. The corresponding *tag switching code* is a heavily-used operation which is worth optimizing as much as possible. This option generates either an automatic C switch (when enabled) or a set of predefined switch patterns based on tag encodings (when disabled).

Connected Continuations [jc]: Tests (or other actions) are sometimes unnecessarily repeated because they appear at the end of an operation and at the beginning of the next one. They are redundant at this point, because they are bound to fail or succeed depending on their behavior in the previous operation. For example, in the fragment `deref(T), (ref(T) -> A ; B)`, T is checked to test whether it is a reference just before exiting `deref/1`. Code can be generated that jumps directly to the implementation of A or B depending on the result of this test. This option enables or disables the optimization.

Read/Write Mode Specialization [rw]: WAM-based implementations sometimes use a flag to test whether heap structures (i.e., the memory representation of functors) are being read (matched against) or written (created). According to the value of this flag, several instructions adapt their behavior with an `if-then-else`. A common optimization is to partially evaluate the switch inside the emulator loop to generate two different, parallel switch structures, one for each of the read/write possibilities. We can generate instruction sets (and emulators) where this optimization has been turned on or off.

5   Experimental Evaluation

We will report here on experimental data regarding the performance which was achieved on a set of benchmarks by a collection of emulators, all of them automatically generated through different combinations of options. In particular, by using all **compatible** possibilities for the transformation and generation options given in Section 4 we generated 96 different emulators (instead of $2^7 = 128$, as not all options are independent; for example, **vo** needs **om** to be performed).

This bears a close relationship with [11], but here we are not changing the internal data structure representation (and of course our instructions are all coded in ImProlog). It is also related to the experiment reported in [10], but the tests we perform are more extensive and cover more variations. Additionally, [10] starts off by being selective about the instructions to merge; this is a point we want to address in the future by using instruction-level profiling.

Our initial point was a "bare" instruction set comprising the "common basic blocks" of a relatively efficient abstract machine (the "stock" abstract machine of Ciao 1.10, itself an independent branch off the original SICStus Prolog 0.5/0.7 emulator, and with performance currently just below modern SICStus versions). Figures 6 to 7 summarize **overall** results for the experiments, as the data gathered —96 emulators × 13 benchmarks = 1248 performance figures— is too large to be examined in detail here. In those figures we plot, for three different cases, the resulting speed of every emulator using a dot per emulator. Every benchmark was run several times on each emulator to arrive at meaningful time measures, in a Linux machine with a Pentium 4 processor and using gcc 3.4 as C compiler. Although most of the benchmarks we used are relatively well known, we include a brief description in [15].

In order to encode emulator generation options in the corresponding dots, each available option in Sections 4.1 and 4.2 is assigned a bit in a binary number (a '1' means activating the option and a '0' means deactivating it). Every value in the y axis of the figures corresponds to a combination of the three options in Section 4.1, but only 6 combinations are plotted due to dependencies among options. Options in Section 4.2, which correspond to transformations in the way code is generated, are represented with four bits which are encoded as 16 different dot shapes (shown in each figure). Every combination of emulator generation options is thus assigned a different 7-bit number and a different dot shape and location. The x coordinate represents the relative speed w.r.t. the hand-coded emulator currently in Ciao 1.10, which is assigned speedup 1.0.

Of course, different selections for the bits assigned to the y coordinate and to the dot shapes would yield a different picture. However, our selection seems intuitively appropriate, as it addresses separately two different families of transformations. Indeed, Figure 6, which uses the geometric average[5] of all benchmarks to determine the overall performance, shows a quite well defined clustering around eight centers. Although it is not immediate from the picture (it has to be "decoded"), poorer speedups come from not activating some instruction creation options (which, for the stock emulator, really means *deactivating* them, since merging and specialization was made by hand quite some time ago, and the resulting instructions are already part of the emulator).

As a side note, while this figure portrays an average behavior, there were benchmarks whose results actually tracked this average behavior quite faithfully. An example is the the doubly recursive Fibonacci, which is often disregarded as unrealistic but which, for this particular experiment, turns out to predict very well the (geometric) average behavior of all benchmarks. All in all, this picture

---

[5] As a means to alleviate the effect of extremely good or bad cases.

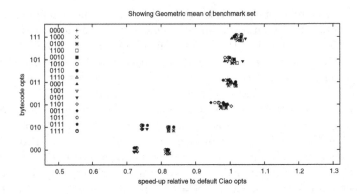

Fig. 6. Geometric average of all benchmarks (a dot per emulator)

(or, rather, the method which led to it) tries to reveal families of optimization options which give similar speed by showing dot clusters. Interestingly enough, once a set of generation options for $\mathcal{L}_B$ is fixed, the changes in the generation of $\mathcal{L}_C$ have (in general – see below) a relatively low impact. The general question *which options should be used for the "stock" emulator to be offered to general users* is answered by selecting a set of options somewhere in the topmost, rightmost cluster.

In any case, there are combinations of code generation options which achieve a speedup of 1.05, on average. While this may appear modest, consider that by starting with a simple instruction set (coded in ImProlog!) and applying systematically a set of transformation and code generation options, we have managed to match (and exceed) the time performance (memory performance was untouched) of an emulator which was hand-coded by very proficient programmers, and in which decisions were thoroughly tested along several years. Moreover, the transformation rules we have applied in our case are of course not the only ones, and we look forward to performing a more aggressive merging guided by profiling (merging is right now limited in depth to avoid a combinatorial explosion in the number of instructions). Similar work, with more emphasis on the production of languages for microprocessors is presented in [16], where a set of benchmarks is used to guide the (constrained) synthesis of such a set of instructions.

Figure 7 shows two cases of particular interest. The plot for *queens11* is a typical case which departs from the average behavior but which still resembles it. As a relevant difference, a much better speedup (around 1.25)[6] is achieved with some combinations of flags. On the other hand, the plot for *crypt* presents a completely different landscape: a plot where variations on the code generation scheme are as relevant as variations on the bytecode itself. This points to the need to find other clustering arrangements which shed some light on the interactions among different emulator code and bytecode generation schemes. Our experiments, however, lead us to think that in some cases the behavior tends to

---

[6] Which of course means that some benchmarks do not get any speedup.

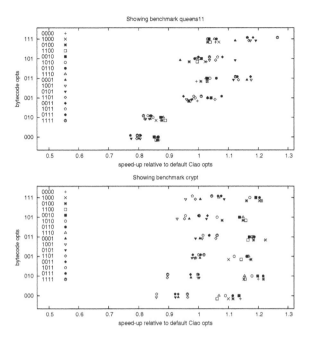

Fig. 7. Crypt: extreme case of spreading. Queens: scattered distribution.

be almost chaotic, as the lack of registers in the target architecture (i86) makes optimization a difficult task for the C compiler. This is supported by similar experiments on a PowerPC architecture, which has more general purpose registers, and in which the results are notably more stable across benchmarks. The overall conclusions for the best options and speedups remain roughly the same, only with less variance.

Table 1 tries to isolate the effects of separate options. It does so by listing, for each benchmark, including the geometric average, which options produced the best and the worst results time-wise. While there is no obvious conclusion, instruction merging is a clear winner, probably followed by having a variable number of operands, and then by specialized calls to built-ins. The first and second options save fetch cycles, while the third one saves processing time in general.

It can come as a surprise that using separate switches for read/write modes, instead of checking the mode in every instruction which needs to do so, does not seem to bring any advantage. A similar result was already observed in [11], and was attributed to modern architectures performing branch prediction and speculative work with redundant units. Therefore, short if-then-else statements might get both branches executed in parallel with the evaluation of the condition. Besides, implementing read/write modes with two switches basically doubles the size of the core of the emulator. A similar size growth happens when extensive merging is performed. In both cases a side effect is that of an increased cache miss ratio and the corresponding reduced performance.

Table 1. Options which gave best/worst performance

Benchmark	Best performance								Worst performance							
	vo	ib	om	ts	jc	ur	rw	Speed-up	vo	ib	om	ts	jc	ur	rw	Speed-down
default	x	x		x	x	x		1.00	x	x		x	x	x		1.00
all (geom.)	x	x	x	x		x		1.05				x		x		0.7
boyer	x		x	x			x	1.18							x	0.70
crypt		x	x	x				1.22		x					x	0.86
deriv	x	x	x	x				1.10	x						x	0.62
factorial	x		x				x	1.02						x	x	0.76
fib	x	x	x	x	x		x	1.02	x	x					x	0.75
knights	x	x	x				x	1.06				x	x	x	x	0.72
nreverse	x	x	x				x	1.03	x					x	x	0.57
poly	x	x	x				x	1.02	x						x	0.56
primes	x		x	x			x	1.10					x	x	x	0.73
qsort		x	x	x			x	1.05				x			x	0.54
queens11	x	x	x	x	x	x	x	1.26					x	x	x	0.77
query		x	x	x	x	x	x	1.06	x						x	0.71
tak	x	x	x	x				1.23				x	x	x	x	0.69

6   Conclusions

We have designed a language (ImProlog, a variation of Prolog with some imperative features) and used it to describe the semantics of instructions of a bytecode interpreter. ImProlog, with the proposed constraints, makes it possible both to perform non-trivial transformations (e.g., partial evaluation, unfolding, merging, etc.) and to generate efficient low-level code (using the cgen compiler) for each of the emulator instructions. Different transformations and code generation options can be applied, which result in different grades of optimization / specialization and different bytecode languages.

The low-level code for each instruction and the definition of the bytecode can be taken as input by a previously developed emulator generator to assemble full, high-quality emulators. Since the process of generating instruction code and bytecode format is automatic, we were able to produce and test different versions thereof to which several combinations of code generation options were applied.

We have also studied how these combinations perform with a series of benchmarks in order to find, e.g., what is the "best" average solution and how independent coding rules affect the overall speed. We have in this way as one case the regular emulator we started with (and which was decomposed to break complex instructions into basic blocks). However, we also found out that it is possible to outperform it by using some code patterns and optimizations not explored in the initial emulator, and, what is more important, starting from abstract machine definitions written in ImProlog. We intend to continue this line of exploration of improved abstract machines and incorporating them in the standard Ciao distributions.

References

1. Taivalsaari, A.: Implementing a Java Virtual Machine in the Java Programming Language. Technical report, Sun Microsystems (1998)
2. Rigo, A., Pedroni, S.: PyPy's Approach to Virtual Machine Construction. In: Dynamic Languages Symposium 2006, ACM Press (2006)
3. Morales, J., Carro, M., Puebla, G., Hermenegildo, M.: A generator of efficient abstract machine implementations and its application to emulator minimization. In Meseguer, P., Larrosa, J., eds.: International Conference on Logic Programming. LNCS, Springer Verlag (2005)
4. Puebla, G., Bueno, F., Hermenegildo, M.: An Assertion Language for Constraint Logic Programs. In Deransart, P., Hermenegildo, M., Maluszynski, J., eds.: Analysis and Visualization Tools for Constraint Programming. Number 1870 in LNCS. Springer-Verlag (2000) 23–61
5. Van Roy, P., Despain, A.: High-Performance Logic Programming with the Aquarius Prolog Compiler. IEEE Computer Magazine (1992) 54–68
6. Taylor, A.: High Performance Prolog Implementation through Global Analysis. Slides of the invited talk at PDK'91, Kaiserslautern (1991)
7. Morales, J., Carro, M., Hermenegildo, M.: Improving the Compilation of Prolog to C Using Moded Types and Determinism Information. In: Proceedings of the Sixth International Symposium on Practical Aspects of Declarative Languages. Number 3057 in LNCS, Heidelberg, Germany, Springer-Verlag (2004) 86–103
8. Van Roy, P.: 1983-1993: The Wonder Years of Sequential Prolog Implementation. Journal of Logic Programming **19/20** (1994) 385–441
9. Hermenegildo, M., Puebla, G., Bueno, F., López-García, P.: Program Development Using Abstract Interpretation (and The Ciao System Preprocessor). In: 10th International Static Analysis Symposium (SAS'03). Number 2694 in LNCS, Springer-Verlag (2003) 127–152
10. Nässén, H., Carlsson, M., Sagonas, K.: Instruction Merging and Specialization in the SICStus Prolog Virtual Machine. In: Proc. 3rd ACM SIGPLAN Int. Conf. on Principles and Practice of Declarative Programming, ACM Press (2001) 49–60
11. Demoen, B., Nguyen, P.L.: So Many WAM Variations, So Little Time. In: Computational Logic 2000, Springer Verlag (2000) 1240–1254
12. Gudeman, D., Bosschere, K.D., Debray, S.: jc: An efficient and portable sequential implementation of janus. In: Proc. of 1992 Joint International Conference and Symposium on Logic Programming, MIT Press (1992) 399–413
13. Henderson, F., Conway, T., Somogyi, Z.: Compiling Logic Programs to C Using GNU C as a Portable Assembler. In: ILPS 1995 Postconference Workshop on Sequential Implementation Technologies for Logic Programming. (1995) 1–15
14. Codognet, P., Diaz, D.: WAMCC: Compiling Prolog to C. In Sterling, L., ed.: International Conference on Logic Programming, MIT PRess (1995) 317–331
15. Morales, J., Carro, M., Hermenegildo, M.: Description and Optimization of Abstract Machines in an Extension of Prolog. Technical Report CLIP8/2006.0, Technical University of Madrid (UPM), School of Computer Science, UPM (2006)
16. Holmer, B.K.: Automatic Design of Computer Instruction Sets. PhD thesis, University of California at Berkeley (1993)

Combining Different Proof Techniques for Verifying Information Flow Security

Heiko Mantel, Henning Sudbrock, and Tina Krauβer

Security Engineering Group, RWTH Aachen University, Germany
{mantel,sudbrock,krausser}@cs.rwth-aachen.de

Abstract. When giving a program access to secret information, one must ensure that the program does not leak the secrets to untrusted sinks. For reducing the complexity of such an information flow analysis, one can employ compositional proof techniques. In this article, we present a new approach to analyzing information flow security in a compositional manner. Instead of committing to a proof technique at the beginning of a verification, this choice is made during verification with the option of flexibly migrating to another proof technique. Our approach also increases the precision of compositional reasoning in comparison to the traditional approach. We illustrate the advantages in two exemplary security analyses, on the semantic level and on the syntactic level.

1 Introduction

Information flow security aims at answering the question: Is a given system sufficiently trustworthy to access secret information? The two main research problems are, firstly, finding adequate, formal characterizations of trustworthiness and, secondly, developing sound and efficient verification techniques based on these characterizations. Information flow security has been a focal research topic in computer security for more than 30 years. Nevertheless, the problem to secure the flow of information in systems is far from being solved. In [28], the state of the art was surveyed for approaches to capturing and analyzing information flow security of concrete programs. For information flow security at the level of more abstract specifications, a broad spectrum of approaches has been developed (see, e.g., [12,19,20,11,26,17,5]). The most popular verification techniques are the unwinding technique on the level of specifications (see, e.g., [13,24,18,4]), and security type systems and program logics on the level of programs (see [28] for a good overview). In this article, we focus on a multi-threaded programming language.

We use the standard scenario for investigating information flow security of imperative programs. That is, the initial values of some variables, the so called *high variables*, constitute the secrets that must be protected while the remaining variables, the *low variables*, initially store public data. We assume an attacker ζ who can observe the values of low variables before and at the end of a program run. The security requirement is that no information flows from the high variables

G. Puebla (Ed.): LOPSTR 2006, LNCS 4407, pp. 94–110, 2007.

into low variables during program execution. We use l to denote low variables and h to denote high variables, i.e. variables that may store secrets.

There are various possibilities for how a program could accidentally or maliciously leak secrets. It could copy a secret into a low variable as, e.g., in $P_1 = l{:}{=}h$. Such leaks are referred to as *intra-command leaks* or *explicit leaks* [9]. More subtly, a secret could influence the flow of control, leading to different assignments to low variables as, e.g., in $P_2 = $ if $h = 0$ then $l{:}{=}0$ else $l{:}{=}1$ fi. If the value of l is 0 at the end of the run, $h = 0$ must have held initially, and if l is 1 then $h \neq 0$ held. Such information leaks are referred to as *inter-command leaks* or *implicit leaks*. Even more subtle leaks originate in a multi-threaded setting.

Verification techniques are often based on characterizations of information flow security that are compositional with respect to the primitives of the programming language. Two well known observations motivated our work:

- Compositionality is indeed helpful, both for making verification techniques efficient and for simplifying the derivation of results at the meta level, e.g., for proving a soundness theorem for a syntactic, type-based analysis.
- Compositionality leads to overly restrictive characterizations of security. Simple programs that are typically rejected include, e.g., while $h \leq 10$ do $h :=$ $h + 1$ od, $l{:}{=}h; l{:}{=}0$, $h{:}{=}0; l{:}{=}h$, and if $h = 0$ then $l := 0$ else $l := 0$ fi (for instance, the security type systems in [32,29] reject all these programs).

More recent work aimed at relaxing security definitions and type systems such that intuitively secure programs like the above examples are not rejected anymore by a security analysis. For instance, [30] and [25] provide solutions for, e.g, while $h \leq 10$ do $h := h + 1$ od (possibly requiring the addition of auxiliary commands to the program), and [15] offers a solution for, e.g., if $h = 0$ then $l :=$ 0 else $l := 0$ fi. While this progress is promising, the approach taken requires the incremental improvement of each individual analysis technique. In this article, we present an alternative approach. We show that and how different analysis techniques can be combined, effectively developing a higher-level security calculus that can be extended with existing verification techniques as plugins. This approach applies to the semantic level, where one applies (semantic) characterizations of security that enjoy desirable meta properties (such as, e.g., compositionality) and uses a calculus for some general-purpose logic for verification. The approach also applies to the syntactic level, where one uses specific security calculi (such as, e.g., security type systems) for verification. Instead of eliminating weaknesses of each individual verification technique, our approach aims at combining the strengths of available techniques.

In summary, the contributions of this article are, firstly, a novel approach to verifying information flow security and, secondly, the illustration of how different verification techniques can be beneficially combined in the information flow analysis of a fairly realistic example program. The article constitutes an initial step in the proposed direction, and some issues such as finding a fully satisfactory baseline characterization will need further investigation.

2   Information Flow Security in an Imperative Language

To make our approach concrete, we introduce a simple, multi-threaded programming language that includes assignments, conditionals, loops, a command for dynamic thread creation, and a sync command. Without sync command and arrays, this language is also used, e.g., in [29]. The set Com of commands is defined by (where V is a command vector in $\textbf{Com} = \bigcup_{n\in\mathbb{N}} Com^n$)

$$C ::= \text{skip} \mid Id{:=}Exp \mid Arr[Exp_1]{:=}Exp_2 \mid C_1; C_2 \mid \text{if } B \text{ then } C_1 \text{ else } C_2 \text{ fi}$$
$$\mid \text{while } B \text{ do } C \text{ od} \mid \text{fork}(CV) \mid \text{sync}.$$

We restrict program variables to Booleans, integers, and arrays. The length of an array Arr is denoted by $Arr.length$ and is treated like a constant. The ith element of Arr is denoted by $Arr[i]$ and treated like a variable. *Expressions* are program variables, constants, and terms resulting from applying operators to expressions: $Exp ::= Const \mid Var \mid Arr[Exp] \mid Arr.length \mid op(Exp_1, \ldots, Exp_n)$.

A *state* is a mapping from variables in a given set Var to values in a given set Val. The set of states is denoted by S. We use $[v = n]s$ to denote the state that maps v to n and all other variables to the same values like the state s. We treat arrays like in [8]: If an array access $a[i]$ is out of bounds (i.e. $i < 0$ or $i \geq a.length$) then a dummy value is returned (0 for integers and False for Booleans), no exception is raised and no buffer overflow occurs. We use the judgment $\langle Exp, s\rangle \downarrow n$ for specifying that expression Exp evaluates to value n in state s. Expression evaluation is assumed to be total and to occur atomically.

$$\frac{}{\langle\text{skip}, s\rangle \twoheadrightarrow \langle\langle\rangle, s\rangle} \qquad \frac{\langle Exp, s\rangle \downarrow n}{\langle Id{:=}Exp, s\rangle \twoheadrightarrow \langle\langle\rangle, [Id = n]s\rangle}$$

$$\frac{\langle Exp', s\rangle \downarrow i \quad 0 \leq i < Arr.length \quad \langle Exp, s\rangle \downarrow n}{\langle Arr[Exp']{:=}Exp, s\rangle \twoheadrightarrow \langle\langle\rangle, [Arr[i] = n]s\rangle} \qquad \frac{\langle Exp', s\rangle \downarrow i \quad (i < 0 \vee i \geq Arr.length)}{\langle Arr[Exp']{:=}Exp, s\rangle \twoheadrightarrow \langle\langle\rangle, s\rangle}$$

$$\frac{\langle C_1, s\rangle \twoheadrightarrow \langle\langle\rangle, t\rangle}{\langle C_1; C_2, s\rangle \twoheadrightarrow \langle C_2, t\rangle} \qquad \frac{\langle C_1, s\rangle \twoheadrightarrow \langle\langle C_1'\rangle V, t\rangle}{\langle C_1; C_2, s\rangle \twoheadrightarrow \langle\langle C_1'; C_2\rangle V, t\rangle} \qquad \frac{}{\langle\text{fork}(CV), s\rangle \twoheadrightarrow \langle\langle C\rangle V, s\rangle}$$

$$\frac{\langle B, s\rangle \downarrow \text{True}}{\langle\text{if } B \text{ then } C_1 \text{ else } C_2 \text{ fi}, s\rangle \twoheadrightarrow \langle C_1, s\rangle} \qquad \frac{\langle B, s\rangle \downarrow \text{False}}{\langle\text{if } B \text{ then } C_1 \text{ else } C_2 \text{ fi}, s\rangle \twoheadrightarrow \langle C_2, s\rangle}$$

$$\frac{\langle B, s\rangle \downarrow \text{True}}{\langle\text{while } B \text{ do } C \text{ od}, s\rangle \twoheadrightarrow \langle C; \text{while } B \text{ do } C \text{ od}, s\rangle} \qquad \frac{\langle B, s\rangle \downarrow \text{False}}{\langle\text{while } B \text{ do } C \text{ od}, s\rangle \twoheadrightarrow \langle\langle\rangle, s\rangle}$$

Fig. 1. Small-step deterministic semantics

$$\frac{\langle C_i, s\rangle \twoheadrightarrow \langle W, t\rangle}{\langle\langle C_0 \ldots C_{n-1}\rangle, s\rangle \rightarrow \langle\langle C_0 \ldots C_{i-1}\rangle W \langle C_{i+1} \ldots C_{n-1}\rangle, t\rangle}$$

$$\frac{\forall i \in \{0, \ldots, n-1\} : (C_i = \text{sync} \wedge V_i' = \langle\rangle) \vee (C_i = \text{sync}; D_i \wedge V_i' = \langle D_i\rangle)}{\langle\langle C_0, \ldots, C_{n-1}\rangle, s\rangle \rightarrow \langle V_0' \ldots V_{n-1}', s\rangle}$$

Fig. 2. Small-step non-deterministic semantics

A *configuration* is a pair $\langle V, s \rangle$ where the vector V specifies the threads that are currently active and s defines the current state of the memory.

The operational semantics is formalized in Figures 1 and 2. *Deterministic judgments* have the form $\langle C, s \rangle \rightarrow \langle W, t \rangle$ expressing that command C performs a computation step in state s, yielding a state t and a vector of commands W, which has length zero if C terminated, length one if it has neither terminated nor spawned any threads, and length greater than one if new threads were spawned. That is, a command vector of length n can be viewed as a *pool of n threads* that run concurrently. *Non-deterministic judgments* have the form $\langle V, s \rangle \twoheadrightarrow \langle V', t \rangle$ (note the new arrow), where V and V' are thread pools, expressing that some thread C_i in V performs a step in state s resulting in the state t and some thread pool W'. The global thread pool V' results then by replacing C_i with W'.

Our sync command blocks a given thread until each other thread has terminated or is blocked. Executing sync unblocks all threads (see the rule in Figure 2).

The following example illustrates the subtle possibilities for leaking information in a multi-threaded setting. It also demonstrates that the parallel composition of two secure programs can result in an insecure program.

Example 1. If $P_3 = h{:=}0; P_2$ (where $P_2 =$ if $h = 0$ then $l{:=}0$ else $l{:=}1$ fi) runs concurrently with $P_4 = h{:=}h'$ under a shared memory and a round robin scheduler then the final value of l is 0 (respectively, 1) given that the initial value of h' is 0 (respectively, not 0). This is illustrated below where $(v_l, v_h, v_{h'})$ denotes the state s with $s(l) = v_l$, $s(h) = v_h$, and $s(h') = v_{h'}$:

$\langle\langle P_3, P_4 \rangle, (0,0,0) \rangle$
$\rightarrow \langle\langle P_2, P_4 \rangle, (0,0,0) \rangle$
$\rightarrow \langle\langle P_2 \rangle, (0,0,0) \rangle$
$\rightarrow \langle\langle l{:=}0 \rangle, (0,0,0) \rangle \rightarrow \langle\langle \rangle, (0,0,0) \rangle$

$\langle\langle P_3, P_4 \rangle, (0,0,1) \rangle$
$\rightarrow \langle\langle P_2, P_4 \rangle, (0,0,1) \rangle$
$\rightarrow \langle\langle P_2 \rangle, (0,1,1) \rangle$
$\rightarrow \langle\langle l{:=}1 \rangle, (0,1,1) \rangle \rightarrow \langle\langle \rangle, (1,1,1) \rangle$

That is, the final value of l equals the initial value of h' and, hence, the attacker is able to reconstruct the secret, initial value of h' from his observation of l. ◇

In the following, we adopt the naming conventions used so far: s and t denote states, Exp denotes an expression, B denotes a Boolean expression, Arr denotes an array, C and D denote commands, and V and W denote command vectors.

2.1 Security Policy, Labelings, and Security Condition

We assume a security lattice that comprises two security domains, a *high level* and a *low level* where the requirement is that no information flows from *high* to *low*. This is the simplest policy for which the problem of information flow security can be investigated. Each program variable is associated with a security domain by means of a *labeling* $lab : Var \rightarrow \{low, high\}$. The intuition is that values of *low variables* can be observed by the attacker and, hence, should only be used to store public data. *High variables* are used for storing secret data and their content is not observable for the attacker. For a given array Arr, the content has a security domain (denoted $lab(Arr)$) and the length has a security domain (denoted $lab(Arr.length)$) that must be at or below the one for the content.

All elements of the array are associated with the same security domain. If Arr : $high$ then $Arr[i]$: $high$ and if Arr : low and i : low then $Arr[i]$: low. If Arr : low and i : $high$ then $Arr[i]$ has no security domain and cannot be typed (see [10]).

As before, h and l denote high and low variables, respectively. An expression Exp has the security domain low (denoted by Exp : low) if all variables in Exp have domain low and, otherwise, has security domain $high$ (denoted by Exp : $high$). The intuition is that values of expressions with domain $high$ possibly depend on secrets while values of low expressions can only depend on public data.

Definition 1. *Two states* $s, t \in S$ *are* low equal *(denoted by* $s =_L t$*) iff*
$$\forall var \in Var : lab(var) = low \implies s(var) = t(var) .$$
Two expressions Exp, Exp' *are* low equivalent *(denoted by* $Exp \equiv_L Exp'$*) iff*
$$\forall s, s' \in S : (s =_L s' \land \langle Exp, s \rangle \downarrow n \land \langle Exp', s' \rangle \downarrow n') \implies n = n' .$$

We decided to use a possibilistic security condition (like in [31]) despite the fact that this condition is not entirely satisfactory from a practical perspective as it does not take scheduling into account (unlike the conditions in, e.g., [32,30]) and, in particular, is not scheduler independent (unlike the condition in [29]). However, possibilistic security is conceptually simple and suitable for illustrating our verification technique, and this is our focus in this article.

Definition 2. *A symmetric relation* R *on command vectors is a* possibilistic low indistinguishability *iff for all* $V, W \in \mathbf{Com}$ *with* $V \ R \ W$ *the following holds:*
$$\forall s, s', t \in S : ((s =_L t \land \langle V, s \rangle \rightarrow^* \langle \langle \rangle, s' \rangle)$$
$$\Rightarrow \exists t' \in S : (\langle W, t \rangle \rightarrow^* \langle \langle \rangle, t' \rangle \land s' =_L t')).$$

The union of all possibilistic low indistinguishabilities, $\sim_L$, is again a possibilistic low indistinguishability. Note that $\sim_L$ is transitive and symmetric, but not reflexive. For instance, $l{:=}h \sim_L l{:=}h$ does not hold. Intuitively, only programs with secure information flow are related to themselves.

Definition 3. *A program* V *is* possibilistic low secure *iff* $V \sim_L V$.

The idea of possibilistic security is that an observer without knowledge of the scheduler cannot infer from the values of low-level variables that some high variable did not have a particular value. That is, any low output that is possible after the system starts in a state s is also possible when the system starts in any other state that is low equal to s.

Example 2. It is easy to see that $P_1 = l{:=}h$ and $P_2 =$ if $h = 0$ then $l{:=}0$ else $l{:=}1$ fi, both are not possibilistic low secure. Moreover, P_3 and P_4 from Example 1, each is possibilistic low secure, but $\langle P_3, P_4 \rangle$ is not (take s and t as in Example 1). ◊

3   Combining Calculus

In general, compositional reasoning about information flow security is not sound. This applies, in particular, to our baseline condition, possibilistic low security, which is neither preserved under parallel composition nor under sequential composition, in general (see Example 2 and below). For making compositional reasoning sound, one must strengthen the definition of secure information flow until one arrives at a compositional property. This approach is taken, e.g., in the derivation of the strong security condition [29]. However, the resulting composable security definitions are over-restrictive in the sense that they are violated by many programs that are intuitively secure.

In this section, we present an approach for deducing the security of a composed program from the fact that each sub-program satisfies some notion of security that is stronger than the baseline property. We derive sufficient conditions for sequential composition, for parallel composition, for conditional branching, and for while loops. This leads us to four compositionality results. These constitute the theoretical basis of our combining calculus, which allows one to flexibly apply available verification techniques during an information flow analysis. We then revisit some available verification techniques and provide plugin-rules that enable the use of these techniques in a derivation with our combining calculus.

3.1 Compositionality Results and Basic Calculus Rules

Auxiliary concepts. If $C \sim_L C'$ and $D \sim_L D'$ hold then $C; D \sim_L C'; D'$ does not necessarily hold because threads spawned during execution of C might still be running when D begins execution, influencing computations in D through shared variables. For instance, the program fork(skip, P_2; $l:=2$); $l':=l$ where $P_2 =$ if $h = 0$ then $l:=0$ else $l:=1$ fi does not satisfy the baseline property (due to the race between the second assignment to l and the assignment to l') although it is the sequential composition of two programs that both satisfy the baseline property. If the main thread is the last thread to terminate before D (respectively D') can begin execution then such problems cannot occur.

Definition 4. *A thread pool V is* main-surviving *(denoted by $MS(V)$), if for arbitrary states s and t as well as for each thread pool $\langle C_0, \ldots, C_{n-1}\rangle$ with $\langle V, s\rangle \rightarrow^* \langle\langle C_0, \ldots, C_{n-1}\rangle, t\rangle$ one of the following two conditions holds:*

- *There is no state t' such that $\langle C_0, t\rangle \twoheadrightarrow \langle\langle\rangle, t'\rangle$.*
- *$n = 1$.*

One can make a program main-surviving by adding sync statements. Consider as an example the program fork($h := 0, \quad h := h'$), which is not main-surviving as both conditions in Definition 4 are violated. Main-surviving programs are, e.g., fork($h := 0, \quad h := h'$); sync and fork(sync; $h := 0, \quad h := h'$).

Parallel composition shares the problems of sequential composition: given $V \sim_L V'$ and $W \sim_L W'$ one does not necessarily obtain $VW \sim_L V'W'$. This is caused by shared variables, which allow one thread to influence the behavior of another thread. Even if the composed thread pools have no low variables in common, we do not obtain a general compositionality theorem (see Example 1). A sufficient condition for preserving low indistinguishability is the disjointness of all variables.

Definition 5. *We say that two thread pools V and W are variable independent $(V \gtrless W)$ if the sets of variables occurring in V respectively W are disjoint.*

Compositionality. We are now ready to present our compositionality results:

Theorem 1. *Let C, C', D, and D' be commands and V, V', W, and W' be thread pools such that $C \sim_L C', D \sim_L D', V \sim_L V'$ and $W \sim_L W'$. Then*

1. *if C and C' are main-surviving then $C; D \sim_L C'; D'$;*
2. *if $V \gtrless W$ and $V' \gtrless W'$ then $VW \sim_L V'W'$;*
3. *if $B \equiv_L B'$ then if B then C else D fi $\sim_L$ if B' then C' else D' fi; and*
4. *if $B \equiv_L B'$ and C and C' are main-surviving, then while B do C od $\sim_L$ while B' do C' od.*

A note with the proof of Theorem 1 is available on the authors' homepage.

Basic calculus rules. We raise the possibility for compositional reasoning about low indistinguishability with Theorem 1 to compositional reasoning about information flow security. This results in the calculus rules depicted below. The judgment $\vdash \mathsf{bls}(V)$ intuitively means that the program V is possibilistic low secure. A soundness result is provided in Section 3.4.

$$[\text{SEQ}] \frac{\vdash \mathsf{bls}(C) \quad \vdash \mathsf{bls}(D) \quad \mathsf{MS}(C)}{\vdash \mathsf{bls}(C; D)} \qquad [\text{PAR}] \frac{\vdash \mathsf{bls}(V) \quad \vdash \mathsf{bls}(W) \quad V \gtrless W}{\vdash \mathsf{bls}(VW)}$$

$$[\text{ITE}] \frac{\vdash \mathsf{bls}(C) \quad \vdash \mathsf{bls}(D) \quad B \equiv_L B}{\vdash \mathsf{bls}(\text{if } B \text{ then } C \text{ else } D \text{ fi})} \qquad [\text{FRK}] \frac{\vdash \mathsf{bls}(\langle C \rangle V)}{\vdash \mathsf{bls}(\text{fork}(CV))}$$

$$[\text{WHL}] \frac{\vdash \mathsf{bls}(C) \quad \mathsf{MS}(C) \quad B \equiv_L B}{\vdash \mathsf{bls}(\text{while } B \text{ do } C \text{ od})} \qquad [\text{SNC}] \frac{\vdash \mathsf{bls}(C)}{\vdash \mathsf{bls}(C; \text{sync})}$$

It should be noted that it is not intended that one proves the security of a complex program solely with the above rules. There are many secure programs for which the side conditions main surviving and variable independence are too restrictive. For analyzing such programs with the combining calculus, one employs plugin rules. The combining calculus is not intended as an alternative to existing security-analysis techniques, but rather as a vehicle for using different analysis techniques in combination. The plugins presented in the following, in particular, allow one to analyze programs that contain races.

3.2   Plugin: Strong Security

Definition 6 ([29]). *The strong low-bisimulation $\approx_L$ is the union of all symmetric relations R on command vectors $V, V' \in \mathbf{Com}$ of equal size, i.e. $V = \langle C_0, \ldots, C_{n-1} \rangle$ and $V' = \langle C'_0, \ldots, C'_{n-1} \rangle$, such that*

$$\forall s, s', t \in S : \forall i \in \{0, \ldots, n-1\} : \forall W \in \mathbf{Com}:$$
$$[(V \, R \, V' \wedge s =_L s' \wedge \langle C_i, s \rangle \rightarrow \langle W, t \rangle)$$
$$\Rightarrow \exists W' \in \mathbf{Com}: \exists t' \in S: (\langle C'_i, s' \rangle \rightarrow \langle W', t' \rangle \wedge W \, R \, W' \wedge t =_L t')] \, .$$

Note that $\approx_L$ is only a partial equivalence relation, i.e. it is transitive and symmetric, but not reflexive. In fact, $\approx_L$ only relates secure programs to themselves (note the structural similarity to the relationship between Definitions 2 and 3).

Definition 7 ([29]). *A program V is strongly secure iff $V \approx_L V$ holds.*

The strong security condition is scheduler independent and enjoys compositionality results that make it a suitable basis for a compositional security analysis.

Theorem 2 ([29,22]). *Let C, D and V be strongly secure programs that do not contain sync statements. If $B \equiv_L B$ then $C; D$, fork(CV), if B then C else D fi, and while B do C od are strongly secure. If $C \approx_L D$ holds then if B then C else D fi is also strongly secure (even for B : high).*

Proof. [22] extends the proof in [29] to the language with arrays. □

The strong security condition constitutes a conservative approximation of our security definition as the following theorem demonstrates.

Theorem 3. *If V is strongly secure and does not contain any sync statements, then V is possibilistic low secure.*

Proof. Let $s =_L t$. If $\langle V, s \rangle \rightarrow^* \langle\langle\rangle, s'\rangle)$ then one can, by applying Definition 6, inductively construct (over the length of the computation sequence) a computation $\langle W, t \rangle \rightarrow^* \langle\langle\rangle, t'\rangle$ of the same length such that $s' =_L t'$. □

While the strong security condition can be suitable for reasoning about secure information flow, there are also situations where it is too restrictive.

Example 3. The programs $l := h; l := 1$, if h then skip else skip; skip fi, and while $h > 0$ do $h := h - 1$ od all have secure information flow (according to Definition 3). However, none of these programs is strongly secure. ◊

The problems in Example 3 can be overcome by applying our combining calculus, in which strong security constitutes only one of several plugins. Its plugin rule is depicted to the right. When this rule is applied, the premise could be proved, e.g., with a security type system (see Section 5), or with some general-purpose theorem prover.

$$[\mathrm{P}_{SLS}] \frac{V \approx_L V \quad V \text{ is sync-free}}{\vdash \mathsf{bls}(V)}$$

3.3 Plugin: Low-Deterministic Security

Roscoe pioneered a characterization of information flow security based on the notion of low determinism. The resulting security definitions for the process algebra CSP [23] are intuitively convincing as they ensure that the low-level behavior of a process is deterministic, no matter what the high-level behavior is. A disadvantage, however, is that it is unnecessarily restrictive with respect to nondeterministic system behavior on the low level. Zdancewic and Myers [33] argue that this disadvantage is acceptable when the approach is applied to concrete programs. We adopt this approach to our setting.

Definition 8. *A program V is* low-deterministic secure *iff*

$$\forall s, t, s', t' \in S : [(s =_L t \wedge \langle V, s\rangle \to^* \langle\langle\rangle, s'\rangle \wedge \langle V, t\rangle \to^* \langle\langle\rangle, t'\rangle) \implies s' =_L t'].$$

That is, if one runs a program that is low-deterministic secure in two arbitrary starting states that are low equal then all final states are also low equal.

Theorem 4. *Let V be a program that is low-deterministic secure. Assume further, that if the program can terminate in some state it can terminate in each low equal state (written $\mathsf{PLT}(V)$). Then V is possibilistic low secure.*

Proof. Let s, s', t, t' be states such that $s =_L t$. Assume that $\langle V, s\rangle \to^* \langle\langle\rangle, s'\rangle$ for some state s'. By assumption, V can terminate in t. Hence, there exists $t' \in S$ such that $\langle V, t\rangle \to^* \langle\langle\rangle, t'\rangle$. From Definition 8, we obtain $s' =_L t'$. $\qquad\square$

In the plugin-rule depicted to the right, we use the judgment $\models \mathit{lds}(V)$. This judgment captures the intuition that V is low-deterministic secure. Again, first-order logic could be used to express and prove the semantic preconditions.

$$[\mathrm{P}_{LDS}]\frac{\models \mathit{lds}(V) \ , \ \mathsf{PLT}(V)}{\vdash \mathsf{bls}(V)}$$

3.4   Soundness and Examples

The combining calculus is sound in the following sense:

Theorem 5. *Let V be a program such that $\vdash \mathsf{bls}(V)$ is derivable in the combining calculus. Then V is possibilistic low secure.*

Proof. The soundness of the rules [SEQ], [PAR], [ITE], and [WHL] follows directly from Theorem 1, while the soundness of rule [FRK] follows from the soundness of [PAR], the definition of possibilistic low security, and the operational semantics. Rule [SNC] is sound since, firstly, a sync statement does not change the state, and, secondly, the sync statement is appended at the end of the command C and therefore does not retard the execution of subsequent commands. The plugin-rules are sound by Theorems 3 and 4. $\qquad\square$

We illustrate the usage of the combining calculus with a simple example. Consider the program fork($l := 0$, $l := 1$); sync; while $h \le 5$ do $h := h + 1$ od. By applying [SEQ] we obtain three new proof obligations, firstly $\vdash$ bls(fork($l := 0$, $l := 1$); sync), secondly $\vdash$ bls(while $h \le 5$ do $h := h + 1$ od), and thirdly MS(fork($l := 0$, $l := 1$); sync). The first one can be proved by the application of [SNC] and subsequently [P_{SLS}], followed by an analysis of strong security, while the second one can be proved by the application of [P_{LDS}], followed by an analysis of low-deterministic security. The third obligation is obviously true. Strong security does not suffice to prove the program secure, since while loops with high guards are rejected; an analysis of the whole program with low-deterministic security would also fail due to the race between $l := 0$ and $l := 1$.

4   Information Flow Security of a PDA Application

In this section, we illustrate how the possibility of combining proof techniques can be exploited in a concrete security analysis. The security of the example program can be successfully verified by combining strong security and low-deterministic security, while none of these security definitions alone provides a suitable basis for the analysis. The example application is a multi-threaded program for managing finances on mobile devices. The program gives an overview of the current stock portfolio, possibly illustrating profits, losses, and other trends with statistics. When the user starts the application he obtains a listing of his portfolio, revealing name and quantity for each stock. In parallel to printing, the current rates of EuroStoxx50 entries are retrieved. When all data is available, informative statistics can be computed. For minimizing idle time during this computation, a background thread already incrementally prepares the printout of the statistics. Finally the statistics is displayed, together with a pay-per-click commercial.

```
fork
 /  //getPortfolio:                    //getEuroStoxx50:
 |                                     j_l:=0; nwOutBuf_l:= getES50;
 |  esOP_l:= getES50old;               while (nwInBuf_l= "") do skip od;
 |  i_h:=0; pfName_h:=getPFNames;      strArr_l:= split(nwInBuf_l, ":");
 |  pfNum_h:=getPFNum;                 while (j_l<50) do
 |  while (i_h<pfName_h.length) do  ,    esName_l[j_l] := strArr_l[2*j_l];
 |    pfTabPrint_h:= pfName_h[i_h] + "|"   esP_l[j_l] := strArr_l[2*j_l+1];
 |     + pfNum_h[i_h];                    j_l:= j_l+1 od;
 \    i_h:= i_h+ 1 od                   coShort_l:= strArr_l[100];
                                        coFull_l:= strArr_l[101]; cold_l:= strArr_l[102]
```

```
;sync;
fork
 /  //computeStatistics:               //generateOutput:
 |  k_l:=0;                            m_l:=0;
 |  while (k_l<50) do                  while (m_l<50) do
 |   IPF_h:= locPF(esName_l[k_l], pfName_h);  while (k_l≤m_l) do skip od;
 |   //calculate profit for stock at position k_l  ,   outL_h[m_l] := m_l+ "|"
 |   st_h[k_l]:=(esOP_l[k_l] -esP_l[k_l])* pfNum_h[IPF_h]  + esName_l[m_l]+ "|"
 \   k_l:= k_l+1 od                     + esP_l[m_l] + "|" +    st_h[m_l];
                                        m_l:= m_l+1 od
```

```
//displayOutputAndCommercial:
;n_l:=0; stTabPrint_h("No. | Name | Price | Profit");
while (n_l<50) do   stTabPrint_h:= outL_h[n_l];  n_l:= n_l+ 1 od;
stTabPrint_h:= coShort_l+ "Press # to get more information.";
while (key_l= ' ') do skip od;
if (key_l≠ '#') then   coDispPrint_h:= coFull_l;   nwOutBuf_l:= "shownComm:"+ cold_l
else skip fi
```

Fig. 3. Implementation

The implementation of the application (Figure 3) is divided into five blocks: reading the portfolio from non-volatile storage (getPortfolio), retrieving current stock rates (getEuroStoxx50), computing statistics (computeStatistics), preparing a printout of the statistics (generateOutput), displaying the printout, advertising the commercial by a preview, and waiting for the user's input (displayOutputAndCommercial). If the user decides to view the commercial, it is displayed in full and a confirmation message is sent to the server.

As an example, we give a detailed description of getEuroStoxx50: After the initialization of the loop variable j_l (where the subscript l indicates that j is a low variable), a request is sent to the network interface represented by the variable $nwOutBuf_l$. Due to the lack of interrupts we have to do busy waiting until the variable $nwInBuf_l$ representing the incoming network stream contains an answer. The answer is a string (sequence of ASCII numbers) containing name and current rate of each stock listed in the EuroStoxx50, separated by colons. To avoid a second network request, the commercial, including the preview, the full version, and a reference ID are already included, again separated by colons. The operation split in the third line of getEuroStoxx50 is similar to the method split of the Java String class. It splits a single string in an atomic step into an array of strings, which then is processed further in the subsequent loop. After extracting the commercial data from the array its memory could be deallocated (but this is outside our language).

We assume that the application is running in a sandbox that protects the memory from programs outside the sandbox. The only exception is the underlying operating system with whom the application communicates via predefined interface variables. Besides the two interface variables for network communication ($nwInBuf_l$, $nwOutBuf_l$), the program uses display variables ($pfTabPrint_h$, $stTabPrint_h$, $coDispPrint_h$), variables that represent parts of the non-volatile storage (getES50old, getPFNames, getPFNum), and the keyboard variable (key_l). Assignments to these variables in the program correspond to the output of the information on the associated interface. Reading these variables corresponds to retrieving input through the operating system.

The parallel execution of getEuroStoxx50 and getPortfolio prevents blocking during time-consuming network activity. Concurrent programming increases efficiency and also complies with programming recommendations for mobile devices like, e.g., [14,16]. For simplicity, computeStatistics calculates only the user's profit for each stock. One could easily imagine more complex statistics. The atomic operation locPF in computeStatistics locates the index of the kth stock value within the portfolio and returns -1 if the value is not present.

The secret to be protected in the given scenario is the content of the portfolio. The sink where this information could be leaked is the network interface (assuming that the display is only accessible for users who are permitted to read the printouts). Both assignments to the $nwOutBuf_l$ are intuitively secure. Hence, there is no direct leakage of secrets and starting a more detailed information flow analysis is appropriate. For the security analysis, we use a combination of low-deterministic security and strong security. The strong security of a program

Fig. 4. Portfolio Tab   **Fig. 5.** Statistics Tab   **Fig. 6.** Commercial Screen

implies that the run-time of this program is independent of the initial value of high variables. This is obviously not the case for the loop in getPortfolio, where the run-time is directly influenced by the value of the high variable $pfName_h.length$. However, each of the five program blocks can be successfully analyzed. The result of this investigation is expressed by the following two theorems. Due to space restrictions we only sketch the proof of the first one.

Theorem 6. *The program* getPortfolio *is low-deterministic secure.*

Proof. Since i_h is incremented in the body of the loop, the loop will eventually terminate. Moreover, the only assignment to a low variable, $esOP_l := $ getES50old, does not depend on the initial high values. Hence the final value of low variables depends deterministically on their initial values. □

Theorem 7. *The programs* getEuroStoxx50, computeStatistics, generateOutput, *and* displayOutputAndCommercial *are strongly secure.*

From these two theorems and the compositionality of strong security, we conclude that the program   fork(computeStatistics, generateOutput); displayOutputAnd-Commercial   is strongly secure. From the plugin-rules $[P_{SLS}]$ and $[P_{LDS}]$, we obtain that getPortfolio and getEuroStoxx50 both satisfy the baseline policy. The parallel execution of these programs also satisfies the baseline policy according to rule [PAR], since variable independence holds. After an application of [FRK], an application of [SNC], and an application of [SEQ], we conclude that the entire program satisfies the baseline property. Hence the program is possibilistic low secure.

The application shows that the combining calculus is applicable for fairly realistic programs. The advantages will become even clearer in Section 5 where we integrate security type systems. Using a type system for the strong security condition, one can efficiently verify four parts of the program and only the remaining part would require a semantic check of low-deterministic security (for which no suitable calculus is available yet).

5   Plugins for Type-Based Analysis Techniques

While Sections 3 and 4 presented plugin rules for semantic security definitions, this section illustrates how syntactic, type-based analysis techniques can be integrated and beneficially exploited. We provide two additional plugins for the combining calculus: one to integrate the security type system proposed in [6] and one to integrate the security type system from [29]. When introducing the second type system, we also illustrate the possibility to integrate transforming type systems. Such type systems may generate a secure program from a given, possibly insecure program. Additionally, we show how to combine transforming and non-transforming analysis techniques.

5.1   Plugin : Boudol and Castellani's Security Type System

In [6] Boudol and Castellani propose a type system that does not generally reject programs containing loops with high guards, unlike the type systems in, e.g., [29] or [31]. The type judgments are of the form $\Gamma \vdash C : (\tau, \sigma)$ *cmd*, where C is a command, τ and σ are security labels, and the context Γ is a mapping from variables to security labels. In the type judgment, τ is a lower bound for the level of the variables to which assignments are made in C, and σ is an upper bound for the security levels occurring in the guards of loops and conditionals in C. After adapting the typing rules to our language, fixing a variable labeling and the induced context Γ, we obtain the following result:

Theorem 8. *Let C be a command that always terminates. If $\Gamma \vdash C : (\tau, \sigma)$ cmd can be derived for some security labels τ and σ, then C is possibilistic low secure.*[1]

For programs that always terminate we obtain the plugin rule depicted to the right. The combining calculus extended by this rule is sound due to Theorem 8.

$$[\mathrm{T}_{BC}] \frac{\Gamma \vdash C : (\tau, \sigma)\ cmd}{\vdash \mathsf{bls}(C)}$$

5.2   Plugin : Sabelfeld and Sand's Security Type System

In [29] Sabelfeld and Sands propose a transforming type system approximating the strong security condition. Its judgments are of the form $V \hookrightarrow V' : Sl$, where V is the program to be checked, V' a transformation of the program, and Sl is the type of V'. The type contains auxiliary information that is used for the transformation of the program. They provide the following theorem:

Theorem 9 ([29]). *Whenever $V \hookrightarrow V' : Sl$, then $V' \cong_L V'$.*

That is, when the type check succeeds, then the transformed program is strongly secure. To integrate plugins for transforming type systems we extend the combining calculus with the transforming rules in Figure 7. The intuition of the judgment $\vdash C \hookrightarrow \mathsf{bls}(C')$ is that the program C is transformed into the possibilistic low secure program C'. The rules [MIX₁] and [MIX₂] permit the combination of

---

[1] The typing rules differ slightly from the ones used in [6]. The adapted rules and the soundness argument will be provided in a technical report.

$$[\text{SEQ'}]\frac{\vdash C \hookrightarrow \mathsf{bls}(C') \quad \vdash D \hookrightarrow \mathsf{bls}(D') \quad \mathsf{MS}(C')}{\vdash C; D \hookrightarrow \mathsf{bls}(C'; D')}$$

$$[\text{PAR'}]\frac{\vdash V \hookrightarrow \mathsf{bls}(V') \quad \vdash W \hookrightarrow \mathsf{bls}(W') \quad V' \gtrsim W'}{\vdash VW \hookrightarrow \mathsf{bls}(V'W')}$$

$$[\text{ITE'}]\frac{\vdash C \hookrightarrow \mathsf{bls}(C') \quad \vdash D \hookrightarrow \mathsf{bls}(D') \quad B \equiv_L B}{\vdash \text{if } B \text{ then } C \text{ else } D \text{ fi} \hookrightarrow \mathsf{bls}(\text{if } B \text{ then } C' \text{ else } D' \text{ fi})}$$

$$[\text{FRK'}]\frac{\vdash \langle C \rangle V \hookrightarrow \mathsf{bls}(\langle C' \rangle V')}{\vdash \mathsf{fork}(CV) \hookrightarrow \mathsf{bls}(\mathsf{fork}(C'V'))} \qquad [\text{SNC'}]\frac{\vdash C \hookrightarrow \mathsf{bls}(C')}{\vdash C; \mathsf{sync} \hookrightarrow \mathsf{bls}(C'; \mathsf{sync})}$$

$$[\text{MIX}_1]\frac{\vdash \mathsf{bls}(C)}{\vdash C \hookrightarrow \mathsf{bls}(C)} \qquad [\text{MIX}_2]\frac{\vdash C \hookrightarrow \mathsf{bls}(C')}{\vdash \mathsf{bls}(C')}$$

Fig. 7. Additional rules for the combining calculus

transforming as well as non-transforming analysis techniques. The first one relies on the fact that a possibilistic low secure program can be securely transformed into itself.

The soundness proof of the extended calculus goes along the same lines as the proof of Theorem 5. We are now ready to add a

$$[\text{T}_{SS}]\frac{V \hookrightarrow V' : Sl \quad V' \text{ is sync-free}}{\vdash V \hookrightarrow \mathsf{bls}(V')}$$

plugin for Sabelfeld's and Sand's proof technique. The addition is sound due to Theorem 9 and Theorem 3.

5.3   Exemplary Type-Based Security Analysis

We exemplify the use of the plugin rules $[\text{T}_{BC}]$ and $[\text{T}_{SS}]$ with a syntactical analysis of the program from Section 4. We already argued that some blocks of the program are strongly secure. Hence we use the combining calculus rules supporting transforming type systems. After applying rule [SEQ']

1. $\mathsf{MS}(\mathsf{fork}(\mathsf{getPortfolio}, \mathsf{getEuroStoxx50}))$,
2. $\vdash \mathsf{fork}(\mathsf{getPortfolio}, \mathsf{getEuroStoxx50}) \hookrightarrow \mathsf{bls}(C)$, and
3. $\vdash \mathsf{fork}(\mathsf{computeStatistics}, \mathsf{generateOutput}); \mathsf{displayOutputAndCommercial} \hookrightarrow \mathsf{bls}(D)$

remain to be derived in the calculus. The first statement can be syntactically shown, since the first thread, getPortfolio, does not contain any conditionals and ends with a sync statement, while the second thread, getEuroStoxx50, does not contain any sync statements.

For the second proof obligation we do not use transforming type systems. We hence instantiate C with fork(getPortfolio, getEuroStoxx50) and apply rule $[\text{MIX}_1]$, obtaining $\vdash \mathsf{bls}(\mathsf{fork}(\mathsf{getPortfolio}, \mathsf{getEuroStoxx50}))$. After applying rule [PAR], we get three new proof obligations, namely getPortfolio $\gtrsim$ getEuroStoxx50, $\vdash \mathsf{bls}(\mathsf{getPortfolio})$ and $\vdash \mathsf{bls}(\mathsf{getEuroStoxx50})$. The first statement can be easily verified syntactically. Since getPortfolio and getEuroStoxx50 are programs that always terminate given that the network always answers the network request and that can be checked automatically with the type system provided by Boudol and Castellani we apply the rule $[T_{BC}]$ to the other two statements and obtain the new proof obligations $\Gamma \vdash$ getPortfolio : (τ, σ) *cmd* and $\Gamma \vdash$ getEuroStoxx50 : (τ', σ') *cmd*. Now we need to continue using rules of the adapted type system from [6]. One can deduce that getPortfolio can be typed with (L, H) *cmd* (getPortfolio contains assignments to low variables and high guards, but the low assignment happens before the loop), while getEuroStoxx50 can be typed with (L, L) *cmd* (getEuroStoxx50 contains assignments to low variables, but no high guards).

For the third proof obligation we apply the rule $[T_{SS}]$, obtaining the obligation fork(computeStatistics, generateOutput); displayOutputAndCommercial $\hookrightarrow D : Sl$. For a deduction we use Sabelfeld's and Sand's transforming type system. Since neither computeStatistics, nor generateOutput, nor displayOutputAndCommercial contain high guards the type system does not perform any modification and we obtain $E \hookrightarrow E : Sl$ for some type Sl and $E =$ fork(computeStatistics, generateOutput); displayOutputAndCommercial.

Due to space restrictions we omit a more detailed derivation.

6   Conclusion

Obviously, the idea of combining different proof techniques is no novelty. The contribution of this article is the illustration of how one can benefit more concretely from combining proof techniques in the information flow analysis of a given program. To our knowledge, no such result was presented before. Moreover, we introduced the combining calculus as a deductive framework that is based on conditional compositionality results and an extensible set of plugin-rules for existing verification techniques. As examples, we presented plugin-rules for restrictive security characterizations (strong security and low-determinism security), which could be verified with general-purpose logics, and plugin-rules for typing judgments that can be derived with security type systems, i.e. special-purpose calculi. We illustrated both possibilities in a fairly realistic example program. The addition of further plugin-rules would be desirable, for instance, to support verification techniques with program-logics (see, e.g., [2,7]).

Based on the experiences gained, our impression is that a baseline characterization of information flow security need not be fully compositional, which is in contrast, e.g., to the opinion stated in [21]. Nevertheless, the baseline characterization employed in the current article, which is a possibilistic property (like, e.g., in [31,6]), requires further improvements, in particular, regarding scheduling aspects. We are currently researching a security definition that is scheduler independent, but less restrictive than strong security or low-determinism security (which are both scheduler independent). Strong security is known to be the least restrictive security definition that is scheduler independent and compositional [27]. However, as we are not requiring full compositionality, less restrictive characterizations that can serve as a justification of our combining calculus exist (without changing the calculus), where the disjunction of strong security and low-determinism security is an obvious candidate.

Another direction is the migration to practically relevant languages such as Java source code or bytecode. In this context, approaches for sequential sublanguages are available (see, e.g., [1,3]), and it is not obvious how to generalize them to a multi-threaded setting. Hence, the possibility of creating a combining calculus for Java with plugin-rules for such approaches is attractive and appears, in principle, possible with the help of a rule like [PAR].

Acknowledgments. This work was funded in part by the German Research Association (DFG) in the Computer Science Action Program and by the Information Society Technologies program of the European Commission, Future and Emerging Technologies under the IST- 2005-015905 MOBIUS project. This article reflects only the authors' views and the Commission, the DFG, and the authors are not liable for any use that may be made of the information contained therein.

References

1. A. Banerjee and D. A. Naumann. Using Access Control for Secure Information Flow in a Java-like Language. In *IEEE Computer Security Foundations Workshop*, pages 155–169, 2003.
2. G. Barthe, P. R. D'Argenio, and T. Rezk. Secure Information Flow by Self-Composition. In *IEEE Computer Security Foundations Workshop*, pages 100–114, 2004.
3. G. Barthe and T. Rezk. Non-Interference for a JVM-like Language. In *ACM SIG-PLAN International Workshop on Types in Languages Design and Implementation*, pages 103–112, 2005.
4. A. Bossi, R. Focardi, C. Piazza, and S. Rossi. Unwinding in Information Flow Security. *ENTCS 99*, pages 127–154, 2004.
5. A. Bossi, D. Macedonio, C. Piazza, and S. Rossi. Secure Contexts for Confidential Data. In *IEEE Computer Security Foundations Workshop*, pages 14–25, 2003.
6. Gérard Boudol and Ilaria Castellani. Noninterference for Concurrent Programs and Thread Systems. *Theoretical Computer Science*, 281(1-2):109–130, 2002.
7. Á. Darvas, R. Hähnle, and D. Sands. A Theorem Proving Approach to Analysis of Secure Information Flow. In *International Conference on Security in Pervasive Computing*, LNCS 3450, pages 193–209, 2005.
8. Z. Deng and G. Smith. Lenient Array Operations for Practical Secure Information Flow. In *IEEE Computer Security Foundations Workshop*, pages 115–124, 2004.
9. D. E. Denning. *Cryptography and Data Security*. Addison-Wesley, 1982.
10. D. E. Denning and P. J. Denning. Certification of Programs for Secure Information Flow. *Communications of the ACM*, 20(7):504–513, 1977.
11. R. Focardi and R. Gorrieri. A Classification of Security Properties for Process Algebras. *Journal of Computer Security*, 3(1):5–33, 1995.
12. J. A. Goguen and J. Meseguer. Security Policies and Security Models. In *IEEE Symposium on Security and Privacy*, pages 11–20, 1982.
13. J. A. Goguen and J. Meseguer. Inference Control and Unwinding. In *IEEE Symposium on Security and Privacy*, pages 75–86, 1984.
14. J. Knudsen. *Networking, User Experience, and Threads*, 2002. http://developers.sun.com/techtopics/mobility/midp/articles/threading/.

15. B. Köpf and H. Mantel. Eliminating Implicit Information Leaks by Transformational Typing and Unification. In *International Workshop: Formal Aspects in Security and Trust, Revised Selected Papers*, LNCS 3866, pages 47–62. Springer-Verlag, 2006.

16. Q. H. Mahmoud. *Preventing Screen Lockups of Blocking Operations*, 2004. http://developers.sun.com/techtopics/mobility/midp/ttips/screenlock/.

17. H. Mantel. Possibilistic Definitions of Security – An Assembly Kit. In *IEEE Computer Security Foundations Workshop*, pages 185–199, 2000.

18. H. Mantel. Unwinding Possibilistic Security Properties. In *European Symposium on Research in Computer Security*, LNCS 1895, pages 238–254, 2000.

19. D. McCullough. Specifications for Multi-Level Security and a Hook-Up Property. In *IEEE Symposium on Security and Privacy*, pages 161–166, 1987.

20. J. D. McLean. A General Theory of Composition for Trace Sets Closed under Selective Interleaving Functions. In *IEEE Symposium on Research in Security and Privacy*, pages 79–93, 1994.

21. J. K. Millen. Hookup Security for Synchronous Machines. In *IEEE Symposium on Research in Security and Privacy*, pages 84–90, 1990.

22. C. Pöpper. A Security Analyzer for Multi-Threaded Programs. Diploma thesis, ETH Zurich, March 2005.

23. A. W. Roscoe. CSP and Determinism in Security Modelling. In *IEEE Symposium on Security and Privacy*, pages 114–127, 1995.

24. J. M. Rushby. Noninterference, Transitivity, and Channel-Control Security Policies. Technical Report CSL-92-02, SRI International, 1992.

25. A. Russo and A. Sabelfeld. Securing Interaction between Threads and the Scheduler. In *IEEE Computer Security Foundations Workshop*, 2006.

26. P. Y. A. Ryan and S. A. Schneider. Process Algebra and Non-interference. In *IEEE Computer Security Foundations Workshop*, pages 214–227, 1999.

27. A. Sabelfeld. Confidentiality for Multithreaded Programs via Bisimulation. In *Andrei Ershov International Conference on Perspectives of System Informatics*, LNCS 2890, pages 260–274, 2003.

28. A. Sabelfeld and A. C. Myers. Language-based Information-Flow Security. *IEEE Journal on Selected Areas in Communication*, 21(1):5–19, 2003.

29. A. Sabelfeld and D. Sands. Probabilistic Noninterference for Multi-threaded Programs. In *IEEE Computer Security Foundations Workshop*, pages 200–215, 2000.

30. G. Smith. Probabilistic Noninterference through Weak Probabilistic Bisimulation. In *IEEE Computer Security Foundations Workshop*, pages 3–13, 2003.

31. G. Smith and D. Volpano. Secure Information Flow in a Multi-threaded Imperative Language. In *ACM Symposium on Principles of Programming Languages*, pages 355–364, 1998.

32. D. Volpano and G. Smith. Probabilistic Noninterference in a Concurrent Language. In *IEEE Computer Security Foundations Workshop*, pages 34–43, 1998.

33. S. Zdancewic and A. C. Myers. Observational Determinism for Concurrent Program Security. In *IEEE Computer Security Foundations Workshop*, pages 29–43, 2003.

On the Automated Synthesis of Proof-Carrying Temporal Reference Monitors

Simon Winwood[1,2], Gerwin Klein[1,2], and Manuel M. T. Chakravarty[1]

[1] University of New South Wales
School of Computer Science & Engineering
Sydney, Australia
[2] National ICT Australia*
{sjw,chak}@cse.unsw.edu.au
gerwin.klein@nicta.com.au

Abstract. We extend the range of security policies that can be guaranteed with proof carrying code from the classical type safety, control safety, memory safety, and space/time guarantees to more general security policies, such as general resource and access control. We do so by means of (1) a specification logic for security policies, which is the past-time fragment of LTL, and (2) a synthesis algorithm generating reference monitor code and accompanying proof objects from formulae of the specification logic. To evaluate the feasibility of our approach, we developed a prototype implementation producing proofs in Isabelle/HOL.

1 Introduction

Proof carrying code (PCC) [1] is inherently trustworthy, independent of its origin or previous opportunities for tampering. The guarantees provided by PCC are, however, not universal: they are relative to a *security policy* agreed upon by the code producer and consumer. It is the code producer's obligation to annotate the code with a *proof object* that establishes the code's compliance with the security policy. This proof object, consisting of steps in a *formal logic,* can be checked with a simple proof checker. Thus, the trustworthiness of the code can be established with mathematical rigour.

Existing research into the generation of proof-carrying code focuses on security policies which can be derived from properties of high-level languages and their type systems, such as type safety [2], control and memory safety [3], and space/time guarantees [4]. The contribution of this paper is to extend the approach to more general security policies, such as general resource and access control. An example of such a policy is one where "a user may perform an operation only if they have been granted a capability for that operation and that capability hasn't been revoked." Such properties are beyond the semantic guarantees of high-level languages; hence, we need (1) a formal device to express such policies and (2) a method for generating proof-carrying code for these policies.

---

* National ICT Australia is funded through the Australian Government's *Backing Australia's Ability* initiative, in part through the Australian Research Council.

G. Puebla (Ed.): LOPSTR 2006, LNCS 4407, pp. 111–126, 2007.

To address Point (1), we introduce a fragment of LTL [5] lacking the usual future operators (*until* and *next*), which we call *propositional pure-past temporal logic* (P3TL), as a specification logic for security policies in Section 3. P3TL can express a wide range of security policies, while enabling the automatic synthesis of reference monitors [6] that enforce P3TL policies. This second property is key to solving Point (2). More precisely, in Section 5, we will give an algorithm to synthesise, firstly, a reference monitor checking a given P3TL policy, and secondly, a proof object demonstrating that the reference monitor code indeed meets the policy. Such a reference monitor in conjunction with a framework to constrain application code to abide by the rules of a reference monitor is sufficient to produce PCC for P3TL policies. To be complete, this framework must also provide machine checkable proof that the application code cannot subvert the reference monitor. We introduced one such framework based on hybrid sandboxing accompanied by a proof in the theorem prover Isabelle/HOL in previous work [7]. We will describe this set up in more detail in Section 2.

The proof of compliance of synthesised reference monitors is in a Hoare-like logic discussed in Section 4 and formalised in Isabelle/HOL. We implemented a prototype synthesis tool in Isabelle/HOL to demonstrate the practical feasibility of our approach.

In summary, our specific contributions are these:

- a formalisation of a simple language and program logic for reference monitors (Section 4); and,
- a synthesis algorithm for reference monitors and proof objects from P3TL formulae (Section 5).

In contrast to previous work on generating reference monitors from temporal logics, we simultaneously generate a proof object that demonstrates that the generated code enforces the security policy. We discuss related work further in Section 6.

2   Our Approach

Fig. 1 shows an application scenario in which our technique is useful. Assume a code producer generating a PCC program, certified for some policy ϕ. The code consumer, however, requires a stronger policy, ψ, where the additional guarantees of ψ over ϕ are beyond those that can be directly included during PCC generation. The method introduced in this paper enables the synthesis of a reference monitor for ψ; this can then be inserted into the PCC program, possibly by rewriting parts of the application, to bridge the gap between ϕ and ψ. This paper presents an algorithm for synthesising such monitors with matching proofs. In previous work [7], we showed how such a monitor can be integrated into an existing application in the special case where that existing application does not use PCC at all; i.e., ϕ is empty. The general case, depicted in Fig. 1, where two policies need to be integrated is left for future work.

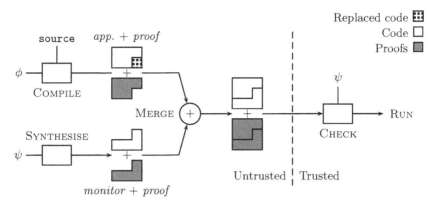

Fig. 1. A possible application of our approach: generate a monitor for the stronger policy ψ and insert it into the application. This paper presents the monitor and proof synthesis component.

2.1   The Monitor Environment

We require that the surrounding PCC infrastructure ensures the monitor invariant, containing assertions about the monitor state, be maintained outside the monitor; in a typical system, we expect the monitor state to be hidden from the rest of the system, either through a module mechanism or through general memory safety — the latter is the option we explored in [7]. If a to be secured operation occurs outside the monitor, the invariant will, in general, be invalidated — this will be detected at proof check time, and the program rejected. Of course, it is perfectly valid for there to be secured operations outside the monitor if the outside code can ensure that the invariant is maintained and that assurance is reflected in the code's proof annotations.

2.2   The Prototype

We have implemented a prototype synthesis tool. The tool generates an Isabelle theory file containing both the monitor code and proofs. The tool is Isabelle-specific, however we expect an implementation for another logical framework to have many similarities. The prototype, along with the Isabelle theory file, is freely available.[1]

While we make extensive use of Isabelle, we have been careful to ensure that there is no intrinsic reliance upon any particular feature. In the generated proofs, we avoid, where possible, use of Isabelle's automated tactics, using them only when the lemma to be proved is Isabelle-specific. This includes, for example, lemmas relating to substitution: because we make use of the meta-logic's substitution (we use a shallow embedding for the assertion logic), the proof will be Isabelle-specific, and thus no general proof is available. Conversely, the monitor's proof obligations are independent of the particular meta-logic, and so we use individual proof rules for the main part of the proof.

---

[1] http://www.cse.unsw.edu.au/~sjw/papers/synthesis.html

3   Policy Logic

In this section we introduce the logic we use for describing security policies.

Example 1. Consider a simple version of the Chinese Wall security policy[8]

> *A user may access files for any client, but once they have done so, they may only access files for that client.*

Given an operator which denotes "at some time in the past", this policy may be expressed as[2]

$$\mathtt{access}(f) \land f \in C \longrightarrow \neg(\mathtt{access}(g) \land g \notin C)$$

which states a policy equivalent to the one above: access to an object belonging to a client is allowed only if at no point in the past has the user accessed an object belonging to another client.

Example 2. Now consider a policy modelling a capability system

> *A user may perform an operation only if they have been granted a capability for that operation and that capability hasn't been revoked.*

We may encode this policy as follows

$$\mathtt{operate}_o \longrightarrow \neg\,\mathtt{revoke}_o\,\mathcal{S}\,\mathtt{grant}_o$$

where $\psi\,\mathcal{S}\,\phi$ means ϕ was true at some point in the past, and ψ ever since.

These policies, like many others, express properties over a *series* of events: the first policy that some event had not occurred in the past; the second policy that some event had occurred, and in the meantime another had not.

Given our general goal of synthesising reference monitors, our policy logic needs to fulfill two requirements: (1) we must be able to use reference monitors to implement all policies that are expressible in the logic and (2) the logic must be powerful enough to express common policies, such as those above.

The latter means that the logic must be able to express properties over behaviours of the program, not just over individual states. The former means that the logic should express safety properties only, as liveness properties cannot be implemented by reference monitors [6].

These two requirements still leave some choice. We have settled on the safety fragment [5] of propositional linear temporal logic (LTL); for the remainder of the paper we will denote this fragment *propositional pure-past temporal logic* (P3TL). As the name signifies, this is a propositional logic containing temporal operators that refer solely to previous worlds. The logic differs from traditional temporal logics in that it lacks the usual future (*until* and *next*) operators — a formula ψ in P3TL is equivalent to $\Box\psi$ in the LTL of Manna and Pnueli [5]. A similar logic (ptLTL) is used by Havelund and Rosu [9].

---

[2] In this section, to simplify the formalisations, we are a little loose with syntax.

$$\langle \sigma, \ n \rangle \models \text{«a»} \qquad\qquad = \text{a } \sigma_{[n]}$$
$$\langle \sigma, \ n \rangle \models \varphi \ [\Rightarrow] \ \psi = \langle \sigma, \ n \rangle \models \varphi \ \longrightarrow \ \langle \sigma, \ n \rangle \models \psi$$
$$\langle \sigma, \ n \rangle \models \varphi \ S \ \psi \quad = \exists i \leq n. \ \langle \sigma, \ i \rangle \models \psi \ \wedge \ (\forall j \in (i..n]. \ \langle \sigma, \ j \rangle \models \varphi)$$
$$\langle \sigma, \ n \rangle \models \ \ \varphi \qquad\qquad = n \neq 0 \ \longrightarrow \ \langle \sigma, \ n \ - \ 1 \rangle \models \varphi$$

Fig. 2. Semantics of P3TL

A more powerful logic, such as a first-order variant of P3TL, would enable more policies and more succinct versions of those already mentioned. Unfortunately, synthesising reference monitors for these logics is much more difficult than for P3TL — the state space for P3TL is fixed, while that of a first-order logic is potentially unbounded. We leave extension of our system to more powerful logics as future work.

The following is the syntax of P3TL

$$\texttt{form} ::= \text{«atom»} \ | \ \texttt{form}_1 \ [\Rightarrow] \ \texttt{form}_2 \ | \ \texttt{form}_1 \ S \ \texttt{form}_2 \ | \ \ \texttt{form}$$

The logic consists of atoms and the operators implication, since, and weak previous. Implication is the usual binary operator; to distinguish it from that of HOL, we write $\varphi \ [\Rightarrow] \ \psi$. The syntax for the since and weak previous operators is standard.

The definition of P3TL is parameterised over the type of states; atoms are HOL predicates on such states. Our implementation of P3TL is then a *deep embedding* into Isabelle/HOL, but uses a *shallow embedding* for atomic propositions.

Example 3. A traditional state space would be a tuple or record of variables. The predicate «λs. x s = 7» then, for instance, states that the variable x in record s should have value 7.

The following gives the definitions for the other propositional connectives (negation, conjunction, disjunction, etc.) as well as the usual temporal operators: *strong previous* (φ), *once* (φ), and *so-far* (φ). The two previous operators (strong and weak) differ only at the initial state: φ is false and φ is true. In particular, $\perp$ is true only at the initial state.

$\top$	= «λs. True»		φ	= [¬] (([¬] φ)) (Previously)
$\perp$	= «λs. False»		φ	= $\top$ S φ (Once)
[¬] φ	= φ [⇒] $\perp$		φ	= [¬] (([¬] φ)) (So-far)
φ [∧] ψ	= [¬] (φ [⇒] [¬] ψ)		φ [∨] ψ	= [¬] φ [⇒] ψ

Fig. 2 gives the semantics of P3TL using an *indexed model* $\langle \sigma, n \rangle$. The first element, σ, is a sequence of worlds, and the second, n, is the index of the current state.

An atom «a» is valid in $\langle \sigma, n \rangle$ iff the function a maps the n-th state in σ (denoted $\sigma_{[n]}$) to true. An implication is valid iff the validity of the premise implies the validity of the conclusion at the same index n. The formula $\varphi \ S \ \psi$ is valid at $\langle \sigma, n \rangle$ iff ψ was valid at some earlier state i and φ was valid at all states j from i to n. The weak previous operator φ is valid iff there is either no previous state ($n = 0$) or φ was valid at index $n - 1$.

4   A Language and Logic for Reference Monitors

4.1   The Programming Language

This section describes the language we use for reference monitors. It is a simple imperative if-while language, using Isabelle/HOL's functions for expressions. Whilst it is usual in expositions on proof-carrying code systems to use a very low-level language (e.g., an assembly language), we chose this comparatively high-level language to simplify the presentation; issues such as memory allocation are orthogonal to the contribution of this work and would only obscure the central points. We expect that low-level languages will present few additional theoretical hurdles — indeed, Barthe et. al. [10] note that, in the absence of optimisations, transformation to a low-level language preserves proof obligations.

The syntax of programs is shown below. The nonterminal *basic* denotes functions from states to states, *bexp* functions from states to booleans, and *form* P3TL formulae.

$$stmt ::= \mathtt{Do}\ basic\ \mid\ stmt_1\ ;\ stmt_2$$
$$\mid\ \mathtt{IF}\ bexp\ \mathtt{THEN}\ stmt_1\ \mathtt{ELSE}\ stmt_2\ \mathtt{FI}\ \mid\ \mathtt{WHILE}\ bexp\ \mathtt{DO}\ stmt\ \mathtt{OD}$$
$$\mid\ \mathtt{Secure}\ form$$

As with P3TL, the syntax is parameterised over the states of the program. The Do statement provides the means to model assignment and simple state transformations directly as HOL functions. The Secure statement represents the operation to be secured, abstracting away from the particular operation's semantics. It is parameterised by a P3TL formula representing the security policy.

Example 4. The following monitor checks the Chinese Wall policy from Example 1

```
IF (λs. ∃f. access s f ∧ f ∈ C) THEN
  IF (λs. seen s = 1) THEN
    Do (λs. s(|error := 1|))
  ELSE
    Secure ψ
  FI
ELSE
  Secure ψ
FI
```

The state variable seen records whether we have previously seen a conflicting access — the code to maintain this is omitted. The expression s(|error := 1|) updates error in record s.

The states over which the language operates are tuples (s, σ), where s is the program state, usually modelled as an Isabelle record[3], and σ a sequence

---

[3] As we use the Do statement to model assignment, taking a state update function as an argument, there is no requirement that a record is used — it merely simplifies use of the language.

$$\boxed{\text{s } -\text{t} \rightarrow \text{ s'}}$$

$$\frac{}{\text{(s, ss) } -\text{Do f} \rightarrow \text{ (f s, ss)}} \qquad \frac{\text{s } -\text{e} \rightarrow \text{ t} \qquad \text{t } -\text{e'} \rightarrow \text{ s'}}{\text{s } -\text{e; e'} \rightarrow \text{ s'}}$$

$$\frac{\text{b (fst s)} \qquad \text{s } -\text{e} \rightarrow \text{ s'}}{\text{s } -\text{IF b THEN e ELSE e' FI} \rightarrow \text{ s'}} \qquad \frac{\neg \text{ b (fst s)} \qquad \text{s } -\text{e'} \rightarrow \text{ s'}}{\text{s } -\text{IF b THEN e ELSE e' FI} \rightarrow \text{ s'}}$$

$$\frac{\neg \text{ b (fst s)}}{\text{s } -\text{WHILE b DO e OD} \rightarrow \text{ s}}$$

$$\frac{\text{b (fst s)} \qquad \text{s } -\text{e} \rightarrow \text{ t} \qquad \text{t } -\text{WHILE b DO e OD} \rightarrow \text{ s'}}{\text{s } -\text{WHILE b DO e OD} \rightarrow \text{ s'}}$$

$$\frac{\text{s'} = (\text{if (s, ss)} \models \varphi \text{ then (s, ss @ [s]) else arbitrary})}{\text{(s, ss) } -\text{Secure } \varphi \rightarrow \text{ s'}}$$

Fig. 3. Semantics of programs

representing a trace of previously seen states. This trace serves as the model when checking P3TL formulae; it records the state at security events only, not all state changes in the program. Note that the trace is only required for reasoning about policies and does *not* appear at runtime.

In monitoring P3TL policies, we interpret the validity of formulae relative to the current state, that is, the last state in the sequence. We thus use an *anchored interpretation* [11]. Satisfaction of P3TL formulae by a program state is then

$$(\text{s, } \sigma) \models \varphi = \langle \sigma \text{ @ [s], } |\sigma| \rangle \models \varphi$$

Fig. 3 shows a big step semantics for our language. The semantics are standard [12], apart from the Secure statement: the effect of Secure φ is to record the current state in the state history. Execution of Secure φ is only defined, however, when the current state satisfies the security policy φ.

A full implementation of our system would replace the Secure statement by, for example, a system call statement. Again, modelling the behaviour of system calls is orthogonal to the aims of this paper; the much-simplified Secure is sufficient.

4.2   The Program Logic

So far we have defined a logic for policies and a language to implement reference monitors. This section introduces a logic for reasoning reasons about programs that allows us to formally verify that safety policies are respected.

The rules of this Hoare-like program logic are shown in Fig 4. The triple ⊢ {P} T {Q} denotes that a statement T that starts execution in a state satisfying P and terminates will finish in a state satisfying Q. Both P and Q are assertions, that is, HOL predicates on states.

As with the semantics in Sect. 4.1, the proof rules are standard apart from the Secure statement. We have one rule for each syntactic construct and the usual rule of consequence.

$$\boxed{\Vdash \{P\}\ T\ \{Q\}}$$

$$\frac{}{\Vdash \{\lambda(s,\ ss).\ P\ (f\ s,\ ss)\}\ Do\ f\ \{P\}}\ \text{DO} \qquad \frac{\Vdash \{P\}\ e\ \{Q\} \qquad \Vdash \{Q\}\ e'\ \{R\}}{\Vdash \{P\}\ e;\ e'\ \{R\}}\ \text{SEQ}$$

$$\frac{\Vdash \{\lambda s.\ P\ s \wedge b\ (\text{fst}\ s)\}\ e\ \{Q\} \qquad \Vdash \{\lambda s.\ P\ s \wedge \neg\ b\ (\text{fst}\ s)\}\ e'\ \{Q\}}{\Vdash \{P\}\ \text{IF}\ b\ \text{THEN}\ e\ \text{ELSE}\ e'\ \text{FI}\ \{Q\}}\ \text{COND}$$

$$\frac{\Vdash \{\lambda s.\ P\ s \wedge b\ (\text{fst}\ s)\}\ e\ \{P\} \qquad Q = (\lambda s.\ P\ s \wedge \neg\ b\ (\text{fst}\ s))}{\Vdash \{P\}\ \text{WHILE}\ b\ \text{DO}\ e\ \text{OD}\ \{Q\}}\ \text{WHILE}$$

$$\frac{\forall s.\ P'\ s \longrightarrow P\ s \qquad \forall s.\ Q\ s \longrightarrow Q'\ s \qquad \Vdash \{P\}\ e\ \{Q\}}{\Vdash \{P'\}\ e\ \{Q'\}}\ \text{CONS}$$

$$\frac{\forall s.\ P\ s \longrightarrow s \models \varphi \qquad \forall s\ ss.\ P\ (s,\ ss) \longrightarrow Q\ (s,\ ss\ @\ [s])}{\Vdash \{P\}\ \text{Secure}\ \varphi\ \{Q\}}\ \text{SECURE}$$

Fig. 4. A Hoare-like logic for the programming language

The new rule for Secure demands that all states that satisfy the precondition be models of the security policy φ; this check links the assertion logic to P3TL, the policy logic. In addition, the rule's postcondition reflects the effect of Secure on the program state, i.e. recording the event in the trace.

Following the standard practise [12] of using a shallow embedding of assertions into Isabelle/HOL means that we can take direct advantage of Isabelle's tactics and libraries to reason about programs. The assertion logic and program expressions, however, are more powerful than strictly required[4].

We have shown this Hoare-logic to be sound in the following sense.

Theorem 1. If $\Vdash \{P\}\ e\ \{Q\}$ and P s and s $-e\rightarrow$ s' then Q s'.

Note that our definition of the semantics of Secure ensures that programs cannot get stuck because of policy violation. The only reason that there might be no s' such that s $-e\rightarrow$ s' in this theorem is non-termination of while loops.

5   Synthesis

In this section we discuss the synthesis algorithm; that is, the algorithm that takes a P3TL formula and emits a reference monitor which enforces the policy, and a proof that the generated monitor does indeed enforce the policy.

We will use the example policy

$$(\ll\lambda s.\ x\ s = 1\gg)\,[\Rightarrow]\,(\ll\lambda s.\ x\ s < 5\gg\ \mathcal{S}\ \ll\lambda s.\ y\ s = 1\gg) \tag{$*$}$$

---

[4] We also have a deep embedding for all logics. We use the shallow embedding as it is much briefer and clearer: the interaction between the assertion logic and P3TL, although non-trivial, is not the main focus of this paper.

as a running example throughout this section. Although this example has no correspondence to a real-world policy (even a small such policy would be too big for the limited space available), it contains enough complexity to be of interest.

5.1 Checking P3TL Satisfaction

In the synthesis of P3TL formulae, the following definition is required

Definition 1. *The* past formulae *of a formula are sub-formulae*

1. *of the form $\phi \, \mathcal{S} \, \psi$; or*
2. *that occur after , e.g. ψ in ψ.*

The number of sub-formulae is linear in the size of the formula.

Example 5. The past formulae for our example policy (*) are «λs. x s = 1» and «λs. x s < 5» $\mathcal{S}$ «λs. y s = 1». Terms in our examples which relate to these formulae will have suffixes 0 and 1, respectively. For example, state_0 is Σ«λs. x s = 1».

Note that a since formula may be unfolded according to the equality:

$$\phi \, \mathcal{S} \, \psi = \psi \, [\vee]((\phi \, \mathcal{S} \, \psi) \, [\wedge] \, \phi)$$

Applying this rule repeatedly yields a formula in which all since formulae occur only after a operator. Thus, truth of the rewritten formula depends only on the truth of propositions in the current world and the truth of sub-formulae in the immediately previous world. Furthermore, note that these sub-formulae are all past formulae.

To check if a sequence σ satisfies a policy, we start by setting all formulae of the form φ to false (as per the semantics of). Starting from the initial state, check and record the truth of all past formulae. At the last state in σ, check the truth of the rewritten policy, using the recorded past formulae from the previous state.

Thus, to monitor a policy, we need only keep track of its past formulae. This implies that we do not require an explicit representation of worlds in our monitor, and that checking a P3TL formula can be done efficiently.

5.2 Monitor Synthesis

The algorithm for constructing a monitor for a P3TL formula is then as follows:

1. For each past formulae ψ, allocate a state bit, Σ_ψ, which records the truth of the formula in the previous world, i.e. $\Sigma_\psi \leftrightarrow \psi$;
2. Construct a program fragment which checks the truth of each past formula ψ in the current world, i.e., with respect to the current program state. When constructing the fragment, if a sub-formula of ψ of the form ϕ is seen, emit code which checks the state bit Σ_ϕ;

```
IF (λs. x s = 1) THEN
   Do (λs. s(|tmp_0 := 1|))
ELSE
   Do (λs. s(|tmp_0 := 0|))
FI
IF (λs. y s = 1) THEN
   Do (λs. s(|tmp_1 := 1|))
ELSE
      IF (λs. state_1 s = 1) THEN
         IF (λs. x s < 5) THEN
            Do (λs. s(|tmp_1 := 1|))
         ELSE
            Do (λs. s(|tmp_1 := 0|))
         FI
      ELSE
         Do (λs. s(|tmp_1 := 0|))
      FI
FI
```

```
                    (CONT.)


IF (λs. state_0 s = 1) THEN
   IF (λs. tmp_1 s = 1) THEN
      Secure policy;
      Do (λs. s(|state_0 := tmp_0 s|));
      Do (λs. s(|state_1 := tmp_1 s|))
   ELSE
      Skip
   FI
ELSE
   Secure policy;
   Do (λs. s(|state_0 := tmp_0 s|));
   Do (λs. s(|state_1 := tmp_1 s|))
FI
```

Fig. 5. Generated code for policy (*). The left hand column contains the state maintenance code, while the right side contains the policy checking code.

3. Construct a monitor fragment for the main formula. In the case that the formula holds, execute the secure statement and update the monitor state, otherwise handle the security violation; and
4. Sequentially compose the fragments to generate the final monitor.

Fig. 6 presents the algorithm for constructing a monitor fragment. The notation $S[\![\psi]\!]_{(tc,fc)}$ denotes the algorithm applied to formula ψ, with arguments tc (true case) and fc (false case). The leaves of the fragment, tc and fc, are assignments in the case of a past formula, and a secure statement along with state update in the case of the policy.

Example 6. The monitor generated for our example policy is shown in Fig. 5. Our implementation includes an optimisation: rather than re-check a formula, monitor fragments may refer to previously established past formula by checking the corresponding variable.

The monitor fragment for the past formula « λs. x s = 1 » (the first 5 lines) of Fig. 5 was generated by

$$S[\![« λs. x s = 1 »]\!]_{(Do (λs. s(|tmp_0 := 1|)), Do (λs. s(|tmp_0 := 0|)))}$$

Not shown are the proof handling aspects; in our prototype, the Do statements are functions taking a proof of « λs. x s = 1 » and ¬« λs. x s = 1 » respectively. These proofs are then stored for later extraction.

If we, for the moment, ignore proof generation, the synthesis algorithm is straightforward: when an atom is seen, generate code which checks the atom and uses

$$S[\![\ll a\gg]\!]_{(tc,\,fc)} = \textbf{IF } a \textbf{ THEN } (tc \text{ ATOMI}) \textbf{ ELSE } (fc \text{ NATOMI})$$

$$S[\![\psi\,[\Rightarrow]\,\phi]\!]_{(tc,\,fc)} = \textbf{let}$$
$$tc' = \lambda\, r.S[\![\phi]\!]_{(tc\,\cdot\,\text{IMPI}_1,\,fc\,\cdot\,(\text{NIMPI }r))}$$
$$\textbf{in}$$
$$S[\![\psi]\!]_{(tc',\,tc\,\cdot\,\text{IMPLI}_2)}$$

$$S[\![[\neg]\psi]\!]_{(tc,\,fc)} = S[\![\psi]\!]_{(fc\,\cdot\,\text{NNEGI},\,tc\,\cdot\,\text{NEGI})}$$

$$S[\![\psi]\!]_{(tc,\,fc)} = \textbf{IF } (\Sigma_\psi) \textbf{ THEN } (tc \text{ INV-}\pi_\psi) \textbf{ ELSE } (fc \text{ NINV-}\pi_\psi)$$

$$S[\![\psi\,\mathcal{S}\,\phi]\!]_{(tc,\,fc)} = S[\\,[\wedge]\,\psi)]\!]_{(tc\,\cdot\,\text{SINCEI},\,fc\,\cdot\,\text{NSINCEI})}$$

Fig. 6. The algorithm for constructing a monitor fragment. It generates both a monitor fragment and proof annotations. The parameters tc and fc are functions which take proof annotations and return the statements to be used in each branch of the conditional; the term tc · SINCEI composes rule SINCEI with tc, thus adding a new rule to the proof tree at tc.

$$\boxed{s \models \varphi}$$

$$\frac{\varphi\ (\text{fst s})}{s \models \ll\varphi\gg}\text{ATOMI} \qquad \frac{\neg\ \varphi\ (\text{fst s})}{\neg\ s \models \ll\varphi\gg}\text{NATOMI}$$

$$\frac{s \models \varphi}{s \models \psi\,[\Rightarrow]\,\varphi}\text{IMPLI}_1 \qquad \frac{\neg\ s \models \psi}{s \models \psi\,[\Rightarrow]\,\varphi}\text{IMPLI}_2 \qquad \frac{s \models \varphi \qquad \neg\ s \models \psi}{\neg\ s \models \varphi\,[\Rightarrow]\,\psi}\text{NIMPLI}$$

$$\frac{\neg\ s \models \varphi}{s \models [\neg]\,\varphi}\text{NEGI} \qquad \frac{s \models \varphi}{\neg\ s \models [\neg]\,\varphi}\text{NNEGI}$$

$$\frac{s \models \psi\,[\vee]\,(\,(\varphi\,\mathcal{S}\,\psi)\,[\wedge]\,\varphi)}{s \models \varphi\,\mathcal{S}\,\psi}\text{SINCEI}$$

$$\frac{\neg\ s \models \psi\,[\vee]\,(\,(\varphi\,\mathcal{S}\,\psi)\,[\wedge]\,\varphi)}{\neg\ s \models \varphi\,\mathcal{S}\,\psi}\text{NSINCEI}$$

Fig. 7. Derived introduction rules for P3TL

tc in the true case, fc in the false case; in the case of a negation, $[\neg]\psi$, generate code for ψ but switch the leaves — if ψ holds, then use fc, otherwise tc. Note that negation produces no extra code; it merely swaps leaves. This means that special cases for conjunction and disjunction are not required: unfolding the definitions results in no additional code; a previous formula, ψ, results in a check of the state component for that formula, Σ_ψ.

5.3 Proof Synthesis

The main monitor theorem is

$$\Vdash \{\text{INV}_\psi\}\ \texttt{monitor}\ \{\text{INV}_\psi\}$$

which states that the monitor preserves the invariant, discussed below. The proof that the monitor enforces the security policy is implicit in the use of any Secure statements: wherever an operation occurs in the monitor, a proof obligation is required which states that the policy holds (c.f. rule SECURE). Thus, as our proof system is sound (Theorem 1), a proof of the main theorem implies that execution of a Secure statement occurs only when the security policy is true.

The proof of the main theorem is generated from the monitor fragments using a verification condition generator style algorithm. The proof requires a number of lemmas for both re-establishing the monitor invariant and for showing the policy holds for Secure statements. The generation of these proof obligations is discussed below.

The monitor invariant. The monitor maintains state between invocations, in particular Σ_ϕ for each past formula ϕ, and so a monitor invariant is required. This invariant relates the value of each state variable to the truth of the corresponding formula in the previous state.

$$\text{INV}_\psi \equiv \bigwedge_{\phi \in past(\psi)} \Sigma_\phi \leftrightarrow \phi$$

where ψ is the security policy and $past(\psi)$ are the past formulae of ψ.

The past formula monitor fragments are then responsible for reestablishing the monitor invariant. This is done in two steps: firstly, the monitor checks the past formula, ϕ, and sets a temporary variable, Δ_ϕ, accordingly; secondly, the monitor updates the real monitor state *after* execution of the Secure statement.

This two-step process is required for a number of reasons: primarily, later monitor fragments may require the state variable to establish the truth of other formulae, past or policy; and, secondly, if the security policy doesn't hold, then the monitor may elect to silently ignore the request. In this case, the initial value of the state variables is still correct — no secure operation is performed, and thus the invariant is still true. This is the behaviour of monitors generated by our prototype. We then define, for each past formula, a pre-invariant $\Xi_\phi \equiv \Delta_\phi \leftrightarrow \phi$. This correspondence is used to generate the invariant — after execution of Secure statement and state update, we can use this to derive $\Sigma_\phi \leftrightarrow \phi$

Example 7. Our prototype generates a number of auxiliary lemmas for manipulating the invariant. These include

- projection rules (the INV-π_ϕ rules mentioned in Fig. 6)

$$\frac{\text{invariant } (s, \sigma) \qquad \text{state\_1 } s = 1}{(s, \sigma) \models (\langle \lambda s.\ x\ s\ <\ 5 \rangle\ S\ \langle \lambda s.\ y\ s\ =\ 1 \rangle)} \text{ INV-}\pi_1$$

- rules for invariance under assignment (X is an arbitrary function)

$$\text{invariant } (s(\!|tmp\_1 := X\ s|\!), \sigma) = \text{invariant } (s, \sigma)$$

Proof obligations. The proof of the main theorem requires, for each assignment in each past formula monitor fragment, a proof obligation of the form

$$\text{INV}_\psi \wedge \Xi_{\phi_1} \wedge \ldots \wedge \Xi_{\phi_m} \wedge a_1 \wedge \ldots \wedge a_n \longrightarrow \text{INV}'_\psi \wedge \Xi'_{\phi_1} \wedge \ldots \wedge \Xi'_{\phi_m} \wedge \Xi'_\phi$$

A formula is primed to denote it's truth after the assignment. The terms $\Xi_{\phi_1} \wedge \ldots \wedge \Xi_{\phi_m}$ are the past formula equivalences established by previous monitor fragments, $a_1, \ldots, a_n$ are the atoms (or their negation, in the case of a false branch) that were checked by the conditionals in the current monitor fragment, and ϕ is the formula from which the monitor fragment was produced, with Δ_ϕ replaced by True or False depending on which branch the assignment occurs.

These proofs state that the monitor fragment correctly establishes Ξ_ϕ and does not invalidate previously established equivalences or the invariant.

The obligations for Secure statements are similar but for the last term in the conjunction: in this case, it is the policy. In addition, the SECURE rule allows us to generate P3TL terms of the form ϕ, assuming we have ϕ — this is how the conversion from pre-invariant to invariant occurs.

Example 8. The following obligation is generated for the fourth assignment in Fig. 5.

```
∀s σ. invariant (s, σ) ∧
        pre_sd0 (s, σ) ∧ y s ≠ 1 ∧ state_1 s = 1 ∧ x s < 5 ⟶
        invariant (s(|tmp_1 := 1|), σ) ∧
        pre_sd0 (s(|tmp_1 := 1|), σ) ∧ pre_sd1 (s(|tmp_1 := 1|), σ)
```

Proof construction. Much of complexity of the algorithm in Fig. 6 arises because the leaves of the tree are annotated with the proof, and the algorithm builds the tree from the leaves up. The proofs require information that is not initially available, i.e., the proofs for sub-formulae, so the arguments to the synthesis function, tc and fc, are *functions* from proofs to program fragments. In particular, if the fragment is checking the truth of ϕ, tc will be a function from a proof of ϕ, and fc a function from a proof of $\neg\phi$.

Fig. 7 shows the P3TL proof rules used by the algorithm, except for the invariant projection lemmas which are described above. All of these rules are derived from the semantics of P3TL (using Isabelle) as lemmas, but are intended to be derivable in a syntactic proof system (such as that in Lichtenstein and Pnueli [13]). Each rule occurs in the positive and negated form, as some proof rules require negated forms of past formulae (e.g., rule NINV-π_ϕ). Note that the atom rules convert assertions into P3TL atoms.

The algorithm assumes these rules are available as functions which build proofs. As the assumptions of the proof are assertions (the invariant and $a_1, \ldots, a_n$ as above), those rules without premises of the form $s \models \psi$ are treated as constants, as in the case for atoms.

In the case of an implication, $\psi [\Rightarrow] \phi$, we construct a function tc' which takes as argument a proof of ψ and produces a fragment which checks ϕ. Note that NIMPI is partially applied to the proof of ψ in the false case; the result is a function from $\neg\phi$ as required. The remaining cases are straightforward.

Example 9. The following is the proof generated for the obligation in Example 8

$$
\dfrac{
\text{INV-}\pi_1 \dfrac{\text{invariant (s, } \sigma) \quad \text{state\_1 s = 1}}{\text{(s, } \sigma) \models \ominus \varphi} \qquad
\dfrac{\dfrac{\text{y s = 1}}{\text{(s, } \sigma) \models \text{«}\lambda\text{s. y s = 1»}}\text{ATOM}I}{\dfrac{\neg \text{ (s, } \sigma) \models \text{[¬] «}\lambda\text{s. y s = 1»}}{\dfrac{\neg \text{ (s, } \sigma) \models \psi}{\dfrac{\text{(s, } \sigma) \models \text{[¬] } \psi}{\dfrac{\text{(s, } \sigma) \models \text{[¬] «}\lambda\text{s. y s = 1» [⇒] [¬] } \psi}{\dfrac{\text{(s, } \sigma) \models \varphi}{(\text{tmp\_1 (s(\!|tmp\_1 := 1|\!)) = 1) = (s, } \sigma) \models \varphi}\text{TMP-1-SUPD}T}\text{SINCE}I}\text{IMPL}I1}\text{NEG}I}\text{NIMPL}I}\text{NNEG}I}
}{}
$$

where $\psi = \text{(«}\lambda\text{s. x s < 5»} \; \mathcal{S} \; \text{«}\lambda\text{s. y s = 1»)} \; \text{[⇒] [¬] «}\lambda\text{s. y s = 1»}$ and $\varphi = \text{«}\lambda\text{s. x}$ s < 5» $\mathcal{S}$ «λs. y s = 1».

The above proof is generated in two steps: firstly (not shown) the previously established facts are shown to be true after the assignment using the assignment invariance rules described above; and secondly, shown above, the new equivalence is established using the proof constructed by the algorithm in Fig. 6.

After the assignment $(\text{tmp\_1 s = 1)} = (s, \sigma) \models \varphi$, as required.

5.4   Discussion

Tableau construction [14] algorithms give an exponential state space due to the use of subset construction, and thus can generate monitors whose worst-case size is exponential in the size of the input formula. Our approach, while tableau-based, has a worst-case size that is $(O(n^2))$ in the size of the input formula. This size reduction is due to the past formula monitor fragments which dynamically calculate the automata transitions. This comes at a cost, however: the time complexity of our approach is quadratic, while that of a simpler automata-based solution is linear in the size of the formula.

6   Related Work

Bernard and Lee [15] present a proof carrying code framework based on temporal logic. In contrast, our system is closer to that of a traditional PCC framework — we require temporal terms only when dealing with the high-level safety policy; this should make extending existing programs simpler. Nevertheless, we envisage no major issues in synthesising monitors for their framework.

Synthesis from temporal logics, traditionally used in the model checking community (e.g. SPIN [16]) has gained recent popularity for constructing program reference monitors [17,18,19].

In particular, our approach is similar to that of the PATHEXPLORER project [9]. They construct monitors for safety properties using an algorithm that is very close to that we presented. These monitors can then be automatically inserted into Java programs for run-time testing. The major difference is that our algorithm also generates proofs.

Peled and Zuck [20] generate a proof from model-checking results. This proof shows properties of the target system; in theory, we may be able to generate the monitor and then apply their technique to generate the proof. It is, however, unclear whether that approach would be feasible in practice.

7   Conclusions and Future Work

In this paper we introduced a temporal logic for formulating security policies — propositional pure past temporal logic — and showed how to automatically generate efficient reference monitor implementations that check the required policy, along with a machine-checkable proof of their safety.

We have implemented a prototype targeting Isabelle/HOL; the majority of formal matter, and all of the theorems, in this paper were generated using Isabelle's presentation mechanism [21] from the Isabelle proofs. This means what we show is what we proved.

The main contribution of this paper is to show how reference monitor synthesis, proof generation, and the policy logic are defined and interact. In future, we are interested in refining the system towards one in which the reference monitors are implemented in a low-level language and inserted into consumer code by binary rewriting, as demonstrated in [7]. Also desirable is a richer policy logic, such as a first order variant of P3TL; finally, a higher-level language that can be compiled into P3TL would ease the job of writing security policies.

Acknowledgements

We wish to thanks Kai Engelhardt and Harvey Tuch, along with the anonymous reviewers, for their valuable comments on earlier versions of this paper.

References

1. Necula, G.C.: Proof-carrying code. In: Proc. of POPL'97, Paris (1997) 106–119
2. Morrisett, G., Walker, D., Crary, K., Glew, N.: From System F to typed assembly language. TOPLAS **21** (1999) 527–568
3. Necula, G.C., Lee, P.: The design and implementation of a certifying compiler. In: Proc. of PLDI'98. Volume 33,5., New York, ACM Press (1998) 333–344
4. Aspinall, D., Gilmore, S., Hofmann, M., Sannella, D., Stark, I.: Mobile resource guarantees for smart devices. In: Proc. of CASSIS'04. Volume 3362 of LNCS., Springer (2005) 1–26
5. Manna, Z., Pnueli, A.: Temporal Verification of Reactive Systems: Safety. Springer-Verlag, New York (1995)
6. Schneider, F.B.: Enforceable security policies. Information and System Security **3** (2000) 30–50
7. Winwood, S., Chakravarty, M.M.T.: Secure untrusted binaries - provably!. In: Proc. of FAST'05. Volume 3866 of LNCS., Springer (2006) 171–186
8. Brewer, D.F.C., Nash, M.J.: The Chinese Wall security policy. In: IEEE Symposium on Security and Privacy. (1989) 206–214

9. Havelund, K., Rosu, G.: Synthesizing monitors for safety properties. In: Proc. of TACAS'02. Volume 2280 of LNCS., Springer (2002) 342–356
10. Barthe, G., Rezk, T., Saabas, A.: Proof obligations preserving compilation. In: Proc. of FAST'05. Volume 3866 of LNCS., Springer (2006) 112–126
11. Manna, Z., Pnueli, A.: The anchored version of the temporal framework. In de Bakker, J.W., de Roever, W.P., Rozenberg, G., eds.: Linear Time, Branching Time and Partial Order in Logics and Models for Concurrency. Volume 354 of LNCS., Springer (1989) 201–284
12. Nipkow, T.: Hoare logics in Isabelle/HOL. In Schwichtenberg, H., Steinbrüggen, R., eds.: Proof and System-Reliability, Kluwer (2002) 341–367
13. Lichtenstein, O., Pnueli, A.: Propositional temporal logics: Decidability and completeness. Logic Journal of the IGPL **8** (2000) 55–85
14. Geilen, M.: On the construction of monitors for temporal logic properties. Volume 55. (2001)
15. Bernard, A., Lee, P.: Temporal logic for proof-carrying code. In: Proc. of CADE'02, London, UK, Springer-Verlag (2002) 31–46
16. Holzmann, G.J.: The model checker spin. IEEE Trans. Software Eng. **23** (1997) 279–295
17. Chen, F., d'Amorim, M., Rosu, G.: A formal monitoring-based framework for software development and analysis. In: Proc. of ICFEM'04. Volume 3308 of LNCS., Springer (2004) 357–372
18. d'Amorim, M., Rosu, G.: Efficient monitoring of omega-languages. Volume 3576 of LNCS. (2005) 364–378
19. Barringer, H., Goldberg, A., Havelund, K., Sen, K.: Program monitoring with LTL in EAGLE. In: Proc. of PADTAD'04. (2004)
20. Peled, D., Zuck, L.: From model checking to a temporal proof. In: Proc. of SPIN'01, New York, NY, USA, Springer (2001) 1–14
21. Nipkow, T., Paulson, L.C., Wenzel, M.: Isabelle/HOL - A Proof Assistant for Higher-Order Logic. Volume 2283 of LNCS. Springer (2002)

Synthesis of Asynchronous Systems*

Sven Schewe and Bernd Finkbeiner

Universität des Saarlandes, 66123 Saarbrücken, Germany
{schewe|finkbeiner}@cs.uni-sb.de

Abstract. This paper addresses the problem of synthesizing an asynchronous system from a temporal specification. We show that the cost of synthesizing a single-process implementation is the same for synchronous and asynchronous systems (2EXPTIME-complete for CTL* and EXPTIME-complete for the μ-calculus) if we assume a full scheduler (i.e., a scheduler that allows every possible scheduling), and exponentially more expensive for asynchronous systems without this assumption (3EXPTIME-complete for CTL* and 2EXPTIME-complete for the μ-calculus). While multi-process synthesis for synchronous distributed systems is possible for certain architectures (like pipelines and rings), we show that the synthesis of asynchronous distributed systems is decidable if and only if at most one process implementation is unknown.

1 Introduction

Synthesis automatically transforms a specification into an implementation that is guaranteed to satisfy the specification. For *synchronous* systems, the synthesis problem is well-understood. Synthesizing single-process implementations is EXPTIME-complete for the μ-calculus [5,9], and 2EXPTIME-complete for linear-time temporal logic (LTL) and computation-tree logic (CTL*) [7,9,6]. Multi-process synthesis, the problem of finding implementations for the processes in a given distributed architecture, has been solved for pipelines [13], rings [10], and in general for all architectures without information forks (i.e., pairs of processes with incomparable information) [3].

By contrast, the problem of synthesizing *asynchronous* systems has so far received very little attention: the synthesis algorithms in the literature are limited to LTL specifications and single-process implementations. The first solution for asynchronous synthesis with specifications in LTL, but without fairness conditions, is due to Pnueli and Rosner [12]. Anuchitanukul and Manna [1] later showed that fairness conditions can be included in a deductive approach; Vardi [14] provided an automata-based algorithm for the same problem.

The question arises if the lack of synthesis algorithms for asynchronous systems is a coincidence or rather an indication of an inherent hardness of the synthesis problem for asynchronous systems. In this paper, we systematically

---

* This work was partly supported by the German Research Foundation (DFG) as part of the Transregional Collaborative Research Center "Automatic Verification and Analysis of Complex Systems" (SFB/TR 14 AVACS).

study the challenges in extending synthesis to the asynchronous case and, in doing so, give a comprehensive answer to this question.

Challenge 1: Synthesizing asynchronous processes for branching-time specifications. We begin by generalizing the synthesis of single-process implementations from linear-time to branching-time specifications. The behavior of an asynchronous process depends on the scheduler: while synchronous processes are aware of each change to their inputs, asynchronous processes may fail to see certain changes (when the writing process is scheduled more often than the reading process) and may see duplicate input values (when the reading process is scheduled multiple times between two writes). For linear-time specifications, asynchronous processes are typically analyzed in combination with a *full* scheduler, which allows every possible scheduling to occur along some path of the computation tree. In our first algorithm, we adapt this setting to branching-time specifications and synthesize an asynchronous process implementation such that the computation tree that results from the combination with a full scheduler satisfies the branching-time specification. The algorithm runs in exponential time for μ-calculus specifications and in double exponential time for CTL*. We thus obtain the result that *under full scheduling, the cost of synthesizing single-process implementations is the same for synchronous and asynchronous systems.*

Challenge 2: Synthesizing scheduler-independent implementations. Dropping the assumption of a full scheduler leads to the problem of synthesizing *scheduler-independent* implementations: we require that the implementation must satisfy the specification for *every* scheduler. For LTL (and, more generally, for universal specifications), the two synthesis problems coincide. For branching-time specifications, scheduler-independent synthesis is the strictly more general problem. Consider the existential specification "there is a path where the output of the process changes in every second step." This specification can trivially be satisfied under the assumption of a full scheduler, but there is no implementation that guarantees this specification for all schedulers. Scheduler-independent synthesis allows us to explicitly state the assumptions on the scheduler as part of the specification. An interesting example for such an assumption is fairness. While synthesis under full scheduling allows us to find implementations that perform correctly on *fair paths* ("there is a *fair scheduling* where the output of the process changes in every second step"), scheduler-independent synthesis allows us to find implementations that perform correctly whenever the scheduling is fair ("if the *scheduler* is *fair* on all paths then there is a path where the output of the process changes in every second step"). In our second algorithm, we synthesize an asynchronous process implementation such that *any* computation tree that results from the combination of the process with some scheduler satisfies the branching-time specification. The algorithm runs in double exponential time for μ-calculus specifications and in triple exponential time for CTL*. We provide matching lower bounds for both logics, obtaining the result that *scheduler-independent synthesis is exponentially harder than synthesis under full scheduling.*

Challenge 3: Synthesizing asynchronous distributed systems. We finally consider the multi-process synthesis problem, where the distributed architecture is given as a directed graph. Each process is either identified as black-box, if its implementation is to be determined by the synthesis algorithm, or as white-box, if the implementation is already known and fixed. In the synchronous case, the distributed synthesis problem is decidable if and only if the architecture does not contain an information fork [3]. We show that in the asynchronous case, *the distributed synthesis problem is decidable if and only if the architecture contains only a single black-box process.*

Our results thus demonstrate that, except for the case of single-process implementations and full scheduling, the synthesis of asynchronous systems is indeed harder than the synthesis of synchronous systems. Our algorithms solve the distributed synthesis problem for architectures with a single black-box process. Since the synthesis problem is undecidable for all architectures with two or more black-box processes, it is impossible to extend our algorithms to a larger set of architectures.

2   The Synthesis Problem

We study the synthesis problem in the general setting of distributed systems. The *synthesis problem* is to decide for the triple $(A, \varphi, \{s_w | w \in W\})$, consisting of an architecture A, a specification φ, and a set of white-box strategies $\{s_w | w \in W\}$, whether there exists a finite-state program (or *strategy*) for each black-box process in A, such that the joint behavior satisfies φ.

Architectures.   An architecture A is a tuple (P, W, p_{env}, E, O, H), where P is a set of processes with a subset $W \subset P$ of white-box processes and a distinguished environment process $p_{env} \in P \setminus W$. (P, E) is a directed graph, $O = \{O_e | e \in E\}$ a set of nonempty sets of (output) variables for every edge and $H = \{H_p | p \in P\}$ a pairwise disjoint set of (possibly empty) sets of hidden variables for every process such that $\bigcup_{e \in E} O_e \cap \bigcup_{p \in P} H_p = \emptyset$ and $e, e' \in E, O_e \cap O_{e'} \neq \emptyset \Rightarrow pr_1(e) = pr_1(e')$ hold (where pr_1 denotes the projection on the first element).

As additional notation, we use $V = \bigcup_{e \in E} O_e \cup \bigcup_{p \in P} H_p$ for the set of variables, $I_p = \bigcup_{p' \in P} O_{(p',p)}$ and $O_p = \bigcup_{p' \in P} O_{(p,p')} \cup H_p$ for the input and output, respectively, of a process p, and $P^- = P \setminus \{p_{env}\}$ for the set of system processes. The set $B = P^- \setminus W$ contains the black-box processes; we assume additionally that, for all $b \in B$, the output of a black-box process O_b is not empty (otherwise, the output is known and we turn b into a white-box process).

Implementations.   A process p is implemented by a *strategy*, i.e., a function $s_p : (2^{I_p})^* \to 2^{O_p}$. A strategy is *finite-state* if it can be represented by a finite-state automaton. An *implementation* of an architecture consists of strategies $S = \{s_p | p \in B\}$ for all black-box processes.

An implementation defines a computation tree. As usual, a *tree* is given as a prefix-closed subset $Y \subseteq \Upsilon^*$ of all finite words over a given set of directions Υ. If Y contains the empty word ε and a successor for every element

$(\forall y \in Y \exists v \in \Upsilon . y \cdot v \in \Upsilon)$, Y is called *total*, and if $Y = \Upsilon^*$, the tree is called *full*. For given finite sets Σ and Υ, a Σ-*labeled* Υ-*tree* is a pair $\langle Y, l \rangle$ with $Y \subseteq \Upsilon^*$ and a labeling function $l : Y \to \Sigma$ that maps every node of Y to a letter of Σ.

Computations. The computation tree identifies the system state (i.e., the values of the system variables and the currently scheduled processes) for every possible history of input assignments and scheduling decisions. For an implementation S and a set of white-box strategies $\{s_w | w \in W\}$, we define the *computation tree* as the full $2^{V \cup P}$-labeled $(2^{O_{env}} \cup \{\bot\}) \times 2^{P^-}$-tree $\langle ((2^{O_{env}} \cup \{\bot\}) \times 2^{P^-})^*, c \rangle$ with the following properties[1]:

- $c(\varepsilon) = \rho_0 \cup \bigcup_{p \in P^-} s_p(\varepsilon)$ and
- $c(x \cdot (v, \pi)) = \widehat{v} \cup \pi \cup \bigcup_{p \in P^-} s_p(vis_p(x))$, with
  - $\widehat{v} = v \cup \{p_{env}\}$, if $v \neq \bot$,
  - $\widehat{v} = c(x) \cap O_{env}$, if $v = \bot$, and
  - $vis_p : ((2^{O_{env}} \cup \{\bot\}) \times 2^{P^-})^* \to (2^{I_p})^*$, which maps a path in the computation tree to the input history of a process p, i.e.,
    * $vis_p(\varepsilon) = \varepsilon$,
    * $vis_p(x \cdot (v, \pi)) = vis_p(x)$ if $p \notin \pi$, and
    * $vis_p(x \cdot (v, \pi)) = vis_p(x) \cdot (c(x) \cap I_p)$ if $p \in \pi$.

Intuitively, $\bot$ denotes that the environment is not scheduled. In this case, the values of its output variables O_{env} remain unchanged.

The Scheduler. In every step, the scheduler makes a (possibly nondeterministic) choice which processes are scheduled. In a *full* scheduler, all choices are possible in each step. In general, some choices may be disabled, and the set of choices may depend on the history of states.

We formalize the scheduler as a function from $((2^{O_{env}} \cup \{\bot\}) \times 2^{P^-})^*$ to the set of potential scheduling decisions $\mathcal{P} = 2^{2^P}$, which consists of the sets of non-empty subsets of the set of processes. We represent the function as a $\mathcal{P}$-labeled Υ_A-tree $\langle \Upsilon_A^*, scheduler \rangle$, where $\Upsilon_A = (2^{O_{env}} \cup \{\bot\}) \times 2^{P^-}$ denotes the set of directions, and the label refers to the nondeterministic choice of the scheduler. A scheduler $\langle \Upsilon_A^*, scheduler \rangle$ defines a subset $Y_{scheduler} \subseteq \Upsilon_A^*$ of reachable nodes of Υ_A^*. $Y_{scheduler}$ can be defined inductively as the smallest subset of Υ_A^* with

- $\varepsilon \in Y_{scheduler}$,
- $\forall y \in Y_{scheduler} . P' \in scheduler(v) \wedge p_{env} \in P'$
    $\Rightarrow \forall O \subseteq O_{env} . y \cdot (O, P' \setminus \{p_{env}\}) \in Y_{scheduler}$, and
- $\forall y \in Y_{scheduler} . P' \in scheduler(v) \wedge p_{env} \notin P' \Rightarrow y \cdot (\bot, P') \in Y_{scheduler}$.

---

[1] For technical convenience, we fix $\rho_0 \subseteq O_{env} \cup P$, called the *fixed-root*, which is comparable to the fixing of a root direction in the synchronous case [7,8].

The Synthesis Problem.   A triple $(A, \varphi, \{s_w | w \in W\})$, consisting of an architecture A, a specification φ, and a set of white-box strategies $\{s_w | w \in W\}$, is called

- *realizable under full scheduling* if there exists an implementation S, such that the computation tree $\langle \Upsilon_A{}^*, c \rangle$ of S satisfies φ; and
- *scheduler-independently realizable* if there exists an implementation S with the computation tree $\langle \Upsilon_A{}^*, c \rangle$ such that, for all schedulers $\langle \Upsilon_A{}^*, scheduler \rangle$, $\langle Y_{scheduler}, c \rangle$ satisfies φ.

We call an architecture A (scheduler-independently) *decidable* if an algorithm exists that decides for all specifications φ and all sets of finite-state white-box strategies $\{s_w | w \in W\}$ if $(A, \varphi, \{s_w | w \in W\})$ is (scheduler-independently) realizable.

3   Single-Process Synthesis Under Full Scheduling

In this section, we show that under the assumption of full scheduling, the cost of synthesizing single-process implementations is the same for synchronous and asynchronous systems. We develop an automata-theoretic synthesis algorithm for asynchronous systems with a single black-box process. The algorithm runs in EXPTIME in the length of a CTL or μ-calculus specification and in 2EXPTIME in the length of a CTL* specification.

3.1   Preliminaries: Tree Automata

An *alternating automaton* $\mathcal{A} = (\Sigma, Q, q_0, \delta, \alpha)$ runs on full Σ-labeled Υ-trees (for a predefined finite set Υ of directions). Q denotes a finite set of states, $q_0 \in Q$ denotes a designated initial state, δ denotes a transition function $\delta : Q \times \Sigma \to \mathbb{B}^+(Q \times \Upsilon_\varepsilon)$, where Υ_ε denotes $\Upsilon \cup \{\varepsilon\}$, and α is an acceptance condition.

A *run tree* on a given Σ-labeled Υ-tree $\langle \Upsilon^*, l \rangle$ is a $Q \times \Upsilon^*$-labeled tree where the root is labeled with (q_0, ε) and where for a node n with a label (q, x) and a set $child(n)$ of children, the labels of these children have the following properties:

- for all children $m \in child(n)$ of n, the label of m is $(q_m, x \cdot v_m)$ for some $q_m \in Q$ and $v_m \in \Upsilon_\varepsilon$ such that (q_m, v_m) is an atom of $\delta(q, l(x))$, and
- the set of atoms defined by the children of n satisfies $\delta(q, l(x))$.

A run tree is *accepting* if all its paths fulfill the acceptance condition. A *parity condition* is a function α from Q to a finite set $C \subset \mathbb{N}$ of colors. A path is accepted if the highest color appearing infinitely often is even.

A full Σ-labeled Υ-tree is accepted if it has an accepting run tree. The set of trees accepted by an alternating automaton $\mathcal{A}$ is called its *language* $\mathcal{L}(\mathcal{A})$. An automaton called is empty, if its language is empty. The acceptance of a tree can also be viewed as the outcome of a game, where player *accept* chooses, for every pair $(q, \sigma) \in Q \times \Sigma$, a set of atoms of $\delta(q, \sigma)$, satisfying $\delta(q, \sigma)$, and player *reject* chooses one of these atoms, which is executed. The input tree is accepted iff player *accept* has a strategy enforcing a path fulfilling α.

If $\delta : Q \times \Sigma \rightarrow \mathbb{B}^+(Q \times \Upsilon)$, i.e., if there are no ε-transitions, the alternating automaton is called *ε-free*. A *nondeterministic* automaton is a special ε-free alternating automaton, where the image of δ consists only of such formulas that, when rewritten in disjunctive normal form, contain exactly one element of $Q \times \{v\}$ for all $v \in \Upsilon$ in every disjunct. For nondeterministic automata, every node of a run tree corresponds to a node in the input tree. The emptiness of a nondeterministic automaton can be checked with the *emptiness game*, where player *accept* also chooses the letter of the input alphabet. A nondeterministic automaton is empty iff the emptiness game is won by *reject*.

Symmetric alternating automata are a variant of alternating automata that run on total Σ-labeled trees. For a symmetric alternating automaton $\mathcal{S} = (\Sigma, Q, q_0, \delta, \alpha)$, Q, q_0, and α are defined as before. The transition function $\delta : Q \times \Sigma \rightarrow \mathbb{B}^+(Q \times \{\Box, \Diamond, \varepsilon\})$ now maps a state and an input letter to a positive boolean combination over atoms that refer to *all* ($\Box$) successor nodes, *some* ($\Diamond$) successor node or the current (ε) node.

3.2 Overview

The algorithm assumes an architecture A with a single black-box process b. It starts by representing a specification φ as a symmetric alternating parity automaton $\mathcal{A}_\varphi$, which is transformed into a nondeterministic automaton $\mathcal{N}_\varphi$ that accepts a tree $\langle (2^{I_b})^*, s_b \rangle$ iff s_b is an implementation of φ. The solution of the emptiness game for $\mathcal{N}_\varphi$ then provides such an implementation.

The following are the main steps of the algorithm:

- **From formulas to automata.** We first construct the symmetric alternating parity automaton $\mathcal{A}_\varphi$, with $\mathcal{L}(\mathcal{A}_\varphi) = \mathcal{M}_\varphi$ (Lemma 1).
  In this section, $\mathcal{A}_\varphi$ is only used for $2^{V \cup P}$-labeled Υ_A-trees, i.e., for trees with the shape and labeling of the computation trees.
- **From computation trees to strategy trees.** We then construct the alternating parity automaton $\mathcal{S}_\varphi$ that accepts a strategy tree $\langle (2^{I_p})^*, s_p \rangle$ iff its computation tree is accepted by $\mathcal{A}_\varphi$ (Lemma 2).
- **Nondeterminization.** In a third step, we construct a nondeterministic parity automaton $\mathcal{N}_\varphi$, with $\mathcal{L}(\mathcal{N}_\varphi) = \mathcal{L}(\mathcal{S}_\varphi)$ (Lemmata 3 and 4).
- **Strategy construction.** Finally, we construct a strategy for the black-box process such that the induced computation tree is a model of φ (or demonstrate that no such strategy exists) by solving the emptiness game for $\mathcal{N}_\varphi$ (Lemma 5).

We now describe the automata transformations of the construction in more detail.

3.3 From Formulas to Automata

The symmetric alternating parity automaton $\mathcal{A}_\varphi$ can be built from a temporal or fixed point specification φ using standard constructions.

Lemma 1. *Given a μ-calculus specification φ, we can construct a symmetric alternating automaton $\mathcal{A}_\varphi$ with $O(|\varphi|)$ states such that $\mathcal{L}(\mathcal{A}_\varphi) = \mathcal{M}_\varphi$ [8,9].*
Given a CTL* specification φ, we can construct a symmetric alternating automaton $\mathcal{A}_\varphi$ with $2^{O(|\varphi|)}$ states such that $\mathcal{L}(\mathcal{A}_\varphi) = \mathcal{M}_\varphi$ [8].   □

$\mathcal{A}_\varphi$ can be transformed into an ordinary alternating automaton over full Υ-trees by replacing each occurrence of $(q, \square)$ and $(q, \diamond)$ in the transition function by $\bigwedge_{v \in \Upsilon}(q, v)$ and $\bigvee_{v \in \Upsilon}(q, v)$, respectively.

3.4   From Computation Trees to Strategy Trees

The central automata transformation for asynchronous synthesis is the transformation of an alternating parity automaton $\mathcal{A}_\varphi$ recognizing a set of computation trees into an alternating parity automaton $\mathcal{S}_\varphi$ that accepts those implementations whose computation trees are accepted by $\mathcal{A}_\varphi$.

We assume that the strategies $\{s_w | w \in W\}$ of the white-box processes are given as a family of *strategy automata* $\{\mathcal{S}_w = (I_w, S_w, s_0^w, d_w, o_w) | w \in W\}$. A strategy automaton is a Moore machine, where

- a state $s \in S_w$ represents the quotient class of equivalent positions in the strategy tree $\langle(2^{I_w})^*, s_w\rangle$;
- the initial state s_0^w represents the quotient class including the root of the strategy tree;
- $o_w : S_w \to 2^{O_w}$ maps each state of $\mathcal{S}_w$ to an output label of the process w;
- upon reading an input $v \in 2^{I_w} \cup \{\varepsilon\}$, the automaton proceeds to the state $s' = d_w(s, v)$, and returns the label $o_w(s')$ of this state.
  An ε-transition does not change the state $(d_w(s, \varepsilon) = s)$.

We construct the automaton $\mathcal{S}_\varphi$ accepting the strategy trees of the black-box process by simulating $\mathcal{A}_\varphi$ on the (implicitly defined) computation tree.

Given a strategy s_b of the black-box process b and a set of strategies $\{s_w | w \in W\}$ for the white-box processes, represented by strategy automata $\{\mathcal{S}_w | w \in W\}$, the computation tree $\langle((2^{O_{env}} \cup \{\bot\}) \times 2^{P^-})^*, c\rangle$ can be constructed by setting
$c : \varepsilon \mapsto \bigcup_{w \in W} \mathcal{S}_w(\varepsilon) \cup s_b(\varepsilon) \cup \rho_0$, and $c : x \cdot (v, \pi) \mapsto \bigcup_{w \in \pi \cap W} \mathcal{S}_w(c(x) \cap (I_p)) \cup$
$\bigcup_{w \in W \smallsetminus \pi} \mathcal{S}_w(\varepsilon) \cup \widehat{v} \cup \pi \cup s_b(vis_b(x))$, where vis_b and $\widehat{v}$ are taken from the definition
of computation trees.

To obtain $\mathcal{S}_\varphi$, we add the output of the environment and of the white-box processes to the states of the automaton.

Lemma 2. *Let $A = (P, W, p_{env}, E, O, H)$ be a given architecture with $B = \{b\}$, let $\{s_w | w \in W\}$ be a given set of white-box strategies represented as strategy automata $\{\mathcal{S}_w = (I_w, S_w, s_0^w, d_w, o_w) | w \in W\}$, and let $\mathcal{A}_\varphi = (2^{V \cup P}, Q, q_0, \delta, \alpha)$ be an alternating parity automaton running on $2^{V \cup P}$-labeled $(2^{O_{env}} \cup \{\bot\}) \times 2^{P^-}$-trees. Then we can, for $S = \bigotimes_{w \in W} S_w$, construct an alternating parity automaton $\mathcal{S} = (2^{O_p}, Q \times S \times 2^{P \cup O_{env}}, q_0', \delta', \alpha')$ running on 2^{O_p}-labeled 2^{I_p}-trees that accepts a strategy tree $\langle(2^{I_p})^*, s_p\rangle$ if its computation tree is accepted by $\mathcal{A}$.*

Proof. We simulate the behavior of $\mathcal{A}_\varphi$ on the computation tree $\langle \Upsilon_A^*, c \rangle$ that is defined by the strategy tree $\langle (2^{I_b})^*, s_b \rangle$. First, we set q_0' to $(q_0, \{s_0^w\}_{w \in W}, \rho_0)$. For $\Sigma = 2^{V \cup P}$, $\Upsilon = \Upsilon_A = (2^{O_{env}} \cup \{\bot\}) \times 2^{P^-}$ and $\delta : Q \times \Sigma \to Q \times \Upsilon_\varepsilon$ with $\delta : (q, \sigma) \mapsto b_{(q,\sigma)}^n (q_i, \upsilon_i)_{i \in \mathbb{N}_n}$ that assigns positive boolean combinations of states and directions to each state and input letter, we define $\delta' : Q \times S \times 2^{O_{env} \cup P} \times 2^{O_b} \to Q \times S \times 2_\varepsilon^{I_p}$ as $\delta' : (q, s, \sigma_{env}, \sigma_b) \mapsto b_{(q, \bigcup_{w \in W} o_w(s) \cup \sigma_{env} \cup \sigma_b)}^n (q_i, f(s, \sigma_{env}, \sigma_b, \upsilon_i), g(s, \sigma_{env}, \sigma_b, \upsilon_i))_{i \in \mathbb{N}_n}$, where f and g are auxiliary functions.

The function f preserves the correct states of the strategy automata $\mathcal{S}_w$ in S and memorizes the values of the variables controlled by the environment ($O_{env} \cup P$). The former is done by applying the correct transition functions to the states of the strategy automata, the latter by storing the correct environment output. $f : \{s^w\}_{w \in W} \times \sigma_{env} \times \sigma_b \times \upsilon \mapsto (\{s^{w\prime}\}_{w \in W}, \sigma_{env}')$ has the following properties:

- $\forall w \in W : w \notin \upsilon \Rightarrow s^{w\prime} = s^w$,
- $\forall w \in W : w \in \upsilon \Rightarrow s^{w\prime} = d_w(s^w, (\bigcup_{w \in W} o_w(s^w) \cup \sigma_{env} \cup \sigma_b) \cap I_w)$;
- $\upsilon = \varepsilon \Rightarrow \sigma_{env}' = \sigma_{env}$,
- $\upsilon \neq \varepsilon \Rightarrow \sigma_{env}' \cap P^- = \upsilon \cap P^-$ and
  - $\bot \in \upsilon \Rightarrow \sigma_{env}' \cap O_{env} = \sigma_{env} \cap O_{env}, p_{env} \notin \sigma_{env}'$ and
  - $\bot \notin \upsilon \neq \varepsilon \Rightarrow \sigma_{env}' \cap O_{env} = \upsilon \cap O_{env}, p_{env} \in \sigma_{env}'$.

The function g maps the label and direction of the computation tree to a direction in the strategy tree of b; if b is scheduled, $g(\upsilon)$ is the I_b part of the label, if b is not scheduled (including the ε-transition), the position in the strategy tree remains unchanged. $g : S \times 2^{O_{env} \cup P} \times 2^{O_b} \times \Upsilon_\varepsilon \to 2_\varepsilon^{I_b}$ has the following properties:

- $g : \upsilon \mapsto \varepsilon$ if $b \notin \upsilon$ and
- $g : \upsilon \mapsto (\bigcup_{w \in W} o_w(s^w) \cup \sigma_{env} \cup \sigma_b) \cap I_b$ if $b \in \upsilon$.

Obviously, for $\alpha' : (q, s, o) \mapsto \alpha(q)$, a strategy tree is accepted by $\mathcal{S}$ iff its computation tree is accepted by $\mathcal{A}$. □

3.5 Nondeterminization

To check $\mathcal{S}_\varphi$ for emptiness, we first eliminate the ε-transitions and then construct an equivalent nondeterministic parity automaton.

Lemma 3. *[15,9] Given an alternating parity automaton $\mathcal{S}$ with n states, we can construct an ε-free alternating parity automaton $\mathcal{S}'$ with at most n^2 states.* □

Lemma 4. *[11,3] Given an alternating parity automaton $\mathcal{S}_\varphi$ with n states, we can construct a nondeterministic parity automaton $\mathcal{N}_\varphi$ with $n^{O(n^2)}$ states and $O(n^2)$ colors.* □

3.6   Strategy Construction

In the last step, we obtain a strategy by solving the emptiness game of the resulting nondeterministic parity automaton $\mathcal{N}_\varphi$.

Lemma 5. *Given a nondeterministic automaton $\mathcal{N} = (\Sigma, Q, q_0, \delta, \alpha)$ running on Σ-labeled Υ-trees with n states and c colors, we can construct a regular tree accepted by $\mathcal{N}$ or show that the language of $\mathcal{N}$ is empty in time $n^{O(c)}$.*

Proof. The nonemptiness problem can be reduced to a parity game with at most $n + n^{|\Upsilon|}$ states and c colors: Player *accept* owns the states Q and chooses a label $\sigma \in \Sigma$ and a conjunction $\bigwedge_{v \in \Upsilon}(q_v, v)$ satisfying $\delta(q, \sigma)$. Player *reject* owns these conjunctions and can move from a state $\bigwedge_{v \in \Upsilon}(q_v, v)$ to a state q_v by choosing a direction $v \in \Upsilon$. The colors of the states of player *accept* are defined by the coloring function α, while all states of player *reject* are colored by the minimum color in the mapping of α. This parity game can be solved in time $n^{O(c)}$ [4].

  $\mathcal{N}$ is empty iff player *reject* has a winning strategy, and the Σ-projection of a memoryless winning strategy for player *accept* defines a regular tree.   □

3.7   Complexity

The construction described in Section 3.2 provides EXPTIME and 2EXPTIME upper bounds for the synthesis problems under full scheduling in case of μ-calculus and CTL* specifications, respectively. Matching lower bounds can be inferred from the known lower bounds for the synthesis problems for CTL and CTL* in synchronous systems by applying linear specification transformations.

Theorem 1. *The distributed synthesis problem under full scheduling for architectures with a single black-box process is EXPTIME-complete for specifications in CTL and the μ-calculus and 2EXPTIME-complete for CTL* specifications.*

Proof. The upper bounds follow from the construction suggested in Section 3.2 together with the Lemmata 1 through 5.

  We establish the lower bound for the special case of architectures without white-box processes. We reduce the synthesis problem for this case from the synthesis problem for the synchronous setting, which is EXPTIME-hard for CTL and 2EXPTIME-hard for CTL* [8]. The reduction is by a linear transformation of each CTL or CTL* formula φ_{sync} that reasons only over the specification variables V, to a CTL or CTL* specification φ_{async}, respectively, such that φ_{async} is realizable iff φ_{sync} if realizable in the synchronous setting.

  For CTL specifications, we replace every occurrence of $A\varphi U\psi$, $E\varphi U\psi$, $AX\psi$ and $EX\psi$ by $A\varphi U(\psi \vee \neg b \vee \neg p_{env})$, $E(\varphi \wedge b \wedge p_{env})U(\psi \wedge b \wedge p_{env})$, $AX(b \wedge p_{env} \rightarrow \psi)$ and $EX(b \wedge p_{env} \wedge \psi)$, respectively.

  For CTL* specifications, we replace every occurrence of $A\pi$ by $A(G(b \wedge p_{env}) \rightarrow \pi)$ and every occurrence of $E\pi$ by $E(G(b \wedge p_{env}) \wedge \pi)$.

  A strategy s_b for the black-box process is obviously a realization for the transformed specification iff s_b realizes the original specification in the synchronous setting.

The EXPTIME lower bound for CTL implies the EXPTIME lower bound for the μ-calculus, and the EXPTIME upper bound for the μ-calculus establishes a matching upper bound for CTL.   □

4   Synthesis of Scheduler-Independent Implementations

We now present an algorithm for *scheduler-independent* synthesis, where we only consider implementations that satisfy the specification for *all* schedulers. Scheduler-independent synthesis can also be used to find implementations that satisfy their specification if the scheduler satisfies assumptions that are explicitly stated in the specification.

4.1   Overview

We again begin with an overview over the main steps of the construction. The algorithm runs in 2EXPTIME and 3EXPTIME in the length of a μ-calculus and CTL* specification, respectively.

- **From formulas to symmetric automata.** We first construct the symmetric alternating parity automaton $\mathcal{A}_\varphi$, with $\mathcal{L}(\mathcal{A}_\varphi) = \mathcal{M}_\varphi$ (Lemma 1).
- **Considering a scheduler.** We then construct the alternating parity automaton $\mathcal{B}_\varphi$ that accepts the product $\langle \varUpsilon_A^*, scheduler \times c \rangle$ of a scheduler $\langle \varUpsilon_A^*, scheduler \rangle$ and a computation tree $\langle \varUpsilon_A^*, c \rangle$ iff $\langle Y_{scheduler}, c \rangle$ is accepted by $\mathcal{A}_\varphi$ (Lemma 6).
- **Quantification over all schedulers.** In a third step, we construct an alternating automaton $\mathcal{C}_\varphi$ that accepts a computation tree $\langle \varUpsilon_A^*, c \rangle$ iff, for all schedulers $\langle \varUpsilon_A^*, scheduler \rangle$, the product $\langle \varUpsilon_A^*, scheduler \times c \rangle$ of the computation tree and the scheduler is accepted by $\mathcal{B}_\varphi$ (Lemmata 3 and 7).
- **Strategy construction.** Finally, we construct a strategy for the black-box process such that the induced computation tree is accepted by $\mathcal{C}_\varphi$ or demonstrate that no such strategy exists (Lemmata 2 through 5).

4.2   Considering a Scheduler

To check whether a symmetric alternating automaton $\mathcal{A}$ accepts $\langle Y_{scheduler}, c \rangle$ for a given scheduler $\langle \varUpsilon_A^*, scheduler \rangle$ and a given a computation tree $\langle \varUpsilon_A^*, c \rangle$, we use the scheduler to determine which successors of a node $y \in Y_{scheduler}$ are contained in $Y_{scheduler}$. For universal atoms $(q, \square)$, the copies are sent only to these successors, and for existential atoms, the copy is sent to one of them.

Lemma 6. *Given a symmetric alternating automaton* $\mathcal{A} = (2^{V \cup P}, Q, q_0, \delta, \alpha)$, *running on total* $2^{V \cup P}$-*labeled trees, we can construct an alternating automaton* $\mathcal{B} = (\mathcal{P} \times 2^{V \cup P}, Q, q_0, \delta', \alpha)$ *running on full* $\mathcal{P} \times 2^{V \cup P}$-*labeled* $\varUpsilon_A$-*trees that accepts a tree* $\langle \varUpsilon_A^*, scheduler \times c \rangle$ *iff* $\langle Y_{scheduler}, c \rangle$ *is accepted by* $\mathcal{A}$.

Proof. $\mathcal{B}$ simply uses the first element of the label of each node in $\langle \Upsilon_A{}^*, scheduler \times c \rangle$ it traverses to determine which successors, according to the definition of $Y_{scheduler}$, really exist.

$\delta'(q'; \pi, \sigma)$ can be constructed from $\delta(q'; \sigma)$ by replacing, for all $q \in Q$,

- each occurrence of $(q, \Box)$ and $(q, \Diamond)$ by $(q, (\bot, \pi))$ if $p_{env} \notin \pi$,
- each occurrence of $(q, \Box)$ by $\bigwedge_{O \subseteq O_{env}} (q, (O, \pi))$ if $p_{env} \in \pi$, and
- each occurrence of $(q, \Diamond)$ by $\bigvee_{O \subseteq O_{env}} (q, (O, \pi))$ if $p_{env} \in \pi$.   □

4.3   Quantification over All Schedulers

We are only interested in implementations that realize the specification for all schedulers.

For a $\Sigma \times \Xi$-labeled Υ-tree $\langle Y, l \rangle$, we denote the Ξ-*projection* $proj_\Xi : \langle Y, l \rangle \mapsto \langle Y, l_\Xi \rangle$ with $l(y) = (\sigma, \xi) \Rightarrow l_\Sigma : y \mapsto \xi$ that maps $\Sigma \times \Xi$-labeled Υ-trees to Ξ-labeled Υ-trees.

Lemma 7. *[2] Given an ε-free alternating automaton $\mathcal{B}$ running on $\Sigma \times \Xi$-labeled Υ-trees, we can construct an ε-free alternating automaton $\mathcal{C}$ that accepts a Ξ-labeled Υ tree $\langle \Upsilon^*, l \rangle$ iff $\mathcal{B}$ accepts all $\Sigma \times \Xi$-labeled Υ-trees $\langle \Upsilon^*, l' \rangle$ with $\langle \Upsilon^*, l \rangle = proj_\Xi(\langle \Upsilon^*, l' \rangle)$. The number of states of $\mathcal{C}$ is exponential in the number of states of $\mathcal{B}$, and the number of colors of $\mathcal{C}$ is quadratic in the number of states of $\mathcal{B}$.*   □

4.4   Complexity

The construction provides 2EXPTIME and 3EXPTIME upper bounds in the length of a specification for the scheduler-independent synthesis problems of μ-calculus and CTL* specifications, respectively.

The 3EXPTIME hardness of scheduler-independent realizability checking for CTL* can be obtained by a reduction from the CTL* synthesis problem for synchronous systems in reactive environments [6].

Theorem 2. *The scheduler-independent realizability and synthesis problem is 2EXPTIME-complete for μ-calculus specifications and in 3EXPTIME-complete for specifications in CTL*.*

Proof. The upper bounds follow from the construction suggested in this section. To establish the lower bound for CTL* specifications, we transform a CTL* specification φ, which reasons only over the communication variables V, into a CTL* specification ψ_φ, which is scheduler-independent realizable iff φ is realizable in a synchronous setting with a reactive environment [6]. The environment is called reactive if it can disable a subset (but not all) of its responses in each turn. A full $2^{O_b \cup I_b}$-labeled 2^{I_b}-tree $\langle (2^{I_b})^*, l \rangle$ is a realization of φ in a reactive environment iff every total subtree of $\langle (2^{I_b})^*, l \rangle$ is a model of φ and the 2^{I_b}-projection of $\langle (2^{I_b})^*, l \rangle$ is a tree, where every node is labeled with its direction $(proj_{2^{I_b}}(\langle (2^{I_b})^*, l \rangle) = \langle (2^{I_b})^*, dir \rangle)$.

Our transformation puts three assumptions on the scheduler: First, we assume that the environment is always scheduled ($\alpha_1 = AG\, p_{env}$). Then, we assume that the process b is scheduled initially and, once it is not scheduled is never scheduled again ($\alpha_2 = b \wedge A\, b\, U\, G\neg b$). And last, we assume that if b is scheduled, then there is a path where b as always scheduled ($\alpha_3 = AG\,(b \rightarrow EG\,b)$).

For architectures without white-box processes and $O_{env} = I_b$, there is a natural bijection between total 2^{I_b}-trees and schedulers that fulfills these assumptions: We simply map a total 2^{I_b}-tree Y to the scheduler $\langle((2^{I_b} \cup \{\bot\}) \times 2^{\{b\}})^*, scheduler_Y\rangle$ that always schedules the environment and b is scheduled iff the 2^{I_b} projection of the input sequence is in Y:

$$b \in scheduler_Y(y) \Leftrightarrow y \in (2^{I_b} \times \{b\})^* \wedge proj_{2^{I_b}}(y) \in Y.$$

The restriction of the scheduler tree of $scheduler_Y$ to those nodes where b is scheduled results in a tree that is isomorphic to Y. Consequently, if we transform a CTL* specification φ to a specification φ' by replacing all quantifications over all paths/some path by quantifications over all paths/some path, where b is constantly scheduled, an implementation $\langle(2^{I_b})^*, s_b\rangle$ realizes φ for a given total tree Y in the synchronous setting iff it realizes φ' for the scheduler $scheduler_Y$. $\langle(2^{I_b})^*, s_b\rangle$ is therefore a realization of φ in a synchronous setting with a reactive environment iff it is a realization of φ for all schedulers which satisfy the assumptions α_1, α_2 and α_3. This is equivalent to realizing $\psi_\varphi = (\alpha_1 \wedge \alpha_2 \wedge \alpha_3) \rightarrow \varphi'$ for all schedulers.

Since φ' can be obtained from φ by replacing each occurrence of $A\pi$ and $E\pi$ in φ by $A(Gb \rightarrow \pi)$ and $E(Gb \wedge \pi)$, respectively, the length of ψ_φ is linear in the length of φ. The 3EXPTIME hardness of scheduler-independent realizability checking for CTL* specifications therefore follows from the 3EXPTIME hardness of realizability checking for CTL* specifications in a synchronous setting with a reactive environment [6]. The 2EXPTIME hardness for realizability checking for the μ-calculus is a direct implication.

4.5   Synthesis with Explicit Assumptions on the Scheduler

We close the discussion of scheduler-independent synthesis with the remark that this type of synthesis can also be used to find implementations that satisfy a specification φ as long as the scheduler satisfies an explicitly stated *assumption* α: we simply weaken the specification to $\varphi' = \alpha \rightarrow \varphi$.

The assumption α might, for example, specifically specify a round-robin scheduler. The most common assumption on schedulers, however, is *fairness*: A scheduling is considered *impartial* towards a process p if p is scheduled infinitely often, *just* if p is infinitely often disabled or scheduled, and *compassionate* if p being enabled infinitely often implies that p is scheduled infinitely often. The enabledness $enabled(p)$ of a process $p \in P^-$ can be expressed using new hidden variables for the processes. Quantifying over all fair schedulers for a specification φ is equivalent to quantifying over all schedulers for a modified specification φ' that is satisfied both if φ is satisfied or if the scheduler is not fair. With the fairness condition expressed as a path formula (for example, justice is expressed by $\pi_p = GF \neg enabled(p) \vee GFp)$, we obtain the fairness constraint $\pi = \bigwedge_{p \in P^-} \pi_p$. The modified specification φ' is the disjunction $\varphi' = \neg A\pi \rightarrow \varphi$.

Synthesis under full scheduling and scheduler-independent synthesis thus give us two different approaches to deal with fairness assumptions. While synthesis under full scheduling allows us to require that a property hold for all fair *schedules* (by replacing all occurrences of $A\psi$ and $E\psi$ in CTL* specifications by $A(\pi \rightarrow \psi)$ and $E(\pi \wedge \psi)$, respectively), scheduler-independent synthesis allows us to require that a property hold for all fair *schedulers*.

5   Multi-process Synthesis

The algorithms from Sections 3 and 4 solve the synthesis problem for all architectures with a single black-box process. We now show that for all architectures with more than one black-box process, the synthesis problem is undecidable. Our synthesis algorithms thus cover all decidable asynchronous architectures.

The following theorem states the undecidability result for synthesis under full scheduling; the undecidability of scheduler-independent synthesis follows as a corollary.

Theorem 3. *The synthesis problem is undecidable for all architectures with at least two black-box processes and CTL or LTL specifications.*

Proof. We prove undecidability with a reduction from Post's Correspondence Problem (PCP). For a given alphabet A, an instance of PCP consists of an indexed set of pairs of words $(u_i, v_i), u_i, v_i \in A^+, i \in I = \{1, \ldots, n\}$, over an alphabet A. A solution of PCP is a sequence of indices $i_1, i_2, \ldots, i_m \in I^+$ such that $u_{i_1} \cdot u_{i_2} \cdot \ldots \cdot u_{i_m} = v_{i_1} \cdot v_{i_2} \cdot \ldots \cdot v_{i_m}$.

We consider architectures that have at least two different black-box processes p and q, where both p and q have at least one binary output or hidden variable. The basic idea of the reduction is to let process p compute the sequence of indices $i_1, i_2, \ldots, i_m$ and to let q produce the corresponding word $u_{i_1} \cdot u_{i_2} \cdot \ldots \cdot u_{i_m} = v_{i_1} \cdot v_{i_2} \cdot \ldots \cdot v_{i_m}$. To check that the word produced by q corresponds to the sequence produced by p, we consider two different schedulings, one in which p produces the indices along the u-words and one in which p produces the indices along the v-words.

We ensure that the two processes always see the constant input 0 along both paths and must therefore produce the same output on both paths. For the white-box processes we fix strategies that map any input history to 0. For all black-box processes except p and q (if any) and the environment, we specify that their output variables are globally set to 0. Let the formulas for this requirement, which are in both LTL and CTL, be denoted by γ_b and γ_{env}, respectively.

Each index produced by process p is preceded and followed by the constant 0, and terminated by the special symbol $\bot$: $0, i_1, 0, \; 0, i_2, 0, \; \ldots, \; 0, i_m, 0, \; \bot$. To each letter l produced by process q, we add a flag f_u indicating if this particular letter is the first letter of the u-word in the sequence, and a flag f_v, if it is the first letter of the v-word. Each letter is again preceded and followed by the constant 0, and the sequence is terminated by $\bot$: $0, l_1, f_{u1}, f_{v1}, 0, \ 0, l_2, f_{u2}, f_{v2}, 0, \ \ldots, \ 0, l_k,$ $f_{uk}, f_{vk}, 0, \ \bot$.

We assume that the encodings of the indices and letters with flags have equal length N. Each encoding of $0, i, 0$ and $0, l, w_i, w_j, 0$ starts with a sequence (say, 0111) that will occur nowhere else in any sequence encoding some sequence of indices or letters with flags, which allows us to identify where the output of an index or letter with flags starts.

LTL. We set $\varphi_u = \alpha_1 \rightarrow (\gamma_1 \wedge (\alpha_2 \rightarrow \gamma_2))$ for the following path assumptions α_1, α_2 and guarantees γ_1, γ_2:

- α_1: globally, the concurrent scheduling of p and q is succeeded by a sequence of $N - 1$ times where only p is scheduled, which is succeeded by a finite sequence where q is not scheduled, which is succeeded by a further concurrent scheduling of p and q;
- γ_1: globally, the concurrent scheduling of p and q initializes the output of an index $i \in I \cup \{\bot\}$;
- α_2: globally, an output sequence of an index $i \in I$ that is started by a concurrent scheduling of p and q is succeeded by $|u_i| \cdot N - 1$ (where $|u_i|$ denotes the length of the word u_i) positions in which only q is scheduled, which is succeeded by a concurrent scheduling of p and q; an output sequence of $\bot$ by p that is started by a concurrent scheduling of p and q is succeeded by $N - 1$ positions in which only q is scheduled;
- γ_2: the concurrent scheduling of p and q initialize the output of an index $i \in I$ followed by the output of u_i, until the concurrent scheduling of p and q initialize the emission of $\bot$ by p, followed by the emission of $\bot$ by q.

If φ_v is defined correspondingly and $\gamma_\bot$ denotes the guarantee that $\bot$ is not immediately emitted, then $\psi = \gamma_b \wedge \gamma_\bot \wedge p \wedge q \wedge \gamma_{env} \rightarrow (\varphi_u \wedge \varphi_v)$ is realizable iff the correspondence problem has a solution.

CTL. For $\varphi_u = E\varphi U\varphi_\bot$, where $\varphi_\bot$ denotes that p and q would start to emit $\bot$, φ is the conjunction of the following assertions:

- if p would (if continously scheduled alone) start to emit u_i, q would start to emit j and the output variables of p and q are set to 0 then $i = j$ and p and q are both scheduled concurrently;
- if p would not start to emit a word u_i and (q would start to output an index or the output variables of p are not set to 0) then only p is scheduled;
- if neither p nor q would start to emit a word or an index, respectively, or the output variables of q are not set to 0 then only q is scheduled;
- the output variables of the environment are all set to 0.

If φ_v is defined correspondingly and γ_0 denotes that the output variables of p and q are set to 0, then $\psi = \gamma_b \wedge \gamma_0 \wedge \varphi_u \wedge \varphi_v \wedge \neg\varphi_\bot$ is realizable iff the correspondence problem has a solution. $\qquad\square$

The undecidability of scheduler-independent synthesis follows because for LTL, realizability under full scheduling and scheduler-independent realizability coincide: Since LTL is a trace language, $\langle \Upsilon_A^*, l \rangle \models \varphi$ implies $\langle Y_{scheduler}, l \rangle \models \varphi$ for every total tree $Y_{scheduler} \subseteq \Upsilon_A^*$ and every LTL specification φ.

The assumption $\alpha = AG \bigwedge_{P' \subseteq P} EX(\bigwedge_{p \in P'} p \wedge \bigwedge_{p \in P \smallsetminus P'} \neg p)$ of a full scheduler can be expressed in CTL, and realizability of a CTL specification φ under full scheduling coincides with the scheduler-independent realizability of $\alpha \to \varphi$.

Corollary 1. *The distributed scheduler-independent synthesis problem is undecidable for all architectures with at least two black-box processes and CTL or LTL specifications.* $\square$

6 Conclusions

The first synthesis algorithms for synchronous and asynchronous systems were introduced almost simultaneously in the late 1980's for trace languages. In the synchronous paradigm, synthesis has received great attention ever since, while, in the asynchronous setting, results have been few and far between. In the introduction, we raised the question whether this is due to an inherent hardness of the problem.

The results of this paper show that the cost of synthesizing asynchronous systems depends on the treatment of the scheduler. Synthesizing asynchronous systems is computationally no more expensive than synthesizing synchronous systems when using the most commonly used semantics, which presumes a full scheduler. Asynchronous synthesis without assumptions on the scheduler, on the other hand, is exponentially harder.

The undecidability of the multi-process synthesis problem underlines that the synthesis of asynchronous systems is indeed more difficult than the synthesis of synchronous systems: while it is possible to solve the distributed synthesis problem for several synchronous architectures with multiple black-box processes (like pipelines and rings), distributed synthesis for asynchronous systems is only decidable if the architecture contains at most one black-box process.

However, we consider the solution of the distributed synthesis problem, even when restricted to only one black-box process, a significant step forward. Model checking (which can be seen as the special case of the distributed synthesis problem where all processes are white-box) has brought formal methods to industrial practice in the test and verification phase. Distributed synthesis allows the application of formal methods in the much earlier design phase. An incompletely implemented system defines an architecture with a single black-box process (representing the unfinished part of the system) in addition to the completed white-box processes. By checking the realizability of the specification for this architecture, we can recognize design errors as soon as they are introduced into the implementation.

References

1. A. Anuchitanukul and Z. Manna. Realizability and synthesis of reactive modules. In *Proc. CAV*, pages 156–168. Springer-Verlag, June 1994.
2. B. Finkbeiner and S. Schewe. Semi-automatic distributed synthesis. In *Proc. ATVA*, pages 263–277. Springer-Verlag, October 2005.
3. B. Finkbeiner and S. Schewe. Uniform distributed synthesis. In *Proc. LICS*, pages 321–330. IEEE Computer Society Press, June 2005.
4. M. Jurdziński. Small progress measures for solving parity games. In *Proc. STACS*, pages 290–301. Springer-Verlag, 2000.
5. D. Kozen and R. J. Parikh. A decision procedure for the propositional μ-calculus. In *Proc. Logic of Programs*, pages 313–325. Springer-Verlag, 1983.
6. O. Kupferman, P. Madhusudan, P. Thiagarajan, and M. Y. Vardi. Open systems in reactive environments: Control and synthesis. In *Proc. 11th Int. Conf. on Concurrency Theory*, pages 92–107. Springer-Verlag, 2000.
7. O. Kupferman and M. Y. Vardi. Synthesis with incomplete informatio. In *Proc. ICTL*, pages 91–106, Manchester, July 1997.
8. O. Kupferman and M. Y. Vardi. Church's problem revisited. *The bulletin of Symbolic Logic*, 5(2):245–263, June 1999.
9. O. Kupferman and M. Y. Vardi. μ-calculus synthesis. In *Proc. MFCS*, pages 497–507. Springer-Verlag, 2000.
10. O. Kupferman and M. Y. Vardi. Synthesizing distributed systems. In *Proc. LICS*, pages 389–398. IEEE Computer Society Press, July 2001.
11. D. E. Muller and P. E. Schupp. Simulating alternating tree automata by non-deterministic automata: new results and new proofs of the theorems of Rabin, McNaughton and Safra. *Theor. Comput. Sci.*, 141(1-2):69–107, 1995.
12. A. Pnueli and R. Rosner. On the synthesis of an asynchronous reactive module. In *Automata, Languages and Programming, 16th International Colloquium*, pages 652–671. Springer-Verlag, 1989.
13. A. Pnueli and R. Rosner. Distributed reactive systems are hard to synthesize. In *Proc. FOCS*, pages 746–757. IEEE Computer Society Press, 1990.
14. M. Y. Vardi. An automata-theoretic approach to fair realizability and synthesis. In *Proc. CAV*, pages 267–278. Springer-Verlag, July 1995.
15. T. Wilke. CTL$^+$ is exponentially more succinct than CTL. In *Proc. FSTTCS*, pages 110–121. Springer-Verlag, Dec. 1999.

A Comparative Study of
Algorithmic Debugging Strategies*

Josep Silva

DSIC, Technical University of Valencia
Camino de Vera s/n, E-46022 Valencia, Spain
jsilva@dsic.upv.es

Abstract. Algorithmic debugging is a debugging technique that has
been extended to practically all programming paradigms. It is based on
the answers of the programmer to a series of questions generated automatically by the algorithmic debugger. Therefore, the performance of
the technique is strongly dependent on the number and the complexity
of these questions. In this work we overview and compare current strategies for algorithmic debugging and we introduce some new strategies and
discuss their advantages over previous approaches.

1 Introduction

Algorithmic debugging is a debugging technique which relies on the programmer having an *intended interpretation* of the program. In other words, some
computations of the program are correct and others are wrong with respect to
the programmer's intended semantics. Therefore, algorithmic debuggers compare the results of sub-computations with what the programmer intended. By
asking the programmer questions or using a formal specification the system can
identify precisely the location of a program's bug.

Essentially, algorithmic debugging is a two-phase process: An *execution tree*
(see, e.g., [12]), ET for short, is built during the first phase. Each node in this
ET corresponds to an equation which consists of a function call with completely
evaluated arguments and results[1]. Roughly speaking, the ET is constructed as
follows: The root node is the *main* function of the program; for each node n
with associated function f, and for each function call in the right-hand side of
the definition of f, a new node is recursively added to the ET as the child of n.
This notion of ET is valid for functional languages but it is insufficient for other
paradigms as the imperative programming paradigm. In general, the information
included in the nodes of the ET incudes all the data needed to determine if the
equations are correct. For instance, in the imperative programming paradigm,

---

* This work has been partially supported by the EU (FEDER) and the Spanish
MEC under grant TIN2005-09207-C03-02, by the ICT for EU-India Cross-Cultural
Dissemination Project ALA/95/23/2003/077-054, and by the Vicerrectorado de
Innovación y Desarrollo de la UPV under project TAMAT ref 5771.
[1] Or as much as needed if we consider a lazy language.

G. Puebla (Ed.): LOPSTR 2006, LNCS 4407, pp. 143–159, 2007.

with the function (or procedure) of each node it is included the value of all global variables when the function was called. Similarly, in object-oriented languages, every node with a method invocation includes the values of the attributes of the object owner of this method (see, e.g., [4]). In the second phase, the debugger traverses the ET asking an oracle (typically the programmer) whether each equation is correct or wrong. At the beginning, the *suspicious area* which contains those nodes that can be buggy (a buggy node is associated with a buggy rule of the program) is empty; but, after every question, some nodes of the ET leave the suspicious area. When all the children of a node with a wrong equation (if any) are correct, the node becomes buggy and the debugger locates the bug in the function definition of this node [14]. If a bug symptom is detected then algorithmic debugging is complete [16]. It is important to say that, once the execution tree is built, the problem of traversing it and selecting a node is independent of the language used; hence algorithmic debugging strategies can theoretically work for any language.

Unfortunately, in practice—for real programs—algorithmic debugging can produce long series of questions which are semantically unconnected (i.e., consecutive questions which refer to different and independent parts of the computation) making the process of debugging too complex.

Furthermore, questions can also be very complex. For instance, during a debugging session with a compiler, the algorithmic debugger of the Mercury language [10]—currently, one of the most advanced algorithmic debuggers—asked a question of more than 1400 lines.

Therefore, new techniques and strategies to reduce the number of questions, to simplify them and to improve the order in which they are asked are a necessity to make algorithmic debuggers usable in practice.

In this paper we review and compare the current algorithmic debugging strategies and propose three new strategies (less YES first, divide by YES and query, and dynamic weighting search) that can further reduce the number of questions asked during an algorithmic debugging session.

The rest of the paper is organized as follows. The next section shows an example of algorithmic debugging session that will be used along the paper. Section 3 reviews current algorithmic debugging strategies and proposes three new strategies. In Section 4 we present a comparison of all techniques and we study their costs. Finally, Section 5 concludes.

2   Algorithmic Debugging

During the algorithmic debugging process, an oracle is prompted with equations and asked about their correctness; it answers "YES" when the result is correct or "NO" when the result is wrong. Some algorithmic debuggers also accept the answer "I don't know" when the programmer cannot give an answer (e.g., because the question is too complex). After every question, some nodes of the ET leave the suspicious area. When there is only one node in the suspicious area, the process finishes reporting this node as buggy. It should be clear that algorithmic debugging finds one bug at a time. In order to find different bugs, the process should be restarted again for each different bug.

```
main = sqrtest [1,2]

sqrtest x = test (computs (listsum x))

test (x,y,z) = (x==y) && (y==z)

listsum [] = 0
listsum (x:xs) = x + (listsum xs)

computs x = ((comput1 x),(comput2 x),(comput3 x))

comput1 x = square x

square x = x*x

comput2 x = listsum (list x x)

list x y | y==0      = []
         | otherwise = x:list x (y-1)

comput3 x = listsum (partialsums x)

partialsums x = [(sum1 x),(sum2 x)]

sum1 x = div (x * (incr x)) 2
sum2 x = div (x + (decr x)) 2

incr x = x + 1
decr x = x - 1
```

Fig. 1. Example program

Let us illustrate the process with an example[2].

Example 1. Consider the buggy program in Fig. 1 adapted to Haskell from [7]. This program sums a list of integers [1,2] and computes the square of the result with three different methods. If the three methods compute the same result the program returns *True*; otherwise, it returns *False*. Here, one of the three methods—the one adding the partial sums of its input number—contains a bug. From this program, an algorithmic debugger can automatically generate the ET

---

[2] While almost all the strategies presented here are independent of the programming paradigm used, in order to be concrete and w.l.o.g. we will base our examples on the functional programming paradigm.

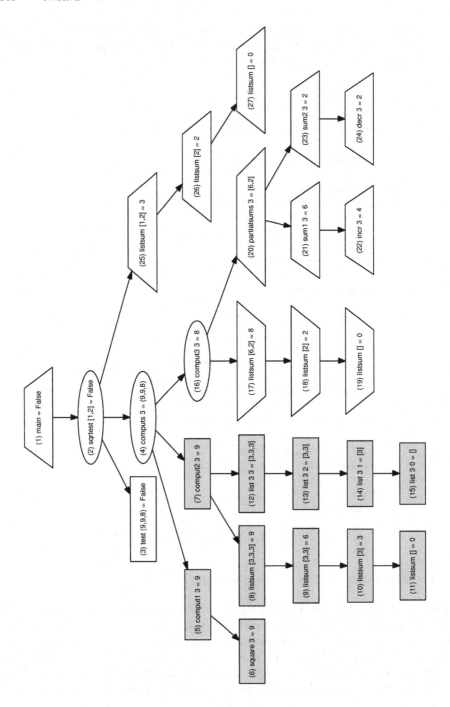

Fig. 2. Execution tree of the program in Fig. 1

```
Starting Debugging Session...

(1)   main = False? NO
(2)   sqrtest [1,2] = False? NO
(3)   test [9,9,8] = False? YES
(4)   computs 3 = [9,9,8]? NO
(5)   comput1 3 = 9? YES
(7)   comput2 3 = 9? YES
(16)  comput3 3 = 8? NO
(17)  listsum [6,2] = 8? YES
(20)  partialsums 3 = [6,2]? NO
(21)  sum1 3 = 6? YES
(23)  sum2 3 = 2? NO
(24)  decr 3 = 2? YES

Bug found in rule:
sum2 x = div (x + (decr x)) 2
```

Fig. 3. Debugging session for the program in Fig. 1

of Fig. 2 (for the time being, the reader can ignore the distinction between different shapes and white and dark nodes) which, in turn, can be used to produce a debugging session as depicted in Fig. 3. During the debugging session, the system asks the oracle about the correctness of some ET nodes w.r.t. the intended semantics. At the end of the debugging session, the algorithmic debugger determines that the bug of the program is located in function "sum2" (node 23). The definition of function "sum2" should be: sum2 x = div (x*(decr x)) 2

3   Algorithmic Debugging Strategies

Algorithmic debugging strategies are based on the fact that the ET can be pruned using the information provided by the oracle. Given a question associated with a node n of the ET, a NO answer prunes all the nodes of the ET except the subtree rooted at n; and a YES answer prunes the subtree rooted at n. Each strategy takes advantage of this property in a different manner.

A correct equation in the tree does not guarantee that the subtree rooted at this equation is free of errors. It can be the case that two buggy nodes caused the correct answer by fluke [6]. In contrast, an incorrect equation does guarantee that the subtree rooted at this equation does contain a buggy node [12]. Therefore, if a program produced a wrong result, then the equation in the root of the ET is wrong and thus there must be at least one buggy node in the ET. We will assume in the following that the debugging session has been started after discovering a bug symptom in the output of the program, and thus the root of the tree contains a wrong equation. Hence, we know that there is at least one bug in the program. We will also assume that the oracle is able to answer all the questions. Then, all the strategies will find the bug.

3.1 Single Stepping *(Shapiro, 1982)*

The first algorithmic debugging strategy to be proposed was *single stepping* [16]. In essence, this strategy performs a bottom-up search because it proceeds by doing a post-order traversal of the ET. It asks first about all the children of a given node, and then (if they are correct) about the node itself. If the equation of this node is wrong then this is the buggy node; if it is correct, then the post-order traversal continues. Therefore, the first node answered NO is identified as buggy (because all its children have already been answered YES).

For instance, the sequence of 19 questions asked for the ET in Fig. 2 would be: 3-YES, 6-YES, 5-YES, 11-YES, 10-YES, 9-YES, 8-YES, 15-YES, 14-YES, 13-YES, 12-YES, 7-YES, 19-YES, 18-YES, 17-YES, 22-YES, 21-YES, 24-YES, 23-NO.

Note that in this strategy questions are semantically unconnected.

3.2 Top-Down Search *(Av-Ron, 1984)*

Due to the fact that questions are asked in a logical order, *top-down search* [1] is the strategy that has been traditionally used (see, e.g., [3,9]) to measure the performance of different debugging tools and methods. It basically consists in a top-down, left-to-right traversal of the ET and, thus, the node asked is always a child or a sibling of the previous question node. When a node is answered NO, one of its children is asked; if it is answered YES, one of its siblings is. Therefore, the idea is to follow the path of wrong equations from the root of the tree to the buggy node. For instance, the sequence of 12 questions asked for the ET in Fig. 2 is shown in Fig. 3.

This strategy significantly improves single stepping because it prunes a part of the ET after every answer. However, it is still very naive, since it does not take into account the structure of the tree (e.g., how balanced it is). For this reason, a number of variants aiming at improving it can be found in the literature:

Top-Down Zooming *(Maeji and Kanamori, 1987)*. During the search of previous strategies, the rule or indeed the function definition may change from one query to the next. If the oracle is human, this continuous change of function definitions slows down the answers of the programmer because he has to switch thinking once and again from one function definition to another. This drawback can be partially overcome by changing the order of the questions: In this strategy [11], recursive child calls are preferred.

The sequence of questions asked for the ET in Fig. 2 is exactly the same as with top-down search (Fig. 3) because no recursive calls are found.

Another variant of this strategy called *exception zooming*, introduced by Ian MacLarty [10], selects first those nodes that produced an exception at runtime.

Heaviest First *(Binks, 1995)*. Selecting always the left-most child does not take into account the size of the subtrees that can be explored. Binks proposed in [2] a variant of top-down search in order to consider this information when selecting a child. This variant is called *heaviest first* because it always selects the child with a bigger subtree. The objective is to avoid selecting small subtrees which have a lower probability of containing the bug.

For instance, the sequence of 9 questions asked for the ET in Fig. 2 would be[3]: 1-NO, 2-NO, 4-NO, 7-YES, 16-NO, 20-NO, 21-YES, 23-NO, 24-YES.

Less YES First *(Silva, 2006)*. This section introduces a new variant of top-down search which further improves heaviest first. It is based on the fact that every equation in the ET is associated with a rule of the source code (i.e., the rule that the debugger identifies as buggy when it finds a buggy node in the ET). Taking into account that the final objective of the process is to find the program's rule which contains the bug—rather than a node in the ET—and considering that there is not a relation one-to-one between nodes and rules because several nodes can refer to the same rule, it is important to also consider the node's rules during the search. A first idea could be to explore first those subtrees with a higher number of associated rules (instead of exploring those subtrees with a higher number of nodes).

Example 2. Consider the following ET:

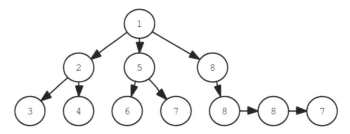

where each node is labeled with its associated rule and where the oracle answered NO to the question in the root of the tree. While heaviest first selects the right-most child because this subtree has four nodes instead of three, less YES first selects the left-most child because this subtree contains three different rules instead of two.

Clearly, this approach relies on the idea that all the rules have the same probability of containing the bug (rather than all the nodes). Another possibility could be to associate a different probability of containing the bug to each rule, e.g., depending on its structure: Is it recursive? Does it contain higher-order calls?.

The probability of a node to be buggy is $q \cdot p$ where q is the probability that the rule associated to this node is wrong, and p is the probability of this rule to execute incorrectly. Therefore, under the assumption that all the rules have the same probability of being wrong, the probability P of a branch b to contain the bug is $P = \frac{\sum_{i=1}^{n} p_i}{R}$ where n is the number of nodes in b, R is the number of rules in the program, and p_i is the probability of the rule in node i to produce a wrong

---

[3] Here, and in the following, we will break the indeterminism by selecting the left-most node in the figures. For instance, the fourth question could be either (7) or (16) because both have a weight of 9. We selected (7) because it is on the left.

result if it is incorrect. Clearly, if we assume that a wrong rule always produces a wrong result[4] we have that $P = \frac{\sum_{i=1}^{r} p_i}{R}$ and $\forall i.p_i = 1$, then the probability is $\frac{r}{R}$ where r is the number of rules in b, and thus, this strategy is (on average) better than heaviest first. For instance, in Example 2 the left-most branch has a probability of $\frac{3}{8}$ to contain a buggy node, while the right-most branch has a probability of $\frac{2}{8}$ despite it has more nodes.

However, in general, a wrong rule can produce a correct result, and thus we need to consider the probability of a wrong rule to return a wrong answer. This probability has been approximated by the debugger Hat-delta (see Section 3.4) by using previous answers of the oracle. The main idea is that a rule answered NO n times out of m is more likely to be wrong than a rule answered NO n' times out of m if $n' < n \leqslant m$.

Here, we use this idea in order to compute the probability of a branch to contain a buggy node. Hence, this strategy is a combination of the ideas from both heaviest first and Hat-delta. However, while heaviest first considers the structure of the tree and does not take into account previous answers of the user, Hat-delta does the opposite; thus, the advantage of less YES first over them is the use of more information (both the structure of the tree and previous answers of the user).

A direct generalization of Hat-delta for branches would result in counting the number of YES answers of a given branch; but this approach would not take into account the number of rules in the branch. In contrast, we proceed as follows: When a node is set correct, we mark its associated rule and all the rules of its descendants as correctly executed. If a rule has been executed correctly before, then it will likely execute correctly again. The debugger associates to each rule of the program the number of times it has been executed in correct computations based on previous answers. Then, when we have to select a child to ask, we can compute the total number of rules in the subtrees rooted at the children, and the total number of answers YES for every rule.

This strategy selects the child whose subtree is less likely to be correct (and thus more likely to be wrong). To compute this probability we calculate for every branch b a weight w_b with the following equation:

$$w_b = \sum_{i=1}^{n} \frac{1}{r_i^{(YES)}}$$

where n is the number of nodes in b and $r_i^{(YES)}$ is the number of answers YES for the rule r of the node i.

As with heaviest first, we select the branch with the biggest weight, the difference is that this equation to compute the weight takes into account previous answers of the user. Moreover, we assume that initially all the rules have been

---

[4] This assumption is valid for instance in those flattened functional languages where all the conditions in the right-hand side of function definitions have been distributed between its rules. This is relatively frequent in internal languages of compilers, but not in source languages.

answered YES once, and thus, at the beginning, this strategy asks those branches with more nodes, but it becomes different as the number of questions asked increases.

With this strategy, the sequence of 9 questions asked for the ET in Fig. 2 is: 1-NO, 2-NO, 4-NO, 7-YES, 16-NO, 20-NO, 21-YES, 23-NO, 24-YES.

3.3 Divide and Query *(Shapiro, 1982)*

In 1982, together with single stepping, Shapiro proposed another strategy: the so-called divide & query (D&Q) [16]. The idea of D&Q is to ask in every step a question which divides the remaining nodes in the ET by two, or, if this is not possible, into two parts with a weight as similar as possible. In particular, the original algorithm by Shapiro always chooses the heaviest node whose weight is less than or equal to $w/2$ where w is the weight of the suspicious area in the ET. This strategy has a worst case query complexity of order $b \, log_2 \, n$ where b is the average branching factor of the tree and n its number of nodes.

This strategy works well with a large search space—this is normally the case of realistic programs—because its query complexity is proportional to the logarithm of the number of nodes in the tree. If the ET is big and unbalanced this strategy is better than top-down search [3]; however, the main drawback of this strategy is that successive questions may have no connection, from a semantic point of view, with each other; requiring the programmer more time for answering the questions.

For instance, the sequence of 6 questions asked for the ET in Fig. 2 is: 7-YES, 16-NO, 17-YES, 21-YES, 24-YES, 23-NO.

Hirunkitti's Divide and Query *(Hirunkitti and Hogger, 1993)*. In [8], Hirunkitti and Hogger noted that Shapiro's algorithm does not always choose the node closest to the halfway point in the tree and addressed this problem slightly modifying the original divide & query algorithm. Their version of divide & query is the same as the one of Shapiro except that their version always chooses a node which produces a least difference between:

- $w/2$ and the heaviest node whose weight is less than or equal to $w/2$
- $w/2$ and the lightest node whose weight is greater than or equal to $w/2$

where w is the weight of the suspicious area in the computation tree.

For instance, the sequence of 6 questions asked for the ET in Fig. 2 is: 7-YES, 16-NO, 17-YES, 21-YES, 24-YES, 23-NO.

Biased Weighting Divide and Query *(MacLarty, 2005)*. MacLarty proposed in his PhD thesis [10] that not all the nodes should be considered equally while dividing the tree. His variant of D&Q divides the tree by only considering some kinds of nodes and/or by associating a different weight to every kind of node.

In particular, his algorithmic debugger was implemented for the functional logic language Mercury [5] which distinguishes between 13 different node types.

Divide by YES and Query *(Silva, 2006)*. The same idea used in less YES first can be applied in order to improve divide & query. Instead of dividing the ET into two subtrees with a similar number of nodes, we can divide it into two subtrees with a similar weight. The problem that this strategy tries to address is the D&Q's assumption that all the nodes have the same probability of containing the bug. In contrast, this strategy tries to compute this probability.

By using the equation to compute the weight of a branch, this strategy computes the weight associated to the subtree rooted at each node. Then, the node which divides the tree into two subtrees with a more similar weight is selected. In particular, the node selected is the node which produces a least difference between:

- $w/2$ and the heaviest node whose weight is less than or equal to $w/2$
- $w/2$ and the lightest node whose weight is greater than or equal to $w/2$

where w is the weight of the suspicious area in the ET.

As with D&Q, different nodes could divide the ET into two subtrees with a similar weights; in this case, we could follow another strategy (e.g., Hirunkitti) in order to select one of them.

We assume again that initially all the rules have been answered YES once. Therefore, at the beginning this strategy is similar to D&Q, but the differences appear as the number of answers increases.

Example 3. Consider again the ET in Example 2. Similarly to D&Q, the first node selected is the top-most "8" because only structural information is available. Let us assume that the answer is YES. Then, we mark all the nodes in this branch as correctly executed. Therefore, the next node selected is "2"; because, despite the subtrees rooted at "2" and "5" have the same number of nodes and rules, we now have more information which allows us to know that the subtree rooted at "5" is more likely to be correct since node "7" has been correctly executed before.

The main difference with respect to D&Q is that divide by YES & query not only takes into account the structure of the tree (i.e., the distribution of the program rules between its nodes), but also previous answers of the user.

With this strategy, the sequence of 5 questions asked for the ET in Fig. 2 is: 7-YES, 16-NO, 21-YES, 23-NO, 24-YES.

3.4   Hat-Delta *(Davie and Chitil, 2005)*

Hat [19] is a tracer for Haskell. Davie and Chitil introduced a declarative debugger tool based on the Hat's traces that includes a new strategy called Hat-delta [6]. Initially, Hat-delta is identical to top-down search but it becomes different as the number of questions asked increases. The main idea of this strategy is to use previous answers of the oracle in order to compute which node has an associated rule that is more likely to be wrong (e.g., because it has been answered NO more times than the others).

This strategy assumes that a rule answered NO n times out of m is more likely to be wrong than a rule answered NO n' times out of m if $n' < n \leqslant m$. During a debugging session, a sequence of questions, each of them related to a particular rule, is asked. In general, after every question, it is possible to compute the total number of questions asked for each rule, the total number of answers YES/NO, and the total number of nodes associated with this rule. Moreover, when a node is set correct or wrong, Hat-delta marks all the rules of its descendants as correctly or incorrectly executed respectively. This strategy uses all this information to select the next question. In particular, three different heuristics have been proposed based on this idea [6]:

- *Counting the number of YES answers.* If a rule has been executed correctly before, then it will likely execute correctly again. The debugger associates to each rule of the program the number of times it has been executed in correct computations based on previous answers.
- *Counting the number of NO answers.* This is analogous to the previous heuristic but collecting wrong computations.
- *Calculating the proportion of NO answers.* This is derived from the previous two heuristics. For a node with associated rule r we have:

$$\frac{number\ of\ answers\ NO\ for\ r}{number\ of\ answers\ NO/YES\ for\ r}$$

If r has not been asked before a value of $\frac{1}{2}$ is assigned.

Example 4. Consider this program:

```
4|0|0        sort [] = []
8|4|⅓        sort (x:xs) = insert x (sort xs)
4|0|0        insert x [] = [x]
             insert x (y:ys)
4|0|0          | x<y = x:y:ys
0|0|½          | otherwise = insert x ys
```

where the left numbers indicate respectively the number of times each rule has been executed correctly, the number of times each rule has failed and the proportion of NO answers for this rule.

With this information, `otherwise = insert x ys` is more likely to be wrong.

3.5 Subterm Dependency Tracking *(MacLarty et al., 2005)*

In 1986, Pereira [15] noted that the answers YES, NO and *I don't know* were insufficient; and he pointed out another possible answer of the programmer: *Inadmissible* (see also [13]). An equation or, more precisely, some of its arguments, are inadmissible if they violate the preconditions of its function definition. For instance, consider the equation `insert 'b' "cc" = "bcc"`, where function `insert` inserts the first argument in a list of mutually different characters (the second argument). This equation is not wrong but inadmissible, since the argument "cc" has repeated characters. Hence, inadmissibility allows us to identify errors in left-hand sides of equations.

However, with only these four possible answers the system fails to get fundamental information from the programmer about *why* the equation is wrong or inadmissible. In particular, the programmer could specify which exact (sub)term in the result or the arguments is wrong or inadmissible respectively. This provides specific information about *why* an equation is wrong (i.e., which part of the result is incorrect? is one particular argument inadmissible?).

Consider again the equation insert 'b' "cc" = "bcc". Here, the programmer could detect that the second argument should not have been computed; he could then mark the second argument ("cc") as inadmissible. This information is essential because it allows the debugger to avoid questions related to the correct parts of the equation and concentrate on the wrong parts.

Based on this idea, MacLarty et al. [10] proposed a new strategy called subterm dependency tracking. Essentially, once the programmer selects a particular wrong subterm, this strategy searches backwards in the computation for the node that introduced the wrong subterm. All the nodes traversed during the search define a *dependency chain* of nodes between the node that produced the wrong subterm and the node where the programmer identified it. The sequence of questions defined in this strategy follows the dependency chain from the origin of the wrong subterm.

For instance, if the programmer is asked question 3 from the ET in Fig. 2, his answer would be YES but he could also mark subexpression "8" as inadmissible. Then, the system would compute the chain of nodes which passed this subexpression from the node which computed it up to question 3. This chain is formed by nodes 2, 4, 16 and 17. The system would ask first 17, then 16, and finally 4 following the computed chain.

In our example, the sequence of 8 questions asked for the ET in Fig. 2, combining this strategy with top-down search, is: 1-NO, 2-NO, 3-YES (the programmer marks "8"), 17-YES, 16-NO, 20-NO (the programmer marks "2"), 23-NO, 24-YES.

3.6 Dynamic Weighting Search *(Silva, 2006)*

Subterm dependency tracking relies on the idea that if a subterm is marked, then the error will likely be in the sequence of functions that produced and passed the incorrect subterm up to the function where the programmer found it. However, the error could also be in any other equation previous to the origin of the dependency chain.

Here, we propose a new strategy which is a generalization of subterm dependency tracking and which can integrate the knowledge acquired by other strategies in order to formulate the next question.

The main idea is that every node in the ET has an associated weight (representing the probability of being buggy). After every question, the debugger gets information that changes the weights and it asks for the node with a higher weight. When the associated weight of a node is 0, then this node leaves the suspicious area of the ET. Weights are modified based on the assumption that those nodes of the tree which produced or manipulated a wrong (sub)term, are more likely to be wrong than those that did not. Here, w.l.o.g., we compute weights instead of probabilities and we assume initially that all the nodes have a weight 1 and that a weight 0 means *"out of the suspicious area"*.

Computing Weights from Subterms

Firstly, as with subterm dependency tracking, we allow the oracle to mark a subterm from an equation as wrong (instead of the whole equation). Let us assume that the programmer is being asked about the correctness of the equation in a node n_1, and he marks a subterm s as wrong (or inadmissible). Then, the suspicious area is automatically divided into four sets. The first set contains the node, say n_2, that introduced s into the computation and all the nodes needed to execute the equation in node n_2. The second set contains the nodes that, during the computation, passed the wrong subterm from equation to equation up to node n_1. The third set contains all the nodes which could have influenced the expression s in node n_2 from the beginning of the computation. Finally, the rest of the nodes form the fourth set. Since these nodes could not produce the wrong subterm (because they could not have influenced it), the nodes in the fourth set are extracted from the suspicious area and, thus, the new suspicious area is formed by the sets 1, 2 and 3.

Each subset can be assigned a different probability of containing the bug. Let us show it with an example.

Example 5. Consider the ET in Fig. 2, where the oracle was asked about the correctness of equation 3 and he pointed out the computed subterm "8" as inadmissible. Then, the four sets are denoted in the figure by using different shapes and colors:

- **Set 1:** those nodes which evaluated the equation 20 to produce the wrong subterm are denoted by an inverted trapezium.
- **Set 2:** those nodes that passed the wrong subterm until the programmer detected it in the equation 3 are denoted by an ellipse.
- **Set 3:** those nodes that could influence the wrong subterm are denoted by a trapezium.
- **Set 4:** the rest of nodes are denoted by a grey rectangle.

The source of a wrong subterm is the equation which computed it. From our experience, all the nodes involved in the evaluation of this equation are more likely to contain the bug. However, it is also possible that the functions that passed this wrong term during the computation should have modified it and they did not. Therefore, they could also contain the bug. Finally, it is also possible (but indeed less likely) that the equation that computed the wrong subterm had a wrong argument and this was the reason why it produced a wrong subterm. In this case, this inadmissible argument should be further inspected. In the example, the wrong term "8" was computed because equation 20 had a wrong argument "[6,2]" which should be "[6,3]"; the nodes which computed this wrong argument have a trapezium shape.

Consequently, in the previous example, after the oracle marked "8" as wrong in equation 3, we could increase the weight of the nodes in the first subset with 3, the nodes in the second subset with 2, and the nodes in the third subset with 1. The nodes in the fourth subset can be extracted from the suspicious area because they could not influence the value of the wrong subterm and, consequently, their probability of containing the bug is zero[5].

These subsets of the ET are in fact slices of different parts of the computation. In [17] it is defined a method to automatically compute each subset. In addition, [17] also introduces an algorithm to combine information from different strategies. This algorithm can help dynamic weighting search to integrate information used by other strategies (e.g., previous answers of the oracle) in order to modify nodes' weights.

4   Comparing Strategies

A summary of the information used by every strategy is shown in Fig. 4. The meaning of each column is the following:

- '*(Struct)ure*' is marked if the strategy takes into account the distribution of nodes (or rules) in the tree;
- '*Rules*' is marked if the strategy considers the rules associated with nodes;
- '*(Sem)antics*' is marked if the strategy follows an order of semantically related questions, the more marks the more strong relation between questions;
- '*(Inadm)issibility*' is marked if the strategy accepts "inadmissible" answers;
- '*History*' is marked if the strategy considers previous answers in order to select the next node to ask (besides cutting the tree);
- '*(Div)isible*' is marked if the strategy can work with a subset of the whole ET. ETs can be huge and thus, it is desirable not to explore the whole tree after every question. Some strategies allow us to only load a part of the tree at a time, thus significatively speeding up the internal processing of the ET; and hence, being much more scalable than other strategies that need to explore the whole tree before every question. For instance, top-down can load the nodes whose depth is less than d, and ask d questions before loading another part of the tree. Note, however, that some of the non-marked strategies could work with a subset of the whole ET if they where restricted. For instance, heaviest first could be restricted by simply limiting the search for the heaviest branch to the loaded nodes of the ET. Other strategies need more simplifications: less YES first or Hat-delta could be restricted by only marking as correctly executed the first d levels of descendants of a node answered YES; and then restricting the search for the heaviest branch (respectively node) to the loaded nodes of the ET. Finally,
- '*Cost*' represents the worst case query complexity of the strategy. Here, n represents the number of nodes in the ET, d its maximum depth and b its branching factor.

---

[5] A proof can be found in [18].

Strategy	Struct.	Rules	Sem.	Inadm.	History	Div.	Cost
Single Stepping	-	-	-	-	-	✓	n
Top-Down Search	-	-	✓	-	-	✓	$b \cdot d$
Top-Down Zooming	-	-	✓✓	-	-	✓	$b \cdot d$
Heaviest First	✓	-	✓	-	-	-	$b \cdot d$
Less YES First	✓	✓	✓	-	✓	-	$b \cdot d$
Divide & Query	✓	-	-	-	-	-	$b \cdot log_2 n$
Biased Weighting D&Q	✓	-	-	-	-	-	$b \cdot log_2 n$
Hirunkitti's D&Q	✓	-	-	-	-	-	$b \cdot log_2 n$
Divide by YES & Query	✓	✓	-	-	✓	-	$b \cdot d$
Hat-delta	-	✓	-	-	✓	-	n
Subterm Dependency Tracking	-	-	✓✓✓	✓	-	-	n
Dynamic Weighting Search	✓	✓	-	✓	✓	-	n

Fig. 4. Comparing algorithmic debugging strategies

The cost of single stepping is too expensive. Its worst case query complexity is order n, and its average cost is $n/2$.

Top-down and its variants have a cost of $b \cdot d$ which is significantly lower than the one of single stepping. The improvement of top-down zooming over top-down is based on the time needed by the programmer to answer the questions; their query complexity is the same.

In contrast, while in the worst case the costs of top-down and heaviest first are equal, in the mean case heaviest first performs an improvement over top-down. In particular, on average, for each wrong node with b children $s_i, 1 \leq i \leq b$:

- Top-down asks $\dfrac{b+1}{2}$ of the children.
- Heaviest first asks $\dfrac{\sum_{i=1}^{b} weight(s_i) \cdot pos(s_i)}{\sum_{i=1}^{b} weight(s_i)}$ of the children.

  where function $weight$ computes the weight of a node and function pos computes the position of a node in a list containing it and all its brothers which is ordered by their weights.

In the case of less YES first, the improvement is based on the fact that the heaviest branch is not always the branch with a higher probability of containing the buggy node. While heaviest first and less YES first have the same worst case query complexity, their average cost must be compared empirically.

D&Q and its variants are optimal in the worst case, with a cost order of $(b \cdot (log_2 n))$. The worst case cost of divide by YES and query is $b \cdot d$; it happens when the ET is completely balanced and the buggy node is in a leaf.

The cost of the rest of strategies is highly influenced by the answers of the user. The worst case of Hat-delta happens when the branching factor is 1 and the buggy node is in the leaf of the ET. In this case the cost is n. However, in normal situations, when the ET is wide, the worst case is still close to n; and it occurs when the first branch explored is answered YES, and the information of YES answers obtained makes the algorithmic debugger explore the rest of the ET bottom up.

Despite subterm dependency tracking is a top-down version enriched with additional information provided by the oracle, this information (that we assume correct here to compute the costs) could make the algorithmic debugger ask more questions than with the standard top-down. In fact, this strategy—and also dynamic weighting search if we assume that top-down is used by default— has a worst case query complexity of n because the expressions marked by the programmer can make the algorithmic debugger explore the whole ET.

5   Conclusions

This article introduces three new strategies and some optimizations for algorithmic debugging. Less YES first tries to improve heaviest first and divide by YES & query tries to improve D&Q by considering previous answers of the oracle during the search. Dynamic weighting search allows the user to specify the exact part of an equation which is wrong. This extra information can produce a much more accurate debugging session.

We have compared the most important algorithmic debugging strategies from a theoretical perspective. The comparison has been done according to seven dimensions including their worst case query complexity; and have produced some objective criteria to determine which strategy is better depending on the context.

We have implemented all the strategies and incorporated them in the algorithmic debugger DDT [3]. As future work, we plan to perform an empirical comparison of all the strategies in order to determine a weighting for their combination. With the knowledge acquired from the experiment we will be able to approximate the strategies' weights and to determine how they should change and on which factors this change depends.

Acknowledgements

I greatly thank Olaf Chitil, Thomas Davie and Yong Luo for many discussions about the contents of this paper. I also want to thank the anonymous referees of LOPSTR'06 for their helpful comments.

References

1. E. Av-Ron. *Top-Down Diagnosis of Prolog Programs*. PhD thesis, Weizmanm Institute, 1984.
2. D. Binks. *Declarative Debugging in Gödel*. PhD thesis, University of Bristol, 1995.
3. R. Caballero.   A Declarative Debugger of Incorrect Answers for Constraint Functional-Logic Programs. In *Proc. of the 2005 ACM SIGPLAN Workshop on Curry and Functional Logic Programming (WCFLP'05)*, pages 8–13, New York, USA, 2005. ACM Press.

4. R. Caballero. Algorithmic Debugging of Java Programs. In *Proc. of the 2006 Workshop on Functional Logic Programming (WFLP'06)*, pages 63–76. Electronic Notes in Theoretical Computer Science, 2006.
5. T. Conway, F. Henderson, and Z. Somogyi. Code Generation for Mercury. In *In Proc. of the International Logic Programming Symposium*, pages 242–256, 1995.
6. T. Davie and O. Chitil. Hat-delta: One Right Does Make a Wrong. In *Seventh Symposium on Trends in Functional Programming, TFP 06*, April 2006.
7. P. Fritzson, N. Shahmehri, M. Kamkar, and T. Gyimóthy. Generalized Algorithmic Debugging and Testing. *LOPLAS*, 1(4):303–322, 1992.
8. V. Hirunkitti and C. J. Hogger. A Generalised Query Minimisation for Program Debugging. In *Proc. of International Workshop of Automated and Algorithmic Debugging (AADEBUG'93)*, pages 153–170. Springer LNCS 749, 1993.
9. G. Kokai, J. Nilson, and C. Niss. GIDTS: A Graphical Programming Environment for Prolog. In *Workshop on Program Analysis For Software Tools and Engineering (PASTE'99)*, pages 95–104. ACM Press, 1999.
10. I. MacLarty. *Practical Declarative Debugging of Mercury Programs*. PhD thesis, Department of Computer Science and Software Engineering, The University of Melbourne, 2005.
11. M. Maeji and T. Kanamori. Top-Down Zooming Diagnosis of Logic Programs. Technical Report TR-290, ICOT, Japan, 1987.
12. L. Naish. A Declarative Debugging Scheme. *Journal of Functional and Logic Programming*, 1997(3), 1997.
13. L. Naish. A Three-Valued Declarative Debugging Scheme. In *Proc. of Workshop on Logic Programming Environments (LPE'97)*, pages 1–12, 1997.
14. H. Nilsson and P. Fritzson. Algorithmic Debugging for Lazy Functional Languages. *Journal of Functional Programming*, 4(3):337–370, 1994.
15. L. M. Pereira. Rational Debugging in Logic Programming. In *Proc. on Third International Conference on Logic Programming*, pages 203–210, New York, USA, 1986. Springer-Verlag LNCS 225.
16. E.Y. Shapiro. *Algorithmic Program Debugging*. MIT Press, 1982.
17. J. Silva. A Classification of Algorithmic Debugging Strategies. Technical Report DSIC-II/12/06, UPV, 2006. Available from URL: http://www.dsic.upv.es/~jsilva/research.htm#techs
18. J. Silva and O. Chitil. Combining Algorithmic Debugging and Program Slicing. In *Proc. of 8th ACM-SIGPLAN International Symposium on Principles and Practice of Declarative Programming (PPDP'06)*, pages 157–166. ACM Press, 2006.
19. M. Wallace, O. Chitil, T. Brehm, and C. Runciman. Multiple-View Tracing for Haskell: a New Hat. In *Proc. of the 2001 ACM SIGPLAN Haskell Workshop*, pages 151–170. Universiteit Utrecht UU-CS-2001-23, 2001.

A Program Transformation for Tracing Functional Logic Computations*

Bernd Brassel, Sebastian Fischer, and Frank Huch

Institute of Computer Science
University of Kiel, 24098 Kiel, Germany
{bbr,sebf,fhu}@informatik.uni-kiel.de

Abstract. Tracing program executions is a promising technique to find bugs in lazy functional logic programs. In previous work we developed an extension of a heap based semantics for functional logic languages which generates a trace reflecting the computation of the program. This extension was also prototypically implemented by instrumenting an interpreter for functional logic programs. Since this interpreter is too restricted for real world applications, we developed a program transformation which efficiently computes the trace by means of side effects during the computation. This paper presents our program transformation.

1 Introduction

Modern functional logic languages provide features like laziness and non-determinism (e.g., Curry [9] and Toy [11]) which makes these languages powerful but also operationally more complex. Although programs are defined on a high level of abstraction, they can still contain bugs. Tools which help finding such bugs (usually called *debuggers*) are needed. Unfortunately, such debuggers cannot be defined as easily as in strict, deterministic or even imperative languages. Because of laziness, sharing and non-determinism it is very difficult to understand the real evaluation performed at execution time. The sophisticated evaluation strategies imply complicated and incomprehensible execution traces. Thus, from the programmer's point of view, following the *actual* trace of a computation is almost useless when debugging lazy functional logic programs. Therefore, tools following this approach, like TeaBag [2], are not useful for real world applications. A naive possibility to cope with this problem would be to manually change to a simpler strategy like strict evaluation. But this will not work in applications actually making use of the advantages of lazy evaluation, e.g. using infinite data structures. In addition to this, a good debugging tool should provide means to selectively browse the program's execution, e.g. the user should be able to choose only those sub computations he is interested in.

For functional logic languages several works have advocated the construction of *declarative* traces that reflect an actual computation and can be presented to the user within a viewing tool, abstracting from the actual lazy execution. The

---

* This work has been partially supported by the DFG under grant Ha 2457/5-1.

main approaches are: Observations (cf. COOSy [3]) and declarative debugging (cf. DDT [5]). Both have predecessors in functional programming, e.g. observations in Hood [7] and declarative debugging in Freja [12]. Declarative debugging was originally developed for logic programming, called algorithmic debugging there [14]. For the functional language Haskell [13] there exists an additional important approach, Hat [15], which enables the exploration of a computation backwards starting at the program output or error message. Recently, Hat has been improved in such a way that it covers all previous three approaches thanks to the construction of an extended trail [6]: the *augmented redex trail* (ART).

In general, these approaches to debugging are based on some program transformation. For instance, Hat's ART is defined (indirectly) through the transformation that enables its creation: the source program is first instrumented and then executed to create the trail. Therefore, it is not easy to understand how the ART of a computation should be constructed (e.g., by hand), it remains unclear which assumptions about the operational semantics are made and, most importantly, there are no correctness results for the transformation [6].

As a consequence, we chose another way and first developed a formal semantics for tracing functional logic computations [4]. This approach defines an instrumentation of the standard operational semantics of lazy functional logic languages. The defined trace is proven to be correct with respect to the operational semantics, i.e., it exactly reflects the operational semantics. Our approach is also prototypically implemented within an interpreter and can be used for tracing small programs. Unfortunately, this interpreter does not scale in practice. Furthermore, many external libraries (e.g., for CGI programming or system calls) are not integrated. Hence, the interpreter is not useful for debugging real-world applications. As a solution, we developed a program transformation which in our case exactly implements the formal and correct specification of [4]. Although the ad-hoc transformations defined for lazy functional computations are a good fundament for our transformation, we have to consider the setting of functional logic computations in which free variables and non-determinism complicates the resulting trace structure and the program transformation considerably.

Although our approach covers tracing for arbitrary lazy functional logic languages, it is implemented in and for Curry [9]. This results in some Curry specific restrictions, e.g., required by the type system, to how we implement the program transformation. Furthermore, there are some additional (unsafe) functions needed to perform IO during a computation or to test whether a value is a free variable. These functions are provided in the Curry implementation PAKCS. Transferring this approach to another functional logic language or another Curry implementation requires similar functions or choosing a different approach.

2   Instrumented Semantics

In this section we briefly introduce the instrumented operational semantics which constructs the trace graph, cf. [4]. The instrumented semantics is shown in Table 1. These rules define a conservative extension of the original semantics [1].

Program	$P ::= D_1 \ldots D_m$	
Definition	$D ::= f(x_1, \ldots, x_n) = e$	
Expression	$e ::= x$	(variable)
	$\mid c(e_1, \ldots, e_n)$	(constructor call)
	$\mid f(e_1, \ldots, e_n)$	(function call)
	$\mid case\ e\ of\ \{\overline{p_n \rightarrow e_n}\}$	(rigid case)
	$\mid fcase\ e\ of\ \{\overline{p_n \rightarrow e_n}\}$	(flexible case)
	$\mid e_1\ or\ e_2$	(disjunction)
	$\mid let\ \overline{x_n = e_n}\ in\ e$	(let binding)
Pattern	$p ::= c(x_1, \ldots, x_n)$	

Fig. 1. Syntax for flat programs

The semantics is defined for a flat core language (Figure 1) for functional logic computations similar to intermediate languages used in common implementations of functional logic languages. Furthermore, the programs are supposed to be normalized which means a variable is introduced for every sub-expression occurring in the right-hand side of a function definition by means of a let expression. The definitions obey the following naming conventions:

$$\Gamma, \Delta, \Theta \in Heap = Var \rightarrow Exp \qquad v \in Value ::= x \mid c(\overline{x_n})$$

A *heap* is a partial mapping from variables to expressions (the *empty heap* is denoted by []). The value associated to variable x in heap Γ is denoted by $\Gamma[x]$. $\Gamma[x \mapsto e]$ denotes a heap with $\Gamma[x] = e$, i.e., we use this notation either as a condition on a heap Γ or as a modification of Γ. In a heap Γ, a free variable x is represented by a circular binding of the form $\Gamma[x] = x$. A *value* is a constructor rooted term or a free variable (w.r.t. the associated heap).

A *configuration* of the semantics is a tuple $\langle \Gamma, e, S, G, r, p \rangle$, where Γ is the current heap, e is the expression to be evaluated (often called the *control*), S is the stack (a list of variable names and case alternatives where the empty stack is denoted by []) which represents the current context, G is a directed graph (the trail built so far), and r, p are references for the *current* and *parent* nodes of the expression in the control. An *initial* configuration has the form: $\langle [], \texttt{main}, [], G_\emptyset, r, \square \rangle$, where $G_\emptyset$ denotes an empty graph, r is a reference and $\square$ denotes the null reference. A *final* configuration has the form: $\langle \Delta, \diamond, [], G, \square, p \rangle$.

Similarly to the ART model, our trail is a directed graph with nodes identified by references[1] that are labeled with expressions. We adopt the following conventions:

- $r \mapsto e$ means that the node with reference r is labeled with expression e.
- $r \overset{q}{\mapsto}$ means that node q is the successor of node r.
- $r \overset{p}{\mapsto}$ means that node p is the parent of node r.

---

[1] The domain for references is not fixed. For instance, we can use natural numbers as references but more complex domains are also possible.

Table 1. Small-Step Tracing Semantics

Rule	Heap	Control	Stack	Graph	Ref.	Par.
varcons	$\Gamma[x \mapsto t]$	x	S	G	r	p
$\Rightarrow$	$\Gamma[x \mapsto t]$	t	S	$G \bowtie (x \rightsquigarrow r)$	r	p
varexp	$\Gamma[x \mapsto e]$	x	S	G	r	p
$\Rightarrow$	$\Gamma[x \mapsto e]$	e	$x:S$	$G \bowtie (x \rightsquigarrow r)$	r	p
val	Γ	v	$x:S$	G	r	p
$\Rightarrow$	$\Gamma[x \mapsto v]$	v	S	G	r	p
fun	Γ	$f(\overline{x_n})$	S	G	r	p
$\Rightarrow$	Γ	$\rho(e)$	S	$G[r \overset{p}{\underset{q}{\uparrow}} f(\overline{x_n})]$	q	r
let	Γ	$let\ \overline{x_k} = e_k\ in\ e$	S	G	r	p
$\Rightarrow$	$\Gamma[\overline{y_k \mapsto \rho(e_k)}]$	$\rho(e)$	S	G	r	p
or	Γ	$e_1\ or\ e_2$	S	G	r	p
$\Rightarrow$	Γ	e_i	S	$G[r \overset{p}{\underset{q}{\uparrow}} e_1\ or\ e_2]$	q	r
case	Γ	$(f)\ case\ x\ of\ \{\overline{p_k \rightarrow e_k}\}$	S	G	r	p
$\Rightarrow$	Γ	x	$(\langle f \rangle \{\overline{p_k \rightarrow e_k}\}, r): S$	$G[r \overset{p}{\underset{q}{\uparrow}} (f)\ case\ x\ of\ \{\overline{p_k \rightarrow e_k}\}]$	q	r
select	Γ	$c(\overline{y_n})$	$(f\{\overline{p_k \rightarrow e_k}\}, r'): S$	G	r	p
$\Rightarrow$	Γ	$\rho(e_i)$	S	$G[r \overset{p}{\underset{q}{\uparrow}} c(\overline{y_n}), r' \underset{q}{\uparrow}]$	q	r'
guess	$\Gamma[y \mapsto y]$	y	$(f\{\overline{p_k \rightarrow e_k}\}, r'): S$	G	r	p
$\Rightarrow$	$\Gamma[y \mapsto \rho(p_i), \overline{y_n \mapsto y_n}]$	$\rho(e_i)$	S	$G[r \overset{p}{\underset{q}{\uparrow}} Free, q \overset{r'}{\mapsto} \rho(p_i), y \rightsquigarrow r, r' \underset{s}{\uparrow}]$	s	r'

where in varcons: t is constructor-rooted

varexp: e is not constructor rooted and $e \neq x$

val: v is constructor rooted or a variable with $\Gamma[v] = v$

fun: $f(\overline{y_n}) = e \in P$ and $\rho = \{\overline{y_n \mapsto x_n}\}$

let: $\rho = \{\overline{x_k \mapsto y_k}\}$ and $\overline{y_k}$ are fresh

or: $i \in \{1, 2\}$

select: $p_i = c(\overline{x_n})$ and $\rho = \{\overline{x_n \mapsto y_n}\}$

guess: $i \in \{1, \ldots k\}$, $p_i = c(\overline{x_n})$, $\rho = \{\overline{x_n \mapsto y_n}\}$, and $\overline{y_n}$ fresh

- Often, we write $r \overset{p}{\underset{q}{\mapsto}} e$ to denote that node r is labeled with expression e, node p is the parent of r, and node q is the successor of r. Similarly, we also write $r \overset{p}{\mapsto} e$ when the successor node is yet unknown (e.g., in rule case) or if there is no successor (e.g., in rule select).
- Argument arrows are denoted by $x \rightsquigarrow r$ which means that variable x points to node r. This is safe in our context since only variables can appear as arguments of function and constructor calls. These arrows are also called *variable pointers*.

In general, given a configuration $\langle \Gamma, e, S, G, r, p \rangle$, G denotes the graph built so far (not yet including the current expression e), r represents a fresh reference to store the current expression e in the control (with some exceptions, see below), and p denotes the parent of r. The basic idea of the graph construction is to record the actual control at the actual reference in every step. A brief explanation for each rule of the semantics follows:

(varcons and varexp) These rules are used to perform a variable lookup in the heap. If one of these rules is applied, it means that the evaluation of variable x is needed in the computation and a variable pointer for x should be added to the current graph G if it does not yet contain such a pointer. For this purpose, we introduce function $\bowtie$ which is defined as follows:

$$G \bowtie (x \rightsquigarrow r) = \begin{cases} G[x \rightsquigarrow r] & \text{if } \not\exists r'. (x \rightsquigarrow r') \in G \\ G & \text{otherwise} \end{cases}$$

Intuitively, function $\bowtie$ is used to take care of sharing: if the value of a given variable has already been demanded in the computation, no new variable pointer is added to the graph.

(val) updates a computed value in the heap. The current graph is not modified.

(fun) performs a simple function unfolding. When this rule is applied, node r (the value in column *Ref.*) is added to the graph. The node is labeled with the function call $f(\overline{x_n})$ and has parent p (the value in column *Par.*) and successor q (a fresh reference). In the new configuration, r becomes the parent reference (*Par.*) and the fresh reference q represents the current reference (*Ref.*).

(let) adds the bindings to the heap (with renamed variables) and proceeds with the evaluation of the main argument of *let*. The graph is not modified.

(or) *non-deterministically* evaluates either the first or the second argument of an *or* expression. A node representing the disjunction is added to the graph.

(case) initiates the evaluation of a case expression by evaluating the case argument and pushing the alternatives on the stack. It adds a node r to the graph which is labeled with the case expression. We set p as the parent of r but include no successor since it will not be known until the case argument is evaluated to head normal form. For this reason, reference r is also stored in the stack (together with the case alternatives) so that rules select and guess may eventually set the right successor for r.

(select) If we reach a constructor-rooted term and the top of the stack contains alternatives of a (f)case expression, rule select is applied to select the appropriate branch and continue with the evaluation of this branch. Furthermore,

a node r is added to the graph which is labeled with the computed value
$c(\overline{y_n})$. It sets p as the parent of r but includes no successor since values are
fully evaluated. Reference r' (stored in the stack) is used to set the right successor for the case expression that initiated the subcomputation: the fresh
reference q. Note that, in the derived configuration, we have r' as a parent
reference—the case expression—rather than r.

(guess) If we reach a free variable and the case expression on the stack is flexible
(i.e., of the form $f\{\overline{p_k \text{->} e_k}\}$), then rule guess is used to non-deterministically
choose one alternative and continue with the evaluation of this branch; more-
over, the heap is updated with the binding of the free variable to the corresponding pattern. This rule modifies the graph in a similar way as the
previous one. The main difference is that the computed value is a *free variable*. Here, we add node r to the graph which is labeled with a special symbol,
Free, and whose successor is a new node q which is labeled with the selected
binding for the free variable.

Finally, the operational semantics provides some rules for copying the result
of a computation into the graph, from which we only present the case for a
constructor rooted term:

Rule	Heap	Control	Stack	Graph	Ref.	Par.
success-c	Γ	$c(\overline{x_n})$	[]	G	r	p
$\Longrightarrow \Gamma$	$\diamond$		[]	$G[r \overset{p}{\mapsto} c(\overline{x_n})]\ \square$		r

Similar rules are defined for failing computations and free variables as results
(see [4]).

We illustrate the tracing semantics with a simple example. For the following
program the computed trail is depicted in Figure 2.

```
mother x = fcase x of { John  -> Christine; Peter -> Monica }
father x = fcase x of { Peter -> John }
main = let x = x, y = father x in mother y
```

Similarly to the original small-step semantics [1], our tracing semantics is
non-deterministic, i.e., it computes a different trail—a graph—for each non-
deterministic computation from the initial configuration. In practice, however,
it is more convenient to build a single graph that comprises all possible non-
deterministic paths (see Section 3.1).

3 Program Transformation

We have implemented a program transformation which converts an arbitrary flat
program into an instrumented flat program. This instrumented program writes
the trace graph as a side effect at runtime. The basic idea is to wrap all sub-
expressions of the program with additional function calls. Semantically, these
wrapper functions are identities but evaluating them initiates the side effects
needed to write the execution trace to a file.

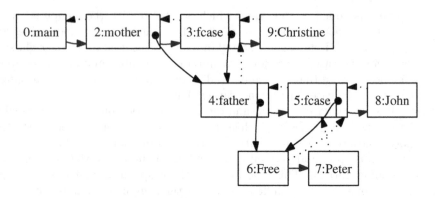

Fig. 2. Trail of a computation

3.1 Path Information

Instead of writing distinct trace graphs for every non-deterministic computation, we generate a *unified graph* that represents all non-deterministic computations at once. The trace corresponding to one non-deterministic computation can be extracted from the unified graph using *path* information that is associated with every trace node.

Initially, the computation starts with the empty path. Whenever a branching is performed, the subsequent computations are distinguished by extended paths. As an example reconsider the example from above with the call

```
main = let x = x in mother x
```

The unified graph for this example is presented in Figure 3. At each node the path (a list of numbers) is added to the label. This unified graph represents two computations, one with path [1] and the other with path [2]. The two graphs can be computed from the unified graph by considering only nodes with a corresponding path prefix. For instance, the node labeled with 1:[]:mother belongs to both graphs while the node labeled with 6:[1]:Christine only belongs to the graph with path [1].

Generating a unified graph instead of a separate graph for each computation has two advantages. Firstly, large parts of the different graphs are identical (e.g., all nodes labeled with the empty path belong to all graphs). Secondly, in the viewer tool, it is not sufficient to present only a single graph to detect errors related to non-determinism. Rather, different results of a computation have to be presented to the programmer. Furthermore, the information about structures that are identical for two non-deterministic branches can be of great help for debugging, too. It is much easier to obtain these results in the unified graph.

Unfortunately, it is not possible to statically determine the order in which non-determinism occurs in the computation, as the following function definition shows:

```
f x y z  = fcase x of { 0 -> fcase y of { 0 -> z };
                        1 -> fcase z of { 1 -> 42 }}
```

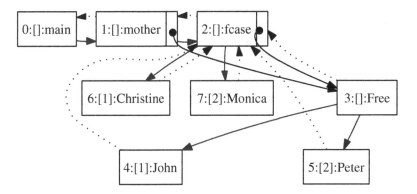

Fig. 3. Unified trace graph

The function branches depending on its first argument x: for 0 the function requires the evaluation of y to 0 and returns z; for 1 the function requires the evaluation of its third argument z and yields 42 without initiating the evaluation of y at all. If the evaluation of the arguments y and z introduces non-determinism, then the order in which this non-determinism is introduced into the concrete computation depends on the value for x. The non-determinism in y may not even be introduced at all if x is bound to 1. Hence, the current path has to be propagated at runtime, independently of the evaluation order.

In our program transformation, we employ the logic features of Curry to compute the path of a non-deterministic computation. To be able to extend the current path when we perform a non-deterministic branching in or or fcase, we pass the current path as an additional parameter to every function. Initially, this argument is a free variable representing the empty path. Non-empty paths are represented by lists that are terminated by a free variable instead of the empty list (cf. message queues in [8]). Hence, a path is represented as a partially instantiated list of numbers. In contrast to other approaches using advanced list implementations like difference lists in PROLOG or functional lists [10], our lists are not supposed to improve efficiency. They are a means to globally extend paths within non-deterministic computations independently of the evaluation order.

The program transformation employs a function extend to extend the path of the current computation. This function is implemented as:

```
extend :: Path -> Int -> a -> a
extend p n x | end p =:= (n:ns) = x where ns free

end :: Path -> Path
end p = if isVar p then p else end (tail p)
```

We use the auxiliary function **end** to return the terminating free variable of a path. The function **isVar** indicates whether the head-normal-form of its argument is a free variable. In order to write a path to a file, we need to replace the free variable that terminates the path with the empty list:

```
path :: Path -> Path
path p = if isVar p then [] else head p : path (tail p)
```

3.2   Labeling Expressions

When writing trace nodes, we need to refer to other nodes in the graph that have not yet been written. For example, to write the node for a function call we need to refer to the function's arguments. However, these may not have been written into the trace graph yet because of lazy evaluation. In the instrumented semantics we use fresh variable names to refer to unevaluated expressions and use a special operation $(x \rightsquigarrow r)$ to map these variables to node references when the corresponding expression is evaluated.

At runtime such variables are not available. Instead, we have to generate similar references and use globally unique labels to represent sub-expressions. New labels are constructed by means of a global state which is accessed by side effects whenever the evaluation of sub-expressions is requested.

As a first approach we can think of references as integer values attached to every expression. Every function is transformed accordingly, i.e., it expects labeled values as arguments instead of the original argument values and returns a labeled result. For example, a function of type **Bool -> Bool -> Bool** would be transformed into a function of type **(Int,Bool) -> (Int,Bool) -> (Int,Bool)** according to this first approach.

Unfortunately, this approach is not sufficient to model compound values. If a component of such a value is selected and passed as argument to some function, we need to be able to determine the label of this sub-term from the original value. In principle, there are two possibilities to store labels for every sub-term of compound values: The first is to provide labeled versions of every datatype and compute with values of this variants instead of the original data-terms. For example, the definition of natural numbers as successor terms

```
data Nat = Z | S Nat
```

can be altered to store labels for each sub-term as follows:

```
data LabeledNat = LZ Int | LS Int LabeledNat
```

Each constructor has an additional argument for the label of the corresponding sub-term. For example, the value (S Z) could be labeled as (LS 1 (LZ 2)). Although this approach is quite intuitive, it also has a severe drawback: It is not possible to write a Curry function that computes the original value from a labeled value of arbitrary type. We need to compute unlabeled values for two reasons: First, the result of the top-level computation should be presented to the user without labels and, second, external functions must be applied to unlabeled values. Although we can define such un-labeling functions for each particular datatype, this is not sufficient for calls to polymorphic external functions where the current argument-types are unknown.

As a solution, we take a different approach: instead of a label, we attach a tree of labels to each expression that represents the labels of all sub-terms of the expression. We define the data-types

```
data Labeled a = Labeled Labels a
data Labels    = Labels Int [Labels]
```

to model labeled values. The label tree has the same structure as the wrapped data structure.

The boolean function mentioned above is transformed into a function of type `Labeled Bool -> Labeled Bool -> Labeled Bool` and we provide wrapper functions for every defined constructor that operates on labeled values. For example, the wrapper functions for the construction of labeled natural numbers have the following types:

```
z :: Labeled Nat                  -- Z :: Nat
s :: Labeled Nat -> Labeled Nat  -- S :: Nat -> Nat
```

Now the value (S Z) is represented as `Labeled (Labels 1 [Labels 2 []])` (S Z). With this representation of labeled values it is no problem to define a function `value :: Labeled a -> a`. Hence, we prefer this solution over the more intuitive approach to label compound values by extending all data types.

3.3   Global State

We provide a library that is imported by every transformed program. This library has two main purposes: a) implement the side effects that write the trace nodes during the computation and b) provide a global state which manages references and labels.

At the beginning of each execution trace, the global state must be initialized, i.e. global counters are set to zero, old trace files are deleted and some header information is written to the new trace file. All this is done by `initState ::` `IO ()`. It is necessary to use a global state instead of passing values through the program, e.g. by a state monad, since tracing must not modify the evaluation order. As already discussed in Section 3.1 the evaluation order is statically unknown. The state cannot be passed and has to be modified by side effects.

There are two global counters, one to provide the references, which corresponds to the *Ref.* column of the tracing semantics, cf. Section 2. The other counter provides labels for arguments which correspond to the variables in the semantics. The counters are accessed by the according IO actions:

```
currentRefFromState, currentLabelFromState :: IO Int
incrementRefCounter, incrementLabelCounter :: IO ()
```

In most cases the access to the current counter is directly followed by increment-ing the counter. Hence, we provide `nextRefFromState, nextLabelFromState` `:: IO Int` which perform those two actions.

In addition to the two counters, there is one more global integer value: the current parent reference. This corresponds to the *Par.* column of the seman-tics and is accessed by the functions `setParentInState :: Int -> IO ()` and `getParentFromState :: IO Int`.

Since all tracing has to be done by side effects, all calls to the library functions are wrapped by a call to the function `unsafe :: IO a -> a`. Therefore, the functions actually called by the transformed programs look like this:

```
nextRef, nextLabel :: Int
nextRef   = unsafe nextRefFromState
nextLabel = unsafe nextLabelFromState
```

As an example for how the global state is used we present the wrapper function for tracing function calls:

```
traceFunc :: Path -> Name -> [Int] -> Labeled a -> Labeled a
traceFunc p name args body = unsafe (do
  l <- nextLabelFromState
  return (Labeled (Labels l (argLabels body))
            (redirect p l (writeFunc p name args (value body)))))

writeFunc :: Path -> Name -> [Int] -> a -> a
writeFunc p name args x = unsafe (do
  ref <- nextRefFromState
  parent <- getParentFromState
  printTrace (showApp ref (path p) parent name args)
  succ <- getRefFromState
  printTrace (showSucc ref succ)
  setParentInState ref
  return x)
```

The function `traceFunc` introduces a new label `l` for the function application, which is redirected to the reference of the application when it is evaluated (dis-cussed in more detail in the next section). `writeFunc` takes this reference from the global state, asks for the current parent and writes a corresponding trace node into the trace file. Since an application is always followed by its result in the trace graph, we then ask for the next reference without incrementing it and write an appropriate successor relation into the trace graph. Similarly, construc-tor applications are traced with the function `traceCons` but without writing a successor relation.

3.4   Redirecting Arguments

One of the key concepts of the instrumented semantics is redirecting variables to references representing their evaluation by means of $\rightsquigarrow$. Function applications can directly be written to the trace without considering which arguments are already evaluated. To write a redirection into the trace, we provide the following function:

```
redirect :: Path -> Int -> a -> a
redirect p l x = unsafe (do
  ref <- getRefFromState
  printTrace (showRedir l (path p) ref)
  return x)
```

The label `l` (representing a variable) is redirected to the current reference (`ref`) to which the next evaluation will be written. The function `printTrace` writes data into the trace file and `showRedir` converts a redirection with respect to the current path into a string.

In the semantics the $\leadsto$ relation is written in the rules varcons, varexp, and guess. In the program transformation these rules are not directly available. However, every expression is labeled as explained in Section 3.2 and can itself write its redirection to the graph when its evaluation is initiated. Hence, every constructed value of type `Labeled` calls redirect. Additionally, the program transformation will introduce a call to redirect to implement the guess rule.

3.5   Transforming Expressions

The key idea of the program transformation is that every expression writes itself when it is evaluated. Each expression is transformed in a way that a corresponding trace node is written as a side effect when the evaluation of the expression is demanded by the computation. In this section, we explain in detail, how arbitrary flat expressions are transformed to generate the instrumented program. The transformed expressions will use functions of the trace library, like `traceFunc`, cf. Section 3.3.

We present the transformation on flat programs and expressions as a function τ and successively discuss τ for the different kinds of expressions. As a first step, we introduce wrapper functions for all defined functions and constructors:

$$\tau(f\ x_1\ \ldots\ x_n = e) =$$
$$f\ p\ x_1 \ldots x_n = \texttt{traceFunc}\ p\ 'f'\ [\texttt{label}\ x_1, \ldots, \texttt{label}\ x_n]\ \tau(e')$$

First, an argument for the path (p) is added to every function definition. Every call to a function in e will also be extended by this path argument such that the current path is available everywhere. In the right-hand side we introduce a call to `traceFunc` which writes a node corresponding to the function call with respect to the current path into the trace graph. The name of the original function is supplied as second argument and a list of argument labels as third. The function `label` returns the label at the root of a labeled value, cf. Section 3.2. After storing the trace information the function `traceFunc` returns its last argument, which is the transformed body of the original function. We wrote e' instead of e for the body because we have to do some additional work, if the function is a projection on one of its arguments. We will consider projections in Section 3.6.

Similarly, for each defined constructor c of arity n we introduce a wrapper function:

$$\tilde{c}\ p\ x_1 \ldots x_n = \text{traceCons}\ p\ 'c'\ [\text{label}\ x_1,\ldots,\text{label}\ x_n]$$
$$(c\ (\text{value}\ x_1)\ \ldots\ (\text{value}\ x_n))$$

Now we consider the different cases of flat expressions for our translation τ. Variables do not need to be transformed at all:

$$\tau(x) = x, \text{ if } x \in Var$$

For the transformation of function and constructor applications, we use the wrapper functions defined above:

$$\tau(f\ e_1 \ldots e_n) = f\ p\ \tau(e_1) \ldots \tau(e_n)$$
$$\tau(c\ e_1 \ldots e_n) = \tilde{c}\ p\ \tau(e_1) \ldots \tau(e_n)$$

Note, that since the path p is an argument of every function, it is always in scope. To trace *or*-expressions (rule or), we need to compute a globally unique reference for the *or*-node in the graph and supply this reference to the non-deterministic sub-computations.

$$\tau(e_1 \text{ or } e_2) = \text{let } r = \text{nextRef}$$
$$\text{in traceOr } p\ r\ ((\text{extend } p\ 1\ (\text{traceBranch } r\ \tau(e_1)))\ \text{or}$$
$$(\text{extend } p\ 2\ (\text{traceBranch } r\ \tau(e_2))))$$

The function traceBranch employs this reference to write successor and parent edges accordingly. The current path is extended by means of extend, cf. Section 3.1.

In our flat language free variables are introduced as cyclic bindings (let x=x in ..., cf. [4]). Free variables have to be introduced as labeled values, which can be realized by introducing the function traceFree:

$$\tau(\text{let } \overline{x_n = e_n} \text{ in } e) = \text{let } \overline{x_n = \tau_{x_n}(e_n)} \text{ in } \tau(e)$$

$$\tau_x(x) = \text{traceFree } p$$
$$\tau_x(e) = \tau(e), \text{ if } e \neq x$$

The transformation of *case*-expressions is a bit more involved. We will explain the transformation of rigid and flexible *case*-expressions separately although the latter is an extension of the former.

When tracing case expressions, different information has to be recorded in the trace. First the case itself has to be stored in the current reference (cf. rule case). Hence, we introduce an application of the function traceCase. Then the branching has to be performed on the original value. In each branch we supplement the successor of the case node as in rule select by introducing the function traceBranch to each case branch. It is not necessary to introduce a stack in our program transformation since both states of the execution (before and after evaluating the case expression) are available at transformation time. The reference stored in the stack in the instrumented semantics can easily be passed into the branches.

$\tau(\text{case } e \text{ of } branches) =$
    $\text{let } r = \text{nextRef}, x = \tau(e), ls = \text{argLabels } x$
        $\text{in traceCase } p \; r \; (\text{label } x) \; (\tau_{select} \; r \; x \; ls \; branches)$

$\tau_{select} \; r \; x \; ls \; \overline{\{c_n \; \overline{x_{m_n}} \; \text{->} \; e_n\}} =$
    $\text{case value } x \text{ of } \{$

        $\dots$

        $c_i \; y_1 \; \dots \; y_{m_i} \text{-> let } [l_1, \dots, l_{m_i}] = ls \; ,$
                            $x_1 = \text{Labeled } l_1 \; y_1,$

                            $\dots$

                            $x_{m_i} = \text{Labeled } l_{m_i} \; y_{m_i}$
                        $\text{in traceBranch } r \; \tau(e_i);$

        $\dots\}$

To reflect pattern matching on the level of the label information as well, we apply the function `argLabels` to the matched expression. It selects all sub-label-trees of the root-label. These label trees are attached to the corresponding sub-terms of the matched value $(y_1, \dots, y_{m_i})$. Note the renaming of the pattern variables: x_k is renamed to y_k and redefined as the corresponding labeled value in each branch of the *case*-expression.

The transformation of flexible case expressions is a bit more complicated but can be implemented with similar techniques. If the case argument evaluates to a constructor rooted term, then the flexible case behaves as a rigid case (select). If the case argument of a flexible case evaluates to a free variable, then this variable is non-deterministically instantiated with the patterns of all branches and the evaluation continues with the right-hand side of the corresponding branches (guess). Both cases can only be distinguished at runtime and have to be reflected in the program transformation. We treat this porblem within the application of `traceFCase`, which branches in dependence of x reducing to a constructor rooted term (τ_{select}) or a free variable (τ_{guess}).

$\tau(\text{fcase } e \text{ of } branches) =$
    $\text{let } v = \text{nextRef},$
        $r = \text{nextRef},$
        $x = \tau(e),$
        $ls = \text{argLabels } x$
    $\text{in traceFCase } p \; r \; v \; x \; (\tau_{select} \; r \; x \; ls \; branches)$
                            $(\tau_{guess} \; v \; r \; x \; ls \; branches)$

$\tau_{guess} \; v \; r \; x \; ls \; \overline{\{c_n \; \overline{x_{m_n}} \; \text{->} \; e_n\}} =$
    $\text{fcase value } x \text{ of } \{$

        $\dots$

        $c_i \; y_1 \; \dots \; y_{m_i} \text{-> extend } p \; i$
            $(\text{let } l_1 = \text{nextLabel}, \dots, l_{m_i} = \text{nextLabel},$
                $x_1 = \text{Labeled } l_1 \; (\text{redirect } p \; l_1 \; y_1),$
                $\dots$

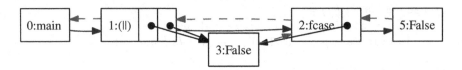

Fig. 4. Trail of a Projection - Tracing Semantics

$$x_{m_i} = \texttt{Labeled}\ l_{m_i}\ (\texttt{redirect}\ p\ l_{m_i}\ y_{m_i})$$
$$\texttt{in traceBind}\ p\ 'c'_i\ v\ [l_1, \dots, l_{m_i}]\ ls\ (\texttt{traceBranch}\ r\ \tau(e_i)));$$
$$\dots\}$$

In contrast to the select case, we have to record three additional kinds of information in the trace: the non-deterministic branching (similar to **or**), the free variable and its bindings.

The function **traceBind** writes trace nodes for the bindings of the free variable, where the free variable is represented by a trace node with reference v and written by the function **traceFCase**. It also unifies the labels $l_1, \dots, l_{m_i}$ with the original argument labels ls of the free variable, which are initially uninstantiated.

3.6   Transforming Projections

The transformation presented so far reflects the behavior of the tracing semantics with one notable exception: projections. Projections are functions that reduce to one of their arguments, as the following example shows:

```
main = let x = False in x || x

(||) :: Bool -> Bool -> Bool
x || y = fcase x of { True -> True; False -> y }
```

Tracing the execution of **main** using the semantics of Section 2 yields the graph shown in Figure 4. When tracing the same program with the transformation introduced so far, the result of the boolean disjunction (||) is not traced. The reason is that if its first argument is **False** the function (||) is a projection. The tracing semantics adds constructor values to the graph *each time* they are demanded. The same is not possible with the approach presented so far; values can only be traced when they are demanded *for the first time*. If a projection is called with a value as argument which has already been evaluated before, then the successor of the projection needs to refer to an already written node.

To solve this problem, we introduce a new kind of trace nodes: projection nodes. Our transformation analyzes the right-hand sides of all defined functions of a program and introduces the special function **traceProj** that writes a projection node as a side effect. This analysis only checks whether there are defining rules with an argument variable as right-hand side and wraps such variables with a call to **traceProj**. For example, the transformation of the identity function is:

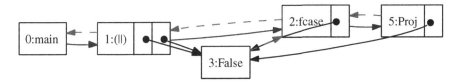

Fig. 5. Trail of a Projection - Transformed Program

```
id :: Path -> Labeled a -> Labeled a
id p x = traceFunc p "id" [label x] (traceProj p x)
```

With this modification, the above example yields the trace shown in Figure 5.

Note, that the resulting graph contains indeed more information than the one of Figure 4: the fact that the value **False** is also shared in the result of (| |). Taking into account the order in which the nodes of the trace graph were written, there exists a simple mapping from the graphs generated by transformed programs to the ones produced by the semantics.

4   Conclusion

We presented a program transformation implementing a tracer for functional logic programs. The transformation exactly reflects a formal tracing semantics defined in previous work except for projections which have to be recorded explicitly. A copying as done in the formal semantics is not possible in the transformed program. However, in the final trace graph projection nodes can be eliminated by copying nodes and we obtain the original, formally defined trace graph. Although our transformation is closely related to the formal semantics it remains to formally prove its equivalence.

Our program transformation is implemented for a (slightly different) flat Curry representation used as intermediate language in the Curry implementation PAKCS. Constructing the trace graph by means of the program transformation performs several times faster than our first implementation within a flat Curry interpreter. However, this is not the only advantage of the new approach. Now the trace generation is integrated into the real environment in which systems are developed and arbitrary Curry programs can be traced, independently of new features possibly not available for the interpreter. In contrast our interpreter only supports the core flat Curry language (with only a small set of external functions), but is a good platform for prototypical implementations of semantic based tools.

At the moment we are working on tracing external functions and want to implement a module-wise transformation with a trusting mechanism for selected modules. Furthermore, we are optimizing our viewing tools to cope with non-determinism and the large size of applications that can now be traced.

References

1. E. Albert, M. Hanus, F. Huch, J. Oliver, and G. Vidal. Operational semantics for declarative multi-paradigm languages. *Journal of Symbolic Computation*, 40(1):795–829, 2005.

2. S. Antoy and S. Johnson. TeaBag: A functional logic language debugger. In Herbert Kuchen, editor, *Proc. of the 13th International Workshop on Functional and (constraint) Logic Programming (WFLP'04)*, pages 4–18, Aachen, Germany, June 2004.

3. B. Braßel, O. Chitil, M. Hanus, and F. Huch. Observing functional logic computations. In *Proc. of the Sixth International Symposium on Practical Aspects of Declarative Languages (PADL'04)*, pages 193–208. Springer LNCS 3057, 2004.

4. B. Braßel, M. Hanus, F. Huch, and G. Vidal. A semantics for tracing declarative multi-paradigm programs. In *Proceedings of the 6th ACM SIGPLAN International Conference on Principles and Practice of Declarative Programming (PPDP'04)*, pages 179–190. ACM Press, 2004.

5. R. Caballero and M. Rodríguez-Artalejo. DDT: a declarative debugging tool for functional-logic languages. In *Proceedings of the 7th International Symposium on Functional and Logic Programming (FLOPS 2004)*, pages 70–84. Springer LNCS 2998, 2004.

6. O. Chitil, C. Runciman, and M. Wallace. Freja, hat and hood – a comparative evaluation of three systems for tracing and debugging lazy functional programs. In *Proc. of the 12th International Workshop on Implementation of Functional Languages (IFL 2000)*, pages 176–193. Springer LNCS 2011, 2001.

7. Andy Gill. Debugging Haskell by observing intermediate datastructures. *Electronic Notes in Theoretical Computer Science*, 41(1), 2001.

8. M. Hanus. Distributed Programming in a Multi-Paradigm Declarative Language. In *Proc. of the International Conference on Principles and Practice of Declarative Programming (PPDP'99)*, pages 376–395. Springer LNCS 1702, 1999.

9. M. Hanus (ed.). Curry: An integrated functional logic language. Available at `http://www-i2.informatik.rwth-aachen.de/~hanus/curry`, 1997.

10. John Hughes. A novel representation of lists and its application to the function "reverse". *Inf. Process. Lett.*, 22(3):141–144, 1986.

11. F. López-Fraguas and J. Sánchez-Hernández. TOY: A multiparadigm declarative system. In *Proc. of RTA'99*, pages 244–247. Springer LNCS 1631, 1999.

12. H. Nilsson and J. Sparud. The Evaluation Dependence Tree as a Basis for Lazy Functional Debugging. *Automated Software Engineering*, 4(2):121–150, 1997.

13. S. Peyton Jones, editor. *Haskell 98 Language and Libraries—The Revised Report*. Cambridge University Press, 2003.

14. E. Shapiro. *Algorithmic Program Debugging*. MIT Press, Cambridge, Massachusetts, 1983.

15. J. Sparud and C. Runciman. Tracing Lazy Functional Computations Using Redex Trails. In *Proc. of the 9th Int'l Symp. on Programming Languages, Implementations, Logics and Programs (PLILP'97)*, pages 291–308. Springer LNCS 1292, 1997.

Automated Termination Analysis for Logic Programs by Term Rewriting*

Peter Schneider-Kamp[1], Jürgen Giesl[1], Alexander Serebrenik[2], and René Thiemann[1]

[1] LuFG Informatik 2, RWTH Aachen, Ahornstr. 55, 52074 Aachen, Germany
{psk,giesl,thiemann}@informatik.rwth-aachen.de
[2] Dept. of Mathematics and Computer Science, TU Eindhoven, P.O. Box 513, 5600 MB Eindhoven, The Netherlands
a.serebrenik@tue.nl

Abstract. There are two kinds of approaches for termination analysis of logic programs: "transformational" and "direct" ones. Direct approaches prove termination directly on the basis of the logic program. Transformational approaches transform a logic program into a term rewrite system (TRS) and then analyze termination of the resulting TRS instead. Thus, transformational approaches make all methods previously developed for TRSs available for logic programs as well. However, the applicability of most existing transformations is quite restricted, as they can only be used for certain subclasses of logic programs. (Most of them are restricted to *well-moded* programs.) In this paper we improve these transformations such that they become applicable for *any* definite logic program. To simulate the behavior of logic programs by TRSs, we slightly modify the notion of rewriting by permitting infinite terms. We show that our transformation results in TRSs which are indeed suitable for *automated* termination analysis. In contrast to most other methods for termination of logic programs, our technique is also sound for logic programming *without occur check*, which is typically used in practice. We implemented our approach in the termination prover AProVE and successfully evaluated it on a large collection of examples.

1 Introduction

Termination of logic programs is widely studied (see, e.g., [12] for an overview and [9,13,20,26,33] for more recent work on "direct" approaches). "Transformational" approaches have been developed in [1,5,8,15,19,23,24,30] and a comparison of these approaches is given in [28]. Transformational methods

(I) should be *applicable* for a class of logic programs as large as possible and
(II) should produce TRSs whose termination is *easy to analyze automatically.*

Concerning (I), the above transformations can only be used for certain subclasses of logic programs. More precisely, all approaches except [23,24] are restricted to *well-moded* programs. [23,24] also consider the classes of *simply well-typed* and

---

* Supported by the Deutsche Forschungsgsmeinschaft DFG under grant GI 274/5-1.

safely typed programs. We present a new transformation which, in contrast to all previous transformations, is applicable for *any* (definite[1]) logic program.

Concerning (II), one needs an implementation and an empirical evaluation to find out whether termination of the transformed TRSs can indeed be verified automatically for a large class of examples. Unfortunately, to our knowledge there is only a single other termination tool available which implements a transformational approach. This tool TALP [29] is based on the transformations of [5,8,15] which are shown to be equally powerful in [28]. So these transformations are indeed suitable for automated termination analysis, but consequently, TALP only accepts well-moded logic programs. This is in contrast to our approach which we implemented in our termination prover AProVE. Our experiments on large collections of examples in Sect. 5 show that our transformation indeed produces TRSs that are suitable for automated termination analysis and that AProVE is currently among the most powerful termination provers for logic programs.

Our transformation is inspired by the transformation of [5,8,15,28]. In this classical transformation, each argument position of each predicate is either labelled as *input* or *output*. As mentioned, the labelling must be such that the labelled program is *well moded* [3]. Well-modedness guarantees that each atom is "sufficiently" instantiated during any derivation with a query that is ground on all input positions. More precisely, a program is well moded iff for any of its clauses $H :\!- B_1, \ldots, B_k$ with $k \geq 0$, we have

(a) $\mathcal{V}_{out}(H) \subseteq \mathcal{V}_{in}(H) \cup \mathcal{V}_{out}(B_1) \cup \ldots \cup \mathcal{V}_{out}(B_k)$ and
(b) $\mathcal{V}_{in}(B_i) \subseteq \mathcal{V}_{in}(H) \cup \mathcal{V}_{out}(B_1) \cup \ldots \cup \mathcal{V}_{out}(B_{i-1})$ for all $1 \leq i \leq k$

$\mathcal{V}_{in}(B)$ and $\mathcal{V}_{out}(B)$ are the variables in terms on B's input and output positions.

Example 1. We illustrate our concepts with a variant of a small example from [28]. Let p's first argument position be input and the second be output.

$$p(X, X)$$
$$p(f(X), g(Y)) :\!- p(f(X), f(Z)), p(Z, g(Y))$$

The program is well moded: This is obvious for the first clause. For the second clause, (a) holds since the output variable Y of the head is also an output variable of the second body atom. Similarly, (b) holds since the input variable X of the first body atom is also an input variable of the head, and the input variable Z of the second body atom is also an output variable of the first body atom.

In the classical transformation from logic programs to TRSs [28], two new function symbols p_{in} and p_{out} are introduced for each predicate p. We write "$p(\boldsymbol{s}, \boldsymbol{t})$" to denote that $\boldsymbol{s}$ and $\boldsymbol{t}$ are the sequences of terms on p's in- and output positions.

---

[1] Like most approaches for termination of logic programs, we restrict ourselves to programs without cut and negation. While there are transformational approaches which go beyond definite programs [24], it is not clear how to transform non-definite logic programs into TRSs that are suitable for *automated* termination analysis, cf. (II).

- For each fact $p(s, t)$, the TRS contains the rule $p_{in}(s) \rightarrow p_{out}(t)$.
- For each clause c of the form $p(s, t) :- p_1(s_1, t_1), \ldots, p_k(s_k, t_k)$, the resulting TRS contains the following rules:

$$p_{in}(s) \rightarrow u_{c,1}(p_{1_{in}}(s_1), \mathcal{V}(s))$$
$$u_{c,1}(p_{1_{out}}(t_1), \mathcal{V}(s)) \rightarrow u_{c,2}(p_{2_{in}}(s_2), \mathcal{V}(s) \cup \mathcal{V}(t_1))$$
$$\ldots$$

$$u_{c,k}(p_{k_{out}}(t_k), \mathcal{V}(s) \cup \mathcal{V}(t_1) \cup \ldots \cup \mathcal{V}(t_{k-1})) \rightarrow p_{out}(t)$$

Here, $\mathcal{V}(s)$ are the variables occurring in s. Moreover, if $\mathcal{V}(s) = \{x_1, ..., x_n\}$, then "$u_{c,1}(p_{1_{in}}(s_1), \mathcal{V}(s))$" abbreviates the term $u_{c,1}(p_{1_{in}}(s_1), x_1, ..., x_n)$, etc.

If the resulting TRS is terminating, then the original logic program terminates for any query with ground terms on all input positions of the predicates, cf. [28].

Example 2. For Ex. 1, the transformation results in the following TRS $\mathcal{R}$.

$$p_{in}(X) \rightarrow p_{out}(X) \qquad\qquad u_1(p_{out}(f(Z)), X) \rightarrow u_2(p_{in}(Z), X, Z)$$
$$p_{in}(f(X)) \rightarrow u_1(p_{in}(f(X)), X) \qquad u_2(p_{out}(g(Y)), X, Z) \rightarrow p_{out}(g(Y))$$

The original logic program is terminating for any query $p(t_1, t_2)$ where t_1 is a ground term. However, the above TRS is not terminating:

$$p_{in}(f(X)) \rightarrow_{\mathcal{R}} u_1(p_{in}(f(X)), X) \rightarrow_{\mathcal{R}} u_1(u_1(p_{in}(f(X)), X), X) \rightarrow_{\mathcal{R}} \ldots$$

In the logic program, after resolving with the second clause, one obtains a query starting with $p(f(\ldots), f(\ldots))$. Since p's output argument $f(\ldots)$ is already partly instantiated, the second clause cannot be applied again for this atom. However, this information is neglected in the translated TRS. Here, one only regards the input argument of p in order to determine whether a rule can be applied. Note that current tools for termination proofs of logic programs like cTI [25], Hasta-La-Vista [32], TALP [29], TermiLog [22], and TerminWeb [10] fail on Ex. 1.[2]

So this example already illustrates a drawback of the classical transformation of [28]: there are several terminating well-moded logic programs which are transformed into non-terminating TRSs. In such cases, one fails in proving the termination of the logic program. Even worse, most of the existing transformations are not applicable for logic programs that are not well moded.[3]

---

[2] They can handle Ex. 1 if one performs a program specialization step before [31]. Our example collection at http://aprove.informatik.rwth-aachen.de/eval/LP/ illustrates the advantages of different tools and also includes several examples where "direct" tools fail because the termination proof requires complex ranking functions.

[3] Ex. 3 is neither well moded nor simply well typed nor safely typed (using the types "*Any*" and "*Ground*") as required by the transformations [1,5,8,15,19,23,24,30].

Example 3. We modify Ex. 1 by replacing $g(Y)$ *with* $g(W)$ *in the body:*

$$\mathsf{p}(X, X)$$
$$\mathsf{p}(\mathsf{f}(X), \mathsf{g}(Y)) :- \mathsf{p}(\mathsf{f}(X), \mathsf{f}(Z)), \mathsf{p}(Z, \mathsf{g}(W))$$

Still, all queries $\mathsf{p}(t_1, t_2)$ *terminate if* t_1 *is ground. But this program is not well moded, as the second clause violates Condition (a):* $\mathcal{V}_{out}(\mathsf{p}(\mathsf{f}(X), \mathsf{g}(Y))) = \{Y\} \not\subseteq \mathcal{V}_{in}(\mathsf{p}(\mathsf{f}(X), \mathsf{g}(Y))) \cup \mathcal{V}_{out}(\mathsf{p}(\mathsf{f}(X), \mathsf{f}(Z))) \cup \mathcal{V}_{out}(\mathsf{p}(Z, \mathsf{g}(W))) = \{X, Z, W\}$. *Transforming the program as before yields a TRS with the rule* $\mathsf{u}_2(\mathsf{p}_{out}(\mathsf{g}(W)), X, Z) \to \mathsf{p}_{out}(\mathsf{g}(Y))$. *So non-well-moded programs result in rules with variables like* Y *in the right- but not in the left-hand side. Such rules are usually forbidden in term rewriting and they do not terminate, since* Y *may be instantiated arbitrarily.*

A natural non-well-moded example is the append-program with the clauses append$([\,], XS, XS)$ and append$([X|XS], YS, [X|ZS]) :- \mathsf{append}(XS, YS, ZS)$. If one only considers append's first argument as input, then this program is not well moded although all queries append(t_1, t_2, t_3) are terminating if t_1 is ground.

Recently, several authors tackled the problem of applying termination techniques from term rewriting for (possibly non-well-moded) logic programs. A framework for integrating orders from term rewriting into direct termination approaches for logic programs is discussed in [13].[4] However, the automation of this framework is non-trivial in general. As an instance of this framework, the automatic application of polynomial interpretations (well-known in rewriting) to termination analysis of logic programs is investigated in [27].

Instead of integrating each termination technique from term rewriting separately, we want to make all these techniques available at once. Therefore, unlike [13,27], we choose a transformational approach. Our goal is a method which

(A) handles programs like Ex. 1 where classical transformations like [28] fail,
(B) handles non-well-moded programs like Ex. 3 where most current transformational techniques are not even applicable,
(C) allows the successful *automated* application of powerful techniques from re writing for logic programs like Ex. 1 and 3 where current tools based on direct approaches fail. For larger and more realistic examples we refer to Sect. 5.

After presenting required preliminaries in Sect. 2, in Sect. 3 we modify the transformation from logic programs to TRSs to achieve (A) and (B). So restrictions like well-modedness, simple well-typedness, or safe typedness are no longer required. Our new transformation results in TRSs where the notion of "rewriting" has to be slightly modified: we regard a restricted form of infinitary rewriting, called *infinitary constructor rewriting*. The reason is that logic programs use *unification*, whereas TRSs use *matching*. For that reason, the logic program $\mathsf{p}(\mathsf{s}(X)) :- \mathsf{p}(X)$ does not terminate for the query $\mathsf{p}(X)$ whereas the TRS

---

[4] But in contrast to [13], we also apply more recent powerful termination techniques from rewriting (e.g., *dependency pairs* [4,16]) for termination of logic programs.

$p(s(X)) \rightarrow p(X)$ terminates for all finite terms. However, the infinite derivation of the logic program corresponds to an infinite reduction of the TRS with the *infinite* term $p(s(s(\ldots)))$ containing infinitely many nested s-symbols. So to simulate unification by matching, we have to regard TRSs where the variables in rewrite rules may be instantiated by infinite constructor terms. It turns out that this form of rewriting also analyzes the termination behavior of logic programs with infinite terms, i.e., of logic programming without occur check.

Sect. 4 shows that the existing termination techniques for TRSs can easily be adapted in order to prove termination of infinitary constructor rewriting. We conclude with an experimental evaluation of our results in Sect. 5 which shows that Goal (C) is achieved as well. In other words, the implementation of our approach can indeed compete with modern tools for direct termination analysis of logic programs and it succeeds for many programs where these tools fail.

2 Preliminaries on Logic Programming and Rewriting

A *signature* is a pair (Σ, Δ) where Σ and Δ are finite sets of function and predicate symbols. Each $f \in \Sigma \cup \Delta$ has an *arity* $n \geq 0$ and we often write f/n instead of f. We always assume that Σ contains at least one constant $f/0$.

Definition 4 (Infinite Terms and Atoms). *A term over Σ is a tree where every node is labelled with a function symbol from Σ or with a variable from $\mathcal{V} = \{X, Y, \ldots\}$. Every node labelled with f/n has n children and leaves are labelled with variables or with $f/0 \in \Sigma$. We write $f(t_1, \ldots, t_n)$ for the term with root f and direct subtrees $t_1, \ldots, t_n$. A term t is* finite *if all paths in the tree t are finite, otherwise it is* infinite. *A term is* rational *if it only contains finitely many subterms. The sets of all finite terms, all rational terms, and all (possibly infinite) terms over Σ are denoted by $\mathcal{T}(\Sigma, \mathcal{V})$, $\mathcal{T}^{rat}(\Sigma, \mathcal{V})$, and $\mathcal{T}^{\infty}(\Sigma, \mathcal{V})$, respectively. If $\boldsymbol{t}$ is the sequence $t_1, \ldots, t_n$, then $\boldsymbol{t} \in \boldsymbol{\mathcal{T}}^{\infty}(\Sigma, \mathcal{V})$ means that $t_i \in \mathcal{T}^{\infty}(\Sigma, \mathcal{V})$ for all i. $\boldsymbol{\mathcal{T}}(\Sigma, \mathcal{V})$ is defined analogously. A position p in a (possibly infinite) term t addresses a subtree $t|_p$ of t where the path from $\text{root}(t)$ to $\text{root}(t|_p)$ is finite. The term $t[s]_p$ results from replacing the subterm $t|_p$ at position p in t by the term s.*

An atom over (Σ, Δ) is a tree $p(t_1, \ldots, t_n)$, where $p/n \in \Delta$ and $t_1, \ldots, t_n \in \mathcal{T}^{\infty}(\Sigma, \mathcal{V})$. $\mathcal{A}^{\infty}(\Sigma, \Delta, \mathcal{V})$ is the set of atoms and $\mathcal{A}^{rat}(\Sigma, \Delta, \mathcal{V})$ (and $\mathcal{A}(\Sigma, \Delta, \mathcal{V})$, resp.) are the atoms $p(t_1, \ldots, t_n)$ where $t_i \in \mathcal{T}^{rat}(\Sigma, \mathcal{V})$ (and $t_i \in \mathcal{T}(\Sigma, \mathcal{V})$, resp.) for all i. We write $\mathcal{A}(\Sigma, \Delta)$ and $\mathcal{T}(\Sigma)$ instead of $\mathcal{A}(\Sigma, \Delta, \varnothing)$ and $\mathcal{T}(\Sigma, \varnothing)$.

A *clause* c is a formula $H :\!- B_1, \ldots, B_k$ with $k \geq 0$ and $H, B_i \in \mathcal{A}(\Sigma, \Delta, \mathcal{V})$. H is c's *head* and $B_1, \ldots, B_k$ is c's *body*. A finite set of clauses $\mathcal{P}$ is a *(logic) program*. A clause with empty body is a *fact* and a clause with empty head is a *query*. We usually omit ":–" in queries and just write "$B_1, \ldots, B_k$". The empty query is denoted $\square$. In queries, we also admit rational instead of finite atoms $B_1, \ldots, B_k$.

Since we are also interested in logic programming without occur check we consider infinite *substitutions* $\theta : \mathcal{V} \rightarrow \mathcal{T}^{\infty}(\Sigma, \mathcal{V})$. Here, we allow $\theta(X) \neq X$ for infinitely many $X \in \mathcal{V}$. Instead of $\theta(X)$ we often write $X\theta$. If θ is a variable renaming (i.e., a one-to-one correspondence on $\mathcal{V}$), then $t\theta$ is a *variant* of t, where

t can be any expression (e.g., a term, atom, clause, etc.). We write $\theta\sigma$ to denote that the application of θ is followed by the application of σ.[5]

We briefly present the procedural semantics of logic programs based on SLD-resolution using the left-to-right selection rule implemented by most Prolog systems. More details on logic programming can be found in [2], for example.

Definition 5 (Derivation, Termination). *Let Q be a query $A_1, \ldots, A_m$, let c be a clause $H :\!- B_1, \ldots, B_k$. Then Q' is a resolvent of Q and c using θ (denoted $Q \vdash_{c,\theta} Q'$) if θ is the mgu[6] of A_1 and H, and $Q' = (B_1, \ldots, B_k, A_2, \ldots, A_m)\theta$.*

A derivation of a program $\mathcal{P}$ and Q is a possibly infinite sequence $Q_0, Q_1, \ldots$ of queries with $Q_0 = Q$ where for all i, we have $Q_i \vdash_{c_{i+1}, \theta_{i+1}} Q_{i+1}$ for some substitution θ_{i+1} and some fresh variant c_{i+1} of a clause of $\mathcal{P}$. For a derivation $Q_0, \ldots, Q_n$ as above, we also write $Q_0 \vdash^n_{\mathcal{P}, \theta_1 \ldots \theta_n} Q_n$ or $Q_0 \vdash^n_{\mathcal{P}} Q_n$, and we also write $Q_0 \vdash_{\mathcal{P}} Q_1$. The query Q terminates for $\mathcal{P}$ if all derivations of $\mathcal{P}$ and Q are finite.

Our notion of derivation coincides with logic programming without occur check [11] as implemented in recent Prolog systems such as SICStus or SWI. Since we consider only definite logic programs, any program which is terminating without occur check is also terminating with occur check, but not vice versa. So if our approach detects "termination", then the program is indeed terminating, no matter whether one uses logic programming with or without occur check. In other words, our approach is sound for both kinds of programs, whereas most other approaches only consider logic programming with occur check.

Example 6. Regard a program $\mathcal{P}$ with the clauses $\mathsf{p}(X) :\!- \mathsf{equal}(X, \mathsf{s}(X))$, $\mathsf{p}(X)$ and $\mathsf{equal}(X, X)$. We obtain $\mathsf{p}(X) \vdash^2_{\mathcal{P}} \mathsf{p}(\mathsf{s}(\mathsf{s}(\ldots))) \vdash^2_{\mathcal{P}} \mathsf{p}(\mathsf{s}(\mathsf{s}(\ldots))) \vdash^2_{\mathcal{P}} \ldots$, where $\mathsf{s}(\mathsf{s}(\ldots))$ is the term containing infinitely many nested s-symbols. So the finite query $\mathsf{p}(X)$ leads to a derivation with infinite (rational) queries. While $\mathsf{p}(X)$ is not terminating according to Def. 5, it would be terminating if one uses logic programming with occur check. Indeed, tools like cTI [25] and TerminWeb [10] report that such queries are "terminating". So in contrast to our technique, such tools are in general not sound for logic programming without occur check, although this form of logic programming is typically used in practice.

---

[5] One can even define the composition of *infinitely* many substitutions $\sigma_0, \sigma_1, \ldots$ such that $t\sigma_0\sigma_1 \ldots$ is an instance of $t\sigma_0 \ldots \sigma_n$ for all terms (or atoms) t and all $n \geq 0$: It suffices to define the symbols at the positions of $t\sigma_0\sigma_1\ldots$ for any term t. Obviously, p is a position of $t\sigma_0\sigma_1\ldots$ iff p is a position of $t\sigma_0\ldots\sigma_n$ for some $n \geq 0$. We define that the symbol of $t\sigma_0\sigma_1\ldots$ at such a position p is $f \in \Sigma$ iff f is at position p in $t\sigma_0\ldots\sigma_m$ for some $m \geq 0$. Otherwise, $(t\sigma_0\ldots\sigma_n)|_p = X_0 \in \mathcal{V}$. Let $n = i_0 < i_1 < \ldots$ be the maximal (finite or infinite) sequence with $\sigma_{i_j+1}(X_j) = \ldots = \sigma_{i_{j+1}-1}(X_j) = X_j$ and $\sigma_{i_{j+1}}(X_j) = X_{j+1}$ for all j. We require $X_j \neq X_{j+1}$, but permit $X_j = X_{j'}$ otherwise. If this sequence is finite (i.e., it has the form $n = i_0 < \ldots < i_m$), then we define $(t\sigma_0\sigma_1\ldots)|_p = X_m$. Otherwise, the substitutions perform infinitely many variable renamings. In this case, we use one special variable Z_∞ and define $(t\sigma_0\sigma_1\ldots)|_p = Z_\infty$. So if $\sigma_0(X) = Y$, $\sigma_1(Y) = X$, $\sigma_2(X) = Y$, $\sigma_3(Y) = X$, etc., we define $X\sigma_0\sigma_1\ldots = Y\sigma_0\sigma_1\ldots = Z_\infty$.

[6] Note that for finite sets of *rational* atoms or terms, unification is decidable, the mgu is unique modulo renaming, and it is a substitution with *rational* terms [18].

Now we define TRSs and introduce the notion of *infinitary constructor rewriting*. For further details on term rewriting we refer to [6].

Definition 7 (Infinitary Constructor Rewriting). *A TRS $\mathcal{R}$ is a finite set of rules $l \rightarrow r$ with $l, r \in \mathcal{T}(\Sigma, \mathcal{V})$ and $l \notin \mathcal{V}$. We divide the signature in defined symbols $\Sigma_D = \{f \mid l \rightarrow r \in \mathcal{R}, \text{root}(l) = f\}$ and* constructors $\Sigma_C = \Sigma \backslash \Sigma_D$. $\mathcal{R}$'s infinitary constructor rewrite relation *is denoted $\rightarrow_{\mathcal{R}}$: for $s, t \in \mathcal{T}^{\infty}(\Sigma, \mathcal{V})$ we have $s \rightarrow_{\mathcal{R}} t$ if there is a rule $l \rightarrow r$, a position p and a substitution $\sigma : \mathcal{V} \rightarrow \mathcal{T}^{\infty}(\Sigma_C, \mathcal{V})$ with $s|_p = l\sigma$ and $t = s[r\sigma]_p$. Let $\rightarrow_{\mathcal{R}}^n, \rightarrow_{\mathcal{R}}^{\geq n}, \rightarrow_{\mathcal{R}}^{*}$ denote rewrite sequences of n steps, of at least n steps, and of arbitrary many steps, respectively (where $n \geq 0$). A term t is* terminating *for $\mathcal{R}$ if there is no infinite sequence of the form $t \rightarrow_{\mathcal{R}} t_1 \rightarrow_{\mathcal{R}} t_2 \rightarrow_{\mathcal{R}} \ldots$ A TRS $\mathcal{R}$ is* terminating *if all terms are terminating for $\mathcal{R}$.*

The above definition of $\rightarrow_{\mathcal{R}}$ differs from the usual rewrite relation in two aspects: (i) We only permit instantiations of rule variables by constructor terms and (ii) we use substitutions with possibly non-rational infinite terms. In Ex. 9 and 10 in the next section, we will motivate these modifications and show that there are TRSs which terminate w.r.t. the usual rewrite relation, but are non-terminating w.r.t. infinitary constructor rewriting and vice versa.

3   Transforming Logic Programs into TRSs

Now we modify the transformation of logic programs into TRSs from Sect. 1 to make it applicable for *arbitrary* (possibly non-well-moded) programs as well. Instead of separating between input and output positions of a predicate p/n, now we keep *all* arguments both for p_{in} and p_{out} (i.e., p_{in} and p_{out} have arity n).

Definition 8 (Transformation). *A logic program $\mathcal{P}$ over (Σ, Δ) is transformed into the following TRS $\mathcal{R}_{\mathcal{P}}$ over $\Sigma_{\mathcal{P}} = \Sigma \cup \{p_{in}/n, p_{out}/n \mid p/n \in \Delta\} \cup \{u_{c,i} \mid c \in \mathcal{P}, 1 \leq i \leq k, \text{ where } k \text{ is the number of atoms in the body of } c\}$.*

- *For each fact $p(\boldsymbol{s})$ in $\mathcal{P}$, the TRS $\mathcal{R}_{\mathcal{P}}$ contains the rule $p_{in}(\boldsymbol{s}) \rightarrow p_{out}(\boldsymbol{s})$.*
- *For each clause c of the form $p(\boldsymbol{s}) :\!- p_1(\boldsymbol{s}_1), \ldots, p_k(\boldsymbol{s}_k)$ in $\mathcal{P}$, $\mathcal{R}_{\mathcal{P}}$ contains:*

$$p_{in}(\boldsymbol{s}) \rightarrow u_{c,1}(p_{1_{in}}(\boldsymbol{s}_1), \mathcal{V}(\boldsymbol{s}))$$
$$u_{c,1}(p_{1_{out}}(\boldsymbol{s}_1), \mathcal{V}(\boldsymbol{s})) \rightarrow u_{c,2}(p_{2_{in}}(\boldsymbol{s}_2), \mathcal{V}(\boldsymbol{s}) \cup \mathcal{V}(\boldsymbol{s}_1))$$

$$\ldots$$

$$u_{c,k}(p_{k_{out}}(\boldsymbol{s}_k), \mathcal{V}(\boldsymbol{s}) \cup \mathcal{V}(\boldsymbol{s}_1) \cup \ldots \cup \mathcal{V}(\boldsymbol{s}_{k-1})) \rightarrow p_{out}(\boldsymbol{s})$$

The following two examples motivate the need for infinitary constructor rewriting in Def. 8, i.e., they motivate Modifications (i) and (ii).

Example 9. For the logic program of Ex. 1, we obtain the following TRS.

$$p_{in}(X, X) \rightarrow p_{out}(X, X)$$
$$p_{in}(f(X), g(Y)) \rightarrow u_1(p_{in}(f(X), f(Z)), X, Y)$$
$$u_1(p_{out}(f(X), f(Z)), X, Y) \rightarrow u_2(p_{in}(Z, g(Y)), X, Y, Z)$$
$$u_2(p_{out}(Z, g(Y)), X, Y, Z) \rightarrow p_{out}(f(X), g(Y))$$

This example shows why rules of TRSs may only be instantiated with constructor terms (Modification (i)). The reason is that local variables like Z (i.e., variables occurring in the body but not in the head of a clause) give rise to rules $l \to r$ where $\mathcal{V}(r) \not\subseteq \mathcal{V}(l)$ (cf. the second rule). Such rules are never terminating in standard term rewriting. However, in our setting one may only instantiate Z with constructor terms. So in contrast to the old transformation in Ex. 2, now all terms $\mathsf{p}_{in}(t_1, t_2)$ terminate for the TRS if t_1 is finite, since now the second argument of p_{in} prevents an infinite application of the second rule. Indeed, constructor rewriting correctly simulates the behavior of logic programs, since the variables in a logic program are only instantiated by "constructor terms".

For the non-well-moded program of Ex. 3, one obtains a similar TRS where $\mathsf{g}(Y)$ is replaced by $\mathsf{g}(W)$ in the right-hand side of the third and the left-hand side of the last rule. Thus, we can now handle programs where the classical transformation of [5,8,15,28] failed, cf. Goals (A) and (B).

Derivations in logic programming use *unification*, while rewriting is defined by *matching*. Ex. 10 shows that to simulate unification by matching, we have to consider substitutions with infinite and even non-rational terms (Modification (ii)).

Example 10. Let $\mathcal{P}$ be ordered($\mathsf{cons}(X, \mathsf{cons}(\mathsf{s}(X), XS))$) :– ordered($\mathsf{cons}(\mathsf{s}(X), XS)$). *If one only considers rewriting with finite or rational terms, then the transformed TRS $\mathcal{R}_\mathcal{P}$ is terminating. However, the query* ordered(YS) *is not terminating for $\mathcal{P}$. Thus, to obtain a sound approach, $\mathcal{R}_\mathcal{P}$ must also be non-terminating. Indeed,* ordered$_{in}$($\mathsf{cons}(X, \mathsf{cons}(\mathsf{s}(X), \mathsf{cons}(\mathsf{s}^2(X), \ldots))))$ *is non-terminating with $\mathcal{R}_\mathcal{P}$'s rule* ordered$_{in}$($\mathsf{cons}(X, \mathsf{cons}(\mathsf{s}(X), XS))$) $\to \mathsf{u}($ordered$_{in}$($\mathsf{cons}(\mathsf{s}(X), XS)), X, XS)$. *This non-rational term corresponds to the infinite derivation with* ordered(YS).

Lemma 11 is needed to prove the soundness of the transformation. It relates derivations with the logic program $\mathcal{P}$ to rewrite sequences with the TRS $\mathcal{R}_\mathcal{P}$.

Lemma 11 (Connecting $\mathcal{P}$ and $\mathcal{R}_\mathcal{P}$). *Let $\mathcal{P}$ be a program, let t be terms from $\mathcal{T}^{rat}(\Sigma, \mathcal{V})$, let $p(t) \vdash_{\mathcal{P}, \sigma}^n Q$. If $Q = \square$, then $p_{in}(t)\sigma \to_{\mathcal{R}_\mathcal{P}}^{\geq n} p_{out}(t)\sigma$. Otherwise, if Q is "$q(v), \ldots$", then $p_{in}(t)\sigma \to_{\mathcal{R}_\mathcal{P}}^{\geq n} r$ for a term r containing the subterm $q_{in}(v)$.*

Proof. Let $p(t) = Q_0 \vdash_{c_1, \theta_1} \ldots \vdash_{c_n, \theta_n} Q_n = Q$ with $\sigma = \theta_1 \ldots \theta_n$. We use induction on n. The base case $n = 0$ is trivial, since $Q = p(t)$ and $p_{in}(t) \to_{\mathcal{R}_\mathcal{P}}^0 p_{in}(t)$.

Now let $n \geq 1$. We first regard the case $Q_1 = \square$ and $n = 1$. Then, c_1 is a fact $p(s)$ and θ_1 is the mgu of $p(t)$ and $p(s)$. Note that such mgu's instantiate all variables with constructor terms (as symbols of Σ are constructors of $\mathcal{R}_\mathcal{P}$). We obtain $p_{in}(t)\theta_1 = p_{in}(s)\theta_1 \to_{\mathcal{R}_\mathcal{P}} p_{out}(s)\theta_1 = p_{out}(t)\theta_1$ where $\sigma = \theta_1$.

Finally, let $Q_1 \neq \square$. Thus, c_1 is $p(s) :– p_1(s_1), \ldots, p_k(s_k)$, Q_1 is $p_1(s_1)\theta_1, \ldots, p_k(s_k)\theta_1$, and θ_1 is the mgu of $p(t)$ and $p(s)$. There is an i with $1 \leq i \leq k$ such that for all j with $1 \leq j \leq i - 1$ we have $p_j(s_j)\sigma_0 \ldots \sigma_{j-1} \vdash_{\mathcal{P}, \sigma_j}^{n_j} \square$. Moreover, if $Q = \square$ then $i = k$ and $p_i(s_i)\sigma_0 \ldots \sigma_{i-1} \vdash_{\mathcal{P}, \sigma_i}^{n_i} \square$ and if Q is "$q(v), \ldots$", then $p_i(s_i)\sigma_0 \ldots \sigma_{i-1} \vdash_{\mathcal{P}, \sigma_i}^{n_i} q(v), \ldots$ Here, $n = n_1 + \ldots + n_i + 1$, $\sigma_0 = \theta_1$, $\sigma_1 = \theta_2 \ldots \theta_{n_1+1}, \ldots$, and $\sigma_i = \theta_{n_1 + \ldots + n_{i-1} + 2} \ldots \theta_{n_1 + \ldots + n_i + 1}$. So $\sigma = \sigma_0 \ldots \sigma_i$.

By the induction hypothesis we have $p_{j_{in}}(s_j)\sigma_0\ldots\sigma_j \to_{\mathcal{R}_{\mathcal{P}}}^{\geq n_j} p_{j_{out}}(s_j)\sigma_0\ldots\sigma_j$ and thus also $p_{j_{in}}(s_j)\sigma \to_{\mathcal{R}_{\mathcal{P}}}^{\geq n_j} p_{j_{out}}(s_j)\sigma$. Moreover, if $Q = \square$ then we also have $p_{i_{in}}(s_i)\sigma \to_{\mathcal{R}_{\mathcal{P}}}^{\geq n_i} p_{i_{out}}(s_i)\sigma$ where $i = k$. Otherwise, if Q is "$q(v),\ldots$", then the induction hypothesis implies $p_{i_{in}}(s_i)\sigma \to_{\mathcal{R}_{\mathcal{P}}}^{\geq n_i} r'$, where r' contains $q_{in}(v)$. Thus

$$\begin{aligned}
p_{in}(t)\sigma = {}& p_{in}(s)\sigma \to_{\mathcal{R}_{\mathcal{P}}} & & u_{c_1,1}(p_{1_{in}}(s_1), \mathcal{V}(s))\sigma \\
& \to_{\mathcal{R}_{\mathcal{P}}}^{\geq n_1} & & u_{c_1,1}(p_{1_{out}}(s_1), \mathcal{V}(s))\sigma \\
& \to_{\mathcal{R}_{\mathcal{P}}} & & u_{c_1,2}(p_{2_{in}}(s_2), \mathcal{V}(s)\cup\mathcal{V}(s_1))\sigma \\
& \to_{\mathcal{R}_{\mathcal{P}}}^{\geq n_2} & & u_{c_1,2}(p_{2_{out}}(s_2), \mathcal{V}(s)\cup\mathcal{V}(s_1))\sigma \\
& \to_{\mathcal{R}_{\mathcal{P}}}^{\geq n_3+\ldots+n_{i-1}} & & u_{c_1,i}(p_{i_{in}}(s_i), \mathcal{V}(s)\cup\mathcal{V}(s_1)\cup\ldots\cup\mathcal{V}(s_{i-1}))\sigma
\end{aligned}$$

Moreover, if $Q = \square$, then $i = k$ and the rewrite sequence yields $p_{out}(t)\sigma$, since

$$\begin{aligned}
u_{c_1,i}(p_{i_{in}}(s_i), \mathcal{V}(s)\cup\ldots\cup\mathcal{V}(s_{i-1}))\sigma \to_{\mathcal{R}_{\mathcal{P}}}^{\geq n_i} {}& u_{c_1,i}(p_{i_{out}}(s_i), \mathcal{V}(s)\cup\ldots\cup\mathcal{V}(s_{i-1}))\sigma \\
\to_{\mathcal{R}_{\mathcal{P}}} {}& p_{out}(s)\sigma = p_{out}(t)\sigma.
\end{aligned}$$

Otherwise, if Q is "$q(v),\ldots$", then rewriting yields a term containing $q_{in}(v)$:

$$u_{c_1,i}(p_{i_{in}}(s_i), \mathcal{V}(s)\cup\ldots\cup\mathcal{V}(s_{i-1}))\sigma \to_{\mathcal{R}_{\mathcal{P}}}^{\geq n_i} u_{c_1,i}(r', \mathcal{V}(s)\sigma\cup\ldots\cup\mathcal{V}(s_{i-1})\sigma). \quad \square$$

For the soundness proof, we need another lemma which states that we can restrict ourselves to non-terminating queries which only consist of a single atom.

Lemma 12 (Form of Non-Terminating Queries). *Let $\mathcal{P}$ be a logic program. Then for every infinite derivation $Q_0 \vdash_{\mathcal{P}} Q_1 \vdash_{\mathcal{P}} \ldots$, there is a Q_i of the form "$q(v),\ldots$" with $i > 0$ such that the query $q(v)$ is also non-terminating.*

Proof. Assume that for all $i > 0$, the first atom in Q_i is successfully proved in n_i steps during the derivation $Q_0 \vdash_{\mathcal{P}} Q_1 \vdash_{\mathcal{P}} \ldots$ (Otherwise, the derivation would not be infinite.) Let m be the number of atoms in Q_1. But then $Q_{1+n_1+\ldots+n_m}$ is the empty query $\square$ which contradicts the infiniteness of the derivation. $\square$

To characterize the classes of queries whose termination we want to analyze, we use *argument filterings*. Related definitions can be found in, e.g., [4,21].

Definition 13 (Argument Filtering). *An argument filtering π over a signature (Σ, Δ) is a function $\pi : \Sigma \cup \Delta \to 2^{\mathbb{N}}$ where $\pi(f/n) \subseteq \{1,\ldots,n\}$ for every $f/n \in \Sigma \cup \Delta$. We extend π to terms and atoms by defining $\pi(x) = x$ if x is a variable and $\pi(f(t_1,\ldots,t_n)) = f(\pi(t_{i_1}),\ldots,\pi(t_{i_k}))$ if $\pi(f) = \{i_1,\ldots,i_k\}$ with $i_1 < \ldots < i_k$. For any TRS $\mathcal{R}$, we define $\pi(\mathcal{R}) = \{\pi(l) \to \pi(r) \mid l \to r \in \mathcal{R}\}$.*

Argument filterings specify those positions which have to be instantiated with finite ground terms. Then, we analyze termination of all queries Q where $\pi(Q)$ is a (finite) ground atom. In Ex. 1, we wanted to prove termination for all queries $p(t_1, t_2)$ where t_1 is finite and ground. These queries are described by the filtering $\pi(h) = \{1\}$ for all $h \in \{p, f, g\}$. Thus, we have $\pi(p(t_1, t_2)) = p(\pi(t_1))$.

Note that argument filterings also operate on *function* instead of just *predicate* symbols. Therefore, they can describe more sophisticated classes of queries than the classical approach of [28] which only distinguishes between input and output positions of predicates. For example, if one wants to analyze all queries $\mathsf{append}(t_1, t_2, t_3)$ where t_1 is a finite list, one would use the filtering $\pi(\mathsf{append}) = \{1\}$ and $\pi(.) = \{2\}$, where "." is the list constructor (i.e., $.(X, L) = [X|L]$). Of course, our method can easily prove that all these queries are terminating.

Now we show the soundness theorem: to prove termination of all queries Q where $\pi(Q)$ is a finite ground atom, it suffices to show termination of all those terms $p_{in}(t)$ for the TRS $\mathcal{R}_\mathcal{P}$ where $\pi(p_{in}(t))$ is a finite ground term and where t only contains function symbols from the logic program $\mathcal{P}$. Here, π has to be extended to the new function symbols p_{in} by defining $\pi(p_{in}) = \pi(p)$.

Theorem 14 (Soundness of the Transformation). *Let $\mathcal{P}$ be a logic program and let π be an argument filtering over (Σ, Δ). We extend π such that $\pi(p_{in}) = \pi(p)$ for all $p \in \Delta$. Let $S = \{p_{in}(t) \mid p \in \Delta, \ t \in \mathcal{T}^\infty(\Sigma, \mathcal{V}), \ \pi(p_{in}(t)) \in \mathcal{T}(\Sigma)\}$. If all terms $s \in S$ are terminating for $\mathcal{R}_\mathcal{P}$, then all queries $Q \in \mathcal{A}^{rat}(\Sigma, \Delta, \mathcal{V})$ with $\pi(Q) \in \mathcal{A}(\Sigma, \Delta)$ are terminating for $\mathcal{P}$.*

Proof. Assume that there is a non-terminating query $p(t)$ as above with $p(t) \vdash_\mathcal{P} Q_1 \vdash_\mathcal{P} Q_2 \vdash_\mathcal{P} \ldots$ By Lemma 12 there is an $i_1 > 0$ with $Q_{i_1} = q_1(v_1), \ldots$ and an infinite derivation $q_1(v_1) \vdash_\mathcal{P} Q'_1 \vdash_\mathcal{P} Q'_2 \vdash_\mathcal{P} \ldots$ From $p(t) \vdash^{i_1}_{\sigma_0, \mathcal{P}} q_1(v_1), \ldots$ and Lemma 11 we get $p_{in}(t)\sigma_0 \to^{\geq i_1}_{\mathcal{R}_\mathcal{P}} r_1$, where r_1 contains the subterm $q_{1in}(v_1)$.

By Lemma 12 again, there is an $i_2 > 0$ with $Q'_{i_2} = q_2(v_2), \ldots$ and an infinite derivation $q_2(v_2) \vdash_\mathcal{P} Q''_1 \vdash_\mathcal{P} \ldots$ From $q_1(v_1) \vdash^{i_2}_{\sigma_1, \mathcal{P}} q_2(v_2), \ldots$ and Lemma 11 we get $p_{in}(t)\sigma_0\sigma_1 \to^{\geq i_1}_{\mathcal{R}_\mathcal{P}} r_1\sigma_1 \to^{\geq i_2}_{\mathcal{R}_\mathcal{P}} r_2$, where r_2 contains the subterm $q_{2in}(v_2)$.

Continuing this reasoning we obtain an infinite sequence $\sigma_0, \sigma_1, \ldots$ of substitutions. For each $j \geq 0$, let $\mu_j = \sigma_j \sigma_{j+1} \ldots$ result from the infinite composition of these substitutions. Since $r_j\mu_j$ is an instance of $r_j\sigma_j \ldots \sigma_n$ for all $n \geq j$ (cf. Footnote 5), we obtain that $p_{in}(t)\mu_0$ is non-terminating for $\mathcal{R}_\mathcal{P}$:

$$p_{in}(t)\mu_0 \to^{\geq i_1}_{\mathcal{R}_\mathcal{P}} r_1\mu_1 \to^{\geq i_2}_{\mathcal{R}_\mathcal{P}} r_2\mu_2 \to^{\geq i_3}_{\mathcal{R}_\mathcal{P}} \ldots$$

As $\pi(p(t)) \in \mathcal{A}(\Sigma, \Delta)$ and thus $\pi(p_{in}(t)\mu_0) \in \mathcal{T}(\Sigma)$, this is a contradiction. □

4 Termination of Infinitary Constructor Rewriting

One of the most powerful methods for automated termination analysis of rewriting is the *dependency pair* (DP) method [4] which is implemented in most current termination tools for TRSs. However, since the DP method only proves termination of term rewriting with *finite* terms, its use is not sound in our setting. Nevertheless, we now show that only very slight modifications are required to adapt dependency pairs from ordinary rewriting to infinitary constructor rewriting. So any rewriting tool implementing dependency pairs can easily be modified in order to prove termination of infinitary constructor rewriting as well. Then, it can also analyze termination of logic programs using the transformation of Def. 8.

Moreover, dependency pairs are a general framework that permits the integration of *any* termination technique for TRSs [16, Thm. 36]. Therefore, instead of adapting each technique separately, it is sufficient only to adapt the DP framework to infinitary constructor rewriting. Then, *any* termination technique can be directly used for infinitary constructor rewriting without adapting it as well.

For a TRS $\mathcal{R}$ over Σ, for each $f/n \in \Sigma_D$ let $f^{\sharp}/n$ be a fresh *tuple symbol*. We often write F instead of $f^{\sharp}$. For $t = g(\boldsymbol{t})$ with $g \in \Sigma_D$, let $t^{\sharp}$ denote $g^{\sharp}(\boldsymbol{t})$.

Definition 15 (Dependency Pair [4]). *The set of* dependency pairs *for a TRS $\mathcal{R}$ is $DP(\mathcal{R}) = \{l^{\sharp} \to t^{\sharp} \mid l \to r \in \mathcal{R}, t \text{ is a subterm of } r, \text{root}(t) \in \Sigma_D\}$.*

Example 16. In the TRS $\mathcal{R}$ of Ex. 9, we have $\Sigma_D = \{p_{in}, u_1, u_2\}$ and $DP(\mathcal{R})$ is

$$\mathsf{P}_{in}(\mathsf{f}(X), \mathsf{g}(Y)) \to \mathsf{P}_{in}(\mathsf{f}(X), \mathsf{f}(Z)) \tag{1}$$
$$\mathsf{P}_{in}(\mathsf{f}(X), \mathsf{g}(Y)) \to \mathsf{U}_1(\mathsf{p}_{in}(\mathsf{f}(X), \mathsf{f}(Z)), X, Y) \tag{2}$$
$$\mathsf{U}_1(\mathsf{p}_{out}(\mathsf{f}(X), \mathsf{f}(Z)), X, Y) \to \mathsf{P}_{in}(Z, \mathsf{g}(Y)) \tag{3}$$
$$\mathsf{U}_1(\mathsf{p}_{out}(\mathsf{f}(X), \mathsf{f}(Z)), X, Y) \to \mathsf{U}_2(\mathsf{p}_{in}(Z, \mathsf{g}(Y)), X, Y, Z) \tag{4}$$

While Def. 15 is from [4], all following definitions and theorems are new. They extend existing concepts from ordinary to infinitary constructor rewriting.

For termination, one tries to prove that there are no infinite *chains* of dependency pairs. Intuitively, a dependency pair corresponds to a function call and a chain represents a possible sequence of calls that can occur during rewriting. Def. 17 extends the notion of chains to infinitary constructor rewriting. To this end, we use an argument filtering π that describes which arguments of function symbols have to be *finite* terms. So if π does not delete arguments (i.e., if $\pi(f) = \{1, \ldots, n\}$ for all f/n), then this corresponds to ordinary (finitary) rewriting and if π deletes all arguments (i.e., if $\pi(f) = \varnothing$ for all f), then this corresponds to full infinitary rewriting. In Def. 17, the TRS $\mathcal{D}$ usually stands for a set of dependency pairs. (Note that if $\mathcal{R}$ is a TRS, then $DP(\mathcal{R})$ is also a TRS.)

Definition 17 (Chain). *Let $\mathcal{D}, \mathcal{R}$ be TRSs and π be a filtering over Σ. A (possibly infinite) sequence of pairs $s_1 \to t_1, s_2 \to t_2, \ldots$ from $\mathcal{D}$ is a $(\mathcal{D}, \mathcal{R}, \pi)$-chain iff*

- *there are substitutions $\sigma_i : \mathcal{V} \to \mathcal{T}^{\infty}(\Sigma_C, \mathcal{V})$ such that $t_i \sigma_i \to^*_{\mathcal{R}} s_{i+1} \sigma_{i+1}$. Here, Σ_C are the constructors of the TRS $\mathcal{R}$.*
- *$\pi(s_i \sigma_i), \pi(t_i \sigma_i) \in \mathcal{T}(\Sigma)$ and for all terms q in the rewrite sequence from $t_i \sigma_i$ to $s_{i+1} \sigma_{i+1}$ we have $\pi(q) \in \mathcal{T}(\Sigma)$ as well. So all terms in the sequence have finite ground terms on those positions which are not filtered away by π.*

In Ex. 16, "(2), (3)" is a chain for any argument filtering π: if one instantiates X and Z with the same finite ground term, then (2)'s instantiated right-hand side rewrites to an instance of (3)'s left-hand side. Note that if one uses an argument filtering π which permits an instantiation of X and Z with the infinite term $\mathsf{f}(\mathsf{f}(\ldots))$, then there is also an infinite chain "(2), (3), (2), (3), ... "

For termination of a program $\mathcal{P}$, by Thm. 14 we have to show that if $\pi(p_{in}(\boldsymbol{t}))$ is a finite ground term and $\boldsymbol{t}$ only contains function symbols from the logic program (i.e., $\boldsymbol{t}$ contains no defined symbols of the TRS $\mathcal{R}_{\mathcal{P}}$), then $p_{in}(\boldsymbol{t})$ is terminating for $\mathcal{R}_{\mathcal{P}}$. Thm. 18 states that one can prove absence of infinite $(DP(\mathcal{R}_{\mathcal{P}}), \mathcal{R}_{\mathcal{P}}, \pi')$-chains instead. Here, π' is a filtering which filters away "at least as much" as π. However, π' has to be chosen in such a way that the filtered TRSs $\pi'(DP(\mathcal{R}_\mathcal{P}))$ and $\pi'(\mathcal{R}_\mathcal{P})$ satisfy the *"variable condition"*, i.e., $\mathcal{V}(\pi'(r)) \subseteq \mathcal{V}(\pi'(l))$ for all $l \to r \in DP(\mathcal{R}_\mathcal{P}) \cup \mathcal{R}_\mathcal{P}$. Then the filtering π' detects all potentially infinite subterms in rewrite sequences (i.e., all subterms which correspond to "non-unification-free parts" of $\mathcal{P}$).

Theorem 18 (Proving Infinitary Termination). *Let $\mathcal{R}$ be a TRS over Σ and let π be an argument filtering over Σ. Let π' be an argument filtering with $\pi'(f) \subseteq \pi(f)$ for all $f \in \Sigma$. Moreover, π' should also be defined on tuple symbols such that $\pi'(F) \subseteq \pi'(f)$ for all $f \in \Sigma_D$. Assume that $\pi'(DP(\mathcal{R}))$ and $\pi'(\mathcal{R})$ satisfy the variable condition.[7] If there is no infinite $(DP(\mathcal{R}), \mathcal{R}, \pi')$-chain, then all terms $f(t)$ with $t \in \mathcal{T}^\infty(\Sigma_C, \mathcal{V})$ and $\pi(f(t)) \in \mathcal{T}(\Sigma)$ are terminating for $\mathcal{R}$.*

Proof. Assume there is a non-terminating term $f(t)$ as above. Since t does not contain defined symbols, the first rewrite step in the infinite sequence is on the root position with a rule $l = f(l) \to r$ where $l\sigma_1 = f(t)$. Since σ_1 does not introduce defined symbols, all defined symbols of $r\sigma_1$ occur on positions of r. So there is a subterm r' of r with defined root such that $r'\sigma_1$ is also non-terminating. Let r' denote the smallest such subterm (i.e., for all proper subterms r'' of r', the term $r''\sigma_1$ is terminating). Then $l^\sharp \to r'^\sharp$ is the first dependency pair of the infinite chain that we construct. Note that $\pi(l\sigma_1)$ and thus, $\pi'(l^\sharp\sigma_1) = \pi'(F(t))$ is a finite ground term by assumption. Moreover, as $l^\sharp \to r'^\sharp \in DP(\mathcal{R})$ and as $\pi'(DP(\mathcal{R}))$ satisfies the variable condition, $\pi'(r'^\sharp\sigma_1)$ is finite and ground as well.

The infinite sequence continues by rewriting $r'\sigma_1$'s proper subterms repeatedly. As $\pi'(\mathcal{R})$ satisfies the variable condition, the terms remain finite and ground when applying the filtering π'. Finally, a root rewrite step is performed again. Repeating this construction infinitely many times results in an infinite chain.

Example 19. We want to prove termination of Ex. 1 for all queries Q where $\pi(Q)$ is finite and ground for the filtering $\pi(h) = \{1\}$ for all $h \in \{\mathsf{p}, \mathsf{f}, \mathsf{g}\}$. By Thm. 14 and 18, it suffices to show absence of infinite $(DP(\mathcal{R}), \mathcal{R}, \pi')$-chains. Here, $\mathcal{R}$ is the TRS from Ex. 9 and $DP(\mathcal{R})$ are Rules (1) – (4) from Ex. 16. The filtering π' has to satisfy $\pi'(\mathsf{p}_{in}) \subseteq \pi(\mathsf{p}_{in}) = \pi(\mathsf{p}) = \{1\}$, $\pi'(h) \subseteq \pi(h) = \{1\}$ for $h \in \{\mathsf{f}, \mathsf{g}\}$, and $\pi'(H) \subseteq \pi'(h)$ for all defined symbols h. Moreover, we have to choose π' such that the variable condition is fulfilled. So while π is always given, π' has to be determined automatically. This can indeed be automated, since there are only finitely many possibilities for π'. In particular, defining $\pi'(h) = \varnothing$ for all symbols h is always possible. But to obtain a successful termination proof afterwards, in our implementation we generate filterings where the sets $\pi'(h)$ are as large as possible, since such filterings provide more information about the finiteness of arguments. So in our example, we use $\pi'(\mathsf{p}_{in}) = \pi'(\mathsf{P}_{in}) = \pi'(\mathsf{f}) = \pi'(\mathsf{g}) = \{1\}$, $\pi'(\mathsf{p}_{out}) = \pi'(\mathsf{u}_1) = \pi'(\mathsf{U}_1) = \{1, 2\}$, and $\pi'(\mathsf{u}_2) = \pi'(\mathsf{U}_2) = \{1, 2, 4\}$. For the non-well-moded Ex. 3 we choose $\pi'(\mathsf{g}) = \varnothing$ instead to satisfy the variable condition.

---

[7] To see why the variable condition is needed in Thm. 18, let $\mathcal{R} = \{\mathsf{g}(X) \to \mathsf{f}(X), \mathsf{f}(\mathsf{s}(X)) \to \mathsf{f}(X)\}$ and $\pi = \pi'$ where $\pi'(\mathsf{g}) = \varnothing$, $\pi'(\mathsf{f}) = \pi'(\mathsf{F}) = \pi'(\mathsf{s}) = \{1\}$. $\mathcal{R}$'s first rule violates the variable condition: $\mathcal{V}(\pi'(\mathsf{f}(X))) = \{X\} \not\subseteq \mathcal{V}(\pi'(\mathsf{g}(X))) = \varnothing$. There is no infinite chain, since π' does not allow us to instantiate the variable X in the dependency pair $\mathsf{F}(\mathsf{s}(X)) \to \mathsf{F}(X)$ by an infinite term. Nevertheless, there is a non-terminating term $\mathsf{g}(\mathsf{s}(\mathsf{s}(\ldots)))$ which is filtered to a finite ground term $\pi'(\mathsf{g}(\mathsf{s}(\mathsf{s}(\ldots)))) = \mathsf{g}$.

Finally, we show how to prove absence of infinite $(DP(\mathcal{R}), \mathcal{R}, \pi)$-chains automatically. To this end, we adapt the *DP framework* of [16] to infinitary rewriting. In this framework, we now consider arbitrary *DP problems* $(\mathcal{D}, \mathcal{R}, \pi)$ where $\mathcal{D}$ and $\mathcal{R}$ are TRSs and π is an argument filtering. Our goal is to show that there is no infinite $(\mathcal{D}, \mathcal{R}, \pi)$-chain. In this case, we call the problem *finite*. Termination techniques should now be formulated as *DP processors* which operate on DP problems instead of TRSs. A DP processor *Proc* takes a DP problem as input and returns a new set of DP problems which then have to be solved instead. *Proc* is *sound* if for all DP problems d, d is finite whenever all DP problems in $Proc(d)$ are finite. So termination proofs start with the initial DP problem $(DP(\mathcal{R}), \mathcal{R}, \pi)$. Then this problem is transformed repeatedly by sound DP processors. If the final processors return empty sets of DP problems, then termination is proved.

In Thm. 22, 24, and 26 we will recapitulate three of the most important existing DP processors [16] and describe how they must be modified for infinitary constructor rewriting.[8] To this end, they now also have to take the argument filtering π into account. The first processor uses an *estimated dependency graph* to estimate which dependency pairs can follow each other in chains.

Definition 20 (Estimated Dependency Graph). *Let* $(\mathcal{D}, \mathcal{R}, \pi)$ *be a DP problem. The nodes of the* estimated $(\mathcal{D}, \mathcal{R}, \pi)$-*dependency graph* are the pairs of $\mathcal{D}$ and there is an arc from $s \to t$ to $u \to v$ iff $CAP(t)$ and a variant u' of u unify with an mgu μ where $\pi(CAP(t)\mu) = \pi(u'\mu)$ is a finite term. Here, $CAP(t)$ replaces all subterms of t with defined root symbol by different fresh variables.*

Example 21. For the DP problem $(DP(\mathcal{R}), \mathcal{R}, \pi')$ from Ex. 19 we obtain:

$$(1) \longleftarrow (3) \qquad (2) \longrightarrow (4)$$

For example, there is an arc $(2) \to (3)$, *as* $CAP(\mathsf{U}_1(\mathsf{p}_{in}(\mathsf{f}(X), \mathsf{f}(Z)), X, Y)) = \mathsf{U}_1(V, X, Y)$ *unifies with* $\mathsf{U}_1(\mathsf{p}_{out}(\mathsf{f}(X'), \mathsf{f}(Z')), X', Y')$ *by instantiating the arguments of* U_1 *with finite terms. But there are no arcs* $(1) \to (1)$ *or* $(1) \to (2)$, *since* $\mathsf{P}_{in}(\mathsf{f}(X), \mathsf{f}(Z))$ *and* $\mathsf{P}_{in}(\mathsf{f}(X'), \mathsf{g}(Y'))$ *do not unify, even if one instantiates* Z *and* Y' *by infinite terms (as permitted by the filtering* $\pi'(\mathsf{P}_{in}) = \{1\}$).

Note that filterings are used to *detect* potentially infinite arguments, but they are not *removed*, since they can still be useful in the termination proof. In Ex. 21, these arguments are needed to determine that there are no arcs from (1).

If $s \to t, u \to v$ is a $(\mathcal{D}, \mathcal{R}, \pi)$-chain then there is an arc from $s \to t$ to $u \to v$ in the estimated dependency graph. Thus, absence of infinite chains can be proved separately for each maximal strongly connected component (SCC) of the graph. This observation is used by the following processor to modularize termination proofs by decomposing a DP problem into sub-problems.

Theorem 22 (Dependency Graph Processor). *For a DP problem* $(\mathcal{D}, \mathcal{R}, \pi)$, *let Proc return* $\{(\mathcal{D}_1, \mathcal{R}, \pi), \ldots, (\mathcal{D}_n, \mathcal{R}, \pi)\}$ *where* $\mathcal{D}_1, \ldots, \mathcal{D}_n$ *are the nodes of the SCCs in the estimated dependency graph. Then Proc is sound.*

---

[8] Their soundness proofs can be found in http://aprove.informatik.rwth-aachen.de/eval/LP/SGST06.ps

Example 23. In Ex. 21, the only SCC consists of (2) and (3). Thus, the dependency graph processor transforms the initial DP problem $(DP(\mathcal{R}), \mathcal{R}, \pi')$ into $(\{(2), (3)\}, \mathcal{R}, \pi')$, i.e., it deletes the dependency pairs (1) and (4).

The next processor is based on *reduction pairs* $(\succsim, \succ)$ where $\succsim$ and $\succ$ are relations on finite terms. Here, $\succsim$ is reflexive, transitive, monotonic (i.e., $s \succsim t$ implies $f(\dots s \dots) \succsim f(\dots t \dots)$ for all function symbols f), and stable (i.e., $s \succsim t$ implies $s\sigma \succsim t\sigma$ for all substitutions σ) and $\succ$ is a stable well-founded order compatible with $\succsim$ (i.e., $\succsim \circ \succ \subseteq \succ$ or $\succ \circ \succsim \subseteq \succ$). There are many techniques to search for such relations automatically (LPO, polynomial interpretations, etc. [14]).

For a DP problem $(\mathcal{D}, \mathcal{R}, \pi)$, we now try to find a reduction pair $(\succsim, \succ)$ such that all filtered $\mathcal{R}$-rules are weakly decreasing (w.r.t. $\succsim$) and all filtered $\mathcal{D}$-dependency pairs are weakly or strictly decreasing (w.r.t. $\succsim$ or $\succ$).[9] Requiring $\pi(l) \succsim \pi(r)$ for all $l \to r \in \mathcal{R}$ ensures that in chains $s_1 \to t_1, s_2 \to t_2, \dots$ with $t_i\sigma_i \to_{\mathcal{R}}^* s_{i+1}\sigma_{i+1}$ as in Def. 17, we have $\pi(t_i\sigma_i) \succsim \pi(s_{i+1}\sigma_{i+1})$. Hence, if a reduction pair satisfies the above conditions, then the strictly decreasing dependency pairs (i.e., those $s \to t \in \mathcal{D}$ where $\pi(s) \succ \pi(t)$) cannot occur infinitely often in chains. So the following processor deletes these pairs from $\mathcal{D}$. For any TRS $\mathcal{D}$ and any relation $\succ$, let $\mathcal{D}_{\succ_\pi} = \{s \to t \in \mathcal{D} \mid \pi(s) \succ \pi(t)\}$.

Theorem 24 (Reduction Pair Processor). *Let $(\succsim, \succ)$ be a reduction pair. Then the following DP processor Proc is sound. For $(\mathcal{D}, \mathcal{R}, \pi)$, Proc returns*

- $\{(\mathcal{D} \setminus \mathcal{D}_{\succ_\pi}, \mathcal{R}, \pi)\}$, *if* $\mathcal{D}_{\succ_\pi} \cup \mathcal{D}_{\succsim_\pi} = \mathcal{D}$ *and* $\mathcal{R}_{\succsim_\pi} = \mathcal{R}$
- $\{(\mathcal{D}, \mathcal{R}, \pi)\}$, *otherwise*

Example 25. For the DP problem $(\{(2), (3)\}, \mathcal{R}, \pi')$ in Ex. 23, one can easily find a reduction pair[10] where the dependency pair (3) is strictly decreasing and where (2) and all rules are weakly decreasing after applying the filtering π':

$$\mathsf{P}_{in}(\mathsf{f}(X)) \succsim \mathsf{U}_1(\mathsf{p}_{in}(\mathsf{f}(X)), X) \qquad \mathsf{p}_{in}(X) \succsim \mathsf{p}_{out}(X, X)$$
$$\mathsf{U}_1(\mathsf{p}_{out}(\mathsf{f}(X), \mathsf{f}(Z)), X) \succ \mathsf{P}_{in}(Z) \qquad \mathsf{p}_{in}(\mathsf{f}(X)) \succsim \mathsf{u}_1(\mathsf{p}_{in}(\mathsf{f}(X)), X)$$
$$\mathsf{u}_1(\mathsf{p}_{out}(\mathsf{f}(X), \mathsf{f}(Z)), X) \succsim \mathsf{u}_2(\mathsf{p}_{in}(Z), X, Z)$$
$$\mathsf{u}_2(\mathsf{p}_{out}(Z, \mathsf{g}(Y)), X, Z) \succsim \mathsf{p}_{out}(\mathsf{f}(X), \mathsf{g}(Y))$$

Thus, the reduction pair processor can remove (3) from the DP problem which results in $(\{(2)\}, \mathcal{R}, \pi')$. By applying the dependency graph processor again, one obtains the empty set of DP problems, since now the estimated dependency graph only has the node (2) and no arcs. This proves that the initial DP problem $(DP(\mathcal{R}), \mathcal{R}, \pi')$ from Ex. 19 is finite and thus, the logic program from Ex. 1 terminates for all queries Q where $\pi(Q)$ is finite and ground. Note that termination of the non-well-moded program from Ex. 3 can be shown analogously since finiteness of the initial DP problem can be proved in the same way. The only difference is that we obtain g instead of $\mathsf{g}(Y)$ in the last inequality above.

---

[9] We only consider *filtered* rules and dependency pairs. Thus, $\succsim$ and $\succ$ are only used to compare those parts of terms which remain *finite* for all instantiations in chains.

[10] One can use the polynomial interpretation $|\mathsf{P}_{in}(t_1, t_2)| = |\mathsf{p}_{in}(t_1, t_2)| = |\mathsf{U}_1(t_1, t_2)| = |\mathsf{u}_1(t_1, t_2)| = |\mathsf{u}_2(t_1, t_2, t_3)| = |t_1|$, $|\mathsf{p}_{out}(t_1, t_2)| = |t_2|$, $|\mathsf{f}(t_1)| = |t_1| + 1$, and $|\mathsf{g}(t_1)| = 0$.

As in Thm. 22 and 24, many other existing DP processors [16] can easily be adapted to infinitary constructor rewriting as well. Finally, one can also use the following processor to transform a DP problem $(\mathcal{D}, \mathcal{R}, \pi)$ for infinitary constructor rewriting into a DP problem $(\pi(D), \pi(R), id)$ for ordinary rewriting. Afterwards, *any* existing DP processor for *ordinary* rewriting becomes applicable.[11] Since any termination technique for TRSs can immediately be formulated as a DP processor [16, Thm. 36], now any termination technique for ordinary rewriting can be directly used for infinitary constructor rewriting as well.

Theorem 26 (Argument Filtering Processor). *Let* $Proc(\,(\mathcal{D}, \mathcal{R}, \pi)\,) = \{(\pi(\mathcal{D}), \pi(\mathcal{R}), id)\}$ *where* $id(f) = \{1, \ldots, n\}$ *for all* f/n. *Then Proc is sound.*

5   Experiments and Conclusion

In this paper, we developed a new transformation from logic programs $\mathcal{P}$ to TRSs $\mathcal{R}_{\mathcal{P}}$. To prove the termination of a class of queries for $\mathcal{P}$, it is now sufficient to analyze the termination behavior of $\mathcal{R}_{\mathcal{P}}$ when using infinitary constructor rewriting. This approach is even sound for logic programming without occur check. We showed how to adapt the DP framework of [4,16] from ordinary term rewriting to infinitary constructor rewriting. Then the DP framework can be used for termination proofs of $\mathcal{R}_{\mathcal{P}}$ and thus, for automated termination analysis of $\mathcal{P}$. Since *any* termination technique for TRSs can be formulated as a DP processor [16], now any such technique can also be used for logic programs.

We integrated our approach in the termination tool AProVE [17] which implements the DP framework. To evaluate our results, we tested AProVE against three other representative termination tools for logic programming: TALP [29] is the only other available tool based on transformational methods (it uses the classical transformation [28] described in Sect. 1), whereas cTI [25] and TerminWeb [10] are based on direct approaches. We ran the tools on a set of 296 examples in fully automatic mode.[12] This set includes all logic programming examples from the *Termination Problem Data Base* which is used in the annual *International Termination Competition*[13] and which contains several collections provided by the developers of other tools. Moreover, we also included all examples from the experimental evaluation of [7]. However, to eliminate the influence of the translation from Prolog to logic programs, we removed all examples that use non-trivial built-in predicates or that are not definite logic programs after ignoring the cut operator. Here, TALP succeeds on 163 examples, cTI proves termination of 167 examples, TerminWeb succeeds on 178 examples, and AProVE verifies termination of 208 examples (including all where TALP is successful).

---

[11] If $(\mathcal{D}, \mathcal{R}, \pi)$ results from the transformation of a logic program, then for $(\pi(D), \pi(R), id)$ it is even sound to apply the existing DP processors for *innermost* rewriting [16]. These processors are usually more powerful than those for ordinary rewriting.

[12] We combined *termsize* and *list-length* norm for TerminWeb and allowed 5 iterations before widening for cTI. Apart from that, we used the default settings of the tools.

[13] For details, see http://www.lri.fr/~marche/termination-competition/

The comparison of APrOVE and TALP shows that our approach improves significantly upon the previous transformational method that TALP is based on, cf. Goals (A) and (B). In particular, TALP fails for all non-well-moded programs.

The comparison with cTI and TerminWeb demonstrates that our new transformational approach is comparable in power to direct approaches. But there is a substantial set of programs where APrOVE succeeds and direct tools fail (cf. Goal (C)) and there is also a substantial set of examples where direct tools succeed and APrOVE fails. More precisely, APrOVE succeeds on 57 examples where cTI fails and on 46 examples where TerminWeb fails. On the other hand, there are 16 examples where cTI succeeds whereas APrOVE cannot prove termination and there are also 16 examples where TerminWeb succeeds and APrOVE fails.

Thus, transformational and direct approaches both have their advantages and the most powerful solution would be to combine direct tools like cTI or Termin-Web with a transformational prover like APrOVE which is based on the contributions of this paper. This also indicates that it is indeed beneficial to use termination techniques from TRSs for logic programs as well. To run APrOVE, for details on our experiments, to access our collection of examples, and for a discussion on the limitations[14] of our approach and its implementation, we refer to http://aprove.informatik.rwth-aachen.de/eval/LP/

Acknowledgements. We thank M. Codish, D. De Schreye, and F. Mesnard for helpful comments and R. Bagnara and S. Genaim for help with the experiments.

References

1. G. Aguzzi and U. Modigliani. Proving termination of logic programs by transforming them into equivalent term rewriting systems. In *Proc. 13th FST & TCS*, LNCS 761, pages 114–124, 1993.
2. K. R. Apt. *From Logic Programming to Prolog*. Prentice Hall, 1997.
3. K. R. Apt and S. Etalle. On the unification free Prolog programs. In *Proc. 18th MFCS*, LNCS 711, pages 1–19, 1993.
4. T. Arts and J. Giesl. Termination of term rewriting using dependency pairs. *Theoretical Computer Science*, 236:133–178, 2000.
5. T. Arts and H. Zantema. Termination of logic programs using semantic unification. In *Proc. 5th LOPSTR*, LNCS 1048, pages 219–233, 1995.
6. F. Baader and T. Nipkow. *Term Rewriting and All That*. Cambridge, 1998.
7. M. Bruynooghe, M. Codish, J. Gallagher, S. Genaim, and W. Vanhoof. Termination analysis of logic programs through combination of type-based norms. *ACM Transactions on Programming Languages and Systems*, 2006. To appear.

---

[14] Our approach could fail for 3 reasons: (1) The transformation of Thm. 14 could fail, i.e., there could be a logic program which is terminating for the set of queries, but not all corresponding terms are terminating in the transformed TRS. We do not know such examples and it could be that this step is indeed complete. (2) The approach via dependency pairs (Thm. 18) can fail to prove termination of the transformed TRS. (3) Our implementation can fail to prove finiteness of the resulting DP problem from Thm. 18. On the website, we give examples for Failures (2) and (3).

8. M. Chtourou and M. Rusinowitch. Méthode transformationelle pour la preuve de terminaison des programmes logiques. Unpublished manuscript, 1993.

9. M. Codish, V. Lagoon, and P. Stuckey. Testing for termination with monotonicity constraints. In *Proc. 21st ICLP*, LNCS 3668, pages 326–340, 2005.

10. M. Codish and C. Taboch. A semantic basis for termination analysis of logic programs. *Journal of Logic Programming*, 41(1):103–123, 1999.

11. A. Colmerauer. Prolog and infinite trees. In K. L. Clark and S. Tärnlund, editors, *Logic Programming*. Academic Press, 1982.

12. D. De Schreye and S. Decorte. Termination of logic programs: The never-ending story. *Journal of Logic Programming*, 19&20:199–260, 1994.

13. D. De Schreye and A. Serebrenik. Acceptability with general orderings. In *Computational Logic. Logic Prog. and Beyond.*, LNCS 2407, pages 187–210, 2002.

14. N. Dershowitz. Termination of rewriting. *J. Symb. Comp.*, 3:69–116, 1987.

15. H. Ganzinger and U. Waldmann. Termination proofs of well-moded logic programs via conditional rewrite systems. *Proc. 3rd CTRS*, LNCS 656, pages 216–222, 1993.

16. J. Giesl, R. Thiemann, and P. Schneider-Kamp. The dependency pair framework: Combining techniques for automated termination proofs. In *Proc. 11th LPAR*, LNAI 3452, pages 301–331, 2005.

17. J. Giesl, P. Schneider-Kamp, R. Thiemann. AProVE 1.2: Automatic termination proofs in the DP framework. In *Proc. 3rd IJCAR*, LNAI 4130, pp. 281–286, 2006.

18. G. Huet. *Résolution d'équations dans les langages d'ordre 1, 2, ..., ω*. PhD, 1976.

19. M. Krishna Rao, D. Kapur, and R. Shyamasundar. Transformational methodology for proving termination of logic programs. *J. Log. Prog.*, 34(1):1–42, 1998.

20. V. Lagoon, F. Mesnard, and P. J. Stuckey. Termination analysis with types is more accurate. In *Proc. 19th ICLP*, LNCS 2916, pages 254–268, 2003.

21. M. Leuschel and M. H. Sørensen. Redundant argument filtering of logic programs. In *Proc. 6th LOPSTR*, LNCS 1207, pages 83–103, 1996.

22. N. Lindenstrauss, Y. Sagiv, and A. Serebrenik. TermiLog: A system for checking termination of queries to logic programs. *Proc. 9th CAV*, LNCS 1254, p. 444-447, 1997.

23. M. Marchiori. Logic programs as term rewriting systems. In *Proc. 4th ALP*, LNCS 850, pages 223–241, 1994.

24. M. Marchiori. Proving existential termination of normal logic programs. In *Proc. 5th AMAST*, LNCS 1101, pages 375–390, 1996.

25. F. Mesnard and R. Bagnara. cTI: A constraint-based termination inference tool for ISO-Prolog. *Theory and Practice of Logic Programming*, 5(1&2):243–257, 2005.

26. F. Mesnard and S. Ruggieri. On proving left termination of constraint logic programs. *ACM Transaction on Computational Logic*, 4(2):207–259, 2003.

27. M. T. Nguyen and D. De Schreye. Polynomial interpretations as a basis for termination analysis of logic programs. *Proc. 21. ICLP*, LNCS 3668, p.311-325, 2005.

28. E. Ohlebusch. Termination of logic programs: Transformational methods revisited. *Appl. Algebra in Engineering, Communication and Computing*, 12:73–116, 2001.

29. E. Ohlebusch, C. Claves, and C. Marché. TALP: A tool for the termination analysis of logic programs. In *Proc. 11th RTA*, LNCS 1833, pages 270–273, 2000.

30. F. van Raamsdonk. Translating logic programs into conditional rewriting systems. In *Proc. 14th ICLP*, pages 168–182. MIT Press, 1997.

31. A. Serebrenik and D. De Schreye. Proving termination with adornments. In *Proc. 13th LOPSTR*, LNCS 3018, pages 108–109, 2003.

32. A. Serebrenik and D. De Schreye. Inference of termination conditions for numerical loops in Prolog. *Theory and Practice of Logic Programming*, 4:719–751, 2004.

33. J.-G. Smaus. Termination of logic programs using various dynamic selection rules. In *Proc. 20th ICLP*, LNCS 3132, pages 43–57, 2004.

Detecting Non-termination of Term Rewriting Systems Using an Unfolding Operator

Étienne Payet

IREMIA - Université de la Réunion, France
epayet@univ-reunion.fr

Abstract. In this paper, we present an approach to non-termination of term rewriting systems inspired by a technique that was designed in the context of logic programming. Our method is based on a classical unfolding operation together with semi-unification and is independent of a particular reduction strategy. We also describe a technique to reduce the explosion of rules caused by the unfolding process. The analyser that we have implemented is able to solve most of the non-terminating examples in the Termination Problem Data Base.

1 Introduction

Proving termination of a term rewriting system (TRS) $\mathcal{R}$ consists in proving that *every* term only has finite rewritings with respect to $\mathcal{R}$ (a particular reduction strategy may be used). Termination of TRS's has been subject to an intensive research (see *e.g.* [10,23] for surveys) that has given rise to several automatic proof methods. One of the most powerful is the dependency pair approach [5], recently extended to the dependency pair framework [14,15], implemented in the termination prover AProVE [16]. In comparison, the dual problem, *i.e.* non-termination, has hardly been studied. It consists in proving that *there exists* a term that *loops*, *i.e.* that leads to an infinite rewriting. Notice that designing non-termination provers is an important issue as this kind of tools can be used to *disprove* termination, *i.e.* to complement any termination prover. In [15], the authors use the dependency pair framework to combine termination and non-termination analyses. In order to detect non-terminating TRS's, they apply forward or backward narrowing to dependency pairs until they find two terms that semi-unify. Some heuristics are used to select forward or backward narrowing and to get a finite search space.

Termination has also been widely studied in the context of logic programming. One of the approaches that have been introduced so far consists in inferring terminating classes of queries, *i.e.* classes where *every* element only has finite left-derivations with respect to a given logic program. Several automatic tools performing termination inference have been designed, *e.g.* TerminWeb [13] or cTI [19]. But as for term rewriting, there are only a few papers about the dual problem, *i.e.* inference of non-terminating classes of queries (classes where *there exists* an element that loops, *i.e.* that has an infinite left-derivation). In [21,20], the authors introduce the unfold & infer approach to infer non-terminating classes of queries. First, they unfold the logic program P of interest to a binary logic program BP using the unfolding operator of [12]. By the results in [9], a query loops with respect to BP if and only if it loops with respect to P. Then, to infer looping queries, they consider every rule $A \leftarrow B$ in BP; if the body B is more general (up to some computed neutral argument positions) than the head A, they conclude that A loops with respect to BP, hence with respect to P.

On the *theoretical* level, it can be noticed that the unfold & infer approach also works with TRS's. Indeed, there exists some techniques to unfold a TRS $\mathcal{R}$ to a TRS $\mathcal{U}$ such that if a term loops with respect to $\mathcal{U}$ then it also loops with respect to $\mathcal{R}$ (see for instance [7,22,3]). Moreover, semi-unification is a powerful tool for detecting looping terms: if there is a rule $l \to r$ in $\mathcal{U}$ where $l\theta_1\theta_2 = r'\theta_1$ for some substitutions θ_1 and θ_2 and some subterm r' of r, then we can deduce that $l\theta_1$ loops with respect to $\mathcal{U}$, hence with respect to $\mathcal{R}$. Notice that the subsumption order is different from that used in logic programming, where the body has to be more general than the head, while here, $l\theta_1$ has to be more general than $r'\theta_1$. This is due to definition of the operational semantics of both paradigms.

On the *practical* level, however, it is not known how the unfold & infer approach behaves in the context of term rewriting. In this paper, we present our experiments on using the narrowing-based unfolding operation described in [3] together with semi-unification to prove non-termination of TRS's. The first analysis that we describe is very simple but leads to an explosion of the number of generated rules. Hence, we refine it into a second one by providing a mechanism that allows us to eliminate some useless rules produced by the unfolding process. The simple and refined analyses are powerful enough to solve most of the non-terminating examples in the Termination Problem Data Base (TPDB) [25], but the refined one runs much faster. We insist that the results we present herein are independent of any particular reduction strategy. This does not mean that our method is parametric in a reduction strategy but that we always consider the whole rewrite relation and not subsets of it.

Our motivations are the following. We want to design a simple formalism for proving non-termination of TRS's (the unfold & infer theory is very simple and clear, as presented above). We do not want any heutistics as in [15]. Moreover, we want another illustration of the unfold & infer technique which was introduced in the context of logic programming. Such an illustration would provide a connection between the paradigm of logic programming and that of term rewriting, by a transfer of a logic programming technique to term rewriting.

The paper is organized as follows. First, in Sect. 2, we give the basic definitions and fix the notations. Then, in Sect. 3 and Sect. 4, we present a non-termination analysis based on an existing unfolding operation together with semi-unification. In Sect. 5, we refine this analysis and in Sect. 6, we present an implementation and some experiments using TRS's from the TPDB. Finally, Sect. 7 discusses related works and concludes the paper.

2   Preliminaries

We briefly present the basic concepts of term rewriting (details can be found *e.g.* in [6]) and the notations that we use in the paper.

We let $\mathbb{N}$ denote the set of non-negative integers and, for any $n \in \mathbb{N}$, $[1, n]$ denotes the set of all the integers i such that $1 \leq i \leq n$ (if $n = 0$, then $[1, n] = \varnothing$).

From now on, we fix a finite *signature* $\mathcal{F}$, *i.e.* a finite set of *function symbols* where every $\mathsf{f} \in \mathcal{F}$ has a unique *arity*, which is the number of its arguments. We write $\mathsf{f}/n \in \mathcal{F}$ to denote that f is an element of $\mathcal{F}$ whose arity is $n \geq 0$. We also fix an infinite countable set $\mathcal{V}$ of *variables* with $\mathcal{F} \cap \mathcal{V} = \varnothing$. The set of terms $\mathcal{T}(\mathcal{F}, \mathcal{V})$ is defined as the smallest set such that:

- $\mathcal{V} \subseteq \mathcal{T}(\mathcal{F}, \mathcal{V})$,
- if $\mathsf{f}/n \in \mathcal{F}$ and $t_1, \ldots, t_n \in \mathcal{T}(\mathcal{F}, \mathcal{V})$ then $\mathsf{f}(t_1, \ldots, t_n) \in \mathcal{T}(\mathcal{F}, \mathcal{V})$.

For $t \in \mathcal{T}(\mathcal{F}, \mathcal{V})$, $root(t)$ denotes the *root symbol* of t and is defined by:

$$root(t) = \begin{cases} \bot & \text{if } t \in \mathcal{V}, \\ \mathsf{f} & \text{if } t = \mathsf{f}(t_1, \ldots, t_n) \end{cases}$$

where $\bot$ is a special symbol not occurring in $\mathcal{F} \cup \mathcal{V}$. We let $Var(t)$ denote the set of variables occurring in t. The *set of positions* in t, denoted by $Pos(t)$, is defined as:

$$Pos(t) = \begin{cases} \{\varepsilon\} & \text{if } t \in \mathcal{V}, \\ \{\varepsilon\} \cup \{i.p \mid 1 \leq i \leq n \text{ and } p \in Pos(t_i)\} & \text{if } t = \mathsf{f}(t_1, \ldots, t_n) \end{cases}.$$

When $p \in Pos(t)$, we write $t|_p$ to denote the subterm of t at position p, with $t|_\varepsilon = t$. We write $t[p \leftarrow s]$ to denote the term obtained from t by replacing $t|_p$ with a term s. We say that p is a *non-variable position of* t if $t|_p$ is not a variable. The set of non-variable positions of t is denoted by $NPos(t)$.

We write substitutions as sets of the form $\{x_1/t_1, \ldots, x_n/t_n\}$ denoting that for each $i \in [1, n]$, variable x_i is mapped to term t_i (note that x_i may occur in t_i). Applying a substitution θ to an object O is denoted by $O\theta$. The *composition* of substitutions θ and η is denoted by $\theta\eta$ and is the substitution that maps any variable x to $(x\theta)\eta$. A term t is *more general than* a term t' when there exists a substitution θ such that $t' = t\theta$. A substitution θ is *more general than* a substitution η when $\eta = \theta\tau$ for some substitution τ. A *renaming* is a substitution that is a 1-1 and onto mapping from its domain to itself. We say that a term t is a *variant* of a term t' if there exists a renaming γ such that $t' = t\gamma$.

Two terms t and t' *unify* when there exists a substitution θ such that $t\theta = t'\theta$. Then we say that θ is a *unifier* of t and t'. A *most general unifier* of t and t' is a unifier of t and t' that is more general than all unifiers of t and t'. We let $mgu(t, t')$ denote the set of most general unifiers of t and t'. We say that t *semi-unifies* with t' if there exists some substitutions θ and θ' such that $t\theta\theta' = t'\theta$.

A *term rewriting system* (TRS) over $\mathcal{F}$ is a set $\mathcal{R} \subseteq \mathcal{T}(\mathcal{F}, \mathcal{V}) \times \mathcal{T}(\mathcal{F}, \mathcal{V})$ of *rewrite rules*, every element $l \rightarrow r$ of which is such that $l \notin \mathcal{V}$ and $Var(r) \subseteq Var(l)$. For every s and t in $\mathcal{T}(\mathcal{F}, \mathcal{V})$, we write $s \underset{\mathcal{R}}{\rightarrow} t$ if there is a rewrite rule

$l \to r$ in $\mathcal{R}$, a substitution θ and a position p in $Pos(s)$ such that $s|_p = l\theta$ and $t = s[p \leftarrow r\theta]$. We let $\xrightarrow[\mathcal{R}]{+}$ (resp. $\xrightarrow[\mathcal{R}]{*}$) denote the transitive (resp. reflexive and transitive) closure of $\xrightarrow[\mathcal{R}]{}$. In this paper, we only consider finite TRS's. We say that a term t *loops* with respect to (w.r.t.) $\mathcal{R}$ when there exists infinitely many terms $t_1, t_2, \ldots$ such that $t \xrightarrow[\mathcal{R}]{} t_1 \xrightarrow[\mathcal{R}]{} t_2 \xrightarrow[\mathcal{R}]{} \cdots$. We say that $\mathcal{R}$ is *non-terminating* when there exists a term that loops with respect to $\mathcal{R}$.

3 Unfolding a TRS

Usually, unfolding a rule of a term rewriting system consists in performing two elementary transformations: instantiation and unfolding (see e.g. [7,22]). These transformations can be combined into a single one using narrowing:

Definition 1 (Unfolding [3]). *Let $\mathcal{R}$ be a TRS and $l \to r \in \mathcal{R}$. If for some $l' \to r' \in \mathcal{R}$ renamed with fresh variables and for some non-variable position p of r we have $\theta \in mgu(r|_p, l')$, then $(l \to r[p \leftarrow r'])\theta$ is an unfolding of $l \to r$.*

The non-termination analysis presented in this paper proceeds by iteratively unfolding sets of rules using a fixed TRS. This is why we rephrase Definition 1 above in the form of an unfolding operator that takes two sets of rules as input: the rules X to be unfolded and the rules $\mathcal{R}$ that are used to unfold:

Definition 2 (Unfolding operator). *For every TRS $\mathcal{R}$, the* unfolding operator $T_{\mathcal{R}}$ *is defined as: for any set X of rewrite rules,*

$$T_{\mathcal{R}}(X) = \left\{ (l \to r[p \leftarrow r'])\theta \;\middle|\; \begin{array}{l} l \to r \in X \\ p \in NPos(r) \\ l' \to r' \in \mathcal{R} \text{ renamed with fresh variables} \\ \theta \in mgu(r|_p, l') \end{array} \right\}.$$

Notice that this operator is not monotone. As in [2], the *unfolding sequence starting from $\mathcal{R}$* is

$$\begin{array}{rcl} T_{\mathcal{R}} \uparrow 0 & = & \mathcal{R} \\ T_{\mathcal{R}} \uparrow (n+1) & = & T_{\mathcal{R}}(T_{\mathcal{R}} \uparrow n) \quad \forall n \in \mathbb{N}. \end{array}$$

Example 1 (Giesl, Thiemann and Schneider-Kamp [15], Example 28). Consider

$$\mathcal{R} = \left\{ \mathsf{f}(x, y, z) \to \mathsf{g}(x, y, z), \; \mathsf{g}(\mathsf{s}(x), y, z) \to \mathsf{f}(z, \mathsf{s}(y), z) \right\}.$$

We have:

- $T_{\mathcal{R}} \uparrow 0 = \mathcal{R}$.
- $T_{\mathcal{R}} \uparrow 1 = T_{\mathcal{R}}(T_{\mathcal{R}} \uparrow 0)$. If we take $\mathsf{f}(x, y, z) \to \mathsf{g}(x, y, z)$ in $T_{\mathcal{R}} \uparrow 0$, $p = \varepsilon$, $l' \to r'$ as $\mathsf{g}(\mathsf{s}(x_1), y_1, z_1) \to \mathsf{f}(z_1, \mathsf{s}(y_1), z_1)$ in $\mathcal{R}$, $\theta = \{x/\mathsf{s}(x_1), y/y_1, z/z_1\}$, we get the rule

$$\mathsf{f}(\mathsf{s}(x_1), y_1, z_1) \to \mathsf{f}(z_1, \mathsf{s}(y_1), z_1)$$

  as an element of $T_{\mathcal{R}} \uparrow 1$. $\square$

Example 2 (Toyama [24]). Consider:

$$\mathcal{R} = \big\{ f(0, 1, x) \to f(x, x, x), \ g(x, y) \to x, \ g(x, y) \to y \big\} \ .$$

We have:

- $T_\mathcal{R} \uparrow 0 = \mathcal{R}$.
- $T_\mathcal{R} \uparrow 1 = T_\mathcal{R}(T_\mathcal{R} \uparrow 0)$. Notice that the rules $g(x, y) \to x$ and $g(x, y) \to y$ in $T_\mathcal{R} \uparrow 0$ cannot be unfolded because there are no non-variable positions in the right-hand side. The rule $f(0, 1, x) \to f(x, x, x)$ cannot be unfolded too because $f(x, x, x)$, the only non-variable subterm in the right-hand side, cannot be unified with any variant of a left-hand side. So, $T_\mathcal{R} \uparrow 1 = \varnothing$. □

In Sect. 4 below, in order to prove non-termination, we consider the rules $l \to r$ in the unfolding sequence. If l semi-unifies with a subterm of r, then we deduce that $\mathcal{R}$ is non-terminating. Notice that using this mechanism directly, one gets a very limited tool that is unable to solve the smallest examples.

Example 3 (Example 2 continued). $\mathcal{R}$ is known to be non-terminating (for instance, $f(0, 1, g(0, 1))$ loops). Note that $T_\mathcal{R} \uparrow 0 = \mathcal{R}$ and for each $n \in \mathbb{N} \setminus \{0\}$, $T_\mathcal{R} \uparrow n = \varnothing$. As no left-hand side in $\mathcal{R}$ semi-unifies with a subterm of the corresponding right-hand side, we cannot conclude. □

In order to get a practical analyser, a solution consists in pre-processing the TRS $\mathcal{R}$ of interest by replacing every variable with the left-hand side of each rule of $\mathcal{R}$. The intuition is that as a variable represents any term, it stands in particular for a term that can be rewritten.

Definition 3 (Augmented TRS). *Let $\mathcal{R}$ be a TRS. The augmented TRS $\mathcal{R}^+$ is defined modulo renaming as follows: $\mathcal{R}^+$ consists of all the rules $(l \to r)\theta$ where $l \to r$ is an element of $\mathcal{R}$ and θ is a substitution of the form $\{x_1/t_1, \ldots, x_n/t_n\}$ (with $n \in \mathbb{N}$) such that $\{x_1, \ldots, x_n\} \subseteq Var(l)$ and for each $i \in [1, n]$, t_i is a variant of a left-hand side in $\mathcal{R}$ and is variable disjoint from $l \to r$ and from every t_j, $j \in [1, n] \setminus \{i\}$. Note that θ can be empty (take $n = 0$).*

Example 4 (Example 2 continued). The rule $f(0, 1, x) \to f(x, x, x)$ only contains variable x. Hence, we consider the substitutions

$$\theta_0 = \varnothing, \ \theta_1 = \{x/f(0, 1, x_1)\} \text{ and } \theta_2 = \{x/g(x_1, y_1)\}$$

and apply them to $f(0, 1, x) \to f(x, x, x)$. This leads, respectively, to:

$$f(0, 1, x) \to f(x, x, x)$$
$$f(0, 1, f(0, 1, x_1)) \to f(f(0, 1, x_1), f(0, 1, x_1), f(0, 1, x_1))$$
$$f(0, 1, g(x_1, y_1)) \to f(g(x_1, y_1), g(x_1, y_1), g(x_1, y_1)) \ .$$

The variables in rules $g(x, y) \to x$ and $g(x, y) \to y$ are x and y. So, we consider the above substitutions $\theta_0, \theta_1, \theta_2$ together with

$$\theta_3 = \{y/f(0, 1, x_1)\} \qquad\qquad \theta_4 = \{y/g(x_1, y_1)\}$$
$$\theta_5 = \{x/f(0, 1, x_1), y/f(0, 1, x_2)\} \quad \theta_6 = \{x/f(0, 1, x_1), y/g(x_2, y_2)\}$$
$$\theta_7 = \{x/g(x_1, y_1), y/f(0, 1, x_2)\} \quad \theta_8 = \{x/g(x_1, y_1), y/g(x_2, y_2)\}$$

that lead to (the rules on the left are obtained from $g(x, y) \to x$ and those on the right from $g(x, y) \to y$):

$$
\begin{array}{lll}
\theta_0 : & g(x, y) \to x & g(x, y) \to y \\
\theta_1 : & g(f(0, 1, x_1), y) \to f(0, 1, x_1) & g(f(0, 1, x_1), y) \to y \\
\theta_2 : & g(g(x_1, y_1), y) \to g(x_1, y_1) & g(g(x_1, y_1), y) \to y \\
\vdots & \vdots & \vdots
\end{array}
$$

Now, we can compute the unfolding sequence starting from $\mathcal{R}^+$ instead of $\mathcal{R}$. From the rule

$$f(0, 1, g(x_1, y_1)) \to f(g(x_1, y_1), g(x_1, y_1), g(x_1, y_1))$$

computed above, using position 1 of the right-hand side and $g(x_2, y_2) \to x_2$ in $\mathcal{R}$, we get $f(0, 1, g(x_1, y_1)) \to f(x_1, g(x_1, y_1), g(x_1, y_1))$ as an element of $T_{\mathcal{R}} \uparrow 1$. Then, from this new rule, using position 2 of the right-hand side together with $g(x_3, y_3) \to y_3$ in $\mathcal{R}$, we get $f(0, 1, g(x_1, y_1)) \to f(x_1, y_1, g(x_1, y_1))$ as an element of $T_{\mathcal{R}} \uparrow 2$. As $f(0, 1, g(x_1, y_1))\theta_1\theta_2 = f(x_1, y_1, g(x_1, y_1))\theta_1$ for $\theta_1 = \{x_1/0, y_1/1\}$ and $\theta_2 = \varnothing$, we conclude that $\mathcal{R}$ is non-terminating.   □

Following the intuitions of the preceding example, we give these new definitions:

Definition 4 (Unfolding semantics). *The* augmented unfolding sequence of $\mathcal{R}$ *is*

$$
\begin{aligned}
T_{\mathcal{R}} \uparrow 0 &= \mathcal{R}^+ \\
T_{\mathcal{R}} \uparrow (n+1) &= T_{\mathcal{R}}(T_{\mathcal{R}} \uparrow n) \quad \forall n \in \mathbb{N}.
\end{aligned}
$$

The unfolding semantics $unf(\mathcal{R})$ *of* $\mathcal{R}$ *is the limit of the unfolding process described in Definition 2, starting from* $\mathcal{R}^+$:

$$unf(\mathcal{R}) = \bigcup_{n \in \mathbb{N}} T_{\mathcal{R}} \uparrow n.$$

Notice that the least fixpoint of $T_{\mathcal{R}}$ is the empty set. Moreover, $unf(\mathcal{R})$ is not a fixpoint of $T_{\mathcal{R}}$. This is because $\mathcal{R}^+ \subseteq unf(\mathcal{R})$ (because $T_{\mathcal{R}} \uparrow 0 = \mathcal{R}^+$) but we do not necessarily have $\mathcal{R}^+ \subseteq T_{\mathcal{R}}(unf(\mathcal{R}))$ because

$$T_{\mathcal{R}}(unf(\mathcal{R})) = T_{\mathcal{R}}(\bigcup_{n \in \mathbb{N}} T_{\mathcal{R}} \uparrow n) = \bigcup_{n \in \mathbb{N}} T_{\mathcal{R}}(T_{\mathcal{R}} \uparrow n) = \bigcup_{n \in \mathbb{N} \setminus \{0\}} T_{\mathcal{R}} \uparrow n.$$

In the logic programming framework, every clause $H \leftarrow B$ of the binary unfoldings specifies that a call to H necessarily leads to a call to B. In the context of term rewriting, we get the following counterpart:

Proposition 1. *Let* $\mathcal{R}$ *be a TRS. If* $l \to r \in unf(\mathcal{R})$ *then* $l \xrightarrow[\mathcal{R}]{+} r$.

This result allows us to prove that the unfoldings exhibit the termination properties of a term rewriting system:

Theorem 1. *Let* $\mathcal{R}$ *be a TRS and* t *be a term. Then,* t *loops w.r.t.* $\mathcal{R}$ *if and only if* t *loops w.r.t.* $unf(\mathcal{R})$.

4   Inferring Looping Terms

The unfoldings of a TRS can be used to infer terms that loop, hence to prove non-termination. It suffices to add semi-unification [18] to Proposition 1. Notice that semi-unification encompasses both matching and unification. A polynomial-time algorithm for semi-unification can be found in [17].

Theorem 2. *Let $\mathcal{R}$ be a TRS. Suppose that for $l \to r \in unf(\mathcal{R})$ there is a subterm r' of r such that $l\theta_1\theta_2 = r'\theta_1$ for some substitutions θ_1 and θ_2. Then, $l\theta_1$ loops w.r.t. $\mathcal{R}$.*

In order to use Theorem 2 as a practical tool, one can for instance fix a maximum number of iterations of the unfolding operator.

Example 5 (Example 4 continued). $\mathsf{f}(0, 1, \mathsf{g}(x_1, y_1)) \to \mathsf{f}(x_1, y_1, \mathsf{g}(x_1, y_1))$ is an element of $T_{\mathcal{R}} \uparrow 2$ with $\mathsf{f}(0, 1, \mathsf{g}(x_1, y_1))\theta_1\theta_2 = \mathsf{f}(x_1, y_1, \mathsf{g}(x_1, y_1))\theta_1$ for $\theta_1 = \{x_1/0, y_1/1\}$ and $\theta_2 = \varnothing$. Hence, $\mathsf{f}(0, 1, \mathsf{g}(x_1, y_1))\theta_1 = \mathsf{f}(0, 1, \mathsf{g}(0, 1))$ loops with respect to $\mathcal{R}$.   □

Example 6 (Example 1 continued). $\mathsf{f}(\mathsf{s}(x_1), y_1, z_1) \to \mathsf{f}(z_1, \mathsf{s}(y_1), z_1)$ is an element of $T_{\mathcal{R}} \uparrow 1$ with $\mathsf{f}(\mathsf{s}(x_1), y_1, z_1)\theta_1\theta_2 = \mathsf{f}(z_1, \mathsf{s}(y_1), z_1)\theta_1$ for $\theta_1 = \{z_1/\mathsf{s}(x_1)\}$ and $\theta_2 = \{y_1/\mathsf{s}(y_1)\}$. Hence, $\mathsf{f}(\mathsf{s}(x_1), y_1, z_1)\theta_1 = \mathsf{f}(\mathsf{s}(x_1), y_1, \mathsf{s}(x_1))$ loops with respect to $\mathcal{R}$.   □

Example 7 (file `Rubio-inn/test76.trs` *in the TPDB).* Consider

$$\mathcal{R} = \left\{ \begin{array}{ll} \mathsf{f}(0, \mathsf{s}(0), x) \to \mathsf{f}(x, +(x, x), x), & +(x, \mathsf{s}(y)) \to \mathsf{s}(+(x, y)), \\ +(x, 0) \to x, \quad \mathsf{g}(x, y) \to x, \quad \mathsf{g}(x, y) \to y \end{array} \right\}.$$

The augmented TRS $\mathcal{R}^+$ contains the rule

$$R_0 = \mathsf{f}(0, \mathsf{s}(0), \mathsf{g}(x_0, y_0)) \to \mathsf{f}(\mathsf{g}(x_0, y_0), +(\mathsf{g}(x_0, y_0), \mathsf{g}(x_0, y_0)), \mathsf{g}(x_0, y_0))$$

obtained from $\mathsf{f}(0, \mathsf{s}(0), x) \to \mathsf{f}(x, +(x, x), x)$ and substitution $\{x/\mathsf{g}(x_0, y_0)\}$.

- If we take position $p = 2.2$ in the right-hand side of R_0, $\mathsf{g}(x_1, y_1) \to x_1$ in $\mathcal{R}$ and $\theta = \{x_1/x_0, y_1/y_0\}$, we get the rule

$$R_1 = \mathsf{f}(0, \mathsf{s}(0), \mathsf{g}(x_0, y_0)) \to \mathsf{f}(\mathsf{g}(x_0, y_0), +(\mathsf{g}(x_0, y_0), x_0), \mathsf{g}(x_0, y_0))$$

  as an element of $T_{\mathcal{R}} \uparrow 1$.
- If we take position $p = 2$ in the right-hand side of R_1, $+(x_2, 0) \to x_2$ in $\mathcal{R}$ and $\theta = \{x_0/0, x_2/\mathsf{g}(0, y_0)\}$, we get the rule

$$R_2 = \mathsf{f}(0, \mathsf{s}(0), \mathsf{g}(0, y_0)) \to \mathsf{f}(\mathsf{g}(0, y_0), \mathsf{g}(0, y_0), \mathsf{g}(0, y_0))$$

  as an element of $T_{\mathcal{R}} \uparrow 2$.
- If we take position $p = 1$ in the right-hand side of R_2, $\mathsf{g}(x_3, y_3) \to x_3$ in $\mathcal{R}$ and $\theta = \{x_3/0, y_3/y_0\}$, we get the rule

$$R_3 = \mathsf{f}(0, \mathsf{s}(0), \mathsf{g}(0, y_0)) \to \mathsf{f}(0, \mathsf{g}(0, y_0), \mathsf{g}(0, y_0))$$

  as an element of $T_{\mathcal{R}} \uparrow 3$.

– If we take position $p = 2$ in the right-hand side of R_3, $\mathsf{g}(x_4, y_4) \to y_4$ in $\mathcal{R}$ and $\theta = \{x_4/0, y_4/y_0\}$, we get the rule

$$R_4 = \mathsf{f}(0, \mathsf{s}(0), \mathsf{g}(0, y_0)) \to \mathsf{f}(0, y_0, \mathsf{g}(0, y_0))$$

as an element of $T_\mathcal{R} \uparrow 4$.

Notice that the left-hand side $\mathsf{f}(0, \mathsf{s}(0), \mathsf{g}(0, y_0))$ of R_4 semi-unifies with the right-hand side $\mathsf{f}(0, y_0, \mathsf{g}(0, y_0))$ for $\theta_1 = \{y_0/\mathsf{s}(0)\}$ and $\theta_2 = \varnothing$. Consequently, $\mathsf{f}(0, \mathsf{s}(0), \mathsf{g}(0, y_0))\theta_1 = \mathsf{f}(0, \mathsf{s}(0), \mathsf{g}(0, \mathsf{s}(0)))$ loops with respect to $\mathcal{R}$.   □

5   Eliminating Useless Rules

The operator of Definition 2 produces many useless rules, *i.e.* rules that cannot be unfolded to $l \to r$ where l semi-unifies with a subterm of r.

Example 8 (Example 4 continued). The augmented TRS $\mathcal{R}^+$ contains the rule

$$\mathsf{f}(0, 1, \mathsf{f}(0, 1, x_1)) \to \mathsf{f}(\mathsf{f}(0, 1, x_1), \mathsf{f}(0, 1, x_1), \mathsf{f}(0, 1, x_1)) \ .$$

The left-hand side does not semi-unify with any subterm of the right-hand side. Applying $T_\mathcal{R}$ to this rule, one gets:

$$\mathsf{f}(0, 1, \mathsf{f}(0, 1, x_1)) \to \mathsf{f}(\mathsf{f}(x_1, x_1, x_1), \mathsf{f}(0, 1, x_1), \mathsf{f}(0, 1, x_1))$$
$$\mathsf{f}(0, 1, \mathsf{f}(0, 1, x_1)) \to \mathsf{f}(\mathsf{f}(0, 1, x_1), \mathsf{f}(x_1, x_1, x_1), \mathsf{f}(0, 1, x_1))$$
$$\mathsf{f}(0, 1, \mathsf{f}(0, 1, x_1)) \to \mathsf{f}(\mathsf{f}(0, 1, x_1), \mathsf{f}(0, 1, x_1), \mathsf{f}(x_1, x_1, x_1)) \ .$$

None of these new rules satisfies the semi-unification criterion. Applying $T_\mathcal{R}$ again, one gets:

$$\mathsf{f}(0, 1, \mathsf{f}(0, 1, x_1)) \to \mathsf{f}(\mathsf{f}(x_1, x_1, x_1), \mathsf{f}(x_1, x_1, x_1), \mathsf{f}(0, 1, x_1))$$
$$\mathsf{f}(0, 1, \mathsf{f}(0, 1, x_1)) \to \mathsf{f}(\mathsf{f}(x_1, x_1, x_1), \mathsf{f}(0, 1, x_1), \mathsf{f}(x_1, x_1, x_1))$$
$$\mathsf{f}(0, 1, \mathsf{f}(0, 1, x_1)) \to \mathsf{f}(\mathsf{f}(0, 1, x_1), \mathsf{f}(x_1, x_1, x_1), \mathsf{f}(x_1, x_1, x_1))$$
$$\mathsf{f}(0, 1, \mathsf{f}(0, 1, x_1)) \to \mathsf{f}(\mathsf{f}(x_1, x_1, x_1), \mathsf{f}(0, 1, x_1), \mathsf{f}(x_1, x_1, x_1)) \ .$$

None of these rules satisfies the semi-unification criterion. Finally, unfolding one more time leads to:

$$\mathsf{f}(0, 1, \mathsf{f}(0, 1, x_1)) \to \mathsf{f}(\mathsf{f}(x_1, x_1, x_1), \mathsf{f}(x_1, x_1, x_1), \mathsf{f}(x_1, x_1, x_1)),$$

a rule that does not satisfy the semi-unification criterion and cannot be unfolded.   □

5.1   Abstraction

The analysis described in the preceding sections leads to an explosion of the number of generated rules (this is illustrated by the results of Sect. 6). A solution to reduce this explosion consists in designing a mechanism that detects, as soon as possible, rules that are useless for proving non-termination. We can also notice that the semi-unification criterion we introduced before consists in checking, for each subterm of a right-hand side, that the corresponding left-hand side semi-unifies. One disadvantage of this technique is that a same semi-unification test may be performed several times.

Example 9 (Example 8 continued). The left-hand side of each rule computed in Example 8 is $f(0, 1, f(0, 1, x_1))$. Moreover, each rule, except the last one, has $f(0, 1, x_1)$ as a subterm of the right-hand side. Consequently, semi-unification of $f(0, 1, f(0, 1, x_1))$ with $f(0, 1, x_1)$ is checked several times. □

In order to avoid any repetition of the same semi-unification test, one solution consists in making those tests explicit by "flattening" each rule $l \to r$ into pairs of terms (l, r') where r' is a subterm of r. Then, semi-unification test on a pair (l, r') is only performed at the root position of r'.

Following these intuitions, we introduce a new domain.

Definition 5 (Abstract domain). *An* abstract TRS *is a finite set, each element of which is either a pair of terms or* true *or* false. *The* abstract domain *$P^{\#}$ is the set of all abstract TRS's.*

The special element true denotes any pair of terms (l, r) such that l semi-unifies with r. The special element false corresponds to any non-useful pair of terms:

Definition 6 (Useful pair). *Let $\mathcal{R}$ be a TRS. A pair (l, r) of terms is* useful *for $\mathcal{R}$ when it can be unfolded, using the rules of $\mathcal{R}$, to a pair (l_1, r_1) where l_1 semi-unifies with r_1.*

The set $P^{\#}$ is a sort of *abstract domain*, the corresponding *concrete domain* of which is the set $P^{\flat}$ of TRS's as defined in Sect. 2. The *abstraction function* that transforms a concrete TRS to an abstract one is defined as follows.

Definition 7 (Abstraction function). *The* abstraction function *α maps every element $\mathcal{R}$ of $P^{\flat}$ to an element of $P^{\#}$ as follows:*

$$\alpha(\mathcal{R}) = \bigcup_{l \to r \in \mathcal{R}} \left\{ \alpha_{\mathcal{R}}(l, r|_p) \mid p \in Pos(r) \right\}$$

where, for any pair (l, r) of terms,

$$\alpha_{\mathcal{R}}(l, r) = \begin{cases} \textit{if } l \textit{ semi-unifies with } r \textit{ then } \mathsf{true} \\ \textit{else if } (l, r) \textit{ is useful for } \mathcal{R} \textit{ then } (l, r) \\ \textit{else } \mathsf{false} \end{cases}$$

The operator that we use to unfold abstract TRS's is defined as follows.

Definition 8 (Abstract unfolding operator). *Let $\mathcal{R}$ be a concrete TRS. For any abstract TRS $X^{\#}$, if $\mathsf{true} \in X^{\#}$ then $T_{\mathcal{R}}^{\#}(X^{\#}) = \{\mathsf{true}\}$, otherwise*

$$T_{\mathcal{R}}^{\#}(X^{\#}) = \left\{ \alpha_{\mathcal{R}}(l\theta, r[p \leftarrow r']\theta) \;\middle|\; \begin{array}{l} (l, r) \in X^{\#} \\ p \in NPos(r) \\ l' \to r' \in \mathcal{R} \textit{ renamed with fresh variables} \\ \theta \in mgu(r|_p, l') \end{array} \right\}$$

This operator allows us to define an abstract semantics.

Definition 9 (Abstract unfolding semantics). *Let $\mathcal{R}$ be a concrete TRS. The abstract unfolding sequence of $\mathcal{R}$ is*

$$
\begin{aligned}
T_{\mathcal{R}}^{\#} \uparrow 0 \quad &= \quad \alpha(\mathcal{R}^{+}) \\
T_{\mathcal{R}}^{\#} \uparrow (n+1) \quad &= \quad T_{\mathcal{R}}^{\#}(T_{\mathcal{R}}^{\#} \uparrow n) \quad \forall n \in \mathbb{N} .
\end{aligned}
$$

The abstract unfolding semantics $unf^{\#}(\mathcal{R})$ of $\mathcal{R}$ is the limit of the unfolding process described in Definition 8:

$$
unf^{\#}(\mathcal{R}) = \bigcup_{n \in \mathbb{N}} T_{\mathcal{R}}^{\#} \uparrow n .
$$

The relevance of a non-termination analysis based on these notions is clarified by the following correctness result.

Proposition 2 (Correctness). *Let $\mathcal{R}$ be a concrete TRS. If true $\in unf^{\#}(\mathcal{R})$, then $\mathcal{R}$ is non-terminating.*

5.2   Detecting Useful Pairs

The intuitions and results of this section rely on the following observation.

Lemma 1. *If (l, r) is a useful pair of terms where l is not a variable, then (l, r) can be unfolded to a pair (l_1, r_1) such that $root(l_1) = root(l)$ and $root(r_1) \in \{root(l), \perp\}$.*

Consider a useful pair of terms (l, r). Then, l semi-unifies with r or (l, r) can be unfolded, in at least one step, to (l_1, r_1) such that l_1 semi-unifies with r_1. By Definition 2, the latter case corresponds to narrowing r to r_1 in at least one step and then in applying to l the computed substitution θ to get l_1. As there is at least one step of narrowing, r cannot be a variable. Hence, r has the form $f(t_1, \ldots, t_n)$. Let us consider the possible forms of the narrowing from r to r_1.

1. There does not exist a step of the narrowing that is performed at the root position, *i.e.* r_1 has the form $f(t'_1, \ldots, t'_n)$ and, roughly, each t_i is narrowed to t'_i, in 0 or more steps.
2. There exists a step of the narrowing that is performed at the root position, *i.e.* (roughly) first each t_i is narrowed (in 0 or more steps) to a term t'_i then $f(t'_1, \ldots, t'_n)$ is narrowed at root position using a rule $f(s_1, \ldots, s_n) \to \cdots$ whose right-hand side further leads to r_1.

Consider the first case above when l is not a variable. As $root(r_1) \neq \perp$, by Lemma 1 $root(r_1) = root(l)$ so l has the form $f(s_1, \ldots, s_n)$. Hence, by Lemma 1 again, l_1 has the form $f(s'_1, \ldots, s'_n)$. Notice that for each $i \in [1, n]$, t_i is narrowed to t'_i and s'_i semi-unifies with t'_i. Consequently, (s_i, t_i) is a useful pair.

Now, consider the second case above, again when l is not a variable. We note that the following result holds.

Lemma 2. *Let* $f(t_1, \ldots, t_n)$ *be a term where each* t_i *can be narrowed to* t'_i, *in 0 or more steps. Suppose that for a term* $f(s_1, \ldots, s_n)$, *we have*

$$mgu(f(t'_1, \ldots, t'_n), f(s_1, \ldots, s_n) \text{ renamed with fresh variables}) \neq \varnothing .$$

Then, each t_i *unifies with any variable disjoint variant of* s_i *or can be narrowed in at least one step to a term whose root symbol is that of* s_i *or* $\bot$.

Moreover, the right-hand side of the rule $f(s_1, \ldots, s_n) \to \cdots$ has to lead to r_1, i.e., by Lemma 1, to a term whose root symbol is that of l or $\bot$. This corresponds to a path in the graph of functional dependencies that we define as follows, in the style of [4,1].

Definition 10 (Graph of functional dependencies). *The* graph of functional dependencies *induced by a concrete TRS* $\mathcal{R}$ *is denoted by* $\mathcal{G_R}$. *The following transformation rules define the edges* E *and the initial vertices* I *of* $\mathcal{G_R}$:

$$\frac{l \to r \in \mathcal{R}}{\langle \mathcal{R}, E, I \rangle \mapsto \langle \mathcal{R} \setminus \{l \to r\}, E \cup \{l \to root(r)\}, I \cup \{l\} \rangle}$$

$$\frac{l \to f \in E \land l' \to g \in E \land l \in I \land l' \in I \land f \notin I \land g \notin I \land (root(l') = f \lor f = \bot)}{\langle \mathcal{R}, E, I \rangle \mapsto \langle \mathcal{R}, E \cup \{f \to l'\}, I \rangle}$$

To build $\mathcal{G_R}$, *the algorithm starts with* $\langle \mathcal{R}, \varnothing, \varnothing \rangle$ *and applies the transformation rules as long as they add new arrows.*

Example 10. Consider Toyama's example again:

$$\mathcal{R} = \{f(0, 1, x) \to f(x, x, x), \ g(x, y) \to x, \ g(x, y) \to y\} .$$

The graph $\mathcal{G_R}$ can be depicted as follows:

$$\boxed{g(x, y)} \longleftrightarrow \bot \longrightarrow \boxed{f(0, 1, x)} \longleftrightarrow f$$

where the boxes correspond to the initial vertices.   □

Notice that the initial vertices of $\mathcal{G_R}$ are the left-hand sides of the rules of $\mathcal{R}$. Hence, a path in $\mathcal{G_R}$ from an initial vertex s to a symbol f indicates that any term s' such that $mgu(s, s'$ renamed with fresh variables$) \neq \varnothing$ *may* be narrowed (using the rules of $\mathcal{R}$) to a term t with $root(t) = f$. The first step of such a narrowing is performed at the root position of s'. We synthesize case 2 above by the following definition.

Definition 11 (The transition relation $\xrightarrow[\mathcal{G_R}]{+}$**).** *Let* $\mathcal{G_R}$ *be the graph of functional dependencies of a concrete TRS* $\mathcal{R}$, $f(t_1, \ldots, t_n)$ *be a term and* g *be a function symbol or* $\bot$. *We write* $f(t_1, \ldots, t_n) \xrightarrow[\mathcal{G_R}]{+} g$ *if there exists a non-empty path in* $\mathcal{G_R}$ *from an initial vertex of the form* $f(s_1, \ldots, s_n)$ *to* g *and, for each* $i \in [1, n]$, *one of these conditions holds:*

- $mgu(t_i, s_i$ renamed with fresh variables$) \neq \varnothing$,
- $t_i \xrightarrow[\mathcal{G_R}]{+} root(s_i)$ or $t_i \xrightarrow[\mathcal{G_R}]{+} \bot$.

Example 11 (Example 10 continued). $g(g(0,0),1) \xrightarrow[\mathcal{G_R}]{+} \bot$ holds as there is a non-empty path from $g(x,y)$ to $\bot$ and $g(0,0) \xrightarrow[\mathcal{G_R}]{+} \bot$ (because there is a non-empty path from $g(x,y)$ to $\bot$ and $g(0,0)$ unifies with $g(x,y)$) and 1 unifies with y. □

Finally, we synthesize both cases 1 and 2 above as follows:

Definition 12 (The relation $useful_\mathcal{R}$). *For any concrete TRS $\mathcal{R}$ and any terms l and r, we write $useful_\mathcal{R}(l,r)$ if one of these conditions holds:*

- *l semi-unifies with r,*
- *$l = f(s_1, \ldots, s_n)$, $r = f(t_1, \ldots, t_n)$ and, for each $i \in [1,n]$, $useful_\mathcal{R}(s_i, t_i)$,*
- *$l = g(s_1, \ldots, s_m)$, $r = f(t_1, \ldots, t_n)$ and $r \xrightarrow[\mathcal{G_R}]{+} g$ or $r \xrightarrow[\mathcal{G_R}]{+} \bot$.*

Note that in the third condition, we may have $g/m = f/n$.

This definition allows us to compute a superset of the set of useful pairs:

Proposition 3 (Completeness). *Let $\mathcal{R}$ be a concrete TRS and (l,r) be a pair of terms. If (l,r) is useful for $\mathcal{R}$, then $useful_\mathcal{R}(l,r)$ holds.*

In order to get a practical tool from the theory of Sect. 5.1, we use the relation $useful_\mathcal{R}$ in function $\alpha_\mathcal{R}$ of Definition 7.

Example 12. Consider Toyama's example. In $\mathcal{R}^+$, one can find the rule:

$$f(0, 1, f(0, 1, x_1)) \to f(f(0, 1, x_1), f(0, 1, x_1), f(0, 1, x_1))$$

(see Example 4). Let l and r be the left and right-hand side of this rule, respectively. Notice that l does not semi-unify with r, so the first condition of Definition 12 is not satisfied. Let us try the second one. As the root symbols of l and r are identical, we check if each argument of l is in relation with the corresponding argument of r. This test fails for the first argument: we do not have $useful_\mathcal{R}(0, f(0, 1, x_1))$ because 0 does not semi-unify with $f(0, 1, x_1)$ and in $\mathcal{G_R}$ there is no path from a vertex of the form $f(\ldots)$ to 0 or to $\bot$. Finally, the third condition of Definition 12 is not satisfied as well because neither $r \xrightarrow[\mathcal{G_R}]{+} f$ nor $r \xrightarrow[\mathcal{G_R}]{+} \bot$ holds. Hence, we do not have $useful_\mathcal{R}(l,r)$, so (l,r) is not useful for $\mathcal{R}$ and we get $\alpha_\mathcal{R}(l,r) = \mathsf{false}$. Consequently, this pair will be eliminated. □

6 Experimental Results

We have implemented two analysers, one performing concrete analyses as described in Sect. 4 and the other performing abstract analyses as described in Sect. 5. Both are written in C++ and are available at

www.univ-reunion.fr/~epayet/Research/TRS/TRSanalyses.html

Our analysers compute the concrete or abstract unfolding sequence until a user-fixed maximum number of iterations is reached or a looping term is found.

Despite its name, the `nontermin` directory of the TPDB [25] contains subdirectories with terminating TRS's:

- in `AG01`, only `#4.2.trs`, `#4.3.trs`, `#4.4.trs`, `#4.5.trs`, `#4.7.trs` and `#4.12a.trs`, `#4.13.trs`, `#4.14.trs`, `#4.15.trs`, `#4.16.trs`, `#4.17.trs`, `#4.18.trs`, `#4.19.trs` are non-terminating;
- in `cariboo`, all the TRS's are non-terminating except `tricky1.trs`;
- in `CSR`, all the TRS's are non-terminating except `Ex49_GM04.trs`;
- in `Rubio-inn`, all the TRS's are non-terminating except `test830.trs`.

We have run our analysers together with APRoVE 1.2 on all the non-terminating TRS's in the `nontermin` directory. We have also run these programs on Example 26, Example 26-2, Example 29, Example 34 and Example 40 of [5] and on Example 28 and footnote 8 of [15]. We fixed a 2 minutes time limit. Using a PowerPC G4, 1.25 GHz, 512 Mo DDR SDRAM, MacOS 10.4.6, we get the results in Table 1. Timings are average over 5 runs. In column "gen" we have reported the number of rules generated by the unfolding process. The abstract analyser runs

Table 1.

directory	concrete analysis			abstract analysis			APRoVE 1.2	
	solved	gen	min:sec	solved	gen	min:sec	solved	min:sec
AG01	12/13	31218	0:56	12/13	9471	0:41	11/13	3:00
cariboo	6/6	833	0:00	6/6	234	0:00	6/6	0:06
CSR	36/36	39937	2:03	36/36	128	0:00	36/36	1:26
HM	1/1	8	0:00	1/1	6	0:00	1/1	0:00
Rubio-inn	8/9	33436	2:04	8/9	19283	2:01	7/9	2:29
TRCSR	1/1	13	0:00	1/1	2	0:00	1/1	0:04
[5]	5/5	397	0:00	5/5	73	0:00	5/5	0:01
[15]	2/2	932	0:00	2/2	292	0:00	2/2	0:00
total	71/73	106774	5:03	71/73	29489	2:42	69/73	7:06

much faster than its counterparts. The best total score in column "solved" is achieved by both the concrete and abstract analysers. As expected, the abstract analyser produces much fewer rules than the concrete one.

The TRS `#4.13.trs` in subdirectory `AG01` was given by Drosten [11]:

$$\mathcal{R} = \left\{ \begin{array}{l} \mathsf{f}(0,1,x) \to \mathsf{f}(x,x,x), \ \mathsf{f}(x,y,z) \to 2, \ 0 \to 2, \ 1 \to 2, \\ \mathsf{g}(x,x,y) \to y, \ \mathsf{g}(x,y,y) \to x \end{array} \right\} .$$

APRoVE answers "maybe" within the time limit when run on this TRS. Both $unf(\mathcal{R})$ and $unf^{\#}(\mathcal{R})$ are finite (for each $n \geq 11$, $T_{\mathcal{R}} \uparrow n = \varnothing$ and for each $n \geq 5$, $T_{\mathcal{R}}^{\#} \uparrow n = \varnothing$). These sets are computed by our analysers before the time limit is reached. No rule in $unf(\mathcal{R})$ satisfies the semi-unification criterion and true $\notin unf^{\#}(\mathcal{R})$. So, this TRS is an example of failure of our method that is not caused by the explosion of the unfolding process.

7   Conclusion

We have presented an automatic technique for proving non-termination of TRS's independently of a particular reduction strategy. It is based on the "unfold & infer" mechanism that was designed in the context of logic programming, thus establishing a connection between both paradigms. We have also described a method for eliminating useless rules to reduce the search space. Notice that we did not implement such a method in our logic programming non-termination tool as unfolding in this context is less explosive than with TRS's (because the particular left-to-right selection rule is classically considered). We have also run our analyser on TRS's from the TPDB; the results are very encouraging as our tool is able to solve 71 over 73 non-terminating examples.

In comparison, the AProVE system solves 69 examples and is slower. The technique implemented in AProVE consists in narrowing dependency pairs until two terms that semi-unify are found. Narrowing operations are performed either directly with the rules of the TRS of interest (forward narrowing) or with the reversed rules (backward narrowing). To select forward or backward narrowing, heuristics are introduced: if the TRS is right and not left-linear, then forward narrowing is performed, otherwise backward narrowing is used. To obtain a finite search space, an upper bound is used on the number of times that a rule can be applied for narrowing. An approximation of the graph of dependency pairs is also constructed and AProVE processes the strongly connected components of this graph separately.

Our approach directly works with the rules (not the dependency pairs) and forward narrowing is sufficient as we pre-process the TRS's. We also do not need heuristics and in order to get a finite search space, we introduce a user-fixed maximum number of iterations. The graph that we use is not a graph of dependency pairs and is closely related to that of [4,1]. In these papers, the authors define a framework for the static analysis of the unsatisfiability of equation sets. This framework uses a loop-checking technique based on a graph of functional dependencies. Notice that in order to eliminate useless rules within our approach, an idea would consist in using the results of [4,1] as we are also interested in a form of satisfiability: is a pair of terms (l, r) unfoldable to (l', r') such that l' semi-unifies with r'? However, [4,1] consider unification instead of semi-unification and both sides of the pairs can be rewritten (whereas the unfolding operation only rewrites the right-hand side). We are also aware of the work described in [8] where the authors consider a graph of terms to detect loops in the search tree. The graph of terms is used within a dynamic approach whereas our paper and [4,1] consider a static approach. Another future work consists in designing a bottom-up technique for proving non-termination of TRS's. What we describe in this paper is a top-down mechanism, as the unfolding process starts from the rules of the TRS $\mathcal{R}$ of interest and then rewrites the right-hand sides down as much as possible. In [21,20], the authors use the unfolding operator T_P^β of [12] that leads to a bottom-up computation of the unfoldings of P starting from the emptyset, instead of P. Given a set of rules X, $T_P^\beta(X)$ unfolds P using the elements of X whereas $T_{\mathcal{R}}(X)$ unfolds X using the rules of $\mathcal{R}$.

Acknowledgements. We greatly thank an anonymous reviewer for many constructive comments. We also thank Fred Mesnard, Germán Puebla and Fausto Spoto for encouraging us to submit the paper.

References

1. M. Alpuente, M. Falaschi, and F. Manzo. Analyses of unsatisfiability for equational logic programming. *Journal of Logic Programming*, 311(1–3):479–525, 1995.
2. M. Alpuente, M. Falaschi, G. Moreno, and G. Vidal. Safe folding/unfolding with conditional narrowing. In *Proc. of ALP/HOA 97*, pages 1–15, 1997.
3. M. Alpuente, M. Falaschi, G. Moreno, and G. Vidal. Rules + strategies for transforming lazy functional logic programs. *Theoretical Computer Science*, 311 (1–3):479–525, 2004.
4. M. Alpuente, M. Falaschi, M. J. Ramis, and G. Vidal. Narrowing approximations as an optimization for equational logic programs. In *Proc. of PLILP 1993*, pages 391–409, 1993.
5. T. Arts and J. Giesl. Termination of term rewriting using dependency pairs. *Theoretical Computer Science*, 236:133–178, 2000.
6. F. Baader and T. Nipkow. *Term rewriting and all that*. Cambridge, 1998.
7. R. M. Burstall and J. Darlington. A transformation system for developing recursive programs. *Journal of the ACM*, 24(1):44–67, 1977.
8. J. Chabin and P. Réty. Narrowing directed by a graph of terms. In G. Goos and J. Hartmanis, editors, *Proc. of RTA'91*, volume 488 of *LNCS*, pages 112–123. Springer-Verlag, Berlin, 1991.
9. M. Codish and C. Taboch. A semantic basis for the termination analysis of logic programs. *Journal of Logic Programming*, 41(1):103–123, 1999.
10. N. Dershowitz. Termination of rewriting. *Journal of Symbolic Computation*, 3 (1 & 2):69–116, 1987.
11. K. Drosten. *Termersetzungssysteme: Grundlagen der Prototyp-Generierung algebraischer Spezifikationen*. Springer Verlag, Berlin, 1989.
12. M. Gabbrielli and R. Giacobazzi. Goal independency and call patterns in the analysis of logic programs. In *Proc. of SAC'94*, pages 394–399. ACM Press, 1994.
13. S. Genaim and M. Codish. Inferring termination conditions for logic programs using backwards analysis. In R. Nieuwenhuis and A. Voronkov, editors, *Proc. of LPAR'01*, volume 2250 of *LNCS*, pages 685–694. Springer-Verlag, Berlin, 2001.
14. J. Giesl, R. Thiemann, and P. Schneider-Kamp. The dependency pair framework: combining techniques for automated termination proofs. In F. Baader and A. Voronkov, editors, *Proc. of LPAR'04*, volume 3452 of *LNAI*, pages 210–220. Springer-Verlag, 2004.
15. J. Giesl, R. Thiemann, and P. Schneider-Kamp. Proving and disproving termination of higher-order functions. In B. Gramlich, editor, *Proc. of FroCoS'05*, volume 3717 of *LNAI*, pages 216–231. Springer-Verlag, 2005.

16. J. Giesl, R. Thiemann, P. Schneider-Kamp, and S. Falke. Automated termination proofs with AProVE. In V. van Oostrom, editor, *Proc. of RTA'04*, volume 3091 of *LNCS*, pages 210–220. Springer-Verlag, 2004.

17. D. Kapur, D. Musser, P. Narendran, and J. Stillman. Semi-unification. *Theoretical Computer Science*, 81:169–187, 1991.

18. D.S. Lankford and D.R. Musser. A finite termination criterion. Unpublished Draft, USC Information Sciences Institute, Marina Del Rey, CA, 1978.

19. F. Mesnard and R. Bagnara. cTI: a constraint-based termination inference tool for iso-prolog. *Theory and Practice of Logic Programming*, 5(1–2):243–257, 2005.

20. E. Payet and F. Mesnard. Non-termination inference for constraint logic programs. In R. Giacobazzi, editor, *Proc. of SAS'04*, volume 3148 of *LNCS*, pages 377–392. Springer-Verlag, 2004.

21. E. Payet and F. Mesnard. Non-termination inference of logic programs. *ACM Transactions on Programming Languages and Systems*, 28, Issue 2:256–289, 2006.

22. A. Pettorossi and M. Proietti. Rules and strategies for transforming functional and logic programs. *ACM Comput. Surv.*, 28(2):360–414, 1996.

23. J. Steinbach. Simplification orderings: history of results. *Fundamenta Informaticae*, 24:47–87, 1995.

24. Y. Toyama. Counterexamples to the termination for the direct sum of term rewriting systems. *Information Processing Letters*, 25(3):141–143, 1987.

25. Termination Problem Data Base. `http://www.lri.fr/~marche/termination-com petition/`

Polytool: Proving Termination Automatically Based on Polynomial Interpretations

Manh Thang Nguyen* and Danny De Schreye

Department of Computer Science, K.U.Leuven
Celestijnenlaan 200A, B-3001, Heverlee, Belgium
{ManhThang.Nguyen, Danny.DeSchreye}@cs.kuleuven.be

1   Introduction

In this system description, we present Polytool, a fully automated system for proving left-termination of definite logic programs (LPs). The aim of Polytool is to extend the power of existing termination analysers by using well-founded orders based on polynomial interpretations. This is a direct extension of the well-founded orders based on (semi-)linear level mappings and norms that are used in most of the existing LP termination analysis systems.

Polytool is based on a termination condition that is rooted on acceptability [2]. More precisely, the system implements the constraint-based approach to termination analysis, presented in [6], but extended to non-linear, polynomial level mappings and norms.

The theoretical foundations of Polytool are formulated and proved in [9]. Space restrictions do not allow us to give a formal account of this theory. We will only present the main intuitions in order to make the paper reasonably self-contained.

In the next section we describe the approach, comment on the various components and illustrate them with fragments of a termination proof. In Section 3, we report on extensive experimentation with the system and comparison with several other systems. We conclude in Section 4.

2   The Polytool System

The main novelty of Polytool is that it uses polynomial interpretations. Instead of ordering atoms and terms by means of associated natural numbers, obtained as function-values under (semi-)linear level mappings and norms, it maps atoms and terms to polynomials. The polynomials are considered as functions $P : \mathbb{N} \rightarrow \mathbb{N}$, and coefficients are also in $\mathbb{N}$. We use the natural well-founded order over such polynomials: $P \geq_{\mathbb{N}} Q$ iff $P(a_1, ..., a_n) \geq Q(a_1, ..., a_m)$, for all $a_1, ..., a_{max(n,m)} \in \mathbb{N}$.

Acceptability-style termination proofs require 3 types of conditions (for a formal presentation, see [9]):

* Manh Thang Nguyen is partly supported by GOA Inductive Knowledge Bases and partly by FWO Termination Analysis: Crossing Paradigm Borders.

G. Puebla (Ed.): LOPSTR 2006, LNCS 4407, pp. 210–218, 2007.

1. For clauses that have intermediate body-atoms between the head and the recursive body-atom, a valid relation between the interpretations of the arguments of the successful instances of these atoms needs to be inferred (valid interargument relations). These can then be used as pre-conditions to prove the decreases in point 2 (to deal with existentially quantified variables).
2. For every clause, the interpretation of the head should be larger than the interpretation of each (mutually) recursive body-atom, given the valid interargument relations of the intermediate body-atoms as pre-conditions.
3. For every non-ground query of interest, we must impose conditions on the interpretation, such that the interpretation of the query cannot grow unboundedly w.r.t. the polynomial order due to instantiations caused by resolutions steps. In Polytool we use rigidity [3] constraints to impose this. Rigidity means that the interpretation of an atom/term should be invariant for any instance of the atom/term.

In the philosophy of the constraint-based approach in [6], we do not *choose* a particular interpretation for the atoms or terms. We introduce a general symbolic form for such interpretations and interargument relations. As an example and assuming that polynomials of degree 2 are selected for the interpretation, instead of assigning an interpretation: $I(p(x, y)) = x^2 + 3xy$, we would assign $I(p(x, y)) = p_1 x^2 + p_2 xy + p_3 y^2$, where p_1, p_2 and p_3 are symbolic coefficients ranging over $\mathbb{N}$. The strategy of the analysis is to:

- introduce symbolic versions of the interpretations (the polynomials associated with each function and predicate symbol),
- introduce symbolic versions of the valid interargument relations,
- express all conditions resulting from steps 1, 2 and 3 above as constraints on the coefficients (e.g. $p_1, p_2, p_3, \ldots$),
- solve the resulting system of constraints to obtain values for the coefficients.

Each solution for this constraint system gives rise to a concrete polynomial interpretation for all atoms and terms and a concrete valid interargument relation for all intermediate body-atoms that respect the termination condition. Therefore, each solution gives a termination proof.

In Polytool, we implement these ideas as follows. On the level of the polynomial interpretations, we need to restrict to fixed types of polynomials, since there does not exist a finite symbolic representation for all possible polynomials. Specifically, we will associate linear polynomials to predicates symbols and simple-mixed polynomials to function symbols. For more details on these classes of polynomials we refer to [13].

Example 1 (permute).

$$perm([], []). \qquad\qquad perm(L, [H|T]) : -del(H, L, L_1), perm(L_1, T).$$
$$del(H, [H|T], T). \qquad\quad del(X, [H|T], [H|T_1]) : -del(X, T, T_1).$$

We use an interpretation in which:

$$I(perm(x, y)) = p_{10} x + p_{01} y + p_{00} \qquad I(del(x, y, z)) = d_{100} x + d_{010} y + d_{001} z + d_{000}$$
$$I(.(x, y)) = _{.11} xy + _{.10} x + _{.01} y + _{.00} \qquad P_{[]} = c_{[]}$$

$\square$

The first component of Polytool (see Fig. 1) does a combined mode and type analysis of the given program. For the given description of the set of (atomic) queries of interest - in terms of modes and types - we need to infer similar descriptions for all calls that may occur during a derivation. We use the rigid types of [8] to represent mode/type-information of the queries and use the type-inference system of [8] to collect the descriptions of all other calls.

Example 2 (permute-continued). Let the query set Q_1 be $\{perm(t_1, t_2)|t_1$ is a nil-terminated list, t_2 is a free variable$\}$. The call set corresponding to Q_1, computed by the type-inference engine, is $S = Q_1 \cup Q_2$, where $Q_2 = \{del(t_1, t_2, t_3)|t_2$ is a nil-terminated list, t_1 and t_3 are free variables$\}$.   □

In the next component of Polytool, we use the computed call patterns to derive the rigidity constraints on the interpretation. The rigidity constraint generator (Fig. 1) derives this set of Diophantine constraints.

Example 3 (permute-continued). Based on the polynomial interpretation in Example 1 and computed call set S in Example 2, the rigidity constraint generator derives the following Diophantine constraints with coefficients as variables:

$$p_{10} * (._{11} + ._{10}) = 0 \qquad p_{01} = 0$$
$$d_{100} = 0 \qquad d_{010} * (._{11} + ._{10}) = 0 \qquad d_{001} = 0$$

     □

In the following component, the polynomial constraint generator translates the other termination conditions, consisting of the valid interargument relations and the head-body decreases, into polynomial constraints.

Example 4 (permute-continued). With the polynomial interpretation of Example 1, for the clause
$$del(X, [H|T], [H|T_1]) :- del(X, T, T_1)$$
the polynomial constraint generator produces the inequation:

$$\forall X, H, T, T_1 \in \mathbb{N}: \tag{1}$$
$$d_{100}X + d_{010}(._{10}H + ._{01}T + ._{11}HT + ._{00}) + d_{001}(._{10}H + ._{01}T_1 + ._{11}HT_1 + ._{00}) + d_{000}$$
$$> d_{100}X + d_{010}T + d_{001}T_1 + d_{000}$$

     □

In the next phase of the system, the generated polynomial constraints are transformed into Diophantine constraints. The point is to eliminate the variables (e.g. X, H, T, T_1 in the example) and to obtain constraints on the coefficients (e.g. $d_{100}, d_{010}, ._{10}, \ldots$) only. This component was by far the hardest one to develop. In general, the generated polynomial constraints are considerably more complex than (1) in Example 4. They most often take the form of implications: a decrease between the polynomial interpretation of a head-atom versus a recursive body-atom holds *if* the valid interargument relations for the intermediate body-atoms hold. As far as we know, no complete solver for such systems of constraint

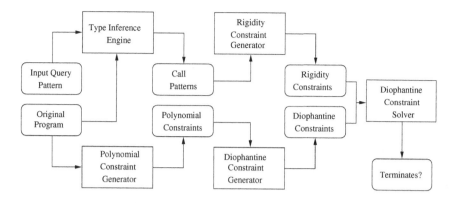

Fig. 1. Overall Structure

exists. A main effort in our work was to provide a set of transformation rules that generate a sufficient system of Diophantine constraints on the coefficients in the polynomial constraints. Here *sufficient* means that any solution of the Diophantine constraints is a solution to the given polynomial constraints (but not conversely). In this component of Polytool, we apply a number of techniques, including the substitution and evaluation rules of [6] but extended to polynomial interpretations, and the technique for testing positiveness of polynomials of [7].

Example 5 (permute-continued). We continue with Example 4 by deriving a set of Diophantine constraints from the constraint (1). Because there is no implication in this constraint, only the technique in [7] is applied. First we need to transform the constraint into the normal form:

$$(d_{100} - d_{100})X + (d_{010} + d_{001}){\cdot}_{10}H + d_{010}({\cdot}_{01} - 1)T + d_{010}{\cdot}_{11}HT$$
$$+ d_{001}({\cdot}_{01} - 1)T_1 + d_{001}{\cdot}_{11}HT_1 + (d_{001}{\cdot}_{00} + d_{010}{\cdot}_{00} - 1){\geq}_\mathbb{N}0$$

Applying the technique for testing positiveness of polynomials (a polynomial $P(x, y, \ldots, z){\geq}_\mathbb{N}0$ iff all its coefficients are not negative), the above constraint holds iff the following Diophantine constraints hold:

$$d_{100} - d_{100}{\geq}0 \qquad (d_{010} + d_{001}){\cdot}_{10}{\geq}0$$
$$d_{010}({\cdot}_{01} - 1){\geq}0 \qquad d_{010}{\cdot}_{11}{\geq}0$$
$$d_{001}({\cdot}_{01} - 1){\geq}0 \qquad d_{001}{\cdot}_{11}{\geq}0 \qquad d_{001}{\cdot}_{00} + d_{010}{\cdot}_{00} - 1{\geq}0$$

$\square$

In the final component, the rigidity and the above generated Diophantine constraints become the input for the CiME 2.02, a Diophantine solver implemented by Contejean, Marché, Tomás and Urbain [4]. A solution for the constraint set implies the existence of a polynomial interpretation, valid interargument relations and a termination proof.

3   Experimental Evaluation

We have implemented a system (Polytool)[1] for automated termination proof based on the approach. It is integrated in the system implementing the constraint-based approach of [6] and consists of four parts. The first part is the type inference engine of Janssens and Bruynooghe [8], coded in MasterProlog (IT Masters 2000). Based on this system, given a program and a set of queries, the call set is computed and the rigid type graph for each call pattern of the call set is generated. The second part, the core of the system, which generates the set of all polynomial conditions, has been done in SICS 3.12.2. Also the third part, which normalises the polynomial conditions and transforms them to Diophantine constraints, is implemented in SICS 3.12.2. The final part is the Diophantine constraint solver (CiME 2.02) of Contejean, Marché, Tomás and Urbain [4]. This part is written in Objective CAML (CAML 3.0.9). We have tested the performance of the system on a number of examples, including benchmarks for LP in Termination Problems Database [1] (Tables 1(b), 2(a), 2(b), 3(a) and 3(b)), and examples collected from other sources (Table 1(a))[2]. The domain of all variables in the generated Diophantine constraints is fixed to the set $D = \{0, 1, 2\}$. The experiments have been performed using SICS 3.12.2, running on Intel Pentium IV 2.80 MHz, 1Gb RAM. We have also performed an experimental evaluation on these examples with other systems, namely: Hasta La Vista [12], TALP [10], and TerminWeb [15]. We do not provide the running times of TALP and TerminWeb on the benchmarks because the tests have been done via the HTTP protocol and there is no information about the configuration of the servers on which these systems are installed. Only the success or failure of these systems w.r.t. the examples is provided. For TALP, polynomial interpretations are chosen. For TerminWeb, all provided semi-linear norms, i.e., node-size, edge-size and list-length norms, are selected. The other options for TALP and TerminWeb remain the same as in their web interfaces. In the tables, the following abbreviations are used:

- *Prog* and *Query* refer to the tested program and the query pattern. For the query pattern, '*g*' and '*f*' denote a ground term and a free variable respectively.
- T_1, T_2 refer to the running time of Polytool and Hasta La Vista.
- R_1, R_2, R_3 and R_4 refer to the results given by the Polytool, Hasta La Vista, TALP and TerminWeb. It contains the symbol '+' if the system reports termination, or the symbol '-' if the system fails to do so.

From the tables, Polytool seems to be quite powerful since it can prove termination of 66 out of 83 terminating cases, in comparison with the performance of Hasta La Vista (53/83), TALP (59/83) and TerminWeb (50/83). For the running times, Polytool is slower than Hasta La Vista in a number of cases.

---

[1] For the source code, please refer to: http://www.cs.kuleuven.be/~manh/polytool

[2] In the table, examples *dist*, *der* were collected from [11], example *taussky* was introduced in [14]. The source of all examples in the tables can be found in http://www.cs.kuleuven.be/~manh/polytool/new_examples.zip

3.1 Comparison Between Hasta La Vista and Polytool

Let us first compare the precision and efficiency between Polytool and Hasta La Vista since these systems have a similar framework of the constraint-based approach. From the theoretical point of view, for the benchmarks without meta-predicates or arithmetic expressions in them, termination analysis of Polytool is at least as precise as the analysis of Hasta La Vista. The claim could come from the fact that the approach based on polynomial interpretations used in Polytool can be considered as a generalization of the semi-linear norm based approach used in Hasta La Vista. The results in Table 1(a) show that there is a class of examples (e.g., *dist, der, SK90_1, taussky*), which can not be solved by Hasta La Vista, but can be solved by Polytool. For those examples, non-linear polynomial interpretations are required.

Observe that independently of whether we choose (semi-)linear norms and level mappings or polynomial interpretations, it still gives rise to nonlinear Diophantine constraints in the final step. Therefore, the requirement for a fast and effective nonlinear Diophantine constraint solver is necessary and C*i*ME 2.02 seems to be a good selection. The only problem is, when the maximum degrees of variables or the domain of each variable in the constraints increases, the performance of the solver decreases considerably. A possible solution is to first apply the **INCLP(R)** [3] implemented by De Koninck, Schrijvers and Demoen [5] to narrow the domain of each variable in the constraint set and then use C*i*ME 2.02 to solve it over the narrowed domains in the following step.

Example 6. Consider the program *normal* with the query pattern *norm(g,f)* in Table 1(b):

$$norm(F, N) : -rewrite(F, F1), norm(F1, N).$$
$$norm(a, a).   \quad   rewrite(op(op(A, B), C), op(A, op(B, C))).$$
$$rewrite(op(A, op(B, C)), op(A, L)) : -rewrite(op(B, C), L).$$

Table 1. Results on Termination Benchmarks

(a) Variously collected examples

Prog	Query	T_1	R_1	T_2	R_2	R_3	R_4
dist	dist(g,f)	0.47	+	0.26	-	+	-
der	d(g,f)	20.02	+	0.25	-	-	-
boolexp	cequiv(g)	43.54	-	0.27	-	-	-
car_1	div(g,g,f)	0.18	-	0.06	-	-	-
car_13	in(g,g,f)	0.06	-	0.04	-	+	-
fac_TRS	fac(g,f)	0.12	-	0.05	-	-	+
fward_ins	f(f,f,f)	0.03	-	0.01	-	-	-
SK90_1	p(g,f)	0.22	+	0.16	-	-	-
SK90_2	p(g,f)	0.68	-	0.35	-	-	-
SK90_3	sum(g,f)	0.13	+	0.44	+	+	-
SK90_4	p(g,f)	0.48	-	0.44	-	+	-
taussky	p(g,f)	0.16	+	0.07	-	+	-
addmul	p(g,f)	0.11	+	0.07	+	-	-
fibo	p(g,f)	0.76	-	0.22	-	+	-
lamdacal	g(g,g,f)	0.17	+	0.16	+	-	-
log-1	log(g,f)	1.33	-	0.16	-	+	-
average1	av(g,g,f)	0.31	+	0.04	-	+	-
average2	av(g,f,g)	0.11	+	0.04	-	+	+
flat	flat(g,f)	0.5	+	0.05	-	+	-
queens	queens(f)	7.21	+	0.65	+	-	+

(b) TALP examples

Prog	Query	T_1	R_1	T_2	R_2	R_3	R_4
ex1	p(f,g)	0.03	+	0.02	+	+	-
ex4	p1(g)	0.02	+	0.01	+	+	+
nat	isNat(g)	0.02	+	0.04	+	+	+
nat	nEq(g,g)	0.03	+	0.03	+	+	+
nat	gt(f,g)	0.02	+	0.04	+	-	+
nat	odd(g)	0.03	+	0.03	+	+	+
nat	fac(g,f)	0.06	+	0.07	+	+	+
normal	norm(g,f)	0.15	+	0.09	-	+	-
perm	perm(g,f)	0.25	+	0.13	+	+	+
permute	perm1(g,f)	0.08	+	0.08	+	+	+
permute	perm2(f,g)	0.09	+	0.1	+	+	+
qsort	qs(g,f)	2.37	+	0.14	+	+	+
t_closure	tc(g,f)	0.03	-	0.02	-	+	-
simple	p(f,g)	0.02	+	0.03	+	-	-
gcd	gcd(g,g,f)	0.03	-	0.03	-	-	+
palind	palind(g)	0.05	+	0.05	+	+	+
slowsort	sort(g,f)	0.1	+	0.08	+	+	+
flat	flat(g,f)	0.73	+	0.08	-	+	-
div	div(g,g,f)	0.09	+	0.09	+	+	+
remind	rem(g,g,f)	11.35	-	0.08	-	-	+

---

[3] Interval-based Nonlinear Constraint Logic Programming over the Reals.

Table 2. Examples from Apt and Plumer

(a) Apt

Prog	Query	T_1	R_1	T_2	R_2	R_3	R_4
list	list(g)	0.01	+	0.01	+	+	+
fold	fold(f,g,f)	0.03	+	0.01	+	+	+
lte	goal	0.04	+	0.04	+	+	+
map	map(g,f)	0.03	+	0.01	+	+	+
member	mem(f,g)	0.03	+	0.01	+	+	+
merg	merg(g,f)	1.01	+	0.37	+	-	-
merg_ap	merg(g,f,g)	300	-	0.82	-	+	-
naiv_rev	reverse(g,f)	0.04	+	0.03	+	+	+
ordered	ordered(g)	0.05	+	0.05	+	+	+
overlap	o_lap(g,g)	0.03	+	0.03	+	+	+
perm	perm(g,f)	0.45	+	0.11	+	+	+
qsort	qs(g,f)	0.07	+	0.13	+	+	+
select	select(f,g,f)	0.01	+	0.02	+	+	+
subset	subset(g,g)	0.06	+	0.05	+	+	+
sum	sum(f,f,g)	0.01	+	0.02	+	+	+

(b) Plumer

Prog	Query	T_1	R_1	T_2	R_2	R_3	R_4
merge_t	merge(g,f)	0.36	+	0.42	+	-	-
pl1.1	append(g,f,f)	0.03	+	0.02	+	-	+
pl1.1	append(f,f,g)	0.03	+	0.03	+	+	+
pl2.3.1	p(g,f)	0.02	+	0.01	-	+	-
pl2.3.1	p(f,f)	0.01	-	0.01	-	-	-
pl3.5.6a	p(f)	0.02	+	0.03	+	-	+
pl4.4.3	merge(g,g,f)	0.08	+	0.02	+	+	+
pl4.4.6a	perm(g,f)	0.04	+	0.03	+	+	+
pl6.1.1	qsort(g,f)	1.12	+	0.19	+	+	+
pl7.2.9	mult(g,g,f)	0.03	+	0.03	+	+	+
pl7.6.2c	reach(g,g,g,g)	4.87	-	0.22	-	+	+
pl8.2.1a	merge(g,f)	0.43	+	0.26	-	+	-
pl8.3.1	minsort(g,f)	0.06	+	0.05	+	-	-
pl8.3.1a	minsort(g,f)	0.05	+	0.07	+	-	+
pl8.4.2	e(g,f)	0.1	+	0.09	+	+	+

Table 3. Examples from TerminWeb and Taboch

(a) TerminWeb

Prog	Query	T_1	R_1	T_2	R_2	R_3	R_4
som	som(g,g,f)	0.04	+	0.03	+	+	+
NJ1	rev(g,f)	0.04	+	0.05	+	+	+
NJ2	f(g,g,f)	0.07	+	0.06	-	+	+
NJ3	ack(g,g,f)	0.16	-	0.1	-	-	+
NJ4	p(g,g,g,f)	0.05	+	0.03	+	+	+
NJ5	f(g,g,f)	0.04	+	0.05	-	+	+
NJ6	f(g,g,f)	0.1	+	0.07	+	+	+

(b) Taboch

Prog	Query	T_1	R_1	T_2	R_2	R_3	R_4
bad_list	sublist(g,g)	0.04	-	0.04	-	-	-
quicksort	qs(g,f)	112.7	+	0.35	+	+	-
queens	queens(g,f)	0.25	+	0.5	+	-	+
rotate	rotate(g,f)	0.05	+	0.05	+	+	+
sameleaves	s_leaves(g,g)	0.09	+	0.13	+	+	-
sublist	sublist(g,g)	0.05	+	0.06	+	+	+
sublist1	sublist(g,g)	0.04	+	0.03	+	+	+

For this example, both Polytool and Hasta La Vista produce nonlinear Diophantine constraints, but only Polytool succeeds. If we take the constraints generated by Hasta La Vista as an input for CiME 2.02, it also gives a positive result. This shows that the constraint solver used in Hasta La Vista, **CLPFD** [4], is not powerful enough to solve such constraint sets.   □

In Hasta La Vista, all constant symbols in the input program are mapped to a same value (zero). Polytool, in contrast, maps different constant symbols to different constants in $\mathbb{N}$. This property allows it to solve examples where constant symbols play an important role in termination behavior of the program. E.g. termination of the example *pl2.3.1* in Table 2(b):

$$p(X, Z) : -q(X, Y), p(Y, Z). \qquad p(X, X). \qquad q(a, b).$$

with the query pattern $Q = p(g, f)$ can be verified by Polytool, but not by Hasta La Vista.

Another issue is the efficiency. Overall, Hasta La Vista is faster than Polytool on a number of benchmarks. A reason could be that termination analysis based on polynomial interpretations increases the number of coefficients of the

---

[4] Constraint Logic Programming over Finite Domain.

polynomials associated with predicates and functors which are variables in the generated Diophantine constraints. This leads to less efficiency of Polytool.

3.2 Comparison Between TALP and Polytool

A point of similarity between Polytool and TALP is that both systems use polynomial interpretations as a basis for the termination proof. However, it is applied indirectly in TALP: given a logic program and a query set, it first transforms them to a TRS. This transformation is termination preserving. Then, a polynomial interpretation technique is applied to the target TRS. A limitation of TALP is that only well-moded logic programs are considered [10]. The results in the tables show that there are a number of examples, which are not well-moded for a specific query pattern, solvable by Polytool, not solvable by TALP (e.g., *pl1.1* with query set *append(g,f,f)* in Table 2(b)).

4 Conclusions

We have presented the development of an automated tool for termination proof of LP based on polynomial interpretations. It is a further extension of the previous work in [9] as we aim at the implementation phase. It has required an intensive work in coding, especially the construction for the symbolic form of the polynomial constraints from the acceptability conditions w.r.t. polynomial interpretations and the transformation from the polynomial constraints to the Diophantine constraints.

Our main contribution is the integration of a number of techniques including the termination framework in [9], the type inference engine in [8], the constraint-based approach in [6] and the Diophantine constraint solver in [4] to provide a completely automated termination analyser.

We have also done an intensive experimental evaluation of Polytool and other termination analysers such as Hasta La Vista, TerminWeb and TALP. It is shown from the evaluation that Polytool is powerful enough to solve a number of terminating benchmarks. It can verify termination of a class of examples in which nonlinear norms are required. In comparison with other tools, the result shows that Polytool has a higher success rate.

References

1. The termination problems database, http://www.lri.fr/~marche/wst2004-competition/tpdb.html, viewed march 2006
2. K. R. Apt and D. Pedreschi. Studies in pure prolog: Termination. In J. W. Lloyd, editor, *Proceedings Symposium in Computational Logic*, pages 150–176. Springe Verlag, Berlin, Heidelberg, 1990.
3. A. Bossi, N. Cocco, and M. Fabris. Proving termination of logic programs by exploiting term properties. In S. A. T. Maibaum, editor, *Proceedings TAPSOFT, volume 494 of Lecture Notes in Computer Science*, pages 153–180. Springer Verlag, 1991.

4. E. Contejean, C. Marché, A. P. Tomás, and X. Urbain. Mechanically proving termination using polynomial interpretations. *Journal of Automated Reasoning*, 2005.
5. L. De Koninck, T. Schrijvers, and B. Demoen. INCLP(R) - Interval-based nonlinear constraint logic programming over the reals. In M. Fink, H. Tompits, and S. Woltran, editors, *Workshop on Logic Programming*, pages 91–100, 2006.
6. S. Decorte, D. De Schreye, and H. Vandecasteele. Constraint based automatic termination analysis of logic programs. *ACM Transactions on Programming Languages and Systems*, 21(6):1137–1195, 1999.
7. H. Hong and D. Jakus. Testing positiveness of polynomials. *Journal of Automated Reasoning*, 21(1):23–38, 1998.
8. G. Janssens and M. Bruynooghe. Deriving descriptions of possible values of program variables by means of abstract interpretation. *Journal of Logic Programming*, 13(2&3):205–258, 1992.
9. M. T. Nguyen and D. De Schreye. Polynomial interpretations as a basis for termination analysis of logic programs. In G. G. M. Gabbrielli, editor, *Proceedings of the 21st International Conference on Logic Programming (ICLP'05)*, volume 3668 of *LNCS*, pages 311–325. Springer Verlag, 2005.
10. E. Ohlebusch, C. Claves, and C. Marché. Talp: A tool for the termination analysis of logic programs. In *Proceedings of the 11th International Conference on Rewriting Techniques and Applications*, volume 1833 of *LNCS*, pages 270–273. Springer Verlag, 2000.
11. A. Serebrenik. *Termination Analysis of Logic Programs*. PhD thesis, Department of Computer Science, K.U.Leuven, Belgium, 2003.
12. A. Serebrenik and D. De Schreye. Hasta-La-Vista: Termination analyser for logic programs. In F. Mesnard and A. Serebrenik, editors, *6th International Workshop on Termination (WLPE'03)*, pages 60–74, 2003.
13. J. Steinbach. Proving polynomials positive. In R. Shyamasundar, editor, *Foundations of Software Technology and Theoretical Computer Science (FSTTCS'92)*, volume 652 of *LNCS*, pages 18–20, 1992.
14. J. Steinbach. On the complexity of simplification orderings. Technical Report SR-93-18 (SFB), SEKI University of Kaiserslautern, 1993.
15. C. Taboch, S. Genaim, and M. Codish. Terminweb: Semantic based termination analyser for logic programs, http://www.cs.bgu.ac.il/~mcodish/terminweb, 2002

Grids: A Domain for Analyzing the Distribution of Numerical Values[*]

Roberto Bagnara[1], Katy Dobson[2], Patricia M. Hill[2], Matthew Mundell[2], and Enea Zaffanella[1]

[1] Department of Mathematics, University of Parma, Italy
{bagnara,zaffanella}@cs.unipr.it
[2] School of Computing, University of Leeds, UK
{katyd,hill,mattm}@comp.leeds.ac.uk

Abstract. This paper explores the abstract domain of *grids*, a domain that is able to represent sets of equally spaced points and hyperplanes over an n-dimensional vector space. Such a domain is useful for the static analysis of the patterns of distribution of the values program variables can take. We present the domain, its representation and the basic operations on grids necessary to define the abstract semantics. We show how the definition of the domain and its operations exploit well-known techniques from linear algebra as well as a dual representation that allows, among other things, for a concise and efficient implementation.

1 Introduction

We distinguish between two kinds of numerical information about the values program variables can take: outer *limits* (or bounds within which the values must lie) and the pattern of *distribution* of these values. Both kinds of information have important applications: in the field of automatic program verification, limit information is crucial to ensure that array accesses are within bounds, while distribution information is what is required to ensure that external memory accesses obey the alignment restriction imposed by the host architecture. In the field of program optimization, limit information can be used to compile out various kinds of run-time tests, whereas distribution information enables several transformations for efficient parallel execution as well as optimizations that enhance cache behavior.

Both limit and distribution information often come in a *relational* form; for instance, the outer limits or the pattern of possible values of one variable may depend on the values of one or more other variables. Domains that can capture relational information are generally much more complex than domains that do not have this capability; in exchange they usually offer significantly more precision, often important for the overall performance of the client application. Relational limit

---

[*] This work has been partly supported by EPSRC project EP/C520726/1 "Numerical Domains for Software Analysis," by MIUR project "AIDA — Abstract Interpretation: Design and Applications," and by a Royal Society (ESEP) award.

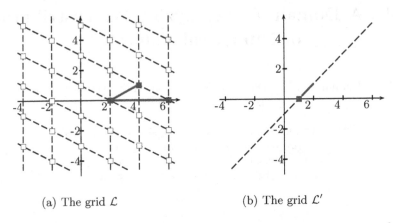

(a) The grid $\mathcal{L}$ (b) The grid $\mathcal{L}'$

Fig. 1. Congruence and generator systems representing two grids in $\mathbb{R}^2$

information can be captured, among other possibilities, by means of *polyhedral do-mains*, that is, domains that represent regions of some n-dimensional vector space bounded by a finite set of hyperplanes [10]. Although polyhedral domains such as the domain of convex polyhedra have been thoroughly researched and are widely used, relational domains for representing the (linear) distribution of numerical val-ues have been less well researched. Moreover, as far as we know and at the time of writing, there is no available implementation providing all the basic operations needed by a relational abstract domain for distribution information. This is in spite of the fact that previous research has shown that a knowledge about the (discrete) distribution of numerical information, especially when combined with that of the limit information, can significantly improve the quality of the analysis results [1].

This paper closes this gap by providing a complete account of the relational domain of *grids*; a domain for capturing numerical distribution information. It includes a detailed survey of previous work in this area; gives two representations for the domain; outlines how these can be reduced and also how to convert between them; and shows how this double description directly supports methods for comparing, joining and intersecting elements of this domain. The paper also outlines affine image and preimage operations and two new widenings for grids.

Grids in a Nutshell. Figure 1 illustrates two ways of describing a grid; either by means of a finite set of congruence relations that all grid points must satisfy (given by dashed lines) or by means of a finite set of generating vectors used for constructing the grid points and lines (given by filled squares and thick lines).

The squares in Figure 1(a) illustrate a grid $\mathcal{L}$ indicating possible values of integer variables x and y resulting from executing the program fragment in Figure 2 for any value of m. The congruence relations $x = 0 \pmod 2$ and $x + 2y = 2 \pmod 4$ are represented by the vertical dashed lines and sloping lines, respectively. The set of congruence relations $\mathcal{C} = \{x = 0 \pmod 2, x + 2y = 2 \pmod 4\}$, called a *congruence system*, is said to *describe* $\mathcal{L}$. The filled squares mark the points $\boldsymbol{p}_1 = \binom{2}{0}$, $\boldsymbol{p}_2 = \binom{6}{0}$ and $\boldsymbol{p}_3 = \binom{4}{1}$ while all the squares (both filled and unfilled) mark points $v = \pi_1 p_1 + \pi_2 p_2 + \pi_3 p_3$, where $\pi_1, \pi_2, \pi_3 \in \mathbb{Z}$ and $\pi_1 + \pi_2 + \pi_3 = 1$. The set of *points* $P = \{p_1, p_2, p_3\}$ is said to *generate* $\mathcal{L}$. Some of these generating points can be replaced by *parameters* that give the gradient and distance between neighboring points. Specifically, by subtracting the point p_1 from each of the other two generating points p_2 and p_3, we obtain the parameters $q_2 = \binom{4}{0}$ and $q_3 = \binom{2}{1}$ for $\mathcal{L}$ that are marked by the thick lines between points p_1 and p_2 and points p_1 and p_3, respectively. It follows that each point $v \in \mathcal{L}$ can be written as $v = p_1 + \pi_2 q_2 + \pi_3 q_3$ for some $\pi_2, \pi_3 \in \mathbb{Z}$.

The dashed line in Figure 1(b) illustrates the grid $\mathcal{L}'$ defining the line $x = y + 1$ and marks the vectors of values of the real variables x and y after an assignment x := y + 1, assuming that nothing is known about the value of y. As equalities are congruences modulo 0, the set $\mathcal{C}' = \{x - y = 1\}$ is also called a congruence system and describes $\mathcal{L}'$. Observe that the grid $\mathcal{L}'$ consists of all points that can be obtained as $\lambda \ell + p'$, for any $\lambda \in \mathbb{R}$, where $\ell = \binom{1}{1}$ and $p' = \binom{1}{0}$; the vector ℓ, called a *line*, defines a gradient and the vector p' is a generating point marking a position for the line (illustrated in Figure 1(b) by the thick line and the filled square, respectively).

```
x := 2; y := 0;   (P1)
for i := 1 to m   (P2)
  if ... then
    x := x + 4    (P3)
  else
    x := x + 2;
    y := y + 1    (P4)
  endif           (P5)
endfor
```

Fig. 2. Fragment based on an example in [10]

From what we have just seen, any grid can be represented both by a congruence system and by a *generator system*. The latter may consist of three components: a set of lines, a set of parameters and a set of points. For instance, the triples $\mathcal{G}_1 = (\varnothing, \varnothing, P)$ and $\mathcal{G}_2 = (\varnothing, \{q_2, q_3\}, \{p_1\})$ are both generator systems for $\mathcal{L}$ while the triple $\mathcal{G}' = (\{\ell\}, \varnothing, \{p'\})$ is a generator system for $\mathcal{L}'$.

Contributions. The paper provides an account of the relational domain of *grids*, fully implemented within the Parma Polyhedra Library [2,4]. In this section we provide the first comprehensive survey of the main research threads concerning these and similar domains. The other contributions are given below.

Minimizing representations. Assuming the grid is represented by a congruence and generator system in an n-dimensional vector space consisting of m congruences or generators, then we outline algorithms for minimizing the representation (based on the Hermite normal form algorithm [29]) that have worst-case complexity $O(n^2 m)$. Note that previous proposals for minimization such as those in [14,23] have worse complexity bounds (see below).

Converting representations. The congruence and generator representations described informally above form the two components of a double description method for the grid domain very similar to that for convex polyhedra [20]. For a double description method, conversion algorithms between the two systems are needed; we show how conversion can be implemented using any matrix inversion algorithm, inheriting the corresponding worst-case complexity. For instance, the complexity is $O(n^3)$ when adopting the standard Gaussian elimination method; since matrix inversion has the same worst-case complexity as matrix multiplication, better theoretical complexity bounds apply [5]. Previous proposals for congruence to generator conversion have complexity no better than $O(n^4)$ [15].

Grid operations. For static analysis, it is useful to provide all the set-theoretic lattice operations for grids (assuming the usual subset ordering) such as comparison, join and meet. We show that these operations are straightforward given the availability of the appropriate representation(s) in minimal form; and hence show that some have complexities strictly better than that of previous proposals [14]. We also describe a grid difference operator which is new to this paper.

Affine transformation operators. Affine image and preimage operators can be used to capture the effect of assignment statements in a program when the expression is linear although, as noted by Müller-Olm and Seidl in [21], analyses that use affine spaces for approximating the semantics of procedures are not sufficiently precise to detect all valid affine relations for programs with procedures. Here we specify, for the domain of grids, the affine image and preimage operators for a *single update* where only one dimension is modified.

Widenings. It was observed by Granger [15], that, if the grid generators can be in the rationals, then the grid domain does not satisfy the ascending chain condition; so, to guarantee termination of the analysis, a widening operation is required. In [15, Proposition 10], a widening is given for non-relational grids that returns a line parallel to an axis whenever the modulus for that dimension changes. It is then proposed that a generalized form of this could be used as a widening for relational grids; however, exactly how this is to be done is unclear. In this paper, we define two possible generalizations which come with simple syntactic checks that have efficient implementations.

Related Work. In [12], Granger shows how a static analysis can usefully employ a simple *non-relational* grid domain (that is a grid described by congruences of the form $x = c \pmod f$ where c and f are integers) and that this domain can obtain more precise information for applications such as automatic vectorization. Larsen et al. [17] also developed a static analyzer over a non-relational grid domain specifically designed to detect when dynamic memory addresses are congruent with respect to a given modulus; they show that, this information helps in the construction of a comprehensive set of program transformations for saving energy on low-power architectures and improving performance on multimedia processors. We note that these applications should carry over to the more complex domain considered here. In addition, Miné has shown how to construct, from the non-relational congruence domain in [12], a zone-congruence domain (that is, a domain that only allows *weakly relational* congruences that have the form $x - y = a \pmod b$ where a and b are rationals) [19].

Concerning *fully relational* domains, note that the use of a domain of linear *equality* relations for program analysis had already been studied by Karr [16]. In [14], Granger generalized this to provide a domain of linear *congruence* relations on an integral domain, i.e., a domain generated by integral vectors in

n-dimensions; and then, in [13,15], generalizes the results to the full grid domain. In [13,14,15], domain elements are represented by congruence and generator systems similar to the ones defined here. Standard algorithms for solving linear equations are used in converting from generator to congruence systems; however, a more complex $O(n^4)$ algorithm is provided for converting from congruence to generator systems. Assuming the number of generators is $n + 1$, the algorithm for minimizing the generator system has complexity $O(n^3 \log_2 n)$. Operators for comparing grids and computing the greatest lower and least upper bounds are also described. In particular, the join operation defined in [14] has complexity $O(n^4 \log_2 n)$, since the generators of one grid are added, one at a time, to the generators of the other; after each addition the minimization algorithm is applied to compute a new linearly independent set. The grid meet operation which also minimizes the addition of one congruence at a time has complexity $O(n^4)$.

The problem of how best to *apply* the grid domain in a program analyzer, has been studied by Müller-Olm and Seidl in [23] also building on the work of Karr [16]. Here, the prime focus is for the design of an *interprocedural* analysis for programs containing assignment statements and procedure calls. The algorithm has three stages: first, for each program point, a matrix M containing a (minimized) set of generators (i.e., vectors of values that hold at that point) is found; secondly, the determinant f of M is computed; thirdly, a congruence system with modulo f that satisfies all the vectors in M is determined. Stage one is similar to that proposed by Granger [14] for minimizing a set of generators. Stages two and three differ from the conversion in [14] in that the modulus f is computed separately and used to reduce the sizes of the coordinates. Note that the framework described in [23] subsumes previous works by the same authors.

Following an independent stream of research, Ancourt [1] considered the domain of $\mathbb{Z}$-*polyhedra*; that is a domain of *integral lattices* intersected with the domain of convex polyhedra (see also [24,25,26]). We are primarily interested here in the "integral lattices" component which may be seen as a subdomain of the domain of grids where the grid is full dimensional and all the grid points are integral vectors. The representation of these integral lattices is a special case of our generator representation where, for n dimensions, there must be exactly one point and n linearly independent parameters, all of which must be integral. There is no support for a congruence representation.

All the operations on $\mathbb{Z}$-polyhedra (and therefore the lattices) require canonic representations; hence Quinton et al. [25,26] define a canonical form for these lattices with a method for its computation. We note that the algorithm for computing the canonic form has complexity $O(n^4)$, where n is the number of dimensions of the vector space. Other operations provided are those of lattice intersection, affine image and affine preimage. As there is no congruence representation, the intersection of two lattices is computed directly from the generator representations [1]; a refined version of this method is provided in [25] which we note that, as for computing the canonic form, has complexity $O(n^4)$. The operations of grid join and grid difference (as defined here) are not considered; instead the union operator takes two lattices $\mathcal{L}_1$ and $\mathcal{L}_2$ and returns the set $\{\mathcal{L}_1, \mathcal{L}_2\}$ unless one (say $\mathcal{L}_1$) is contained in the other, in which case they return the larger, $\mathcal{L}_2$. Similarly the difference operation returns a set of lattices representing the set difference $\mathcal{L}_1 \setminus \mathcal{L}_2$. The domain of integral lattices has been implemented in PolyLib [18] following the approach in [25,26]. This means that only the generator representation is supported and some operations return *sets* of lattices while others manipulate and simplify these sets.

The *homogeneous form* of a representation given in Section 4, is required by the conversion algorithm. This form is not new to this paper; in fact several researchers have observed this. For instance, Granger [14] describes a map from a linear congruence system in n variables to a homogeneous one in $n+1$ variables; Nookala and Risset [24] explain that the PolyLib [18] adds a dimension to make the (generator) representation homogeneous; while Müller-Olm and Seidl [23] consider *extended states* where vectors have an extra 0'th component.

Plan of the Paper. Preliminary concepts and notation are given in Section 2. Section 3 introduces a grid together with its congruence and generator representations while Section 4 provides the main algorithms needed to support the double description. Section 5 introduces grid widening and the paper concludes in Section 6. A long version of the paper containing all proofs is available at `http://www.comp.leeds.ac.uk/hill/Papers/papers.html`

2   Preliminaries

The *cardinality* of a set S is denoted by $\# S$. The set of integers is denoted by $\mathbb{Z}$, rationals by $\mathbb{Q}$ and reals by $\mathbb{R}$. The complexities will assume a unit cost for every arithmetic operation.

Matrices and Vectors. If H is a matrix in $\mathbb{R}^{n \times m}$, the *transposition* of H is denoted by $H^{\mathrm{T}} \in \mathbb{R}^{m \times n}$. A vector $\boldsymbol{v} = (v_1, \dots, v_n) \in \mathbb{R}^n$ is also regarded as a matrix in $\mathbb{R}^{n \times 1}$. The *scalar product* of vectors $\boldsymbol{v}$ and $\boldsymbol{w} \in \mathbb{R}^n$, denoted by $\langle \boldsymbol{v}, \boldsymbol{w} \rangle$, is the real number $\boldsymbol{v}^{\mathrm{T}} \boldsymbol{w} = \sum_{i=1}^n v_i w_i$. The vector $\boldsymbol{e}_i \in \mathbb{R}^n$ has 1 in the i-th position and 0 in every other position. We let

$$\mathrm{piv}_<(\boldsymbol{v}) := \begin{cases} 0 & \text{if } \boldsymbol{v} = 0 \\ \max\{i \mid 1 \le i \le n, v_i \ne 0\} & \text{if } \boldsymbol{v} \ne \boldsymbol{0} \end{cases}$$

$$\mathrm{piv}_>(\boldsymbol{v}) := \begin{cases} n+1 & \text{if } \boldsymbol{v} = 0 \\ \min\{i \mid 1 \le i \le n, v_i \ne 0\} & \text{if } \boldsymbol{v} \ne \boldsymbol{0}. \end{cases}$$

We write $\boldsymbol{v} \Uparrow \boldsymbol{v}'$, if $\mathrm{piv}_<(\boldsymbol{v}) = \mathrm{piv}_<(\boldsymbol{v}') = k$ and either $k = 0$ or $v_k = v_k'$ and $\boldsymbol{v} \Downarrow \boldsymbol{v}'$, if $\mathrm{piv}_>(\boldsymbol{v}) = \mathrm{piv}_>(\boldsymbol{v}') = k$ and either $k = n+1$ or $v_k = v_k'$.

Integer Combinations. The set $S = \{\boldsymbol{v}_1, \dots, \boldsymbol{v}_k\} \subseteq \mathbb{R}^n$ is *affinely independent* if, for all $\boldsymbol{\lambda} \in \mathbb{R}^k$, $\boldsymbol{\lambda} = 0$ is the only solution of $\{\sum_{i=1}^k \lambda_i \boldsymbol{v}_i = \boldsymbol{0}, \sum_{i=1}^k \lambda_i = 0\}$. For all $\boldsymbol{\lambda} \in \mathbb{R}^k$, the vector $\boldsymbol{v} = \sum_{j=1}^k \lambda_j \boldsymbol{v}_j$ is said to be a *linear* combination of S.

This combination is *affine*, if $\sum_{j=1}^{k} \lambda_j = 1$; and *integral*, if $\boldsymbol{\lambda} \in \mathbb{Z}^k$. The set of all linear (resp., affine, integral, integral and affine) combinations of S is denoted by linear.hull (resp., affine.hull(S), int.hull(S), int.affine.hull(S)).

Congruences and Congruence Relations. For any $a, b, f \in \mathbb{R}$, $a \equiv_f b$ denotes the *congruence* $\exists \mu \in \mathbb{Z} \,.\, a - b = \mu f$. Let $\mathbb{S} \in \{\mathbb{Q}, \mathbb{R}\}$. For each vector $\boldsymbol{a} \in \mathbb{S}^n$ and scalars $b, f \in \mathbb{S}$, the notation $\langle \boldsymbol{a}, \boldsymbol{x} \rangle \equiv_f b$ stands for the *linear congruence relation in* $\mathbb{S}^n$ defined by the set $\{ \boldsymbol{v} \in \mathbb{R}^n \mid \exists \mu \in \mathbb{Z} \,.\, \langle \boldsymbol{a}, \boldsymbol{v} \rangle = b + \mu f \}$; when $f \neq 0$, the relation is said to be *proper*; $\langle \boldsymbol{a}, \boldsymbol{x} \rangle \equiv_0 b$ denotes the equality $\langle \boldsymbol{a}, \boldsymbol{x} \rangle = b$. Thus, provided $\boldsymbol{a} \neq \boldsymbol{0}$, the relation $\langle \boldsymbol{a}, \boldsymbol{x} \rangle \equiv_f b$ defines the set of affine hyperplanes $\{ (\langle \boldsymbol{a}, \boldsymbol{x} \rangle = b + \mu f) \mid \mu \in \mathbb{Z} \}$; when $\boldsymbol{a} = \boldsymbol{0}$, we assume that $b \neq 0$; if $b \equiv_f 0$, $\langle \boldsymbol{0}, \boldsymbol{x} \rangle \equiv_f b$ defines the universe $\mathbb{R}^n$ and the empty set, otherwise.

Any vector that satisfies $\langle \boldsymbol{a}, \boldsymbol{x} \rangle = b + \mu f$ for some $\mu \in \mathbb{Z}$ is said to *satisfy* the relation $\langle \boldsymbol{a}, \boldsymbol{x} \rangle \equiv_f b$. Congruence relations in $\mathbb{S}^n$, such as $\langle \boldsymbol{a}, \boldsymbol{x} \rangle \equiv_1 b$ and $\langle 2\boldsymbol{a}, \boldsymbol{x} \rangle \equiv_2 2b$, defining the same hyperplanes are considered equivalent.

The pivot notation for vectors is extended to congruences: if $\beta = (\langle \boldsymbol{a}, \boldsymbol{x} \rangle \equiv_f a_0)$ then $\text{piv}_<(\beta) := \text{piv}_<(\boldsymbol{a})$; if $\gamma = (\langle \boldsymbol{c}, \boldsymbol{x} \rangle \equiv_g c_0)$ and $g\boldsymbol{a} \Uparrow f\boldsymbol{c}$, then we write $\beta \Uparrow \gamma$; so that β and γ are either both equalities or both proper congruences.

3   The Grid Domain

Here we introduce grids and their representation. Note that the use of the word 'grid' here is to avoid confusion with the meaning of 'lattice' (used previously for elements similar to a grid) in its set-theoretic context (particularly relevant when working in abstract interpretation).

Grids and the Congruence Representation. A *congruence system in* $\mathbb{Q}^n$ is a finite set of congruence relations $\mathcal{C}$ in $\mathbb{Q}^n$. As we do not distinguish between syntactically different congruences defining the same set of vectors, we can assume that all proper congruences in $\mathcal{C}$ have modulus 1.

Definition 1. *Let $\mathcal{C}$ be a congruence system in $\mathbb{R}^n$. If $\mathcal{L}$ is the set of vectors in $\mathbb{R}^n$ that satisfy all the congruences in $\mathcal{C}$, we say that $\mathcal{L}$ is a* grid *described by a congruence system $\mathcal{C}$ in $\mathbb{Q}^n$. We also say that $\mathcal{C}$ is a congruence system for $\mathcal{L}$ and write $\mathcal{L} = \text{gcon}(\mathcal{C})$. If $\text{gcon}(\mathcal{C}) = \varnothing$, then we say that $\mathcal{C}$ is* inconsistent.

The grid domain $\mathbb{G}_n$ *is the set of all grids in $\mathbb{R}^n$ ordered by the set inclusion relation, so that $\varnothing$ and $\mathbb{R}^n$ are the bottom and top elements of $\mathbb{G}_n$ respectively.*

The vector space $\mathbb{R}^n$ is called the *universe* grid. In set theoretical terms, $\mathbb{G}_n$ is a *lattice* under set inclusion. Many algorithms given here will require the congruence systems not only to have minimal cardinality but also such that the coefficients of (a permutation of) the congruences can form a triangular matrix.

Definition 2. *Suppose $\mathcal{C}$ is a congruence system in $\mathbb{Q}^n$. Then we say that $\mathcal{C}$ is in* minimal form *if either $\mathcal{C} = \{\langle \boldsymbol{0}, \boldsymbol{x} \rangle \equiv_0 1\}$ or $\mathcal{C}$ is consistent and, for each congruence $\beta = (\langle \boldsymbol{a}, \boldsymbol{x} \rangle \equiv_f b) \in \mathcal{C}$, the following hold:*

1. *if* $\mathrm{piv}_<(\beta) = k$, *then* $k > 0$ *and* $a_k > 0$;
2. *for all* $\beta' \in \mathcal{C} \setminus \{\beta\}$, $\mathrm{piv}_<(\beta') \neq \mathrm{piv}_<(\beta)$.

Proposition 1. *Let $\mathcal{C}$ be a congruence system in $\mathbb{Q}^n$ and $m = \#\mathcal{C}$. Then there exists an algorithm for finding a congruence system $\mathcal{C}'$ in minimal form with worst-case complexity $O(n^2 m)$ such that $\mathrm{gcon}(\mathcal{C}) = \mathrm{gcon}(\mathcal{C}')$.*

Note that the algorithm mentioned in Proposition 1, is based on the Hermite normal form algorithm; details about the actual algorithm are given in the proof. Note also, that when $m < n$, the complexity of this algorithm is just $O(m^2 n)$.

The Generator Representation. Let $\mathcal{L}$ be a grid in $\mathbb{G}_n$. Then

- a vector $\boldsymbol{p} \in \mathcal{L}$ is called a *point* of $\mathcal{L}$;
- a vector $\boldsymbol{q} \in \mathbb{R}^n \setminus \{\boldsymbol{0}\}$ is called a *parameter* of $\mathcal{L}$ if $\mathcal{L} \neq \varnothing$ and $\boldsymbol{p} + \mu\boldsymbol{q} \in \mathcal{L}$, for all points $\boldsymbol{p} \in \mathcal{L}$ and all $\mu \in \mathbb{Z}$;
- a vector $\boldsymbol{\ell} \in \mathbb{R}^n \setminus \{\boldsymbol{0}\}$ is called a *line* of $\mathcal{L}$ if $\mathcal{L} \neq \varnothing$ and $\boldsymbol{p} + \lambda\boldsymbol{\ell} \in \mathcal{L}$, for all points $\boldsymbol{p} \in \mathcal{L}$ and all $\lambda \in \mathbb{R}$.

If L, Q and P are finite sets of vecors in $\mathbb{R}^n$ and

$$\mathcal{L} := \mathrm{linear.hull}(L) + \mathrm{int.hull}(Q) + \mathrm{int.affine.hull}(P)$$

where the symbol '+' denotes the Minkowski's sum,[1] then $\mathcal{L} \in \mathbb{G}_n$ is a grid (see [29, Section 4.4] and also Proposition 7). The 3-tuple (L, Q, P), where L, Q and P denote sets of lines, parameters and points, respectively, is said to be a *generator system* in $\mathbb{Q}^n$ for $\mathcal{L}$ and we write $\mathcal{L} = \mathrm{ggen}((L, Q, P))$. Note that, for any grid $\mathcal{L}$ in $\mathbb{G}_n$, there is a generator system (L, Q, P) in $\mathbb{Q}^n$ for $\mathcal{L}$ (see again [29, Section 4.4] and also Proposition 6). Note also that the grid $\mathcal{L} = \mathrm{ggen}((L, Q, P)) = \varnothing$ if and only if the set of points $P = \varnothing$. If $P \neq \varnothing$, then $\mathcal{L} = \mathrm{ggen}((L, \varnothing, Q_{\boldsymbol{p}} \cup P))$ where, for some $\boldsymbol{p} \in P$, $Q_{\boldsymbol{p}} = \{\boldsymbol{p} + \boldsymbol{q} \in \mathbb{R}^n \mid \boldsymbol{q} \in Q\}$.

As for congruence systems, for many procedures in the implementation, it is useful if the generator systems have a minimal number of elements.

Definition 3. *Suppose $\mathcal{G} = (L, Q, P)$ is a generator system in $\mathbb{Q}^n$. Then we say that $\mathcal{G}$ is in minimal form if either $L = Q = P = \varnothing$ or $\#P = 1$ and, for each generator $\boldsymbol{v} \in L \cup Q$, the following hold:*

1. *if* $\mathrm{piv}_>(\boldsymbol{v}) = k$, *then* $v_k > 0$;
2. *for all* $\boldsymbol{v}' \in (L \cup Q) \setminus \{\boldsymbol{v}\}$, $\mathrm{piv}_>(\boldsymbol{v}') \neq \mathrm{piv}_>(\boldsymbol{v})$.

Proposition 2. *Let $\mathcal{G} = (L, Q, P)$ be a generator system in $\mathbb{Q}^n$ and $m = \#L + \#Q + \#P$. Then there exists an algorithm for finding a generator system $\mathcal{G}'$ in minimal form with worst-case complexity $O(n^2 m)$ such that $\mathrm{ggen}(\mathcal{G}') = \mathrm{ggen}(\mathcal{G})$.*

As for Proposition 1, the algorithm mentioned in Proposition 2 is based on the Hermite normal form algorithm. Note also that, when $m < n$, the complexity of this algorithm is again just $O(m^2 n)$.

---

[1] This is defined, for each $S, T \subseteq \mathbb{R}^n$, by $S + T := \{\boldsymbol{s} + \boldsymbol{t} \in \mathbb{R}^n \mid \boldsymbol{s} \in S, \boldsymbol{t} \in T\}$.

Double Description. We have shown that any grid $\mathcal{L}$ can be described by using a congruence system $\mathcal{C}$ and also generated by a generator system $\mathcal{G}$. For the same reasons as for the polyhedral domain, it is useful to represent the grid $\mathcal{L}$ by the *double description* $(\mathcal{C}, \mathcal{G})$. Just as for the double description method for convex polyhedra, in order to maintain and exploit such a view of a grid, an implementation must include algorithms for converting a representation of one kind into a representation of the other kind and for minimizing both representations. Note that having easy access to both representations is assumed in the implementation of many grid operators including those described here.

Suppose we have a double description $(\mathcal{C}, \mathcal{G})$ of a grid $\mathcal{L} \in \mathbb{G}_n$, where both $\mathcal{C}$ and $\mathcal{G}$ are in minimal form. Then, it follows from the definition of minimal form that $\#\mathcal{C} \leq n + 1$ and $\#L + \#Q \leq n$. In fact, we have a stronger result.

Proposition 3. *Let $(\mathcal{C}, \mathcal{G})$ be a double description where both $\mathcal{C}$ and $\mathcal{G}$ are in minimal form. Letting $\mathcal{C} = \mathcal{E} \cup \mathcal{F}$, where $\mathcal{E}$ and $\mathcal{F}$ are sets of equalities and proper congruences, respectively, and $\mathcal{G} = (L, Q, P)$, then $\#\mathcal{F} = \#Q = n - \#L - \#\mathcal{E}$.*

Example 1. Consider the grids $\mathcal{L}$ and $\mathcal{L}'$ in Figure 1. The congruence systems $\mathcal{C}$ and $\mathcal{C}'$ are in minimal form and the generator systems $\mathcal{G}_2$ and $\mathcal{G}'$ are also in minimal form; however, $\mathcal{G}_1$ is not in minimal form as it contains more than one point. Furthermore, for $i = 1, 2$, the pairs $(\mathcal{C}, \mathcal{G}_i)$ are double descriptions for $\mathcal{L}$ while $(\mathcal{C}', \mathcal{G}')$ is a double description for $\mathcal{L}'$.

Comparing Grids. For any pair of grids $\mathcal{L}_1 = \mathrm{ggen}\big((L, Q, P)\big)$, $\mathcal{L}_2 = \mathrm{gcon}(\mathcal{C})$ in $\mathbb{G}_n$, we can decide whether $\mathcal{L}_1 \subseteq \mathcal{L}_2$ by checking if every generator in (L, Q, P) satisfies every congruence in $\mathcal{C}$. Note that a parameter or line $\boldsymbol{v}$ *satisfies* a congruence $\langle \boldsymbol{a}, \boldsymbol{x} \rangle \equiv_f b$ if $\langle \boldsymbol{a}, \boldsymbol{v} \rangle \equiv_f 0$. Therefore, assuming the systems $\mathcal{C}$ and $\mathcal{G}$ are already in minimal form, the complexity of comparison is $\mathrm{O}\big(n^3\big)$.

Given that it is known that one grid is a subset of another, there are quicker tests for checking equality - the following definition is used in their specification.

Definition 4. *Let $\mathcal{C}_1, \mathcal{C}_2$ be congruence systems in minimal form. Then $\mathcal{C}_1, \mathcal{C}_2$ are said to be* pivot equivalent *if, for each $i, j \in \{1, 2\}$ where $i \neq j$, for each $\beta \in \mathcal{C}_i$, there exists $\gamma \in \mathcal{C}_j$ such that $\beta \Uparrow \gamma$.*

Let $\mathcal{G}_1 = \big(L_1, Q_1, \{\boldsymbol{p}_1\}\big)$ and $\mathcal{G}_2 = \big(L_2, Q_2, \{\boldsymbol{p}_2\}\big)$ be generator systems in minimal form. Then $\mathcal{G}_1, \mathcal{G}_2$ are said to be pivot equivalent *if, for each $i, j \in \{1, 2\}$ where $i \neq j$: for each $\boldsymbol{q}_i \in Q_i$, there exists $\boldsymbol{q}_j \in Q_j$ such that $\boldsymbol{q}_i \Downarrow \boldsymbol{q}_j$; and, for each $\boldsymbol{\ell}_i \in L_i$, there exists $\boldsymbol{\ell}_j \in L_j$ such that $\mathrm{piv}_>(\boldsymbol{\ell}_i) = \mathrm{piv}_>(\boldsymbol{\ell}_j)$.*

Proposition 4. *Let $\mathcal{L}_1 = \mathrm{gcon}(\mathcal{C}_1) = \mathrm{ggen}(\mathcal{G}_1)$ and $\mathcal{L}_2 = \mathrm{gcon}(\mathcal{C}_2) = \mathrm{ggen}(\mathcal{G}_2)$ be non-empty grids in $\mathbb{G}_n$ such that $\mathcal{L}_1 \subseteq \mathcal{L}_2$. If $\mathcal{C}_1$ and $\mathcal{C}_2$ are pivot equivalent congruence systems in minimal form or $\mathcal{G}_1$ and $\mathcal{G}_2$ are pivot equivalent generator systems in minimal form, then $\mathcal{L}_1 = \mathcal{L}_2$.*

It follows from Proposition 4, that provided $\mathcal{L}_1 \subseteq \mathcal{L}_2$ and $\mathcal{L}_1$ and $\mathcal{L}_2$ have both their generator or congruence systems already in minimal form, then the complexity of checking if $\mathcal{L}_1 = \mathcal{L}_2$ is just $\mathrm{O}(n)$. Moreover, if it is found that one pair of corresponding pivot elements of the congruence or generator systems differ, then we can immediately deduce that the grids they describe also differ.

Intersection and Grid Join. For grids $\mathcal{L}_1, \mathcal{L}_2 \in \mathbb{G}_n$, the *intersection* of $\mathcal{L}_1$ and $\mathcal{L}_2$, defined as the set intersection $\mathcal{L}_1 \cap \mathcal{L}_2$, is the largest grid included in both $\mathcal{L}_1$ and $\mathcal{L}_2$; similarly, the *grid join* of $\mathcal{L}_1$ and $\mathcal{L}_2$, denoted by $\mathcal{L}_1 \oplus \mathcal{L}_2$, is the smallest grid that includes both $\mathcal{L}_1$ and $\mathcal{L}_2$. In theoretical terms, the intersection and grid join operators are the binary *meet* and *join* operators on the lattice $\mathbb{G}_n$. They can easily be computed; if $\mathcal{L}_1 = \mathrm{gcon}(\mathcal{C}_1) = \mathrm{ggen}(\mathcal{G}_1)$ and $\mathcal{L}_2 = \mathrm{gcon}(\mathcal{C}_2) = \mathrm{ggen}(\mathcal{G}_2)$, then $\mathcal{L}_1 \cap \mathcal{L}_2 = \mathrm{gcon}(\mathcal{C}_1 \cup \mathcal{C}_2)$ and $\mathcal{L}_1 \oplus \mathcal{L}_2 = \mathrm{ggen}(\mathcal{G}_1 \cup \mathcal{G}_2)$.

In practice, the cost of computing the grid intersection and join depends on a number of factors: if generator systems $\mathcal{G}_1$ and $\mathcal{G}_2$ for $\mathcal{L}_1$ and $\mathcal{L}_2$ are known, then the complexity of computing $\mathcal{L}_1 \oplus \mathcal{L}_2$ is linear in either $\# \mathcal{G}_1$ or $\# \mathcal{G}_2$; if, however, only congruence systems $\mathcal{C}_1$ and $\mathcal{C}_2$ for $\mathcal{L}_1$ and $\mathcal{L}_2$ (not necessarily in minimal form) are known, then the complexity is that of minimizing and converting them which is, at worst, $\mathrm{O}\big(n^2 \max(\# \mathcal{C}_1, \# \mathcal{C}_2, n)\big)$. A similar argument applies to the complexities of the meet operation. However, the above operations are not directly comparable with the meet and join operations given in [14]. For such a comparison, for instance for the join operation, we assume that generator systems for $\mathcal{L}_1$ and $\mathcal{L}_2$ in minimal form are available (i.e., each with at most $n+1$ generators) and the operation returns a generator system in minimal form for $\mathcal{L}_1 \oplus \mathcal{L}_2$. Then the complexity is $\mathrm{O}\big(n^3\big)$, the complexity of minimizing a generator system with at most $2n + 2$ generators, which is strictly better than $\mathrm{O}\big(n^4 \log_2 n\big)$, the complexity of the equivalent operation in [14].

Example 2. Consider the grids $\mathcal{L}_1 = \mathrm{gcon}(\mathcal{C}_1)$ and $\mathcal{L}_2 = \mathrm{gcon}(\mathcal{C}_2)$ in $\mathbb{G}_2$ where $\mathcal{C}_1 := \{x \equiv_2 0, \ -x + y \equiv_3 0\}$ and $\mathcal{C}_2 := \{x \equiv_4 0, \ -x + 2y \equiv_6 0\}$. Then the grid intersection is $\mathcal{L}_1 \cap \mathcal{L}_2 = \mathrm{gcon}(\mathcal{C}_1 \cup \mathcal{C}_2)$; thus, as $\mathcal{C} = \{x \equiv_{12} 0, \ y \equiv_3 0\}$ is a reduced form of $\mathcal{C}_1 \cup \mathcal{C}_2$, we have $\mathcal{L}_1 \cap \mathcal{L}_2 = \mathrm{gcon}(\mathcal{C})$.

Consider $\mathcal{L}_1 = \mathrm{ggen}\big((\varnothing, \varnothing, P_1)\big)$ and $\mathcal{L}_2 = \mathrm{ggen}\big((\varnothing, \varnothing, P_2)\big)$ in $\mathbb{G}_2$, where $P_1 := \left(\begin{smallmatrix} 2 & 0 & 0 \\ 2 & 3 & 0 \end{smallmatrix}\right)$ and $P_2 := \left(\begin{smallmatrix} 4 & 0 & 0 \\ 2 & 3 & 0 \end{smallmatrix}\right)$. Then the grid join $\mathcal{L}_1 \oplus \mathcal{L}_2$ is generated by $(\varnothing, \varnothing, P_1 \cup P_2)$; thus, the generator system $\mathcal{G} := \big(\varnothing, \left(\begin{smallmatrix} 2 & 0 \\ 0 & 1 \end{smallmatrix}\right), \left(\begin{smallmatrix} 0 \\ 0 \end{smallmatrix}\right)\big)$ is a minimal form of $(\varnothing, \varnothing, P_1 \cup P_2)$ and $\mathcal{L}_1 \oplus \mathcal{L}_2 = \mathrm{ggen}(\mathcal{G})$. Note that here $\mathcal{L}_1 \oplus \mathcal{L}_2 \neq \mathcal{L}_1 \cup \mathcal{L}_2$.

Grid Difference. For grids $\mathcal{L}_1, \mathcal{L}_2 \in \mathbb{G}_n$, the *grid difference* $\mathcal{L}_1 \ominus \mathcal{L}_2$ of $\mathcal{L}_1$ and $\mathcal{L}_2$ is the smallest grid containing the set-theoretic difference of $\mathcal{L}_1$ and $\mathcal{L}_2$.

Proposition 5. *The grid $\mathcal{L}_1 \ominus \mathcal{L}_2$ is returned by the algorithm in Figure 3.*

Assuming $\mathcal{C}_1$ and $\mathcal{C}_2$ are available and in minimal form, it follows from the complexities of minimization, conversion and comparison operations that the grid difference algorithm in Figure 3 has worst-case complexity $\mathrm{O}\big(n^4\big)$.

Affine Images and Preimages. Affine transformations for the vector space $\mathbb{R}^n$ will map hyperplanes to hyperplanes and preserve intersection properties between hyperplanes; such transformations can be represented by matrices in

Input: Nonempty grids $\mathcal{L}_1 = \mathrm{gcon}(\mathcal{C}_1)$ and $\mathcal{L}_2 = \mathrm{gcon}(\mathcal{C}_2)$ in $\mathbb{G}_n$.
Output: A grid in $\mathbb{G}_n$.
(1) $\mathcal{L}' := \varnothing$
(2)   **while** $\exists \beta = (e \equiv_f 0) \in \mathcal{C}_2$
(3) $\mathcal{C}_2 := \mathcal{C}_2 \setminus \{\beta\}$
(4)   **if** $\mathcal{L}_1 \nsubseteq \mathrm{gcon}(\{\beta\})$
(5)   **if** $\mathcal{L}_1 \subseteq \mathrm{gcon}(\{2e \equiv_f 0\})$
(6) $\mathcal{L}_\beta := \mathrm{gcon}(\mathcal{C}_1 \cup \{2e - f \equiv_{2f} 0\})$
(7) $\mathcal{L}' := \mathcal{L}' \oplus \mathcal{L}_\beta$
(8)   **else**
(9)   **return** $\mathcal{L}_1$
(10)   **return** $\mathcal{L}'$

Fig. 3. The grid difference algorithm

$\mathbb{R}^{n \times n}$. It follows that the set $\mathbb{G}_n$ is closed under the set of all affine transformations for $\mathbb{R}^n$. Simple and useful linear affine transformations for numerical domains, including the grids, are provided by the 'single update' affine image and affine preimage operators.

Given a grid $\mathcal{L} \in \mathbb{G}_n$, a variable x_k and linear expression $e = \langle a, x \rangle + b$ with coefficients in $\mathbb{Q}$, the *affine image operator* $\phi(\mathcal{L}, x_k, e)$ maps the grid $\mathcal{L}$ to

$$\left\{ (p_1, \ldots, p_{k-1}, \langle a, p \rangle + b, p_{k+1}, \ldots, p_n)^{\mathrm{T}} \in \mathbb{R}^n \mid p \in \mathcal{L} \right\}.$$

Conversely, the *affine preimage operator* $\phi^{-1}(\mathcal{L}, x_k, e)$ maps the grid $\mathcal{L}$ to

$$\left\{ p \in \mathbb{R}^n \mid (p_1, \ldots, p_{k-1}, \langle a, p \rangle + b, p_{k+1}, \ldots, p_n)^{\mathrm{T}} \in \mathcal{L} \right\}.$$

Observe that the affine image $\phi(\mathcal{L}, x_k, e)$ and preimage $\phi^{-1}(\mathcal{L}, x_k, e)$ are invertible if and only if the coefficient a_k in the vector a is non-zero.

Program Analysis Using Grids. We show how the grid domain can be used to find properties of the program variables not found using the polyhedra domain [10], constraint-based analysis [28] or polynomial invariants [27].

Example 3. The program fragment in Figure 2 is annotated with program points Pj, for $j = 1, \ldots, 5$. Let $\mathcal{L}_j^i \in \mathbb{G}_2$ denote the grid computed at the i-th iteration executed by the point Pj. Initially, $\mathcal{L}_j^0 = \varnothing = \mathrm{gcon}(\{1 = 0\})$, for $j = 1, \ldots, 5$. After one and two iterations of the loop we have:

$$\mathcal{L}_1^1 = \mathrm{gcon}(\{x = 2, \ y = 0\}), \quad \mathcal{L}_2^1 = \mathrm{gcon}(\{x = 2, \ y = 0\}),$$
$$\mathcal{L}_3^1 = \mathrm{gcon}(\{x = 6, \ y = 0\}), \quad \mathcal{L}_4^1 = \mathrm{gcon}(\{x = 4, \ y = 1\}),$$
$$\mathcal{L}_5^1 = \mathrm{gcon}(\{x = 4, \ y = 1\}) \oplus \mathrm{gcon}(\{x = 6, \ y = 0\})$$
$$\quad = \mathrm{gcon}(\{x + 2y = 6, \ x \equiv_2 0\}),$$
$$\mathcal{L}_2^2 = \mathrm{gcon}(\{x = 2, y = 0\}) \oplus \mathrm{gcon}(\{x + 2y = 6, x \equiv_2 0\})$$
$$\quad = \mathrm{gcon}(\{x + 2y \equiv_4 2, x \equiv_2 0\}).$$

Subsequent computation steps show that an invariant for P2 has already been computed since $\mathcal{L}_3^2 = \mathcal{L}_3^1$, $\mathcal{L}_4^2 = \mathcal{L}_4^1$, $\mathcal{L}_5^2 = \mathcal{L}_5^1$ so that $\mathcal{L}_2^3 = \mathcal{L}_2^2$. Thus at the end of the program, the congruences $x + 2y \equiv_4 2$ and $x \equiv_2 0$ hold.

Observe that, using convex polyhedra, a similar analysis will find instead that the inequalities $x - 2y \geq 2$, $x + 2y \geq 6$ and $y \geq 0$ hold [10].

4   Implementation

In this section, we describe convenient internal representations of the congruence and generator systems in terms of arrays (i.e., matrices) and show how matrix inversion provides a basis for converting between these representations.

Homogeneous Representations. A congruence system $\mathcal{C}$ is *homogeneous* if, for all $(\langle a, x \rangle \equiv_f b) \in \mathcal{C}$, we have $b = 0$. Similarly, a generator system (L, Q, P) is *homogeneous* if $\mathbf{0} \in P$. For the implementation, it is convenient to work with a homogeneous system. Thus we first convert any congruence or generator system in $\mathbb{Q}^n$ to a homogeneous system in $\mathbb{Q}^{n+1}$. The extra dimension is denoted with a 0 subscript; the vector $\hat{x} = (x_0, \ldots, x_n)^{\mathrm{T}}$; and e_0 denotes the vector $(1, \mathbf{0}^{\mathrm{T}})^{\mathrm{T}}$.

Consider the congruence system $\mathcal{C} = \mathcal{E} \cup \mathcal{F}$ in $\mathbb{Q}^n$, where $\mathcal{E}$ is a set of equalities and $\mathcal{F}$ is a set of proper congruences. Then the *homogeneous form* for $\mathcal{C}$ is the congruence system $\hat{\mathcal{C}} = \hat{\mathcal{E}} \cup \hat{\mathcal{F}}$ in $\mathbb{Q}^{n+1}$ defined by:

$$\hat{\mathcal{E}} := \left\{ \langle (-b, a^{\mathrm{T}})^{\mathrm{T}}, \hat{x} \rangle = 0 \,\middle|\, (\langle a, x \rangle = b) \in \mathcal{E} \right\},$$

$$\hat{\mathcal{F}} := \left\{ \langle f^{-1}(-b, a^{\mathrm{T}})^{\mathrm{T}}, \hat{x} \rangle \equiv_1 0 \,\middle|\, (\langle a, x \rangle \equiv_f b) \in \mathcal{F} \right\} \cup \left\{ \langle e_0, \hat{x} \rangle \equiv_1 0 \right\}.$$

The congruence $\langle e_0, \hat{x} \rangle \equiv_1 0$ expresses the fact that $1 \equiv_1 0$. By writing $\hat{\mathcal{E}} = (E^{\mathrm{T}} x = \mathbf{0})$ and $\hat{\mathcal{F}} = (F^{\mathrm{T}} x \equiv_1 \mathbf{0})$, where $E, F \subseteq \mathbb{Q}^{n+1}$, it can be seen that the pair (F, E), called the *matrix form* of $\hat{\mathcal{C}}$, is sufficient to determine $\mathcal{C}$.

Consider next a generator system $\mathcal{G} = (L, Q, P)$ in $\mathbb{Q}^n$. Then the *homogeneous form* for $\mathcal{G}$ is the generator system $\hat{\mathcal{G}} := (\hat{L}, \hat{Q} \cup \hat{P}, \{\mathbf{0}\})$ in $\mathbb{Q}^{n+1}$ where

$$\hat{L} := \{(0, \ell^{\mathrm{T}})^{\mathrm{T}} \mid \ell \in L\}, \quad \hat{Q} := \{(0, q^{\mathrm{T}})^{\mathrm{T}} \mid q \in Q\}, \quad \hat{P} := \{(1, p^{\mathrm{T}})^{\mathrm{T}} \mid p \in P\}.$$

The original grid $\mathcal{L} = \mathrm{gcon}(\mathcal{C})$ (resp., $\mathcal{L} = \mathrm{ggen}(\mathcal{G})$) can be recovered from the grid $\hat{\mathcal{L}} = \mathrm{gcon}(\hat{\mathcal{C}})$ (resp., $\hat{\mathcal{L}} = \mathrm{ggen}(\hat{\mathcal{G}})$) since $\mathcal{L} = \{v \in \mathbb{R}^n \mid (1, v^{\mathrm{T}})^{\mathrm{T}} \in \hat{\mathcal{L}}\}$. Note that, if $(\mathcal{C}, \mathcal{G})$ is a double description for a grid and $\hat{\mathcal{C}}$ and $\hat{\mathcal{G}}$ are homogeneous forms for $\mathcal{C}$ and $\mathcal{G}$, then $(\hat{\mathcal{C}}, \hat{\mathcal{G}})$ is also a double description.

Converting Representations. By considering the matrix forms of the (homogeneous forms of the) representations, we can build the conversion algorithms on top of those for matrix inversion. For an informal explanation why this is appropriate, suppose that the generator system $\mathcal{G} = (\varnothing, Q, \{\mathbf{0}\})$ in $\mathbb{Q}^n$ is in minimal form and Q is a non-singular square matrix. Letting $\mathcal{L} = \mathrm{ggen}(\mathcal{G}) = \{Q\pi \mid \pi \in \mathbb{Z}^n\}$, then we also have $\mathcal{L} = \{v \in \mathbb{R}^n \mid Q^{-1}v \equiv_1 0\}$, so that $(Q^{-1}, \varnothing)$ is the matrix form of a congruence system for the same grid $\mathcal{L}$. Similarly we can use matrix inversion to convert the matrix form of a homogeneous congruence system in minimal form consisting of n proper congruences for a grid $\mathcal{L}$ to a generator system for $\mathcal{L}$. When the matrices to be inverted have less than n linearly independent columns, the algorithms first add vectors e_i where $1 \leq i \leq n$, as necessary, so as to make the matrices non-singular and hence invertible.

Proposition 6. *Let $\mathcal{C}$ be a congruence system in $\mathbb{Q}^n$ in minimal form; (F, E) the matrix form of the homogeneous form for $\mathcal{C}$; N a matrix in $\mathbb{Z}^{n+1}$ whose vectors are of the form e_i, $i \in \{0, \ldots, n\}$, and such that $(N, \hat{F}, \hat{E})$ is square and nonsingular; and $(\hat{L}, \hat{Q}, M) := \left((N, \hat{F}, \hat{E})^{-1}\right)^{\mathrm{T}}$ where $\#\hat{L} = \#N$, $\#\hat{Q} = \#\hat{F}$ and $\#M = \#\hat{E}$. Then $\hat{\mathcal{G}} = (\hat{L}, \hat{Q}, \{\mathbf{0}\})$ is the homogeneous form for a generator system $\mathcal{G}$ in minimal form and $\mathrm{ggen}(\mathcal{G}) = \mathrm{gcon}(\mathcal{C})$.*

Proposition 7. *Let $\mathcal{G}$ be a generator system in $\mathbb{Q}^n$ in minimal form; $\hat{\mathcal{G}} = (\hat{L}, \hat{Q}, \{\mathbf{0}\})$ the homogeneous form for $\mathcal{G}$; M a matrix in $\mathbb{Z}^{n+1}$ whose vectors are of the form e_i, $i \in \{0, \ldots, n\}$, and such that $(\hat{L}, \hat{Q}, M)$ is square and non-singular; and $(N, \hat{F}, \hat{E}) := \left((\hat{L}, \hat{Q}, M)^{-1}\right)^{\mathrm{T}}$ where $\#N = \#\hat{L}$, $\#\hat{F} = \#\hat{Q}$ and $\#\hat{E} = \#M$. Then $(\hat{F}, \hat{E})$ is the matrix form of the homogeneous form for a congruence system $\mathcal{C}$ in minimal form and $\mathrm{gcon}(\mathcal{C}) = \mathrm{ggen}(\mathcal{G})$.*

Both algorithms just perform matrix inversion; so their complexity depends on the inversion algorithm adopted in the implementation. As far as we know, the current best theoretical worst-case complexity is $\mathrm{O}(n^{2.376})$ [5]. Note that, in the current implementation in the PPL, the conversion algorithm is based on the Gaussian elimination method, which has complexity $\mathrm{O}(n^3)$.

5   Grid Widening

A simple and general characterization of a widening for enforcing and accelerating convergence of an upward iteration sequence is given in [6,7,8,9]. We assume here a minor variation of this classical definition (see footnote 6 in [9, p. 275]).

Definition 5 (Widening). *Let $\langle D, \vdash, \mathbf{0}, \oplus \rangle$ be a join-semilattice. The partial operator $\nabla \colon D \times D \rightarrowtail D$ is a widening if*

1. *for each $d_1, d_2 \in D$, $d_1 \vdash d_2$ implies that $d_1 \nabla d_2$ is defined and $d_2 \vdash d_1 \nabla d_2$;*
2. *for each increasing chain $d_0 \vdash d_1 \vdash \cdots$, the increasing chain defined by $d_0' := d_0$ and $d_{i+1}' := d_i' \nabla (d_i' \oplus d_{i+1})$, for $i \in \mathbb{N}$, is not strictly increasing.*

In addition to the formal requirements in Definition 5, it is also important to have a widening that has an efficient implementation, preferably, one that depends on a simple syntactic mapping of the representations. At the same time, so that the widening is well-defined, the result of this operation should be independent of the actual representation used. For this reason, the two widenings we propose assume specific minimal forms for the congruence and generator systems.

Definition 6. *A congruence system C is in strong minimal form if, for each pair of distinct proper congruences, $\langle a, x \rangle \equiv_1 b$ and $\langle c, x \rangle \equiv_1 d$ in C, if $\mathrm{piv}_<(c) = k > 0$, then $-c_k < 2a_k \leq c_k$. A generator system $G = \left((L, Q, P) \right)$ in $\mathbb{Q}^n$ is in strong minimal form if G is in minimal form and, for each pair of distinct parameters $u, v \in Q$, if $\mathrm{piv}_>(v) = k \leq n$, then $-v_k < 2u_k \leq v_k$.*

Proposition 8. *There exists an algorithm with complexity $O(n^3)$ for converting a congruence system C (resp., generator system G) in minimal form to a congruence system C' (resp., generator system G') in strong minimal form such that $\mathrm{gcon}(C) = \mathrm{gcon}(C')$ (resp., $\mathrm{ggen}(G) = \mathrm{ggen}(G')$).*

The widenings defined below use either the congruence or the generator systems.

Definition 7. *Let $\mathcal{L}_1 = \mathrm{gcon}(C_1)$ and $\mathcal{L}_2 = \mathrm{gcon}(C_2)$ be two grids in $\mathbb{G}_n$ such that $\mathcal{L}_1 \subseteq \mathcal{L}_2$, C_1 is in minimal form and C_2 is in strong minimal form. Then the grid widening $\mathcal{L}_1 \, \nabla_c \, \mathcal{L}_2$ is defined by*

$$\mathcal{L}_1 \, \nabla_c \, \mathcal{L}_2 := \begin{cases} \mathcal{L}_2, & \text{if } \mathcal{L}_1 = \varnothing \text{ or } \dim(\mathcal{L}_1) < \dim(\mathcal{L}_2), \\ \mathrm{gcon}(C_s), & \text{otherwise,} \end{cases}$$

where $C_s := \{ \gamma \in C_2 \mid \exists \beta \in C_1 \, . \, \beta \Uparrow \gamma \}$.

Definition 8. *Let $\mathcal{L}_1 = \mathrm{ggen}(G_1)$ and $\mathcal{L}_2 = \mathrm{ggen}(G_2)$ be two grids in $\mathbb{G}_n$ such that $\mathcal{L}_1 \subseteq \mathcal{L}_2$, $G_1 = (L_1, Q_1, P_1)$ is in minimal form and $G_2 = (L_2, Q_2, P_2)$ is in strong minimal form. Then the grid widening $\mathcal{L}_1 \, \nabla_g \, \mathcal{L}_2$ is defined by*

$$\mathcal{L}_1 \, \nabla_g \, \mathcal{L}_2 := \begin{cases} \mathcal{L}_2, & \text{if } \mathcal{L}_1 = \varnothing \text{ or } \dim(\mathcal{L}_1) < \dim(\mathcal{L}_2); \\ \mathrm{ggen}(G_s), & \text{otherwise,} \end{cases}$$

where $G_s := \left(L_2 \cup (Q_2 \setminus Q_s), Q_s, P_2 \right)$ and $Q_s := \{ v \in Q_2 \mid \exists u \in Q_1 \, . \, u \Downarrow v \}$.

Proposition 9. *The operators '∇_c' and '∇_g' are both widenings on $\mathbb{G}_n$.*

In Definition 7, it is required that C_2 is in strong minimal form. The following example shows that this is necessary for the operator '∇_c' to be well-defined.

Example 4. Let $\mathcal{L}_1 := \mathrm{gcon}(C_1)$, $\mathcal{L}_2 := \mathrm{gcon}(C_2)$ and $\mathcal{L}_2' := \mathrm{gcon}(C_2')$ where $C_1 = \{x \equiv_2 0, \; y \equiv_2 0\}$, $C_2 = \{x \equiv_1 0, \; x + y \equiv_2 0\}$, $C_2' = \{x \equiv_1 0, \; 3x + y \equiv_2 0\}$; then $\mathcal{L}_2 = \mathcal{L}_2'$. Note that only C_1 and C_2 are in strong minimal form. Therefore, assuming C_s (resp., C_s') is defined as in Definition 7 using C_1 and C_2 (resp., C_1 and C_2'), we have $C_s = \{x + y \equiv_2 0\}$ and $C_s' = \{3x + y \equiv_2 0\}$. Thus $\mathcal{L}_1 \, \nabla_c \, \mathcal{L}_2 = \mathrm{gcon}(C_s) \neq \mathrm{gcon}(C_s')$.

Example 5. To see that the widenings depend on the variable ordering, consider the grids $\mathcal{L}_1 = \mathrm{gcon}(C_1) = \mathrm{gcon}(C_1')$ and $\mathcal{L}_2 = \mathrm{gcon}(C_2) = \mathrm{gcon}(C_2')$ in $\mathbb{G}_2$, where

$$C_1 := \{5x + y \equiv_1 0, \; 22x \equiv_1 0\}, \quad C_2 := \{5x + y \equiv_1 0, \; 44x \equiv_1 0\},$$
$$C_1' := \{9y + x \equiv_1 0, \; 22y \equiv_1 0\}, \quad C_2' := \{9y + x \equiv_1 0, \; 44y \equiv_1 0\}.$$

Assume for C_1 and C_2 that the variables are ordered so that x precedes y, as in the vector $(x, y)^T$; then, C_1 and C_2 are in strong minimal form and, according to Definition 7, we obtain $\mathcal{L}_1 \mathbin{\nabla_{\!c}} \mathcal{L}_2 = \mathrm{gcon}(\{5x + y \equiv_1 0\})$. On the other hand, C_1' and C_2' are in strong minimal form when taking the variable order where y precedes x. In this case, by Definition 7, $\mathcal{L}_1 \mathbin{\nabla_{\!c}} \mathcal{L}_2 = \mathrm{gcon}(\{9y + x \equiv_1 0\})$.

6 Conclusion

We have defined a domain of *grids* and shown that any element may be represented either by a congruence system which is a finite set of congruences (either equalities or proper congruences); or a generator system which is a triple of finite sets of vectors (denoting sets of lines, parameters and points). Assuming such a system in $\mathbb{Q}^n$ has m congruences or generators, then the minimization algorithms have worst-case complexity $\mathrm{O}(n^2 m)$. It is shown that any matrix inversion algorithms such as Gaussian elimination which has complexity $\mathrm{O}(n^3)$, can be used for converting between generator and congruence systems in minimal form. Thus, the complexity of converting any system with m elements is no worse than $\mathrm{O}(n^2 m)$ if $m > n$ and $\mathrm{O}(n^3)$, otherwise.

The minimization and conversion algorithms, form the basis for a double description method for grids so that any generator or congruence systems, possibly in minimal form, can be provided on demand; the complexity of such a provision being as stated above. Assuming this method, we have shown that operations for comparison, intersection and grid join are straightforward. The complexity of comparing two grids is $\mathrm{O}(n^3)$ but, for just checking equality when it is already known that one of the grids is a subset of the other, we have described simpler procedures with complexity $\mathrm{O}(n)$. The intersection and grid join just take the union of the congruence or generator systems, respectively, so that, from a theoretical perspective, these have complexity $\mathrm{O}(n)$. However, in the implementation, we assume a common divisor for all the coordinates or coefficients in the system; hence, combining the systems requires changing the denominators of both components to their least common multiple with a consequential need to scale all the numerators in the representation; giving a worst-case complexity of $\mathrm{O}(n^2)$. We have also described an algorithm for computing the grid difference with complexity $\mathrm{O}(n^4)$. Observe that this operator is useful in the specification of the certificate-based widening for the grid powerset domain [3].

The grid domain is implemented in the PPL [2,4] following the approach described in this paper. Among the tests available in the PPL are the examples in this paper and implementations of the running examples in [22,23]. The PPL provides full support for lifting any domain to the powerset of that domain, so that a user of the PPL can experiment with powersets of grids and the extra precision this provides. An interesting line of research is the combination of the grids domain with the polyhedral domains provided by the PPL: not only the $\mathbb{Z}$-polyhedra domain, but also many variations such as the grid-polyhedra, grid-octagon, grid-bounded-difference, grid-interval domains and their powersets.

References

1. C. Ancourt. *Génération Automatique de Codes de Transfert pour Multiprocesseurs à Mémoires Locales.* PhD thesis, Université de Paris VI, March 1991.
2. R. Bagnara, P. M. Hill, and E. Zaffanella. *The Parma Polyhedra Library User's Manual.* Department of Mathematics, University of Parma, Parma, Italy, release 0.9 edition, March 2006. Available at http://www.cs.unipr.it/ppl/.
3. R. Bagnara, P. M. Hill, and E. Zaffanella. Widening operators for powerset domains. *Software Tools for Technology Transfer*, 2006. To appear.
4. R. Bagnara, E. Ricci, E. Zaffanella, and P. M. Hill. Possibly not closed convex polyhedra and the Parma Polyhedra Library. In M. V. Hermenegildo and G. Puebla, editors, *Static Analysis: Proceedings of the 9th International Symposium*, volume 2477 of *Lecture Notes in Computer Science*, pages 213–229, Madrid, Spain, 2002. Springer-Verlag, Berlin.
5. D. Coppersmith and S. Winograd. Matrix multiplication via arithmetic progressions. *Journal of Symbolic Computation*, 9(3):251–280, 1990.
6. P. Cousot and R. Cousot. Static determination of dynamic properties of programs. In B. Robinet, editor, *Proceedings of the Second International Symposium on Programming*, pages 106–130, Paris, France, 1976. Dunod, Paris, France.
7. P. Cousot and R. Cousot. Abstract interpretation: A unified lattice model for static analysis of programs by construction or approximation of fixpoints. In *Proceedings of the Fourth Annual ACM Symposium on Principles of Programming Languages*, pages 238–252, New York, 1977. ACM Press.
8. P. Cousot and R. Cousot. Abstract interpretation frameworks. *Journal of Logic and Computation*, 2(4):511–547, 1992.
9. P. Cousot and R. Cousot. Comparing the Galois connection and widening/narrowing approaches to abstract interpretation. In M. Bruynooghe and M. Wirsing, editors, *Proceedings of the 4th International Symposium on Programming Language Implementation and Logic Programming*, volume 631 of *Lecture Notes in Computer Science*, pages 269–295, Leuven, Belgium, 1992. Springer-Verlag, Berlin.
10. P. Cousot and N. Halbwachs. Automatic discovery of linear restraints among variables of a program. In *Conference Record of the Fifth Annual ACM Symposium on Principles of Programming Languages*, pages 84–96, Tucson, Arizona, 1978. ACM Press.
11. R. Giacobazzi, editor. *Static Analysis: Proceedings of the 11th International Symposium*, volume 3148 of *Lecture Notes in Computer Science*, Verona, Italy, 2004. Springer-Verlag, Berlin.
12. P. Granger. Static analysis of arithmetical congruences. *International Journal of Computer Mathematics*, 30:165–190, 1989.
13. P. Granger. *Analyses Sémantiques de Congruence.* PhD thesis, École Polytechnique, 921128 Palaiseau, France, July 1991.
14. P. Granger. Static analysis of linear congruence equalities among variables of a program. In Samson Abramsky and T. S. E. Maibaum, editors, *TAPSOFT'91: Proceedings of the International Joint Conference on Theory and Practice of Software Development, Volume 1: Colloquium on Trees in Algebra and Programming (CAAP'91)*, volume 493 of *Lecture Notes in Computer Science*, pages 169–192, Brighton, UK, 1991. Springer-Verlag, Berlin.

15. P. Granger. Static analyses of congruence properties on rational numbers (extended abstract). In P. Van Hentenryck, editor, *Static Analysis: Proceedings of the 4th International Symposium*, volume 1302 of *Lecture Notes in Computer Science*, pages 278–292, Paris, France, 1997. Springer-Verlag, Berlin.

16. M. Karr. Affine relationships among variables of a program. *Acta Informatica*, 6:133–151, 1976.

17. S. Larsen, E. Witchel, and S. P. Amarasinghe. Increasing and detecting memory address congruence. In *Proceedings of the 2002 International Conference on Parallel Architectures and Compilation Techniques (PACT'02)*, pages 18–29, Charlottesville, VA, USA, 2002. IEEE Computer Society Press.

18. V. Loechner. *PolyLib*: A library for manipulating parameterized polyhedra. Available at http://icps.u-strasbg.fr/~loechner/polylib/, March 1999. Declares itself to be a continuation of [30].

19. A. Miné. A few graph-based relational numerical abstract domains. In M. V. Hermenegildo and G. Puebla, editors, *Static Analysis: Proceedings of the 9th International Symposium*, volume 2477 of *Lecture Notes in Computer Science*, pages 117–132, Madrid, Spain, 2002. Springer-Verlag, Berlin.

20. T. S. Motzkin, H. Raiffa, G. L. Thompson, and R. M. Thrall. The double description method. In H. W. Kuhn and A. W. Tucker, editors, *Contributions to the Theory of Games – Volume II*, number 28 in Annals of Mathematics Studies, pages 51–73. Princeton University Press, Princeton, New Jersey, 1953.

21. M. Müller-Olm and H. Seidl. Precise interprocedural analysis through linear algebra. In N. D. Jones and X. Leroy, editors, *Proceedings of the 31st ACM SIGPLAN-SIGACT Symposium on Principles of Programming Languages (POPL 2004)*, pages 330–341, Venice, Italy, 2004. ACM Press.

22. M. Müller-Olm and H. Seidl. Analysis of modular arithmetic. In M. Sagiv, editor, *Programming Languages and Systems, Proceedings of the 14th European Symposium on Programming*, volume 3444 of *Lecture Notes in Computer Science*, pages 46–60, Edinburgh, UK, 2005. Springer-Verlag, Berlin.

23. M. Müller-Olm and H. Seidl. A generic framework for interprocedural analysis of numerical properties. In C. Hankin and I. Siveroni, editors, *Static Analysis: Proceedings of the 12th International Symposium*, volume 3672 of *Lecture Notes in Computer Science*, pages 235–250, London, UK, 2005. Springer-Verlag, Berlin.

24. S. P. K. Nookala and T. Risset. A library for Z-polyhedral operations. *Publication interne* 1330, IRISA, Campus de Beaulieu, Rennes, France, 2000.

25. P. Quinton, S. Rajopadhye, and T. Risset. On manipulating Z-polyhedra. Technical Report 1016, IRISA, Campus Universitaire de Bealieu, Rennes, France, July 1996.

26. P. Quinton, S. Rajopadhye, and T. Risset. On manipulating Z-polyhedra using a canonic representation. *Parallel Processing Letters*, 7(2):181–194, 1997.

27. E. Rodríguez-Carbonell and D. Kapur. An abstract interpretation approach for automatic generation of polynomial invariants. In Giacobazzi [11], pages 280–295.

28. S. Sankaranarayanan, H. Sipma, and Z. Manna. Constraint-based linear-relations analysis. In Giacobazzi [11], pages 53–68.

29. A. Schrijver. *Theory of Linear and Integer Programming*. Wiley Interscience Series in Discrete Mathematics and Optimization. John Wiley & Sons, 1999.

30. D. K. Wilde. A library for doing polyhedral operations. Master's thesis, Oregon State University, Corvallis, Oregon, December 1993. Also published as IRISA *Publication interne* 785, Rennes, France, 1993.

Author Index

Lecture Notes in Computer Science

For information about Vols. 1–4316

please contact your bookseller or Springer

Tuyls, R. Westra, Y. Saeys, A. Nowé
ledge Discovery and Emergent Complex-
.formatics. IX, 183 pages. 2007. (Sublibrary

.364: T. Kühne (Ed.), Models in Software Engineer-
. XI, 332 pages. 2007.

Vol. 4362: J. van Leeuwen, G.F. Italiano, W. van der
Hoek, C. Meinel, H. Sack, F. Plášil (Eds.), SOFSEM
2007: Theory and Practice of Computer Science. XXI,
937 pages. 2007.

Vol. 4361: H.J. Hoogeboom, G. Păun, G. Rozenberg, A.
Salomaa (Eds.), Membrane Computing. IX, 555 pages.
2006.

Vol. 4360: W. Dubitzky, A. Schuster, P.M.A. Sloot,
M. Schroeder, M. Romberg (Eds.), Distributed, High-
Performance and Grid Computing in Computational Bi-
ology. X, 192 pages. 2007. (Sublibrary LNBI).

Vol. 4358: R. Vidal, A. Heyden, Y. Ma (Eds.), Dynamical
Vision. IX, 329 pages. 2007.

Vol. 4357: L. Buttyán, V. Gligor, D. Westhoff (Eds.),
Security and Privacy in Ad-Hoc and Sensor Networks.
X, 193 pages. 2006.

Vol. 4355: J. Julliand, O. Kouchnarenko (Eds.), B 2007:
Formal Specification and Development in B. XIII, 293
pages. 2006.

Vol. 4354: M. Hanus (Ed.), Practical Aspects of Declarative Languages. X, 335 pages. 2006.

Vol. 4353: T. Schwentick, D. Suciu (Eds.), Database Theory – ICDT 2007. XI, 419 pages. 2006.

Vol. 4352: T.-J. Cham, J. Cai, C. Dorai, D. Rajan, T.-S.
Chua, L.-T. Chia (Eds.), Advances in Multimedia Modeling, Part II. XVIII, 743 pages. 2006.

Vol. 4351: T.-J. Cham, J. Cai, C. Dorai, D. Rajan, T.-S.
Chua, L.-T. Chia (Eds.), Advances in Multimedia Modeling, Part I. XIX, 797 pages. 2006.

Vol. 4349: B. Cook, A. Podelski (Eds.), Verification,
Model Checking, and Abstract Interpretation. XI, 395
pages. 2007.

Vol. 4348: S.T. Taft, R.A. Duff, R.L. Brukardt, E. Ploedereder, P. Leroy (Eds.), Ada 2005 Reference Manual.
XXII, 765 pages. 2006.

Vol. 4347: J. Lopez (Ed.), Critical Information Infrastructures Security. X, 286 pages. 2006.

Vol. 4346: L. Brim, B. Haverkort, M. Leucker, J. van de
Pol (Eds.), Formal Methods: Applications and Technology. X, 363 pages. 2007.

Vol. 4345: N. Maglaveras, I. Chouvarda, V. Koutkias, R.
Brause (Eds.), Biological and Medical Data Analysis.
XIII, 496 pages. 2006. (Sublibrary LNBI).

Vol. 4344: V. Gruhn, F. Oquendo (Eds.), Software Architecture. X, 245 pages. 2006.

Vol. 4342: H. de Swart, E. Orłowska, G. Schmidt, M.
Roubens (Eds.), Theory and Applications of Relational
Structures as Knowledge Instruments II. X, 373 pages.
2006. (Sublibrary LNAI).

Vol. 4341: P.Q. Nguyen (Ed.), Progress in Cryptology -
VIETCRYPT 2006. XI, 385 pages. 2006.

Vol. 4340: R. Prodan, T. Fahringer, Grid Computing.
XXIII, 317 pages. 2007.

Vol. 4339: E. Ayguadé, G. Baumgartner, J. Ramanujam,
P. Sadayappan (Eds.), Languages and Compilers for Parallel Computing. XI, 476 pages. 2006.

Vol. 4338: P. Kalra, S. Peleg (Eds.), Computer Vision,
Graphics and Image Processing. XV, 965 pages. 2006.

Vol. 4337: S. Arun-Kumar, N. Garg (Eds.), FSTTCS
2006: Foundations of Software Technology and Theoretical Computer Science. XIII, 430 pages. 2006.

Vol. 4336: V.R. Basili, H.D. Rombach, K. Schneider, B.
Kitchenham, D. Pfahl, R.W. Selby, Empirical Software
Engineering Issues. XVII, 194 pages. 2007.

Vol. 4335: S.A. Brueckner, S. Hassas, M. Jelasity, D.
Yamins (Eds.), Engineering Self-Organising Systems.
XII, 212 pages. 2007. (Sublibrary LNAI).

Vol. 4334: B. Beckert, R. Hähnle, P.H. Schmitt (Eds.),
Verification of Object-Oriented Software. XXIX, 658
pages. 2007. (Sublibrary LNAI).

Vol. 4333: U. Reimer, D. Karagiannis (Eds.), Practical
Aspects of Knowledge Management. XII, 338 pages.
2006. (Sublibrary LNAI).

Vol. 4332: A. Bagchi, V. Atluri (Eds.), Information Systems Security. XV, 382 pages. 2006.

Vol. 4331: G. Min, B. Di Martino, L.T. Yang, M. Guo, G.
Ruenger (Eds.), Frontiers of High Performance Computing and Networking – ISPA 2006 Workshops. XXXVII,
1141 pages. 2006.

Vol. 4330: M. Guo, L.T. Yang, B. Di Martino, H.P. Zima,
J. Dongarra, F. Tang (Eds.), Parallel and Distributed Processing and Applications. XVIII, 953 pages. 2006.

Vol. 4329: R. Barua, T. Lange (Eds.), Progress in Cryptology - INDOCRYPT 2006. X, 454 pages. 2006.

Vol. 4328: D. Penkler, M. Reitenspiess, F. Tam (Eds.),
Service Availability. X, 289 pages. 2006.

Vol. 4327: M. Baldoni, U. Endriss (Eds.), Declarative
Agent Languages and Technologies IV. VIII, 257 pages.
2006. (Sublibrary LNAI).

Vol. 4326: S. Göbel, R. Malkewitz, I. Iurgel (Eds.), Technologies for Interactive Digital Storytelling and Entertainment. X, 384 pages. 2006.

Vol. 4325: J. Cao, I. Stojmenovic, X. Jia, S.K. Das (Eds.),
Mobile Ad-hoc and Sensor Networks. XIX, 887 pages.
2006.

Vol. 4323: G. Doherty, A. Blandford (Eds.), Interactive
Systems. XI, 269 pages. 2007.

Vol. 4322: F. Kordon, J. Sztipanovits (Eds.), Reliable
Systems on Unreliable Networked Platforms. XIV, 317
pages. 2007.

Vol. 4320: R. Gotzhein, R. Reed (Eds.), System Analysis
and Modeling: Language Profiles. X, 229 pages. 2006.

Vol. 4319: L.-W. Chang, W.-N. Lie (Eds.), Advances in
Image and Video Technology. XXVI, 1347 pages. 2006.

Vol. 4318: H. Lipmaa, M. Yung, D. Lin (Eds.), Information Security and Cryptology. XI, 305 pages. 2006.

Vol. 4317: S.K. Madria, K.T. Claypool, R. Kannan, P.
Uppuluri, M.M. Gore (Eds.), Distributed Computing and
Internet Technology. XIX, 466 pages. 2006.

Lecture Notes in Computer Science

For information about Vols. 1–4316

please contact your bookseller or Springer

Vol. 4366: K. Tuyls, R. Westra, Y. Saeys, A. Nowé (Eds.), Knowledge Discovery and Emergent Complexity in Bioinformatics. IX, 183 pages. 2007. (Sublibrary LNBI).

Vol. 4364: T. Kühne (Ed.), Models in Software Engineering. XI, 332 pages. 2007.

Vol. 4362: J. van Leeuwen, G.F. Italiano, W. van der Hoek, C. Meinel, H. Sack, F. Plášil (Eds.), SOFSEM 2007: Theory and Practice of Computer Science. XXI, 937 pages. 2007.

Vol. 4361: H.J. Hoogeboom, G. Păun, G. Rozenberg, A. Salomaa (Eds.), Membrane Computing. IX, 555 pages. 2006.

Vol. 4360: W. Dubitzky, A. Schuster, P.M.A. Sloot, M. Schroeder, M. Romberg (Eds.), Distributed, High-Performance and Grid Computing in Computational Biology. X, 192 pages. 2007. (Sublibrary LNBI).

Vol. 4358: R. Vidal, A. Heyden, Y. Ma (Eds.), Dynamical Vision. IX, 329 pages. 2007.

Vol. 4357: L. Buttyán, V. Gligor, D. Westhoff (Eds.), Security and Privacy in Ad-Hoc and Sensor Networks. X, 193 pages. 2006.

Vol. 4355: J. Julliand, O. Kouchnarenko (Eds.), B 2007: Formal Specification and Development in B. XIII, 293 pages. 2006.

Vol. 4354: M. Hanus (Ed.), Practical Aspects of Declarative Languages. X, 335 pages. 2006.

Vol. 4353: T. Schwentick, D. Suciu (Eds.), Database Theory – ICDT 2007. XI, 419 pages. 2006.

Vol. 4352: T.-J. Cham, J. Cai, C. Dorai, D. Rajan, T.-S. Chua, L.-T. Chia (Eds.), Advances in Multimedia Modeling, Part II. XVIII, 743 pages. 2006.

Vol. 4351: T.-J. Cham, J. Cai, C. Dorai, D. Rajan, T.-S. Chua, L.-T. Chia (Eds.), Advances in Multimedia Modeling, Part I. XIX, 797 pages. 2006.

Vol. 4349: B. Cook, A. Podelski (Eds.), Verification, Model Checking, and Abstract Interpretation. XI, 395 pages. 2007.

Vol. 4348: S.T. Taft, R.A. Duff, R.L. Brukardt, E. Ploedereder, P. Leroy (Eds.), Ada 2005 Reference Manual. XXII, 765 pages. 2006.

Vol. 4347: J. Lopez (Ed.), Critical Information Infrastructures Security. X, 286 pages. 2006.

Vol. 4346: L. Brim, B. Haverkort, M. Leucker, J. van de Pol (Eds.), Formal Methods: Applications and Technology. X, 363 pages. 2007.

Vol. 4345: N. Maglaveras, I. Chouvarda, V. Koutkias, R. Brause (Eds.), Biological and Medical Data Analysis. XIII, 496 pages. 2006. (Sublibrary LNBI).

Vol. 4344: V. Gruhn, F. Oquendo (Eds.), Software Architecture. X, 245 pages. 2006.

Vol. 4342: H. de Swart, E. Orłowska, G. Schmidt, M. Roubens (Eds.), Theory and Applications of Relational Structures as Knowledge Instruments II. X, 373 pages. 2006. (Sublibrary LNAI).

Vol. 4341: P.Q. Nguyen (Ed.), Progress in Cryptology - VIETCRYPT 2006. XI, 385 pages. 2006.

Vol. 4340: R. Prodan, T. Fahringer, Grid Computing. XXIII, 317 pages. 2007.

Vol. 4339: E. Ayguadé, G. Baumgartner, J. Ramanujam, P. Sadayappan (Eds.), Languages and Compilers for Parallel Computing. XI, 476 pages. 2006.

Vol. 4338: P. Kalra, S. Peleg (Eds.), Computer Vision, Graphics and Image Processing. XV, 965 pages. 2006.

Vol. 4337: S. Arun-Kumar, N. Garg (Eds.), FSTTCS 2006: Foundations of Software Technology and Theoretical Computer Science. XIII, 430 pages. 2006.

Vol. 4336: V.R. Basili, H.D. Rombach, K. Schneider, B. Kitchenham, D. Pfahl, R.W. Selby, Empirical Software Engineering Issues. XVII, 194 pages. 2007.

Vol. 4335: S.A. Brueckner, S. Hassas, M. Jelasity, D. Yamins (Eds.), Engineering Self-Organising Systems. XII, 212 pages. 2007. (Sublibrary LNAI).

Vol. 4334: B. Beckert, R. Hähnle, P.H. Schmitt (Eds.), Verification of Object-Oriented Software. XXIX, 658 pages. 2007. (Sublibrary LNAI).

Vol. 4333: U. Reimer, D. Karagiannis (Eds.), Practical Aspects of Knowledge Management. XII, 338 pages. 2006. (Sublibrary LNAI).

Vol. 4332: A. Bagchi, V. Atluri (Eds.), Information Systems Security. XV, 382 pages. 2006.

Vol. 4331: G. Min, B. Di Martino, L.T. Yang, M. Guo, G. Ruenger (Eds.), Frontiers of High Performance Computing and Networking – ISPA 2006 Workshops. XXXVII, 1141 pages. 2006.

Vol. 4330: M. Guo, L.T. Yang, B. Di Martino, H.P. Zima, J. Dongarra, F. Tang (Eds.), Parallel and Distributed Processing and Applications. XVIII, 953 pages. 2006.

Vol. 4329: R. Barua, T. Lange (Eds.), Progress in Cryptology - INDOCRYPT 2006. X, 454 pages. 2006.

Vol. 4328: D. Penkler, M. Reitenspiess, F. Tam (Eds.), Service Availability. X, 289 pages. 2006.

Vol. 4327: M. Baldoni, U. Endriss (Eds.), Declarative Agent Languages and Technologies IV. VIII, 257 pages. 2006. (Sublibrary LNAI).

Vol. 4326: S. Göbel, R. Malkewitz, I. Iurgel (Eds.), Technologies for Interactive Digital Storytelling and Entertainment. X, 384 pages. 2006.

Vol. 4325: J. Cao, I. Stojmenovic, X. Jia, S.K. Das (Eds.), Mobile Ad-hoc and Sensor Networks. XIX, 887 pages. 2006.

Vol. 4323: G. Doherty, A. Blandford (Eds.), Interactive Systems. XI, 269 pages. 2007.

Vol. 4322: F. Kordon, J. Sztipanovits (Eds.), Reliable Systems on Unreliable Networked Platforms. XIV, 317 pages. 2007.

Vol. 4320: R. Gotzhein, R. Reed (Eds.), System Analysis and Modeling: Language Profiles. X, 229 pages. 2006.

Vol. 4319: L.-W. Chang, W.-N. Lie (Eds.), Advances in Image and Video Technology. XXVI, 1347 pages. 2006.

Vol. 4318: H. Lipmaa, M. Yung, D. Lin (Eds.), Information Security and Cryptology. XI, 305 pages. 2006.

Vol. 4317: S.K. Madria, K.T. Claypool, R. Kannan, P. Uppuluri, M.M. Gore (Eds.), Distributed Computing and Internet Technology. XIX, 466 pages. 2006.